WALRASIAN AND
NON-WALRASIAN EQUILIBRIA

For
Lionel W. McKenzie

WALRASIAN AND NON-WALRASIAN EQUILIBRIA

An Introduction to General Equilibrium Analysis

ANJAN MUKHERJI

CLARENDON PRESS · OXFORD

1990

Oxford University Press, Walton Street, Oxford OX2 6DP
Oxford New York Toronto
Delhi Bombay Calcutta Madras Karachi
Petaling Jaya Singapore Hong Kong Tokyo
Nairobi Dar es Salaam Cape Town
Melbourne Auckland
and associated companies in
Berlin Ibadan

Oxford is a trade mark of Oxford University Press

Published in the United States
by Oxford University Press, New York

British Library Cataloguing in Publication Data
Mukherji, Anjan
Walrasian and non-walrasian equilibria: an
introduction to general equilibrium analysis.
1. General equilibrium theory
I. Title
330.15'43
ISBN 0–19–877290–4
ISBN (0–19–877289–0 pbk.)

Library of Congress Cataloging in Publication Data
Mukherji, Anjan.
Walrasian and non-Walrasian equilibria: an introduction to
general equilibrium analysis/Anjan Mukherji.
Includes bibliographical references.
1. Equilibrium (Economics)   2. Walras, Léon, 1834–1910.
I. Title.
HB145.M85   1990   339.5—dc20   89-16290
ISBN 0–19–877290–4
ISBN 0–19–877289–0 (pbk.)

Typeset by Macmillan India Ltd, Bangalore 25
Printed in Great Britain
by Courier International Ltd.,
Tiptree, Essex

Preface

The book grew out of a course on general equilibrium analysis taught to students in the first year of the M.A. (Economics) programme at the Centre for Economic Studies and Planning of the Jawaharlal Nehru University, New Delhi. The course was a compulsory one, and the mathematical training and aptitude of the students varied over a wide range with a clear upper bound; to most of them, for example, Debreu's (1959) fundamental work and Arrow and Hahn's (1971) definitive treatment were well beyond it. General equilibrium analysis for such students thus usually meant Edgeworth boxes involving apples and oranges and little else; consequently, richer methods of analysis were never available to the non-specialist student. The course, and then the book, were developed to provide such students with a more adequate introduction.

Accordingly, the chapters of the book are so devised that only the simpler material is covered in the body of the chapters; the more involved derivations and general treatments are contained in the mathematical notes to each chapter. Since the text draws on the results demonstrated in these notes, it is hoped that students will be motivated to delve into the mathematical notes as well as sampling some of the items mentioned in the bibliographical notes at the end of each chapter. All mathematical results have been collected together so that a statement of the relevant mathematical theorem or concept is readily available.

During the year 1982–3, Jawaharlal Nehru University granted me a year's sabbatical which was spent at the Department of Economics at Cornell University, Ithaca, New York. The excellent secretarial facilities enabled me to prepare the first draft there. I am deeply indebted to the Department of Economics at Cornell for this opportunity, and to JNU for allowing me to avail myself of it.

The present form of the book is largely due to the very helpful comments received on earlier versions from Krishna Bharadwaj, Pradipta Chaudhury, Amal Sanyal, and the anonymous adviser of the Oxford University Press. In particular, Pradipta Chaudhury kindly agreed to use a part of the manuscript for his course at Hyderabad, and his experience played a major role in the revision. Also, had it not been for Amal Sanyal's collaboration, Chapter 7 would not have taken its present form. In addition, it is my very pleasant duty to record my indebtedness to

— members of the faculty during 1969–73 of the Department of Economics at the University of Rochester, Rochester, New York, for having provided an extremely rewarding graduate programme;
— my students, for suffering patiently through the development of the book;
— Amitava Bose, Dipankar Dasgupta, Bhaskar Dutta, Satish Jain, Mukul Majumdar, Tapas Majumdar, Tapan Mitra, and Amartya Sen, for encouragement and advice during the preparation of the manuscript;
— P. S. Rajagopalan, for typing the final version;
— the editors of Oxford University Press, for their patient help and suggestions;
— Mritiunjoy Mahanty and Jhaljit Singh for help with the proofs;
— finally, my wife Shormila, our son Arnab and my parents, Achalendranath and Dipti Mukharji, for making adjustments and allowances without which the book could not have been completed.

None of the above mentioned can be held responsible for the pages that follow; unfortunately, I must bear this responsibility alone.

A.M.

Contents

Contents

1 Firms, Individuals, and Markets: An Overview

1.1 Activities and Agents

There are many types of objects that we require for our daily life: food and clothing, the services of a doctor when we fall ill, the services of an architect if we wish to build a house, and so on. Over the years this list has grown, and there does not seem to be any limit to what we might consider essential for our existence in the years ahead. Basically, however, there are only two types of items named above: some are *goods*, such as food and clothing; the others are *services*, which involve receiving help from others such as the doctor. We shall hereafter use the term *commodities* to mean both goods and services. Commodities, then, will cover a large variety of objects.

Some commodities are useful in making other commodities; these are called *factors*. The commodities made with the help of factors are the *produced commodities*. Some factors may themselves be produced commodities, for example steel; these are the *intermediate goods*. Other produced commodities are required for the satisfaction of people's needs; these are called *consumption goods*. Given the diverse nature of many commodities, some consumption goods could also be intermediate goods. For example, electricity is used to run machines that make other goods, and it is also used to run televisions and stereos for our entertainment at home. But even though there are overlaps between the types of commodities mentioned above, we shall find the distinction useful.

An activity that involves factors to make produced commodities is a *production activity*. A person or group of persons or an organization primarily engaged in production activities will be called a *firm*. Thus, firms produce whenever they find it advantageous to do so. How they decide this and what they produce are questions that will be taken up later.

In addition to firms, individuals need commodities to meet their personal wants; an activity that ends with the satisfaction of some need involves the acquisition of consumption goods and is called a *consumption activity*. Persons engaged primarily in such activities are *consumers*, or *households*, or *individuals*.

We may now think of an *economy* as a collection of firms and individuals; these are the *agents* of the economy. Often, a third type of agent called the *government* or *planner* should also be considered. The government may produce, may consume, and may do various other things such as framing rules that are binding on other agents, imposing taxation, and so on. The outcome of various activities by such diverse agents will be investigated in the following pages.

Although I have not described how individuals decide on their consumption activity, nor have I disclosed how firms decide on their production activity, it should be clear that the decisions made by agents may be implemented successfully only if there is some compatibility between them. Arriving at such a match of plans or activities can be quite difficult if there are many firms and individuals. To properly appreciate the nature of this problem, consider the island economy of Robinson Crusoe before the advent of Friday. Crusoe, the individual, owned the land and labour; Crusoe, the farmer (the firm), produced corn with the help of land and labour obtained from Crusoe the individual. So long as he could produce as much as he required for his consumption, there were no problems. This was essentially because the objective of the individual and the firm were identical, namely, to keep Crusoe as satisfied as possible. The addition of a second agent, Friday, would not alter Crusoe's stranglehold over the island economy, for even then his desires would dominate. However, if there are two agents, neither of which is subservient to the other, the outcome as well as the objectives of such activities and plans become less transparent. With more than two agents, the outcome may even be obscure. To analyse the possible outcome when there are many agents, we need to visualize some more structures for our economy. One such structure is the institution of markets.

1.2 Markets

The necessity for exchange among agents arises because of an assumption that agents are not completely satisfied with what they have. The farmer requires some meat from the butcher; however, for a bilateral transaction between the two, the butcher must be ready to accept corn in exchange for meat. The trading of commodities against commodities is known as the system of *barter*. As indicated above, a barter system runs into problems whenever there are many commodities. With many commodities, we shall assume that the agents decide to designate one of the commodities, say commodity N, as a unit of account or *numeraire*. In addition, agents accept to take units of N in exchange for any other commodity i; thus N serves as the *medium of exchange*. Now, if an agent, a, decides to give up p_i units of N for each unit of i, we shall say that a has decided to *purchase* i at the *price* p_i. The place where buyers and sellers of i meet would be the *market* for i; in such a market, commodity i is exchanged against commodity N. Hence, if there are n non-numeraire commodities, there would be n markets.

In any market, therefore, there would be buyers and sellers and, apart from the initial chaotic bidding, a single price. The determination of such a price will be examined in greater detail later. For the present, let us consider the behaviour of agents in each market. Clearly, some will buy and the others will sell. It turns out that the classification of agents introduced above contains information about which agents would buy and which would sell in a given market. As Figure 1.1 indicates, typically, firms sell produced commodities and buy factors, whereas individuals buy produced commodities and sell factors. Here the problem of overlap among the types of commodities should be recalled. Usually, individuals sell factors such as labour and land. In the figure, the conflicts between different agents emerge into sharp focus. It should be noted also that the markets are interconnected; for the wage that an individual gets while selling his labour surely affects his decision regarding purchases of bread and clothing.

Even if a single market were to be taken up for examination, the conflict between buyers and sellers would naturally emerge. But in the examination of a single market, there is a basic difficulty. Let us consider one such market, in isolation, to examine this claim. Traditionally, a rich variety of assumptions have been employed to describe a market, ranging from *perfect competition* to *monopoly*. Let us consider the assumption of perfect competition, where buyers and sellers are assumed to be so numerous that no single agent can influence the outcome to his advantage. What is of interest, of course, is the amount of the good bought and sold and the price. For a competitive market, demand and supply curves are constructed: these curves represent the plans

Markets for → / Agents ↓	Consumption goods	Intermediate goods	Factors
Firms	Seller	Buyer/seller	Buyer/seller
Individuals	Buyer	Buyer	Seller

FIG. 1.1

of buyers and sellers at each level of price, *every thing else held constant*. Among 'everything else' are the prices of other commodities that buyers may purchase, the prices of factors used to produce this particular commodity, and so on. Given all these things, if demand and supply curves intersect at a price, then this is the price at which buyers and sellers find that their plans match. Such a price may be called an 'equilibrium price'; it depends on all the magnitudes given. But, given the interconnections mentioned above, some of the things held constant may be affected by this equilibrium price. Then we can not hold other things constant. This is the problem referred to earlier. Thus, we must consider all markets simultaneously; this is the method of *general equilibrium analysis*.

It should be pointed out that we could have proceeded differently. The introduction of markets is not really essential. We could have introduced an alternative institution—the planning authority, or the planner. The planner decides what is best for the economy, and this may or may not take into account the wishes of the agents in the economy. Having come to a decision, the planner issues appropriate instructions regarding what ought to be produced and who should consume and in what quantity. In short, the planner lays down an activity plan for each agent in this economy. Even in such a scheme as this, the planner would have to resort to general equilibrium analysis in order to choose appropriate instructions. While we shall not adopt such a framework, we shall see that in certain situations a planner has distinct advantages over a system of markets; these advantages will be made precise later on. However, at this point it should be emphasized that the method of general equilibrium analysis does not depend on either the institution of markets or that of the planner.

1.3   General Equilibrium Analysis

Consider the system of markets introduced above. An economy where transactions are so organized would be called a *market economy*. We shall use such an economy to examine the methods of general equilibrium analysis.

Assume, for the sake of concreteness, that our market economy is perfectly competitive. In such a situation, consider the behaviour of agents when confronted by a price configuration (a system of prices, one for each non-numeraire commodity). Each agent makes a comprehensive plan regarding its activities when it knows the prices; thus, individuals plan how much to buy and how much of a factor to supply, while firms plan how much of a factor to buy and how much to sell. The purchase plans would be referred to as *demands*, while sales plans would be referred to as *supplies*. In the previous section, while restricting attention to a single market, we considered demand and supply curves. Now, when we wish to examine all markets simultaneously, we need to consider *demand and supply functions*, that is, we must take into account all the variables that influence demand and supply. And a general equilibrium configuration of these variables is such that demand and supply match in every market.

Thus, by a general competitive equilibrium we shall mean a configuration where the plans of all agents are compatible. It is only at such configurations that agents can carry out their plans. Hence the existence of a general competitive equilibrium—hereafter, a *competitive equilibrium*—constitutes a consistency check of all our assumptions. This is the first such check, and we shall subject our construction to other checks later.

I should mention here that a competitive equilibrium as defined above is a general equilibrium for competitive markets. Changing the assumption of perfect competition leads to a different type of general equilibrium. In each case, a general equilibrium is a configuration where plans of agents are compatible. It is when the plans of agents are specified by demands and supplies that the resulting general equilibrium is termed a 'competitive equilibrium'.

Having defined a general equilibrium, and having satisfied ourselves that the concept is non-vacuous, we need to examine whether such a configuration is unique. If such configurations are non-unique, then how can one such configuration be distinguished from another? Also, if there are changes in the parameters of the system, how would the equilibrium configurations alter? Finally, beginning with a disequilibrium configuration, are there forces that drive the system towards an equilibrium? These are some of the issues that will be discussed within the context of a competitive equilibrium.

Most of the questions considered above originate from the contribution of Walras (1877). It is for this reason that the competitive equilibrium is often called a *Walrasian equilibrium*. A substantial part of the analysis below will follow Walras, but there will be some features of it that have a non-Walrasian flavour. It will turn out that these departures from Walrasian traditions have some benefits.

1.4 A Brief Résumé of the Book

In view of the above discussion, we shall begin, in Chapter 2, to consider a simple economy. It is simple in the sense that there is only one class of agents: individuals. There are no firms, and hence no production occurs; thus, the total stock of commodities available in the economy is fixed and is owned by individuals. The bundle of commodities owned by individual i will be called i's *endowment*. It will be assumed that at least some individuals are not satisfied with their endowment and will, therefore, seek to exchange goods in order to obtain a more preferred bundle. What are the possible outcomes of such an exchange problem? Two distinct methods of approach to answering this question are presented. The first utilizes the notion of a *coalition* of individuals and their powers of *blocking* a particular outcome. The second is based on the markets of the type sketched above and, assuming competitive individuals, seeks to determine an equilibrium price configuration at which demand and supply match. These two approaches are shown to lead to the same solution when there are many individuals: strictly speaking, it is when the number of individuals is infinite that the outcomes via the two methods coincide. One may, therefore, conclude that the assumption of competitive markets is appropriate when there are many agents, and this provides a justification at one level of using the competitive assumption. The properties of *demand functions* are analysed in some detail in the set of mathematical notes at the end of the chapter; these properties are then used to investigate how a change in the distribution of endowments affects the equilibrium configuration.

Chapter 3 looks at production. Here, in contrast to the previous chapter, we consider the behaviour of firms. Two basic types of behaviour are discussed. The first is an aggregative structure for the production side of an economy. Here individual firms play no role; rather, assuming that there are many competitive firms, we examine the relationship between prices of produced commodities or *outputs* and factor prices, between the quantities of factors available and the full-employment levels of outputs, and so on. A special case of such an aggregative model, the Leontief model, merits a detailed and systematic analysis in the mathematical notes to the chapter. We shall spend some time with such production structures, since such models are used to examine various planning situations and, in addition, much of the pure theory of international trade and growth rest on the various special features of the model developed here. The second type of behaviour is that of an individual competitive firm, and the methods of Chapter 2 are re-employed to obtain the *profit function* and the *supply function* and to study their relationship.

Chapter 4 integrates the individuals of Chapter 2 with the firms of Chapter 3 to form a single framework of a model where factors are privately owned. We shall establish, first, that there exists a set of prices at which demand and supply match in each market: the existence of a Walrasian equilibrium. Next, conditions under which this equilibrium configuration is unique are examined. This, then, is the second check of consistency. Moreover, the concepts of global and local stability are presented. In a unified treatment of these topics it is shown how both non-uniqueness and instability may be attributed to income effects. Finally, some results on comparative statics of equilibrium prices are presented. Technically, this chapter is perhaps the most demanding, since the propositions covered are among the more difficult ones. An elementary approach to these questions was presented in Chapter 2, so Chapter 4 brings us to relatively more general situations.

Chapter 5 is devoted to the welfare aspects of competitive equilibria. The usual relationships between competitive equilibria and Pareto optima are considered at an elementary level in the text and at a more general level in the chapter's mathematical notes. These results provide another justification for an interest in a competitive equilibrium. It should be made clear that the term 'optimum' is somewhat unfortunate, as the word conjures up an image of something good, whereas a Pareto-optimal state could be socially quite unbearable; for at such a state, to make some individual better off, some one else has to be made worse off. The point is that society may prefer to better the lot of a deserving citizen at the expense of a not-so-deserving member. This, therefore, leads to questions of comparability among different optimal states; such attempts are discussed and problems created by such comparisons are presented.

Next, examples of externalities are considered and the consequent failure of the markets to realize an optimal configuration is exposed. Not only this, but the very existence of competitive equilibrium is in jeopardy. With external effects, an individual's decisions cannot be taken in isolation; they have to be taken after a consideration of what actions the other may take. Such interdependence can be properly handled within the context of a non-cooperative game, and the appropriate equilibrium concept is that of a *non-cooperative equilibrium*. In the examples considered, the non-cooperative equilibrium is shown to be inoptimal. The restoration of optimality is discussed, and it becomes clear that we need a third agent, the government or the planner, to step in. A particular problem, the production of public goods, is considered in some detail. Even the planner may fail to attain the right output for public goods if he has no information regarding individuals' tastes. For the individual has some incentive in misrepresenting his preferences. This leads us to a consideration of the problem of revelation of preferences and strategic behaviour of individuals. Once again, we find that the game-theoretic formulation is useful in analysing such situations.

Up to now we have considered topics that may be broadly classified under Walrasian economics. Let us take a quick stock of what may be the more important deficiencies of such an approach. First, there has been an emphasis on equilibrium configurations. But, as we will have seen in Chapter 4, getting to such a configuration is not easy. So what happens if we cannot attain an equilibrium? Do individuals make transactions at prices that are not market-clearing? Answers to these questions have to be sought outside the Walrasian context. In particular, we must try to explain the existence of configurations with imbalances; clearly, if such configurations are designated to be equilibria, then they cannot be Walrasian. Consider the contribution of Keynes (1936), for example, and his concept of an equilibrium with unemployment. General equilibrium analysis should be able to admit such situations.

Next, do we consider individuals as being in the market only once? Is there no future? Is it not the case that agents generally take decisions over a sequence of time? Here again, the notion of a Walrasian equilibrium may have to be extended. Suppose we consider commodities to have a location and time dimension. In otherwords, not only do we consider a 500 g loaf of bread, but we consider a 500 g loaf of bread available in London in 1990, and this should be taken to be different from a 500 g loaf of bread available in London in 1992. With separate markets for each such distinct commodity, the Walrasian equilibrium guarantees the matching of demand and supply in each of these markets. But surely, many such markets may not exist. An alternative, more meaningful, procedure may be to consider two periods; T (for today) and F (for future). Agents believe that in F some things are more likely to happen than others, and based on these expectations, they may take decisions today. So we may study whether, given some expectations regarding F, the markets today are equilibrated; if they are, then we have a *temporary equilibrium* in the T-markets. We will call such equilibria 'Hicksian', since these ideas may be traced to the contribution of Hicks (1946). Naturally, expectations regarding the future raise many complex issues.

Consider also the question of money, a commodity that figures very importantly in our daily routine. Have we been able to accommodate such a commodity into the Walrasian framework? To answer this, we need to recognize that money has two distinct roles: as a medium of exchange, and as a store of value. Our numeraire commodity satisfies the former but not the latter role. For the validity of the store-of-value argument, we need to admit a future for our agents.

In Chapters 6 and 7, some of the points raised above are covered. Chapter 6, on non-Walrasian equilibria, marks the first point of departure from Walrasian traditions. The major relaxation is that transactions may occur at prices that are not market-clearing. Beginning with some simple axioms which may be considered meaningful, the various notions of non-Walrasian equilibria are discussed and their relationship examined. In the mathematical notes to the chapter, we consider the question of why prices may get stuck and why trades occur at such prices. The answer involves the idea that agents are actually in search of information regarding the overall nature of the market imbalances; this information is obtained by taking part in trading. Only when some agents are constrained in making a transaction do they realize the nature of the imbalance. Armed with this information, they decide to bid the price up or down depending on whether purchases or sales have been constrained. Such an approach, we believe, would be the first step in building up a systematic account of price formation in a general equilibrium context.

Chapter 7 presents an aggregative model of unemployment equilibrium. The individual plans over two periods, a present and a future. This allows the introduction of a demand for money, a commodity that provides satisfaction not directly, but through what it may purchase in the future. Although the model is quite simplistic, by its very nature it allows people to hold money to tide them over anticipated difficulties in the future. First, the Walrasian temporary equilibrium is studied. Next, we consider price and money wage rigidity. The constructs of Chapter 6 are used to characterize the nature of the resulting non-Walrasian temporary equilibrium. It is shown that two distinct forms of unemployment can result in the current markets: one has Keynesian features and the other, classical properties. An intermediate situation with price flexibility and money wage rigidity is also analysed. The mathematical notes to the chapter discuss the properties of the consumption function or the effective demand for goods in the current markets.

Chapter 8 is in the nature of a mathematical appendix. It contains a collection of the various mathematical concepts used, their definitions, and the statements of the theorems invoked either in the text or in the mathematical notes to the various chapters.

At the end of every chapter except the first and the last, there are two sets of notes. The first is a collection of mathematical notes while the second consists of biographical notes. The former has allowed me to separate some of the more involved bits of derivations and applications from the text. In the latter, further readings and references are provided.

Finally, it should be pointed out that the coverage as described above is not exhaustive. Nor was this ever intended. But it is hoped that the areas and topics covered will expose readers to the core of general equilibrium analysis.

BIBLIOGRAPHICAL NOTES

For a set of readings on general equilibrium analysis, see Hahn (1984, ch. 3), Koopmans (1957, Essay I), Chipman (1965), and Arrow (1974), arranged in order of their technical contents, beginning with the least technical. For readings on individual topics, the bibliographical notes at the end of each chapter below are to be consulted. Perhaps the most glaring omission among the topics covered is the treatment of imperfect competition in a general equilibrium context. Hart (1985) contains a discussion of such issues.

2 Exchange

2.1 Introduction

In the light of our earlier discussion, consider an economy with only one type of agent, either individuals or households. We shall analyse, at first, the classical problem of exchange of commodities in a very simple context. Two persons meet in order to trade, and each of them possesses a commodity bundle, or *endowment*, which he wishes to exchange for a 'better' bundle. Within the period in which exchange is to occur, the total stock of each commodity is fixed; this postulate implies that no person can alter his endowment. Thus these commodities are desired for final consumption. Let the persons be designated by A and B and the two commodities by F (food) and C (clothing). Suppose that the endowment of A is (f_a, c_a) and that of B, (f_b, c_b); i.e., A has f_a units of food and c_a units of clothing; similarly, B has f_b units of food and c_b units of clothing initially. Each individual is assumed to possess an ordering over the set of all consumption bundles (f, c). For simplicity, any $(f, c) \geqq 0$ would be a possible consumption bundle. In particular, we shall assume that this ordering is representable by a continuous real valued function u_i $(i = \text{A, B})$ defined over the non-negative orthant. In particular, we shall assume that each $u_i(\cdot)$ satisfies

(a) the assumption that more is always better, i.e. that $(f', c') \geq (f, c)$ or $(f', c') \geqq (f, c)$, with strict inequality in at least one component, implies that

$$u_i(f', c') > u_i(f, c);$$

(b) strict quasi-concavity; i.e.,

$$u_i(f', c') \geqq u_i(f, c)$$
$$\Rightarrow u_i\{\lambda f' + (1 - \lambda)f, \lambda c' + (1 - \lambda)c\} > u_i(f, c)$$

for all λ, $0 < \lambda < 1$.

Thus, each person has an extremely well behaved indifference map of which a representative indifference curve $(u_i(f, c) = \text{const.})$ is shown in Figure 2.1. Assumption (a) means that a movement to the right (horizontally) and/or up (vertically) leads to more desirable bundles; thus, indifference curves slope downwards; assumption (b) ensures that these contain no straight-line segments.

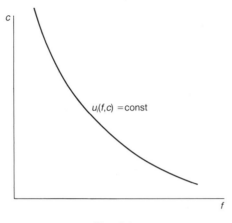

c

$u_i(f,c) = \text{const}$

f

FIG. 2.1

To analyse the exchanges possible in such a situation, we take the help of a device due to Edgeworth: the box diagram (Figure 2.2). The box is of length $f(= f_a + f_b)$ and breadth $c(= c_a + c_b)$; i.e., the dimensions of the box correspond to the total availability of the two goods.

A's indifference curve is superimposed on the box with the origin at the lower left-hand corner, while B's indifference map is turned through 180° and superimposed on the box with its origin at the top right-hand corner. Thus, in contrast to A, B becomes worse off as he moves north-east and better off as he moves south-west. The point E shows the initial shares of A and B and is the endowment point. Any possible exchange is a redistribution of these fixed stocks; and any point in the box denotes such a redistribution; henceforth, we shall refer to any point in the box as an *allocation*.

The following questions may now be posed: Are there allocations that make both A and B better off than at E? Which are they? Answers may be derived by focusing attention on the indifference curves AA and BB through E; if these intersect at E as shown above, then the region bounded by these curves contains exactly those redistributions that leave no one worse off when compared with E.

If, however, AA and BB were to touch (be tangential to one another) at E, then any redistribution that benefits one harms the other, and hence no voluntary transactions can occur. The locus of points of tangencies of indifference curves of A and B is called the *efficiency locus*, and unless E is a point off the efficiency locus, no transactions would occur. Thus, E must be as in the diagram, so that A and B may profitably engage in exchange.

Given that A and B may profitably engage in trade, what are the possible outcomes? Notice that the only possibilities lie along the portion CC of the efficiency locus. This follows, since any redistribution leading to a point such

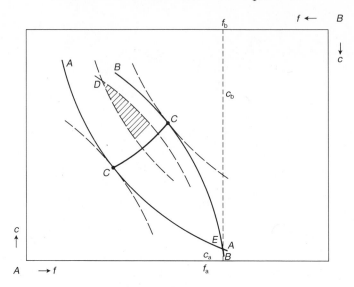

FIG. 2.2

as D, a point not on CC, may be improved upon, since anything in the shaded region must be preferred by both A and B to the allocation at D. Thus, *any allocation not on CC may be improved upon*, whereas the only allocations that cannot be improved upon lie on CC. Clearly, the outcome must be on CC, the *contract locus*. The concept of improving upon an allocation has narrowed the possibilities, but there are still far too many on CC.

In our two-agent economy, it is clear how one may improve upon a given allocation. What if there are many agents? The concept of improving upon then needs to be examined more carefully. Suppose that there are N individuals indexed $i = 1, 2, \ldots, N$; the endowment bundle for i is denoted by $e^i \in R_+^2$; thus, $e^i = (e_1^i, e_2^i)$. And let $e = \sum_i e^i$. A redistribution of e among N individuals, or an allocation $x^i, i = 1, \ldots, N$, is feasible, provided that $x^i \geqq 0$ and $\sum_i x^i = e$.

Consider a feasible allocation $\{x^i, i = 1, \ldots, N\}$; a subset of individuals S is said to *block* $\{x^i, i = 1, \ldots, N\}$ if there is $\{y^i, i \in S\}$ such that

$$\sum_{i \in S} y^i = \sum_{i \in S} e^i,$$

and if $u^i(y^i) \geqq u^i(x^i)$ for all $i \in S$ with strict inequality for some $i \in S$. S is said to form a *blocking coalition*, and $\{y^i, i \in S\}$ improves upon $\{x^i, i \in S\}$ in the sense used earlier.

The *core* for the economy is the set of all feasible allocations for which no blocking coalition exists.

Clearly, for the world of two persons, the contract locus CC in Figure 2.2 constitutes the core. And, as noted above, there are still too many possibilities that are candidates for the solution to the exchange problem. We shall return to this question soon, but first we need to look at another approach to the same question.

2.2 Competitive Allocations and Equilibrium Conditions

We begin by giving a concrete formulation of the plans that A and B make when they are competitive agents; if p_f and p_c denote, respectively, the prices of F and C, we assume that A and B respond passively to these prices by announcing their requirements: (x_f, x_c) (by A) and (y_f, y_c) (by B). We postpone for the time a discussion of why A and B are such docile persons. Thus, A chooses (x_f, x_c) to maximize $u_A(x_f, x_c)$, subject to

$$p_f x_f + p_c x_c \lessgtr p_f f_a + p_c c_a.$$

From this maximum problem, x_f, x_c are obtained as functions of p_f, p_c (the prices) and f_a, c_a (the endowments). Similarly for B. The maximizing bundle (x_f, x_c) for A would in general depend on the prices p_f, p_c and endowments f_a, c_a. Thus, total demand for food is $x_f + y_f$, obtained from maximum problems noted above; the total demand for clothing, obtained similarly, is $x_c + y_c$. The property of an equilibrium configuration (p_f^*, p_c^*) is that total demands match total supplies.

Formally, $\{x_f^*, x_c^*; y_f^*, y_c^*; p_f^*, p_c^*\}$ constitute an equilibrium if

$$x_f^* + y_f^* = f_a + f_b \tag{2.1}$$

and

$$x_c^* + y_c^* = c_a + c_b, \tag{2.2}$$

the market balance conditions, hold, and if

$$\left. \frac{\partial u_a / \partial x_f}{\partial u_a / \partial x_c} \right|_{(x_f^*, x_c^*)} = \frac{p_f^*}{p_c^*}, \tag{2.3}$$

$$p_f^* x_f^* + p_c^* x_c^* = p_f^* f_a + p_c^* c_a, \tag{2.4}$$

$$\left. \frac{\partial u_b / \partial y_f}{\partial u_b / \partial y_c} \right|_{(y_f^*, y_c^*)} = \frac{p_f^*}{p_c^*}, \tag{2.5}$$

and

$$p_f^* y_f^* + p_c^* y_c^* = p_f^* f_b + p_c^* c_b, \tag{2.6}$$

which are the demand conditions. Equations (2.3) and (2.4) characterize the demand of A, namely the familiar equality of the marginal rate of substitution to the relative prices and the budget equations, assuming that demands are positive. Similarly, (2.5) and (2.6) characterize the demand of B.

Notice that we have six equations to determine six variables. But (2.4), (2.6), and (2.2) $\Rightarrow$ (2.1) if $p_f^* > 0$; similarly, (2.4), (2.6), and (2.1) $\Rightarrow$ (2.2) if $p_c^* > 0$. This may be seen by adding (2.4) and (2.6) and comparing with the market balance equations. Thus there are at most five independent equations which may determine at most five variables. The number of variables may be reduced by introducing the relative price $p^* = p_f^*/p_c^*$ of food and clothing—which is the only price involved in utility maximization. Thus, one may expect p^*, x_f^*, x_c^*, y_f^*, y_c^* to be determined.

2.3 Excess Demand Functions

To enable us to answer the existence question posed above, it becomes necessary to reformulate (2.1)–(2.6) somewhat. By combining (2.3) and (2.4), we have the demand functions

$$x_f = F_A(p;\, pf_a + c_a),$$

$$x_c = G_A(p;\, pf_a + c_a)$$

where p is the price of food relative to clothing; i.e., $p = p_f/p_c$. Since (f_a, c_a) the endowments do not alter; we drop these and write

$$x_f = F_A(p);\ x_c = G_A(p).$$

Similarly,

$$y_f = F_B(p);\ y_c = G_B(p).$$

We next define $Z_f(p) = F_A(p) + F_B(p) - f_a - f_b$ to be the *excess demand* for food, the difference between aggregate demand and supply. Similarly, $Z_c(p) = G_A(p) + G_B(p) - c_a - c_b$, is the excess demand for clothing.

Also, for any p, notice that (2.4) and (2.6) imply that

$$pZ_f(p) + Z_c(p) = 0, \tag{2.7}$$

which was first noted by Walras and is called *Walras's Law*. In view of (2.7), we can characterize the equilibrium p^* as the solution to

$$Z_f(p) = 0. \tag{2.8}$$

We are therefore interested in solving (2.8); if such an equation has a solution, then we can go back and obtain the demands of A and B and so derive the equilibrium configuration. On the face of it, there is nothing to guarantee that a solution exists to (2.8) or, if there is a solution, that it is unique. Figures 2.3–2.5 should convince readers that any of the states illustrated is possible. If no equilibrium exists, then our assumptions regarding individual behaviour

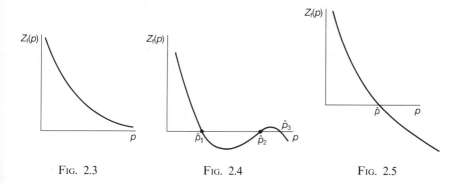

FIG. 2.3   FIG. 2.4   FIG. 2.5

are inconsistent; so we need to guarantee that an equilibrium exists. If there are multiple equilibria such as $\hat{p}_1$, $\hat{p}_2$, and $\hat{p}_3$, can we differentiate between them?

Specifically, to differentiate between points of multiple equilibria, Walras introduced a hypothesis regarding the adjustment of prices at disequilibrium (see e.g., Walras 1877: Lesson 5). We may state this, in terms of our notation, as follows:

If $Z_f(p) > 0$, then p rises; if $Z_f(p) < 0$, then p falls; if $Z_f(p) = 0$, then p does not change.

Thus, at disequilibrium prices, according to Walras, there would be a pressure on the price to be bid up or down; it is to be bid up in the face of an excess demand that is positive; it is to be bid down in the face of excess demand that is negative. Thus, in the vicinity of $\hat{p}_1$ (and $\hat{p}_3$), prices always move towards $\hat{p}_1$ (and $\hat{p}_3$). In this sense, and given the above adjustment rule, $\hat{p}_1, \hat{p}_3$ are said to be *stable* equilibria while $\hat{p}_2$ is an *unstable* equilibrium. Thus, alternatively, if, at an equilibrium $\hat{p}$, $Z_f(p)$ is downward-sloping, then $\hat{p}$ is a stable equilibrium.

2.4 Existence of a Stable Equilibrium

To guarantee the existence of equilibrium, we need further restrictions. The kind of restrictions required may be seen by the following:

A: $Z_f(p)$, $Z_c(p)$ are continuous functions of p for all $p > 0$.
B: There is some small $\varepsilon > 0$ such that $p < \varepsilon \Rightarrow Z_f(p) > 0$ whereas $p > 1/\varepsilon \Rightarrow Z_c(p) > 0$, where $\varepsilon < 1/\varepsilon$.

The mathematical notes at the end of this chapter discuss conditions under which demand functions and excess demand functions are continuous functions of prices. Restriction B above says that, if the price of one good is small relative to the other, then that good is in a state of positive excess demand.

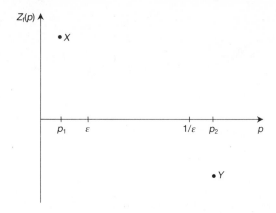

Fɪɢ. 2.6

Under the above conditions, it should be clear from Figure 2.6 that, for $p < \varepsilon$, $Z_f(p)$ should pass through a point such as X in the figure; for $p > 1/\varepsilon$, since $Z_c(p) > 0$, Walras's Law implies that $Z_f(p) < 0$; so that for $p > 1/\varepsilon$, $Z_f(p)$ should pass through a point such as Y. The curve $Z_f(p)$, being continuous, when passing through X and Y must cut the p-axis at some point, say p^*, in $(\varepsilon, 1/\varepsilon)$; clearly, $Z_f(p^*) = 0$. But $Z_f(p)$ may cross and recross the p-axis at many points in $(\varepsilon, 1/\varepsilon)$; all such points are equilibrium prices. In particular, since $Z_f(p)$ must travel from above the p-axis to below it, the curve $Z_f(p)$ must cross at least once, with a negative slope. Let such a crossing occur at a point $\hat{p}^*$; then $\hat{p}^*$ is a stable equilibrium.

Next, we try to see whether unstable positions of equilibria can be ruled out under meaningful assumptions, because then, if an equilibrium exists, it must be unique.

For this, we would like to guarantee that the excess demand function is downward-sloping at equilibrium; in other words, if $\hat{p}$ is an equilibrium, and if $Z_f(p)$ has a derivative at $\hat{p}$ (the prime sign denotes a derivative), then

$$Z_f'(\hat{p}) = \frac{dZ_f}{dp}(\hat{p}) < 0.$$

But $Z_f'(\hat{p}) = F_A'(\hat{p}) + F_B'(\hat{p})$, since supplies are fixed; so

$$Z_f'(\hat{p}) = \left\{\frac{\partial F_A}{\partial p}\right\}_{du_A = 0} - \{F_a(\hat{p}) - f_a\}\left(\frac{\partial F_A}{\partial I}\right)_{dp = 0}$$

$$+ \left(\frac{\partial F_B}{\partial p}\right)_{du_B = 0} - \{F_b(\hat{p}) - f_b\}\left(\frac{\partial F_B}{\partial I}\right)_{dp = 0},$$

from the Slutsky equation derived in the mathematical notes to this chapter. Thus,

$$Z_f'(\hat{p}) = \text{(two substitution terms)} + \{F_a(\hat{p}) - f_a\}\left(\frac{\partial F_B}{\partial I} - \frac{\partial F_a}{\partial I}\right),$$

assuming $F_a(\hat{p}) - f_a > 0$, since $F_b(\hat{p}) - f_b = -\{F_a(\hat{p}) - f_a\}$. So even if goods are normal, the net seller (i.e. B) might have a large enough income effect to offset the two negative substitution terms. Thus there is a serious problem with the excess demand function; as we shall see later, a lot of the indeterminacy stems from this particular source.

Increasing the number of individuals (or goods) creates no additional problems as long as each of them behaves competitively. Thus, with individuals $i = 1, 2, \ldots, N$, each with an endowment $w^i \in R_+^n$ and a utility function $u^i(\cdot)$, each i may be taken to be solving the problem

$$\max \quad u^i(x)$$

$$\text{s.t.} \quad px \leqslant pw^i$$

$$x \geqslant 0$$

where $p = (p_1, \ldots, p_n)$ is the price vector and we assume $p_j > 0$ for all j. This problem has a solution $x^i = x^i(p)$ (the demand function) and, as above,

$$X(p) = \sum_i x^i(p): \text{the aggregate demand,}$$

leading to the following definition of excess demand:

$$Z(p) = X(p) - W$$

where $W = \Sigma_i w^i$ and an equilibrium $p*$ is defined by the equations

$$Z(p) = 0$$

or

$$Z_j(p) = 0, \quad j = 1, 2, \ldots, n.$$

We may also note that Walras's Law holds; i.e.,

$$pZ(p) = 0,$$

for every $p > 0$, by methods noted earlier, so that we may define at best $n - 1$ relative prices at equilibrium since there are at most $n - 1$ independent equations.

Up to this point, it has been plain sailing, just a question of altering the dimension of the problem; but the demonstration that a solution exists for the system of equations provided above is more difficult to prove in these higher dimensions. These issues will be taken up in Chapter 4.

2.5 The Equivalence Theorem

We have seen above two distinct lines of approach to the resolution of the exchange problem. The first takes us to the *core* of the economy, and the second takes us to a *competitive equilibrium* for the economy. It should be clear that these two approaches are reached through different sets of assumptions; for example, the second requires individuals to go through markets and arrive at a competitive equilibrium price, whereas the first requires the introduction of neither markets nor a price. Thus, competitive assumptions are not made. However, it is necessary to assume (when there are many individuals) that all possible coalitions can form. Given these distinctive lines of approach, how can we compare the two solutions? Before answering this, let us call an allocation in the core a *core allocation* and the demands achieved at a competitive equilibrium a *competitive allocation*.

First, it may be noted that *any competitive allocation is also a core allocation*.

Suppose this is not the case, i.e. that there is a competitive allocation $\{x^{i*}, i = 1, 2, \ldots, N\}$ which is not in the core. Since x^{i*} is a competitive allocation, there are prices $p_j^*(p^* = (p_j^*))$ such that, for each i, x^{i*} solves

$$\max \quad u^i(x)$$

$$\text{s.t.} \quad p^* x \leqslant p^* e^i$$

$$x \geqslant 0.$$

Again, if $\{x^{i*}\}$ is not in the core, it means that there is a blocking coalition, S; i.e., there is some

$$\{y^i, i \in S\}, \quad \sum_{i \in S} y^i = \sum_{i \in S} e^i$$

such that $u^i(y^i) \geqslant u^i(x^{i*})$ for all $i \in S$ with strict inequality for some $i \in S$.

Let us say that the strict inequality holds for $i_1 \in S$. Now $p^* y^{i_1} > p^* x^{i_1*}$ (by virtue of the utility-maximizing nature of x^{i_1*}). Also, $p^* y^i \not< p^* x^{i*}$ for all $i \in S$; for $p^* y^i < p^* x^{i*} \leqslant p^* e^i$ implies that, by spending more, one may get a higher level of utility than at y^i and hence more utility than x^{i*} is feasible. Therefore

$$p^* y^i \geqslant p^* x^{i*} = p^* e^i, \quad i \in S$$

and

$$p^* y^{i_1} > p^* x^{i_1*} = p^* e^{i_1}$$

where the equality follows from property 3 (Section 2.6.1 below), or

$$p^* \sum_{i \in S} y^i > p^* \sum_{i \in S} e^i$$

which cannot be—hence no such blocking coalition can exist.

We have seen that core allocations contain as a subset the competitive allocations. What is the nature of the other allocations in the core? It turns out that, if there are many individuals, the core allocations are mostly made up of competitive allocations, and with an infinite number of individuals the core allocations and competitive allocations coincide. This is the *Equivalence Theorem*, and we shall consider it next.

As a first step, returning to our two-person (AB) economy, consider an economy where there are two more agents, one of whom a replica of A and other a replica of B. The new A is identical to the previous A in all respects, especially endowment and tastes; similarly, the new B is identical to the earlier one. Let us now call them Al, A2 and B1, B2. How does the core for this economy relate to the core of the AB economy?

Recall that in the AB economy the core consists of $C_1 C_2$, (Figure 2.7). First of all, in the $\{A1, A2; B1, B2\}$ economy, the core would provide identical bundles to individuals of the same type; i.e., each A-type would receive the same x whereas each B-type would receive the same y (the *Equal Treatment Property*). This property may be seen to follow from the property of strict quasi-concavity of the utility functions. For consider an allocation $\{x^1, x^2; y^1, y^2\}$, $x^1 \neq x^2$, say. Now $u^A(x^1) \geqq u^A(x^2)$ and $u^B(y^1) \geqq u^B(y^2)$, say; then $u^A(\frac{1}{2}x^1 + \frac{1}{2}x^2) > u^A(x^2)$ and $u^B(\frac{1}{2}y^1 + \frac{1}{2}y^2) \geqq u^B(y^2)$; moreover,

$$\tfrac{1}{2}\{x^1 + x^2 + y^1 + y^2\} = \tfrac{1}{2}(2e^A + 2e^B) = e^A + e^B,$$

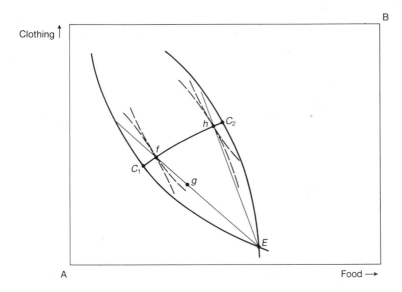

Fig. 2.7

so that a coalition of A2 and B2 can block. Hence $\{x^1, x^2, y^1, y^2\}$ is a core allocation, necessarily means that $x^1 = x^2$ and $y^1 = y^2$.

Thus, if we have an equal number of individuals of each type, then when considering core allocations it is sufficient to consider the allocation to one representative of each type. This is the major analytical advantage when we increase the number of agents by replicating the economy. Also note that C_1, which was in the core for the AB economy, has now been removed from the core for the $\{A1, A2; B1, B2\}$ economy. For, suppose that C_1 corresponds to A receiving $\bar{x}$ and B receiving $\bar{y}$. Does $\{\bar{x}, \bar{x}, \bar{y}, \bar{y}\}$ belong to the core? core?

Consider the coalition of A1, A2, and say B1: from Figure 2.7, Ai prefers z to $\bar{x}$, where $z = \frac{1}{2}\bar{x} + \frac{1}{2}e^A$. Also,

$$2z + \bar{y} = \bar{x} + e^A + \bar{y} = e^A + e^A + e^B,$$

so that $\{A1, A2, B1\}$ form a blocking coalition.

A similar argument establishes the fact that C_2 in Figure 2.7 can no longer be in the core of the economy with A1, A2, B1, B2 as agents. Suppose next that we keep on increasing the number of agents in a special manner; i.e., the number of A and B types are increased so that we always obtain a replica of the original AB economy. In otherwords, there will always be the two distinct types, A and B, and in each type there are n agents. Let these agents be represented by Ai if the agent is of type A and by Bi otherwise, with $i = 1$, $2, \ldots, n$. Now when $n = 2$ we have seen that C_1 and C_2, which are in the core for $n = 1$, do not remain in the core. Consider next non-competitive allocations in the core for $n = 1$. Examples of such allocations are provided by the allocations f or h as shown in Figure 2.7. Suppose f depicts an allocation f^A to A and f^B to B. Consider

$$g = \frac{1}{n}e + \left(1 - \frac{1}{n}\right)f, \quad n > 1,$$

as indicated with an allocation g^A to A. Clearly, for n large, g^A would be preferred to f^A by every member of the type A. So consider a coalition with n A's and $(n - 1)$ B's; such a coalition can offer g^A to each A and f^B to each B since

$$ng^A + (n-1)f^B = e^A + (n-1)(f^A + f^B)$$
$$= e^A + (n-1)(e^A + e^B)$$
$$= ne^A + (n-1)e^B,$$

and hence the allocation f or f^A to each A and f^B to each B would be blocked for n large enough.

Similarly, the allocation h or h^A to each A and h^B to each B can be blocked by a coalition of $(n-1)$ A's and n B's for n large enough.

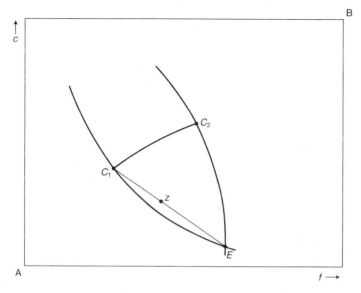

F<small>IG</small>. 2.8

Thus, any non-competitive allocation in the core for $n = 1$ is blocked for n large enough, so that only the competitive allocations in the core for $n = 1$ remain in the core for all n. Thus, as $n \to \infty$, the core shrinks to the set of competitive allocations. This is the *Equivalence Theorem*.

One may think that the way in which number of agents have been increased (keeping types of agents fixed—in our case to two) is crucial for the result; but this is not so. The bibliographical notes at the end of this chapter contain references that consider this result in greater generality.

Having settled doubts on this score, let us consider the significance of the result. In this chapter, we have considered two distinct approaches to the analysis of the exchange problem. One, via the markets where agents are assumed to be competitive, leads to the competitive equilibrium; the other considers a setup where agents co-operate to obtain allocations that cannot be improved upon (or blocked). The spirit of co-operation, embodied in the acts of forming coalitions and putting forward alternatives that are improvements on proposed allocations, is not present in the market economy, with agents considering their interests and reacting to prices. The Equivalence Theorem guarantees that, with large number of agents, the 'appropriate' solution is the competitive allocation.

This, then, is the first reason for being preoccupied with competitive behaviour. As we proceed, we shall encounter other reasons for being concerned with such behaviour; for the present, the Equivalence Theorem and this chapter, in general, will have served their purpose if we can conclude from our elementary discussion of the competitive equilibrium that we have introduced an important concept which merits serious consideration.

MATHEMATICAL NOTES

2.6   Demand Functions and Their Properties

2.6.1   *The Classical Approach*

An individual has an endowment vector $w = (w_1, \ldots, w_n)$ of the n commodities and is assumed to possess tastes that enable him to rank all possible consumption bundles. We assume that his consumption possibility set is R^n_+, the *non-negative orthant* of the Euclidean space; further, his tastes are represented by a real valued function, the utility function $u(\cdot)$, defined over R^n_+. We shall use the notation $x > y$ to mean $x_i > y_i$ for all components, $x \geqq y$ to mean $x_i \geqq y_i$ for all components with strict inequality for some i, and $x \geqq y$ to imply that $x_i \geqq y_i$ for all i. The price vector $p = (p_1, \ldots, p_n)$ will be assumed to satisfy $p > 0$. (0 would be used to denote zero, the scalar as well as the vector with all components zero.) The endowment vector w would be taken to satisfy $w \geqq 0$. Further, we assume that

 (i) $u(x) = 0$ if $x_i = 0$ for some i, and $u(x) > 0$ if $x > 0$;
(ii) there is strict quasi-concavity in the interior of R^n_+ (R^n_{++}): $x > 0, y > 0$, $x \neq y$, and $u(x) = u(y) \Rightarrow u\{\lambda x + (1-\lambda)y\} > u(x)$ for any λ such that $0 < \lambda < 1$;
(iii) $u(x)$ is strictly increasing in R^n_{++}: $x \geqq y > 0 \Rightarrow u(x) > u(y)$.
(iv) $u(x)$ is continuously differentiable of the second order for all $x > 0$.

The consumer's problem may now be written as

$$\max \quad u(x) \tag{C}$$

$$\text{s.t.} \quad px \leqq pw$$

$$x \geqq 0.$$

The constraint set $X = \{x \geqq 0; px \leqq pw\}$ is non-empty and compact, given the positivity of the prices; thus $u(x)$ attains a maximum on X and (C) has a solution (by the Extremum Theorem; see Section 8.5) with the following properties.

1 *If x solves (C), then $x > 0$.*
2 *(C) has a unique solution*; let it be denoted by $x(p, w)$.
3 $px(p, w) = pw$.
4 $x(\mu p, w) = x(p, w)$ *for all $\mu > 0$.*

To see the above results, note first of all $pw > 0$; hence there exists $\bar{x}$ in X such that $\bar{x} > 0$ and hence $u(\bar{x}) > 0$. So if x solves (C), $u(x) \geqq u(\bar{x}) > 0 \Rightarrow x > 0$. Let $\bar{x}, \hat{x}, \bar{x} \neq \hat{x}$ solve (C). Then $\bar{x}, \hat{x} > 0$ and $u(\bar{x}) = u(\hat{x})$. Consequently, $u\{\lambda\bar{x} + (1-\lambda)\hat{x}\} > u(\bar{x})$ for any λ, $0 < \lambda < 1$, and $p\{\lambda\bar{x} + (1-\lambda)\hat{x}\} = \lambda p\bar{x} + (1-\lambda)p\hat{x} \leqq pw$, so that $\bar{x}$ cannot solve (C). Hence $\bar{x} = \hat{x}$.

Property (3) is a trivial consequence of (iii); since $x(p, w) > 0$ and $px(p, w) < pw$, there is $z \in X$ such that $z \geqq x(p, w)$ so that $u(z) > u\{x(p, w)\}$.

For Property (4), notice that replacing p by μp does not alter the constraint set. $x(p, w)$ constitutes the *demand function*.

2.6.2 The Slutsky Equation

By virtue of property 1, $x(p, w) > 0$ implies the validity of the classical Lagrangean method of solving problem (C). Thus, if we write $L(x, \lambda) = u(x) + \lambda(pw - px)$, the solution to (C), $x(p, w)$ (*or* $\hat{x}$), must necessarily satisfy

$$\nabla u(\hat{x}) = \hat{\lambda}p \tag{2.9}$$

$$p\hat{x} = pw$$

for some $\hat{\lambda} \geqq 0$.

It is useful to note from (2.9), and from our assumptions on u, that

$$\hat{\lambda} > 0. \tag{2.10}$$

If

$$\nabla^2 u(x) = \left\{\frac{\partial^2 u(x)}{\partial x_i \partial x_j}\right\},$$

then it must be the case that

$$(x - \hat{x})\nabla^2 u(\hat{x})(x - \hat{x}) \leqq 0$$

for all x such that $px = pw$ (the necessary second-order conditions for a maximum subject to a constraint).

As indicated in the Mathematical Appendix (Section 8.6), a sufficient second-order condition which we shall assume is that

$$(x - \hat{x})\nabla^2 u(\hat{x})(x - \hat{x}) < 0 \tag{2.11}$$

for all x such that

$$x \neq \hat{x}, \quad px = pw = p\hat{x}.$$

As I hope to demonstrate, (2.11) would enable us to obtain the partial derivatives of the demand functions; indeed, (2.11) guarantees that the demand function is a differentiable function of prices. Differentiating (2.9) totally and evaluating the derivatives at $\hat{x}$, we have

$$\begin{bmatrix} \nabla^2 u(\hat{x}) & -p \\ -p & 0 \end{bmatrix} \cdot \begin{bmatrix} dx \\ d\lambda \end{bmatrix} = \begin{bmatrix} \hat{\lambda} dp \\ (\hat{x}-w)dp - pdw \end{bmatrix}. \qquad (2.12)$$

Basically, (2.11) guarantees that the (bordered hessian) matrix on the right of (2.12) is non-singular. For suppose, to the contrary, that it is singular; then there exists (y, α) such that $(y, \alpha) \neq 0$ and

$$\nabla^2 u(\hat{x})y = \alpha p$$

$$py = 0$$

Thus,

$$y\nabla^2 u(\hat{x})y = \alpha yp = 0,$$

which implies by (2.11) that $y = 0$; whence $\alpha = 0$.

Thus the matrix on the right is non-singular, and one may use Cramer's Rule (Section 8.3.3) to obtain

$$d\hat{x}_k = \frac{\hat{\lambda}\sum\limits_{i=1}^{n} A_{ik}\,dp_i + A_{n+1\,k}\{(\hat{x}-w)dp - pdw\}}{\det A} \qquad (2.13)$$

where A is the matrix on the right of (2.12) and A_{ij} denotes the co-factor of the i–jth element in A. Setting $dp_i = 0$, $i \neq j$, and $dw = 0$, we have from (2.13)

$$\left.\frac{\partial \hat{x}_k}{\partial p_j}\right|_{dw=0} = \frac{\hat{\lambda} A_{jk}}{\det A} + (\hat{x}_j - w_j)\frac{A_{n+1\,k}}{\det A}. \qquad (2.14)$$

Let us write $M = pw$; then $dM = pdw$ if $dp = 0$, so we may write

$$\left.\frac{\partial \hat{x}_k}{\partial M}\right|_{dp=0} = -\frac{A_{n+1\,k}}{\det A}. \qquad (2.15)$$

Finally, we wish to consider a compensated price change, that is, a change in p_j together with a change in M so as to leave the individual exactly as well off as before:

$$du(\hat{x}) = 0$$

i.e., $\nabla u(\hat{x})d\hat{x} = 0$ or $\hat{\lambda}pd\hat{x} = 0$ by (2.9), or $pd\hat{x} = 0$ by (2.10). Since

$$p\hat{x} = pw,$$

$$pd\hat{x} + dp\hat{x} = pdw + wdp.$$

Therefore

$$pd\hat{x} = 0 \Rightarrow dp\hat{x} = pdw + wdp$$

or

$$dp(\hat{x} - w) - pdw = 0.$$

Substituting the above into (2.13), we have, after setting $dp_i = 0$ for all $i \neq j$,

$$\left.\frac{\partial \hat{x}_k}{\partial p_j}\right|_{du=0} = \frac{\lambda A_{jk}}{\det A}. \tag{2.16}$$

Thus (2.14) may be written as

$$\left.\frac{\partial \hat{x}_k}{\partial p_j}\right|_{dw=0} = \left.\frac{\partial \hat{x}_k}{\partial p_j}\right|_{du=0} - (\hat{x}_j - w_j)\left.\frac{\partial \hat{x}_k}{\partial M}\right|_{dp=0}. \tag{2.17}$$

This equation occupies a central place in the theory of demand; following Hicks, we shall refer to it as the *Slutsky equation*. Expression (2.17) provides us with the decomposition of the *price effect* into a *substitution effect* and an *income effect*. The results of demand theory are all in terms of the elements of the substitution matrix,

$$W = \left(\frac{\partial \hat{x}_k}{\partial p_j}\right)_{du=0}, \quad k, j = 1, 2, \dots, n, \tag{2.18}$$

and we proceed next to derive these.

2.6.3   The Substitution Matrix

The martix W defined in (2.18) has the following properties:

1   W is symmetric and $p'W = 0$;
2   $x'Wx < 0 \; \forall \, x \neq 0, x \neq \alpha p$ for any scalar α (i.e., W is negative semi-definite with rank $n - 1$).

We shall denote by a prime any matrix transposition; thus p is a column whereas p' is a row.

Property 1 follows easily; for

$$W_{ij} = \left.\frac{\partial \hat{x}_i}{\partial p_j}\right|_{du=0} = \frac{A_{ji}}{\det A} = \frac{A_{ij}}{\det A} \text{ as } A \text{ is symmetric}$$

$$= \left.\frac{\partial \hat{x}_j}{\partial p_i}\right|_{du=0} = W_{ji}.$$

Also,

$$\sum_{i=1}^{n} p_i \left.\frac{\partial x_i}{\partial p_j}\right|_{du=0} = \sum_{i=1}^{n} p_i \frac{A_{ji}}{\det A} = 0,$$

from the property of expansion of determinants.

For property 2, suppose, to the contrary, that there is $\bar{y} \neq 0$, $\bar{y} \neq \alpha p$ for any α and $\bar{y}' W \bar{y} \geqslant 0$. Define $z' = (\bar{y}, 0)$. Since A is non-singular (see above), there is x such that

$$x'A = z'.$$

$$\therefore \quad x'Ax = x'AA^{-1}Ax$$

$$= z'A^{-1}z$$

$$= (\bar{y}, 0)' \begin{bmatrix} \dfrac{A_{ji}}{\det A} & \dfrac{A_{n+1i}}{\det A} \\[3mm] \dfrac{A_{in+1}}{\det A} & \dfrac{A_{n+1n+1}}{\det A} \end{bmatrix} (\bar{y}, 0)$$

$$= \bar{y}' \left(\dfrac{A_{ji}}{\det A} \right) \bar{y}$$

$$= \bar{y}' W \bar{y} \gtreqless 0. \tag{2.19}$$

Also,

$$x'A = (\bar{y}, 0)' \Rightarrow x = (\bar{x}, \alpha) \text{ for some } \alpha,$$

$$\bar{x} \nabla^2 u(\hat{x}) - \alpha p' = \bar{y}',$$

and

$$\bar{x} p = 0.$$

Clearly, $\bar{x} \neq 0$, since otherwise $\bar{y} = -\alpha p$ and $\alpha \neq 0$.

$$\therefore \quad x'Ax = \bar{y}'\bar{x}$$

$$= \bar{x}' \nabla^2 u(\hat{x}) \bar{x},$$

and since $p\bar{x} = 0$, we have, by virtue of (2.11), $x'Ax < 0$. But this violates (2.19). Consequently no such $\bar{y}$ exists and property 2 is established.

Notice that, as a consequence of property 2,

$$\left. \frac{\partial x_i}{\partial p_i} \right|_{du=0} < 0 \text{ for all } i.$$

That is, the own-price substitution effect is negative. This follows by considering

$$x = (0, 0, \ldots, 0, 1, 0, \ldots, 0),$$
$$_{i}$$

and since $p > 0$, $x'Wx < 0$ immediately provides us with the above.

2.7 The Axiomatic Approach

2.7.1 *Existence and Continuity of Demand Functions*

One may obtain the results of the last section by beginning with a more basic idea—that of the ranking over the set S of all possible consumption bundles. We shall take S to be a subset of R^n. We assume that

(i) S is convex and bounded from below; i.e., there is $c \in R^n$ such that $x \in S \Rightarrow x \geqslant c$;

(ii) S is completely ordered by a preference relation $\mathscr{R}$; i.e., there is a binary relation $\mathscr{R}$ defined on S satisfying

(a) $x \mathscr{R} x$ for all $x \in S$ (*reflexivity*);

(b) for any pair $(x, y) \in S \times S$, either $x \mathscr{R} y$ or $y \mathscr{R} x$ or both (*completeness*);

(c) $x, y, z \in S$, $x \mathscr{R} y$, $y \mathscr{R} z \Rightarrow x \mathscr{R} z$ (*transitivity*).

We shall interpret $\mathscr{R}$ as the 'no worse than' relation; i.e., $x \mathscr{R} y$ would be interpreted as 'x is no worse than y'. Given $\mathscr{R}$, one may define relations $\mathscr{P}$ (preferred to) and $\mathscr{I}$ (indifferent to) as follows:

$$x \mathscr{P} y \Leftrightarrow x \mathscr{R} y \text{ and not } y \mathscr{R} x$$

$$x \mathscr{I} y \Leftrightarrow x \mathscr{R} y \text{ and } y \mathscr{R} x.$$

We shall also employ an additional requirement on $\mathscr{R}$:

(iii) If (x^n), (y^n) are two sequences in S with $x^n \mathscr{R} y^n$ for all n, and if $x^n \to \hat{x}$, $y^n \to \hat{y}$ as $n \to \infty$ where $\hat{x}, \hat{y} \in S$, then $\hat{x} \mathscr{R} \hat{y}$. (The relation $\mathscr{R}$ is *continuous*.)

Given an endowment w and price p, where $w \in S$, $p > 0$, let $B(p, w) = \{z : pz \leqslant pw, z \in S\}$: *the budget set*. Then $f(p, w) = \{x \in B(p, w) : x \mathscr{R} z$ for all $z \in B(p, w)\}$: *the demand correspondence*. (The term 'correspondence' is used to indicate that $f(p, w)$ need not contain a unique element.) We first seek to establish the fact that $f(p, w) \neq \varnothing$ and then demonstrate that demand varies continuously with prices, in some sense to be made precise. Let

$$C_x = \{y \in S : y \mathscr{R} x\}, \quad C^x = \{z \in S : x \mathscr{R} z\}.$$

1: If $\mathscr{R}$ is continuous, then C_x, C^x are closed subsets of S.

To show that C_x is a closed subset of S, we need to establish that every limit point of C_x is contained in C_x. So let $\hat{y}$ be a limit point of C_x; i.e., there is a sequence $y^n \in C_x$ and $y^n \to \hat{y}$. Since $y^n \mathscr{R} x^n$ for all n, $\hat{y} \mathscr{R} \hat{x}$ by continuity of $\mathscr{R}$; i.e. $\hat{y} \in C_x$ and the claim follows. The closure of C_x may be similarly established. $\square$

Let B be any subset of S, and let $x^1, \ldots, x^k$ be a finite subset of B. $[x^1, \ldots, x^k]$ would be defined to be *dominated in B* if there is $y \in B$ such that $y \mathscr{R} x^j$ for all $j = 1, \ldots, k$.

2: Let S be bounded below, $p > 0$, and $\mathscr{R}$ be continuous. Then $f(p, w) \neq \varnothing$ if and only if every finite subset of $B(p, w)$ is dominated in $B(p, w)$.

In case $x^* \in f(p, w)$, since $x^* \mathscr{R} x$ for all $x \in B(p, w)$, it is clear that every finite subset of $B(p, w)$ is dominated in B. For the other part, note that $p > 0 \Rightarrow B(p, w)$ is compact; suppose, to the contrary, that it is not so: since $B(p, w)$ is closed, there must be a sequence $z^n \in B(p, w)$ and $z_j^n \to +\infty$. (This is the only possibility, as $B(p, w) \subseteq S$ and S is bounded below.) Hence

$\Sigma p_j z_j^n \leqslant \Sigma p_j w_j$ must be violated for n large enough. So no such sequence can exist.

Let $\{x^1, \ldots, x^m\}$ be a finite subset of $B(p, w)$; since it is dominated in $B(p, w)$, there is $y \in B(p, w)$ such that $y \in C_x$ for all i. For any $x \in B(p, w)$, let $\bar{C}_x = C_x \cap B(p, w)$. From continuity of $\mathcal{R}$, $\{\bar{C}_x, x \in B(p, w)\}$ forms a family of non-empty closed subsets of a compact set $B(p, w)$. Moreover, for any finite $x^1, \ldots, x^m$

$$\bigcap_{j=1}^{m} \bar{C}_x \neq \varnothing.$$

Then it follows (see Section 8.4.1) that

$$\bigcap_{x \in B(p, w)} \bar{C}_x \neq \varnothing;$$

Let

$$y \in \bigcap_{x \in B(p, w)} \bar{C}_x;$$

then $y \in f(p, w)$. $\square$

Notice that we have established the existence of demand under extremely general conditions; $\mathcal{R}$ need not satisfy any of the standard assumptions such as transitivity or completeness. The crucial property for a continuous $\mathcal{R}$ is the domination of every finite subset of the budget set.

To provide the demand correspondence with greater structure, we need to strengthen our requirements on $\mathcal{R}$ from the meagre restrictions imposed in the last two results. We shall also find it easier to confine our attention to the case of a demand function. With this in mind, we shall use assumptions (i)–(iii); we also need

(iv) $x, y \in S$, $x \neq y$, and $x \mathcal{R} y \Rightarrow \{\lambda x + (1 - \lambda)y\} \mathcal{P} x$ for any λ where $0 < \lambda < 1$ (*strict quasi-concavity*).

 3: Under (iv), $\bar{x}, \hat{x} \in f(p, w) \Rightarrow \bar{x} = \hat{x}$.

The proof follows the lines of the argument presented in Section 2.6 for proving the corresponding result. Consequently, we may speak of the demand function; our next aim is to establish that it varies continuously with respect to (p, w). Before we do so, an important step consists of the following:

 4: If $p > 0$ and $w \in S$ is such that there is $\bar{x} \in S$ and $p\bar{x} < pw$, then for any sequence $(p^r, w^r) \to (p, w)$ and for any $z \in B(p, w)$ there is $z^r \in B(p^r, w^r)$ and $z^r \to z$ (the lower hemi-continuity of the budget set correspondence).

Proof. Choose $z \in B(p, w)$ and a sequence $(p^r, w^r) \to (p, w)$. In case $pz < pw$, $p^r z < p^r w^r$ for all r large enough and $z \in B(p^r, w^r)$ for all $r > N$, say, for an appropriate N. So let $pz = pw$; consider $\bar{x} \in S$ such that $p\hat{x} < pw$. Define $z^r = t^r z + (1 - t^r)\bar{x}$, $t^r \in [0, 1]$, and assume that t^r is the maximum number between 0 and 1 such that $p^r z^r \leqslant p^r w^r$.

Since S is convex, $z^r \in S$; hence $z^r \in B(p^r, w^r)$. Notice also that $t^r < 1 \Rightarrow p^r z^r = p^r w^r$ as otherwise t^r is not maximal. Since (t^r) is a bounded sequence, limit points exist by virtue of (BW) (see Section 8.4.1). Let $\hat{t}$ be one such; if possible, let $t < 1$. Then there is a subsequence,

$$t^{r_k} \to \hat{t} < 1;$$

$$z^{r_k} \to \hat{z} = \hat{t}z + (1 - \hat{t})\bar{x};$$

and

$$p\hat{z} = \hat{t}pz + (1 - \hat{t})p\bar{x} < pw \Rightarrow p^{r_k} z^{r_k} < p^{r_k} w^{r_k},$$

for all k large enough; i.e., $t^{r_k} = 1$ for all k large enough so that $\hat{t} = 1$: a contradiction. Thus $t^r \to 1$ and $z^r \to z$, and the claim is established. □

5: If $\bar{p} > 0$ and $\bar{w} \in S$ is such that there is $\bar{x} \in S$ and $\bar{p}\bar{x} < \bar{p}\bar{w}$, then $f(p, w)$ is a continuous function of (p, w) at $(\bar{p}, \bar{w})$.

Proof. The claim would be established if, given any sequence $(p^r, w^r) \to (\bar{p}, \bar{w})$, $x^r = f(p^r, w^r) \Rightarrow x^r \to \hat{x}$ and $\hat{x} = f(\bar{p}, \bar{w})$. First of all, let $\bar{p}_k = \min_i \bar{p}_i$ and $\bar{p}_j = \max_i \bar{p}_i$; choose $\varepsilon > 0$ such that $\bar{p}_k - \varepsilon > 0$, and define $p_* = (p_{i*})$ such that $p_{i*} = \bar{p}_k - \varepsilon$ for all i; also, define $p^* = (p_i^*)$ where $p_i^* = \bar{p}_j + \varepsilon$ for all i. Then $x^r \in B = \{x: p_* x \leqslant \Sigma p_i^*(\bar{w}_i + \varepsilon)\}$ for all r large enough; this follows since

$$p_* x^r < p^r x^r \leqslant p^r w^r \leqslant \Sigma_i p_i^*(\bar{w}_i + \varepsilon)$$

for all r large; since B is compact, x^r must have a convergent subsequence $x^{r_k} \to x^*$ as $k \to \infty$. Suppose $x^* \neq f(\bar{p}, \bar{w})$. Since $p^r x^r \leqslant p^r w^r$, $\bar{p}x^* \leqslant \bar{p}\bar{w}$ so that $x^* \in B(\bar{p}, \bar{w})$; moreover, there exists $\tilde{x} \in B(\bar{p}, \bar{w})$ and $\tilde{x} \mathscr{P} x^*$. Since result 4 is applicable, there is $\tilde{x}^r \in B(p^r, w^r)$ such that $\tilde{x}^r \to \tilde{x}$. Again, $x^r \mathscr{R} \tilde{x}^r \Rightarrow x^* \mathscr{R} \tilde{x}$. This is a contradiction. So no such $\tilde{x}$ can exist, and consequently $x^* = f(\bar{p}, \bar{w})$. Since this is true for any arbitrary limit point, $x^r \to \hat{x} = f(\bar{p}, \bar{w})$. □

When (iv) does not hold, the demand set $f(p, w)$ need not consist of a single element, but an argument exactly similar to the one above may be provided to conclude that the demand correspondence would be closed. The demand correspondence $f: R^n_{++} \times S \to S$ is said to be closed at $(\bar{p}, \bar{w})$ if, for any sequence $(p^r, w^r) \to (\bar{p}, \bar{w})$ and $x^r \in f(p^r, w^r)$, $x^r \to \bar{x}$ such that $\bar{x} \in f(\bar{p}, \bar{w})$.

2.7.2 *The Expenditure Function and the Slutsky Equation*

The assumptions for this section are assumptions (i)–(iii) made in the last section.

Define $M_x(p) = \text{Inf } [pz: z \in C_x]$, i.e. the infimum of the expenditure required to be just as well off as at x. First of all, we may note the following.

6: There is $w \in C_x$ such that $pw = M_x(p)$ when $p > 0$.

Note result 1 in the last section; hence $B_x(p) = \{z \in S: pz \leqslant px\} \cap C_x$ is closed and bounded, given that S is bounded below. Thus pz attains a minimum on $B_x(p)$ by virtue of ET (Section 8.5).

$M_x(p)$ may now be defined with the infimum replaced by minimum, whenever $p > 0$; henceforth we consider only $p > 0$. $M_x(p)$ has rather interesting properties which may be used for an alternative route to the Slutsky equation. This method is entirely due to McKenzie (1956), and we shall follow his analysis. In addition to assumptions (i)–(iii), we shall use two further restrictions:

(v) For any (p, x) and any arbitrary neighbourhood U of x, there is $\tilde{x} \in U \cap S$ such that $p\tilde{x} < px$.
(vi) For any $x \in S$, U an arbitrary neighbourhood of x, there is $x' \in U \cap S$, such that $x' \mathscr{P} x$.

The properties of $M_x(p)$ may now be stated.

7: (a) $M_x(p)$ is concave in p and $M_x(tp) = tM_x(p)$ for any scalar $t > 0$.
   (b) Under (v), $z \in f_x(p) = \{z: z \in f[p, M_x(p)]\} \Rightarrow z \mathscr{I} x$.
   (c) If (vi) holds at $z \in f(p, M)$, then $pz = M$; if (vi) holds at all $z \in f(p, M)$, then $pz = M_z(p)$.

Proof. First of all, $M_x(tp) = tM_x(p)$ follows from definition. Next, by result 6, let

$$p = \lambda p^1 + (1 - \lambda)p^2, 0 \leqslant \lambda \leqslant 1.$$

$$M_x(p) = pw = \lambda p^1 w + (1 - \lambda)p^2 w \geqslant \lambda M_x(p^1) + (1 - \lambda)M_x(p^2)$$

since $w \in C_x$.

For (b), note first that $z \in f\{p, M_x(p)\}$ and $w \in C_x$ being available implies $z \mathscr{R} x$. Next, assumption (v) allows us to generate a sequence $z^i \to z$, such that $pz^i < pz$; hence $pz^i < M_x(p) \Rightarrow z^i \notin C_x$ or $x \mathscr{P} z^i$; i.e., $x \mathscr{R} z$. Combining the two, (b) follows.

Part (c) follows by noting that $pz \leqslant M$; in case of strict inequality, (vi) allows the choice of z' such that $pz' \leqslant M$ and $z' \mathscr{P} z$: a contradiction. Thus $pz = M$.

Next, $M_z(p) \leqslant pz = M$; if $M_z(p) < M$, there is $w \in C_z$ such that $pw = M$; thus, $w \in f(p, M)$, which contradicts the first part, given assumption (vi). Thus $pz = M_z(p) = M$. $\square$

The remaining properties of $M_x(p)$ deal with the derivatives of $M_x(p)$ and $f_x(p)$, so the statement is contingent upon these derivatives existing.

8: (a) $\tilde{p} \left\{ \dfrac{\partial f_{x_i}(\tilde{p})}{\partial p_j} \right\} = 0.$

 (b) $\left\{ \dfrac{\partial f_{x_i}(\tilde{p})}{\partial p_j} \right\}$ is symmetric and negative semi-definite.

Proof. For $p \in N_\delta(\tilde{p})$, $z = f_x(p) \Rightarrow z \in C_x$. Therefore $M_x(\tilde{p}) \leqslant \tilde{p}z$; i.e., $\tilde{p}f_x(\tilde{p}) \leqslant \tilde{p}f_x(p)$ for all p close to $\tilde{p}$; hence $\tilde{p}f_x(p)$ takes on a minimum at $p = \tilde{p}$; (a) is just the first-order condition.

Next, note that

$$\frac{\partial M_x(\tilde{p})}{\partial p_i} = f_{x_i}(\tilde{p}) + \tilde{p} \left\{ \frac{\partial f_{x_i}(\tilde{p})}{\partial p_k} \right\}$$

$$= f_{x_i}(\tilde{p}),$$

by (a). So

$$\frac{\partial^2 M_x(\tilde{p})}{\partial p_i \partial p_k} = \frac{\partial f_{x_i}(\tilde{p})}{\partial p_k}.$$

Part (b) now follows from the above and the concavity of $M_x(p)$. □
Since $M_x(p)$ is concave, $\partial^2 M_x(p)/\partial p_i \partial p_k$ exists almost everywhere. (Section 8.5.2)
Finally, consider the demand function, $x = f(p, M)$. Then we have

$$\frac{\partial f_i(p, M)}{\partial p_j} = \frac{\partial f_{x_i}}{\partial p_j} - f_j(p)\frac{\partial f_i(p, M)}{\partial M}.$$

By definition, $f_x(p) = f\{p, M_x(p)\} = f(p, M)$ (see result 7(c)). Therefore

$$\frac{\partial f_{x_i}(p)}{\partial p_j} = \frac{\partial f_i\{p, M_x(p)\}}{\partial p_j} + \frac{\partial f_i}{\partial M}\frac{\partial M_x(p)}{\partial p_j}$$

$$= \frac{\partial f_i}{\partial p_j} + f_{x_j}(p)\frac{\partial f_i(p, M)}{\partial M}.$$

Therefore

$$\frac{\partial f_i(p, M)}{\partial p_j} = \frac{\partial f x_i}{\partial p_j} - f_j(p, M)\frac{\partial f_i(p, M)}{\partial M},$$

which is the Slutsky equation. □

2.8   Equilibrium Price and the Distribution of Endowments

2.8.1   *The Problem*

Given a particular distribution of goods among individuals, and given the assumptions made in the text, an equilibrium may exist. Although we have not yet presented an argument to demonstrate the existence of equilibrium in the general case, we have already seen an argument that establishes the existence of equilibrium for the case of two goods. If the distribution of endowments is altered, then the equilibrium configuration alters too. The object of this section is to look into this connection between equilibrium and the distribution of endowments.

Consider the situation analysed in the text. A and B, the two persons, have a distribution of endowments $(\bar{f}_a, \bar{c}_a)$ and $(\bar{f}_b, \bar{c}_b)$ of the two goods. Given their preferences, one may derive the excess demand for food and represent it as $z_f(p; e)$, where $e \in E = \{(f_a, c_a), (f_b, c_b): f_a + f_b = \bar{f}_a + \bar{f}_b, c_a + c_b = \bar{c}_a + \bar{c}_b, f_a, f_b, c_a, c_b > 0\}$, the set of possible endowment distributions, and p, the relative price of food to clothing. p^* is an equilibrium, given $e \in E$, if

$$z_f(p^*; e) = 0.$$

We define $X(e) = \{p: p \geqslant 0 \text{ such that } z_f(p; e) = 0\}$ for any distribution of endowments $e \in E$. Under the assumptions of Section 2.4, $X(e) \neq \varnothing$ for any e; i.e., equilibrium exists. The specific aim of this section is to study the relationship $X(e)$. In particular, two specific forms of changes of e and their effects on the welfare of A and B are considered. One type of change may be called 'transfer'. This concerns a change in the distribution of endowments wherein one of the agents, say A, makes a gift to B; A would be *the donor* and B *the recipient*. The other type of change would be called 'growth'; i.e., only one agent experiences a change in his endowment. In transfer, the endowment shifts from one point in the box diagram to another point within the same box; in growth, the dimensions of the box alter. Such changes have been considered in international trade theory, and questions such as transfer making the donor better off and growth being immiserizing have been widely discussed. We shall take up the question of transfer first. In each case there is a change in the endowment followed by a change in equilibrium price.

2.8.2   *Preliminary Results*

We first establish a continuity property of $X(e)$. For each $e \in E$, $X(e)$ denotes the equilibrium price (of food relative to clothing). Let e^s be a sequence in E and $e^s \to \bar{e} \in S$; let $p^s \in X(e^s)$, $p^s \to \bar{p}$. We shall show that $\bar{p} \in X(\bar{e})$, under some conditions. For suppose to the contrary that $\bar{p} \notin X(\bar{e})$: then $z_f(\bar{p}, \bar{e}) \neq 0$. By virtue of the result demonstrated in Section 2.7.1 (the continuity of demand functions), $z_f(p, e)$ is a continuous function of (p, e) if $pf_a + c_a > 0$ and

$pf_b + c_b > 0$. From the definition of the excess demand function, that would be continuous too. So $z_f(\bar{p}, \bar{e}) \neq 0$ implies that $z_f(p^s, e^s)$ has the same sign as $z_f(\bar{p}, \bar{e})$ and hence $p^s \notin X(e^s)$: a contradiction. Thus

9: The correspondence $X : E \to R_+$ is closed at every $e \in E$.

In what follows, we shall assume that

$$\bar{p}, \hat{p} \in X(e) \Rightarrow \bar{p} = \hat{p} \tag{u}$$

or that equilibrium is unique; this makes $X(e)$ a continuous function on E. Let $\hat{e}$ then denote the initial distribution of endowments, $X(\hat{e}) = \hat{p}$, and $\bar{e}$, the altered distribution of endowments, $X(\bar{e}) = \bar{p}$; further, let

$$\hat{e} = \{(\hat{f}_a, \hat{c}_a); \quad (\hat{f}_b, \hat{c}_b)\} \quad \text{and} \quad \bar{e} = \{(\bar{f}_a, \bar{c}_a); \quad (\bar{f}_b, \bar{c}_b)\}.$$

Using the notation of Section 2.3, let

$$\left. \begin{array}{l} \hat{X}_f = F_A(\hat{p}, \hat{p}\hat{f}_a + \hat{c}_a) \\ \hat{X}_c = G_A(\hat{p}, \hat{p}\hat{f}_a + \hat{c}_a) \end{array} \right\} \qquad \text{the consumption of A at the initial equilibrium configuration}$$

$$\left. \begin{array}{l} \hat{Y}_f = F_B(\hat{p}, \hat{p}\hat{f}_b + \hat{c}_b) \\ \hat{Y}_c = G_B(\hat{p}, \hat{p}\hat{f}_b + \hat{c}_b) \end{array} \right\} \qquad \text{the consumption of B at the initial equilibrium configuration}$$

and let

$$\bar{X}_f = F_A(\bar{p}, \bar{p}\bar{f}_a + \bar{c}_a), \quad \bar{X}_c = G_A(\bar{p}, \bar{p}\bar{f}_a + \bar{c}_a);$$
$$\bar{Y}_f = F_B(\bar{p}, \bar{p}\bar{f}_b + \bar{c}_b), \quad \bar{Y}_c = G_B(\bar{p}, \bar{p}\bar{f}_b + \bar{c}_b).$$

What we wish to investigate is the effect of the change on A and B: how are they placed at $(\bar{p}, \bar{e})$ when compared to their position at $(\hat{p}, \hat{e})$? To answer this question, we introduce

$$M_{\hat{u}}^A(p) = \min(px_f + x_c) \quad \text{s.t.} \quad U^A(x_f, x_c) \geqslant U^A(\hat{X}_f, \hat{X}_c) = \hat{U}^A$$
$$M_{\hat{u}}^B(p) = \min(py_f + y_c) \quad \text{s.t.} \quad U^B(y_f, y_c) \geqslant U^B(\hat{Y}_f, \hat{Y}_c) = \hat{U}^B.$$

These are, of course, the minimum expenditure functions whose properties were discussed in the last section.

In particular, we may recall that

(a) $M_{\hat{u}}^i(p)$ is concave in p;

(b) $\dfrac{\partial M_{\hat{u}}^i}{\partial p} = \left\{ \begin{array}{ll} x_f(p, \hat{U}^i), & i = A \\ y_f(p, \hat{U}^i), & i = B \end{array} \right\}$ the compensated demand functions;

$$\frac{\partial^2 M_{\hat{u}}^i(p)}{\partial p^2} = \left\{ \begin{array}{ll} \dfrac{\partial x_f(p, \hat{U}^i)}{\partial p} < 0, & i = A \\[2mm] \dfrac{\partial y_f(p, \hat{U}^i)}{\partial p} < 0, & i = B \end{array} \right.$$

so that $M_a^i(p)$ is strictly concave in p; see for example, the treatment of the properties of the substitution terms provided in Section 2.7.

To establish the change in welfare of A and B, we need to examine the sign of

$$\theta^i = M_a^i(\bar{p}) - (\bar{p}\bar{f}_i + \bar{c}_i), \qquad i = A, B;$$

or, writing $\bar{p} = \hat{p} + \Delta p, \bar{f}_i = \hat{f}_i + \Delta f_i, \ \bar{c}_i = \hat{c}_i + \Delta c_i$, we need to sign the expression

$$\begin{aligned}
\theta^i &= M_a^i(\bar{p}) - \{(\hat{p} + \Delta p)(\hat{f}_i + \Delta f_i) + \hat{c}_i + \Delta c_i\} \\
&= M_a^i(\bar{p}) - (\hat{p}\hat{f}_i + \hat{c}_i) - \{\Delta p(\hat{f}_i + \Delta f_i) + \Delta c_i\} + \hat{p}\Delta f_i \\
&= M_a^i(\bar{p}) - M_a^i(\hat{p}) - \{\Delta p(\hat{f}_i + \Delta f_i) + \hat{p}\Delta f_i + \Delta c_i\}.
\end{aligned}$$

Now

$$\begin{aligned}
\theta^A &< \{x_f(\hat{p}, \hat{U}^A) - \hat{f}_a\}\Delta p - \{\hat{p}\Delta f_a + \Delta c_a\} - \Delta p \Delta f_a \\
&= \alpha^A, \text{ say,}
\end{aligned}$$

and

$$\begin{aligned}
\theta^B &< \{y_f(\hat{p}, \hat{U}^B) - \hat{f}_b\}\Delta p - \{\hat{p}\Delta f_b + \Delta c_b\} - \Delta p \Delta f_b \\
&= \alpha^B, \text{ say.}
\end{aligned}$$

Notice the clear breakup of α^i into the sets of terms, the 'price effect', the 'endowment effect', and a 'combined effect'. Our point of focus below will be whether one of these effects always dominates.

2.8.3 *The Welfare Effects of Transfer*

For the case of two individuals, $i = A, B$, if changes in endowments satisfy

$$\left.\begin{aligned}
\Delta f_a + \Delta f_b &= 0 \\
\Delta c_a + \Delta c_b &= 0,
\end{aligned}\right\} \tag{T}$$

then we have the transfer problem; moreover, we shall designate A to be the donor if $\hat{p}\Delta f_a + \Delta c_a \leqslant 0$; as in the last section, $\hat{p}$ denotes the pre-change equilibrium. Moreover, for the sake of viability, we need to have

$$\hat{f}_a + \Delta f_a \geqslant 0 \qquad \hat{f}_b + \Delta f_b \geqslant 0$$

$$\hat{c}_a + \Delta c_a \geqslant 0 \qquad \hat{c}_b + \Delta c_b \geqslant 0.$$

Notice now that specifying any $(\Delta f_a, \Delta c_a)$ such that

$$\hat{p}\Delta f_a + \Delta \hat{c}_a \leqslant 0$$

specifies, via (T), $(\Delta f_b, \Delta c_b)$; hence the new distribution $\{(\bar{f}_a, \bar{c}_a), (\bar{f}_b, \bar{c}_b)\}$ becomes determined; consequently, the new equilibrium price ratio $\bar{p}$ is fixed, given condition (u). Thus the expressions $\alpha^i (i = A, B)$ become continuous functions of $(\Delta f_a, \Delta c_a)$, given the preliminary results of the last section.

By virtue of A being the donor, the set of all possible $(\Delta f_a, \Delta c_a)$ lies in the shaded part of Figure 2.9. X corresponds to $(-\hat{f}_a, -\hat{c}_a)$ i.e. to a gift from A to B of A's total stock of goods. Clearly, it would be the case that, if A were to give everything away, A would be worse off at the new equilibrium after the transfer. Thus $\alpha^A(-\hat{f}_a, -\hat{c}_a) > 0$. Moreover,

$$\alpha^A(\Delta f_a, \Delta c_a) + \alpha^B(\Delta f_a, \Delta c_a) = \{x_f(\hat{p}, \hat{U}^A) - \hat{f}_a + y_f(\hat{p}, \hat{U}^B) - \hat{f}_b)\} \Delta p$$
$$- \{\Delta p(\Delta f_a + \Delta f_b) + \hat{p}(\Delta f_a + \Delta f_b)$$
$$+ (\Delta c_a + \Delta c_b)\} = 0,$$

using the equilibrium conditions and the transfer condition.

Thus, $\alpha^A(\Delta f_a, \Delta c_a) \leqslant 0$ implies that A is better off after the transfer; whereas $\alpha^A(\Delta f_a, \Delta c_a) > 0 \Rightarrow \alpha^B(\Delta f_a, \Delta c_a) < 0$, i.e. that B is better off after the transfer; then it must be the case that A is worse off—since, basically, we are comparing points along the contract locus of a given box diagram.

For A to be better off after the transfer, there must exist $(\Delta f_a, \Delta c_a)$ in S such that $\alpha^A(\Delta f_a, \Delta c_a) \leqslant 0$; since $\alpha^A(\cdot)$ is continuous on S, and $\alpha^A(\cdot) > 0$ at X, it

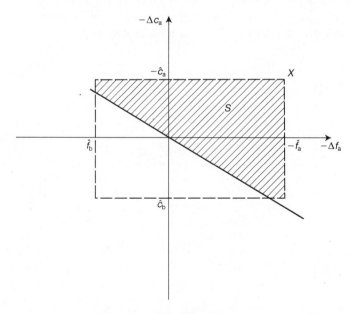

Fɪɢ. 2.9

follows that, for A to be better off, $\alpha^A(\cdot)$ must be zero somewhere in S, i.e. that $\alpha^A(\cdot)$ must change sign, or that, for some $(\Delta \tilde{f}_a, \Delta \tilde{c}_a)$,

$$\alpha^A(\Delta \tilde{f}_a, \Delta \tilde{c}_a) = 0;$$

and for any neighbourhood $N(\Delta \tilde{f}_a, \Delta \tilde{c}_a) \cap S$, there would exist $(\Delta f_a, \Delta c_a)$ in this neighbourhood such that $\alpha^A(\Delta f_a, \Delta c_a) > 0$. But $\alpha^A(\Delta \tilde{f}_a, \Delta \tilde{c}_a) = 0$, which means that there is $\tilde{p}$ such that

$$M_{\tilde{u}}^A(\tilde{p}) - (\tilde{p}\tilde{f}_a + \tilde{c}_a) < 0$$

where $\tilde{p}$ is the post-transfer equilibrium corresponding to a transfer $(\Delta \tilde{f}_a, \Delta \tilde{c}_a)$; or that

$$U^A\{X_f(\tilde{p}; \tilde{f}_a, \tilde{c}_a), X_c(\tilde{p}; \tilde{f}_a, \tilde{c}_a)\} > U^A\{X_f(\hat{p}; \hat{f}_a, \hat{c}_a), X_c(\hat{p}; \hat{f}_a, \hat{c}_a)\};$$

i.e., there exists a small neighbourhood N_δ of $(\Delta \tilde{f}_a, \Delta \tilde{c}_a)$ such that, for all $(\Delta f_a, \Delta c_a)$ in $N_\delta \cap S$,

$$U^A\{X_f(p; f_a, c_a), X_c(p; f_a, c_a)\} > U^A\{X_f(\hat{p}; \hat{f}_a, \hat{c}_a), X_c(\hat{p}, \hat{f}_a, \hat{c}_a)\},$$

or $\alpha^A(\Delta f_a, \Delta c_a) \lesseqgtr 0$. This follows, given the continuity of the various demand functions and equilibrium price function. So $\alpha^A(-\hat{f}_a, -\hat{c}_a) > 0 \Rightarrow \alpha^A(\cdot) > 0$ on the entire shaded areas (except, of course, for the origin).

Thus, the recipient will always be better off after the transfer. Basically, condition (u) is crucial for the above result to go through; that condition (u) is violated whenever the donor is better off after transfer may be seen in Figure 2.10. Let e denote the initial distribution of endowments, x the equilibrium demands at e, $\bar{e}$ the post-transfer distribution of endowments,

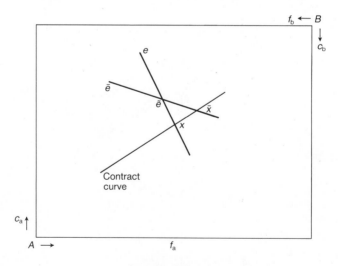

F<small>IG</small>. 2.10

and $\bar{x}$ the equilibrium demands at $\bar{e}$. Thus A, the donor, is better off after the transfer. Notice then that, necessarily, there must exist $\tilde{e}$ such that at $\tilde{e}$ there are two positions of equilibrium, so that condition (u) is violated at $\tilde{e}$.

2.8.4 *The Welfare Effects of Growth*

Growth would be interpreted generally to mean a change in the endowment pattern of one individual only; suppose for example that $\Delta f_a \geqslant 0$, $\Delta c_a \geqslant 0$ with strict inequality at least once, and that $\Delta f_b = 0$, $\Delta c_b = 0$. Returning to our basic equations in Section 2.8.2,

$$\alpha^A = \{x_f(\hat{p}, \hat{U}^A) - \hat{f}_a\}\Delta p - \{\hat{p}\Delta f_a + \Delta c_a\} - \Delta p \Delta f_a$$
$$\alpha^B = y_f(\hat{p}, \hat{U}^B)\Delta p$$

so that, as far as A is concerned, there are two possible sources of $\alpha^A < 0$ (i.e. of A being better off after growth): either $\{x_f(\hat{p}, \hat{U}^A) - \hat{f}_a\}\Delta p < 0$ (the price effect), or the negativity of α^A arising from the other terms (the endowment and combined effects). So far as B is concerned, there is only the price effect.

Notice that the nature of our enquiry is as before: whether a beneficial endowment change can be swamped by an adverse price change. Unfortunately, no general results follow here, as the following simple example shows. The two individuals are provided with the following tastes. Let $U^A(x, y) = xy$. B consumes goods in the proportion 1:1, A has 2 units of good x, and B has 3 units of good y. One may compute B's demand for x to be

$$x_B = \frac{3}{p+1}$$

where p is the price of x relative to y. Further,

$$x_A = 1 \text{ if } p \neq 0,$$

so that excess demand for x is

$$\frac{3}{p+1} + 1 - 2,$$

which vanishes if and only if $\hat{p} = 2$. Also, the excess demand may be noted to be downward-sloping at $\hat{p} = 2$. At this equilibrium, A consumes $(1, 2)$ of x and y, respectively; on the other hand, B consumes $(1, 1)$. Suppose now that A's endowment goes up to 4 units of x. Then $x_A = 2$ if $p \neq 0$; excess demand for x is given by $\{3/(p+1)\} - 2$, which vanishes if and only if $p^* = \frac{1}{2}$. At this equilibrium, A consumes $(2, 1)$ and is no worse off than before; B consumes $(2, 2)$ and is better off.

In fact, if A's endowment were to go up to 5 units of x, the resultant equilibrium would be one where A is worse off than at $\hat{p} = 2$; the details may be worked out to show that, with A's endowment at 5 units, the equilibrium price $p=0.2$ and A consumes (2.5, 0.5) of x and y. The same example may be used to demonstrate that, if A were to destroy some units of x, then the disadvantageous endowment effect would be swamped by an advantageous price effect. Such examples have been noted in the literature, too; for readers interested in examples such as these, some items are provided in the bibliographical notes that follow.

BIBLIOGRAPHICAL NOTES

The text contains material which is considered by now to be classical; the basic reference in this connection is Walras (1877: Lessons 5–20); Newman (1965) contains a more modern and an equally clear exposition. On the existence of a competitive equilibrium in a simple framework, see Arrow and Hahn (1977: ch. 2) and the discussion in Chipman (1965). The stability question in the two-goods case is traditionally discussed in the area of international trade theory; see Jones (1961), for example. The final section of the chapter contains an elementary discussion of the Equivalence Theorem due to Debreu and Scarf (1963). For a more detailed and highly readable account, see Hildenbrand and Kirman (1976).

The mathematical notes to Chapter 2 contain an analysis of the properties of demand functions; the classical approach is due to Hicks (1946: chs. 1–3 and relevant mathematical appendices). The axiomatic approach covers three sets of issues: (a) existence, (b) continuity, and (c) derivative properties of demand. The result, so far the first is considered, is from Mukherji (1977); for some other results in this connection, see Sonnenschein (1971) and Gale and Mas-Colell (1975). The continuity property was first clearly demonstrated in its current form by Debreu (1959). The derivative properties obtained via the expenditure function are due to McKenzie (1956). Such an analysis is of wider relevance; see e.g. Diewert (1982) for a discussion of the duality theory.

The importance of the expenditure function is best exhibited by applications to particular areas; see for example Willig (1976) for an application to the mesurement of consumer's surplus, and Diamond and McFadden (1974) for an application to the area of public finance. In the mathematical notes to this chapter, the expenditure function has been exploited to study the dependence of equilibrium price on the pattern of the initial endowment structure. This is related to two topics in international trade theory: the *transfer problem*, and the *effects of growth*. In contrast to the more traditional approaches to such problems, this method enables us to handle 'large' changes in endowments. In this connection, see Majumdar and Mitra (1985), from which I have borrowed Figure 2.10, Jones and Kenen (1985: chs. 1 and 2), Gale (1974), and Guesnerie and Laffont (1978).

Two topics have not been discussed at all: (1) under what conditions on individual preferences would there be a continuous utility indicator (see Debreu 1959 in this connection), and (2) under what conditions may one recover the individual's preference ordering given the demand function (on this topic see Uzawa 1971).

3 Production

Our economy of the last chapter had a very simple setup as we had allowed only one type of agents: individuals. We shall now consider another important type of agents: firms. Such agents have access to a *technology*—the book of blueprints—which tells them how commodities may be combined to make other commodities. It is on the basis of this technology that firms buy factors and convert them into other products which in turn are sold to earn profits. We shall assume that firms are interested in earning the maximum possible profit. We shall also assume that firms are competitive, i.e. that they take the prices of factors and their outputs as given and accordingly formulate their plans to buy factors and sell outputs.

If production in the entire economy is organized through such competitive firms, then one may enquire into the nature of the various alternative configurations of outputs that the economy is capable of producing. It should be evident that the scarcity of various factors, together with the nature of the technology, limit the configuration of feasible outputs. Hence changes in the availability of scarce factors would naturally lead to changes in the feasible alternatives, and we shall discuss and analyse this and related issues below in the first three sections.

We shall then shift our focus from what the economy can achieve to what the individual competitive firm plans to attain. Such a shift of focus is necessary to allow us to derive and analyse the *supply function*. Together with the demand function of Chapter 2, the supply function constitute the main ingredients of our analysis of general equilibrium in Chapter 4. Accordingly, we shall examine the supply function in Section 3.4.

3.1 A Simple Production Model

As a convenient point of departure, consider the following simple model: two commodities, F (food) and C (clothing), are produced under competitive conditions by means of two scarce factors, L (labour) and T (land). Such simple production models have been used primarily in the area of international trade theory; because of its simple structure, the model allows us to obtain very striking results regarding the connections between outputs and factor supplies and between commodity and factor prices. However, these are extremely special results and depend crucially on the simple two-by-two structure.

Each sector produces one output, and the technology that governs production is as follows: production of 1 unit of F requires a_{LF} units of L and a_{TF} units of T; while production of 1 unit of C requires a_{LC} units of L and a_{TC} units of T. These are the only methods of production available in each sector; i.e., to produce x units of i, xa_{Li} units of L and xa_{Ti} units of T have to be used. Moreover, it is not unreasonable to require that food production is essentially different from clothing production; that is, we must have $a_{LF}/a_{TF} \neq a_{LC}/a_{TC}$. To keep things definite, we might as well assume that

$$a_{LF}/a_{TF} > a_{LC}/a_{TC}. \tag{3.1}$$

This condition would be interpreted to mean that the food sector is *labour-intensive*. Although (3.1) appears quite harmless at this stage, we shall see later how crucial it is for the entire analysis.

Let $\bar{L}, \bar{T}$ denote the total amounts of L and T available in any given period; full employment of factors requires that the outputs x_F, x_C of F and C satisfy

$$\left. \begin{array}{l} x_F a_{LF} + x_C a_{LC} = \bar{L} \\ x_F a_{TF} + x_C a_{TC} = \bar{T} \end{array} \right\} \tag{3.2}$$

Figure 3.1 has been drawn to show that equations (3.2) have a solution $(\bar{x}_F, \bar{x}_C)$, the full-employment outputs; by (3.1), the labour constraint must be steeper than the land constraint and there can be at most one set of full-employment outputs. A natural question to investigate at this stage is how the full employment configuration alters when $\bar{L}, \bar{T}$ change. Figure 3.2 helps us to answer this.

To point out how much labour and land have to be used to produce x units of F, one may simply mark off x times OB along the F-ray; alternatively, any point such as B' corresponds to OB'/OB units of food output. The C-ray may

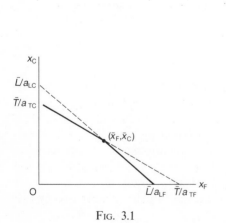

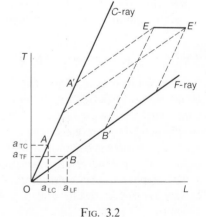

FIG. 3.1   FIG. 3.2

be similarly used. Notice also that the fact that the *C*-ray is steeper than the *F*-ray follows from (3.1). Now if the coordinates of *E* are $(\bar{L}, \bar{T})$, then the full-employment outputs $\bar{x}_F$, $\bar{x}_C$ are given by $\bar{x}_F = OB'/OB$, $\bar{x}_C = OA'/OA$. So if the labour supply were to alter, with no change in *T*, then the new supply of factors would be represented by a point such as *E'*. The full-employment outputs corresponding to *E'* are provided by drawing through *E'* lines parallel to the two rays; the result would be that the food output has gone up while the clothing output has decreased. The output of the labour-intensive commodity goes up and the other output declines when the supply of labour increases; at the heart of this result lies the fact that it requires both labour and land to produce both commodities and that food is labour-intensive.

We turn next to the connection between factor prices and commodity prices. If both commodities are to be produced at a given set of prices (p_F, p_C), prices in each sector must exactly match marginal cost under perfect competition; i.e.,

$$\left.\begin{array}{l} p_F = wa_{LF} + ra_{TF} \\ p_C = wa_{LC} + ra_{TC} \end{array}\right\} \tag{3.3}$$

where *w* and *r* are prices of L and T, respectively. By virtue of (3.1), fixing (p_F, p_C) amounts to fixing (w, r); this unique link between commodity prices and factor prices received a lot of attention at one time; it is easy to see why this is so in the present context. To study the effect of a change in commodity prices on factor prices, let us refer to Figure 3.3. Again by virtue of (3.1), the *r*-ray must lie above the *w*-ray; along the *w*-ray, we can measure wage costs corresponding to various wage rates; e.g., *D* represents wage costs when *w* = 1;

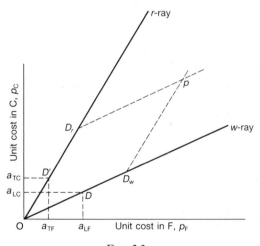

FIG. 3.3

for the wage costs when $w=2$, we simply look along the ray at a point that is twice as far away from O as D. The r-ray serves a similar purpose.

If the coordinates of P denote commodity prices, then, drawing lines through P parallel to the two rays, we obtain the equilibrium $w = OD_w/OD$ and $r = OD_r/OD'$. And as in our earlier analysis, an increase only in p_F leads to a higher w and a lower r. Thus, an increase in the price of food leads to an increase in the real return of the factor used intensively in food production.

In a sense, the diagram with the w, r-rays is a dual to Figure 3.2 with its F, C-rays. By exploiting geometry a bit further, it is possible to demonstrate that

(a) an increase in $\bar{L}$ with constant $\bar{T}$ increases $\bar{x}_F$ more than proportionately; and

(b) an increase in p_F with constant p_C increases w more than proportionately.

Thus in both cases there is a magnified response.

3.2   Substitution Among Factors under Constant Returns to Scale

The treatment of the last section is of course quite special. Here we shall consider a somewhat more general situation. The generalization consists of allowing factor substitution in both sectors, although retaining the assumption of constant returns to scale. In particular, we shall assume that the technology is specified by *production functions* that are *strictly quasi-concave* (see Section 8.5.2 below). Thus,

$$x_F = g_f(L_F, T_F)$$

and
$$x_C = g_c(L_C, T_C)$$

where L_i, T_i are, respectively, the amounts of L and T employed in sector i, $i = F, C$. Moreover, $g_f(\lambda L_F, \lambda T_F) = \lambda g_f(L_F, T_F)$ for any $\lambda > 0$, and the set $\{(L_F, T_F): g_f(L_F, T_F) \geqslant \bar{x}_F\}$ is a strictly convex set (see Section 3.4. below) for any level of output $\bar{x}_F$. The function $g_c(\cdot)$ is assumed to satisfy an identical set of conditions.

First of all, owing to constant returns to scale, the level of the output produced in any sector plays no role in the process chosen for production; i.e., if, at $(\bar{w}, \bar{r})$, $(\bar{a}_{LF}, \bar{a}_{TF})$ is the minimum cost technique of producing 1 unit of F, then, so long as the factor price ratio remains $\bar{w}/\bar{r}$, one would always use labour and land in the proportion $\bar{a}_{LF}/\bar{a}_{TF}$, regardless of the scale of output. Figure 3.4 may be used to establish this result.

Suppose to the contrary that, at a given w/r, A is chosen to produce 1 unit, whereas at the same w/r B is chosen to produce x units. Since the triangles OAX, $OA'X'$ are similar,

$$\frac{OA'}{OA} = \frac{OX'}{OX} = \frac{A'X'}{AX} = k \text{ (say)}.$$

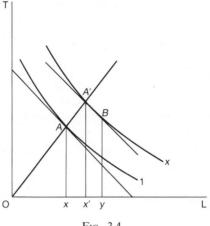

F<small>IG</small>. 3.4

From constant returns to scale, $OX' = xOX$, $A'X' = xAX$; hence $x = k$. Again, Figure 3.4 tells us that

$$wOX' + rA'X' > wOY + rBY \Rightarrow w\frac{OX'}{x} + r\frac{A'X'}{x} > w\frac{OY}{x} + r\frac{BY}{x}$$

$$\Rightarrow wOX + rAX > w\left(\frac{OY}{x}\right) + r\left(\frac{BY}{x}\right).$$

This means that A cannot be the least-cost method of producing 1 unit.

Thus, given any w, r, one may consider the unit isoquants, using the notation of the last section,

$$1 = g_f(a_{LF}, a_{TF})$$

$$1 = g_c(a_{LC}, a_{TC}),$$

where a_{ij} denotes the quantity of factor i required to produce 1 unit of output j, $i = L, T$, and $j = F, C$. Given the factor prices, the problem of minimizing cost, namely,

$$\text{min} \quad wa_{Lj} + ra_{Tj}$$

$$\text{s.t.} \quad g_j(a_{Lj}, a_{Tj}) = 1,$$

leads to the chosen (a_{Lj}, a_{Tj}). Given our restriction on $g_j(\cdot)$, such a problem leads to a unique combination, and we shall henceforth write

$$a_{ij} = f_{ij}(w/r), \quad i = L, T; \quad j = F, C$$

to denote the solutions to the above cost-minimizing problem.

Also, given w, r, a chosen technique (a land/labour ratio) is defined in each sector and may be compared across sectors. *If, at any w/r,*

$$a_{LF}/a_{TF} > a_{LC}/a_{TC},$$

then F-production is labour-intensive. This is the only way in which we can extend expression (3.1) to the present context. In particular, we must have the situation depicted in Figure 3.5. With variations in w/r, a_{LF}/a_{TF} and a_{LC}/a_{TC} vary—*but the curves never intersect.* This, then, reveals the true nature of the assumption that the sector producing F is always labour-intensive.

Thus, the system of equations of the last section become:

$$a_{ij} = f_{ij}(w/r), \qquad\qquad i = L, T; \quad j = F, C \qquad\qquad (3.4)$$

$$\left.\begin{array}{l} x_F a_{LF} + x_C a_{LC} = \bar{L} \\ x_F a_{TF} + x_C a_{TC} = \bar{T} \end{array}\right\} \qquad\qquad (3.5)$$

$$\left.\begin{array}{l} p_F = w a_{LF} + r a_{TF} \\ p_C = w a_{LC} + r a_{TC} \end{array}\right\} \qquad\qquad (3.6)$$

Expressions (3.4) are the least-cost conditions, as explained above; (3.5) are the full-employment conditions, and (3.6) are the profit maximization conditions. To analyse the relationships, we shall assume that the F-sector is always labour-intensive; i.e.,

$$a_{LF}/a_{TF} > a_{LC}/a_{TC}, \qquad \text{for all } w/r. \qquad\qquad (3.7)$$

Now,

$$p = p_F/p_C = \frac{w a_{LF} + r a_{TF}}{w a_{LC} + r a_{TC}} = \frac{(w/r) a_{LF} + a_{TF}}{(w/r) a_{LC} + a_{TC}}.$$

Thus using (3.4), $p = g(s)$ where $s = w/r$. Differentiating, we can see that

$$\text{Sign of } \frac{dp}{ds} = \text{sign of } (a_{TC} a_{LF} - a_{TF} a_{LC}),$$

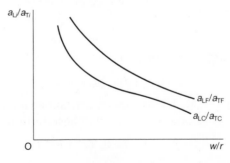

FIG. 3.5

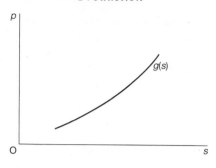

F<small>IG</small>. 3.6

which is positive, from (3.7). Thus the situation depicted in Figure 3.6 obtains, and, given p, $p = g(s)$ defines s uniquely. However, if the F-sector is not always labour-intensive, we may have $g(s)$ as shown in Figure 3.7. In this case, for a given p, $p = g(s)$ may define two values of s, and the unique link between commodity and factor prices is lost.

Analysing the effect of a change in $\bar{L}$ alone at constant commodity prices amounts to fixing all a_{ij}, and hence our earlier results apply so long as the F-sector is labour-intensive. However, now, full-employment output may be affected by a change in commodity prices, even if $\bar{L}$, $\bar{T}$ are held constant. To see how this happens, we proceed as follows.

First, differentiating totally the equations in (3.6), we have

$$\left.\begin{array}{l} dp_F = a_{LF}dw + a_{TF}dr + w\,da_{LF} + r\,da_{TF} \\ dp_C = a_{LC}dw + a_{TC}dr + w\,da_{LC} + r\,da_{TC}. \end{array}\right\} \tag{3.8}$$

We introduce the notation $\hat{z} = dz/z$ for any variable z; also, we let $\theta_{Li} = wa_{Li}/p_i$, $\theta_{Ti} = ra_{Ti}/p_i$, $i = \text{F, C}$. By virtue of (3.6), $\theta_{Li} + \theta_{Ti} = 1$. θ_{ji} denotes

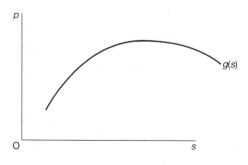

F<small>IG</small>. 3.7

the share of factor j in sector i, and by virtue of the factor intensity condition (3.7),

$$\frac{wr}{p_F p_C}(a_{LF}a_{TC} - a_{LC}a_{TF}) = \theta_{LF}\theta_{TC} - \theta_{TF}\theta_{LC}$$

$$= \theta_{LF}(1 - \theta_{LC}) - (1 - \theta_{LF})\theta_{LC}$$

$$= \theta_{LF} - \theta_{LC} > 0. \tag{3.9}$$

Also, by virtue of the least-cost conditions, assuming an interior minimum,

$$w\,da_{Li} + r\,da_{Ti} = 0$$

or

$$\theta_{Li}\hat{a}_{Li} + \theta_{Ti}\hat{a}_{Ti} = 0. \tag{3.10}$$

From the equations in (3.8), by virtue of (3.9),

$$\left.\begin{aligned}\hat{p}_F &= \theta_{LF}\hat{w} + \theta_{TF}\hat{r}\\ \hat{p}_C &= \theta_{LC}\hat{w} + \theta_{TC}\hat{r}\end{aligned}\right\} \tag{3.11}$$

so that

$$\hat{p}_F - \hat{p}_C = (\theta_{LF} - \theta_{LC})(\hat{w} - \hat{r}), \tag{3.12}$$

which expresses the relationship between a change in commodity prices and the change in factor prices; and, given that (3.9) holds, and since $\theta_{ji} < 1$ for all j and i, we have

$$\hat{w} - \hat{r} = \frac{1}{\theta}(\hat{p}_F - \hat{p}_C)$$

where $\theta = \theta_{LF} - \theta_{LC} < 1$, the magnified response, referred to in the last section.

Again, let

$$\sigma_i = \frac{\hat{a}_{Ti} - \hat{a}_{Li}}{\hat{w} - \hat{r}}, \quad i = F, C.$$

Then σ_i is the elasticity of substitution between T and L in sector i and measures the percentage change in a_{Ti}/a_{Li} brought about owing to a 1 per cent change in the factor price ratio w/r. Clearly,

$$\hat{a}_{Ti} = \hat{a}_{Li} + \sigma_i(\hat{w} - \hat{r}),$$

or

$$\theta_{Ti}\hat{a}_{Ti} = \theta_{Ti}\hat{a}_{Li} + \theta_{Ti}\sigma_i(\hat{w} - \hat{r}).$$

So, by virtue of (3.10),

$$\hat{a}_{Li} = -\theta_{Ti}\sigma_i(\hat{w} - \hat{r})$$

and

$$\hat{a}_{Ti} = \theta_{Li}\sigma_i(\hat{w} - \hat{r}) \qquad (3.13)$$

provide us with the relationship between proportional changes in a_{Li}, a_{Ti} and proportional changes in w/r.

Returning to (3.5), we have

$$dL = dx_F a_{LF} + dx_C a_{LC} + x_F da_{LF} + x_C da_{LC}$$

$$dT = dx_F a_{TF} + dx_C a_{TC} + x_F da_{TF} + x_C da_{TC}$$

or

$$\hat{L} = \lambda_{LF}\hat{x}_F + \lambda_{LC}\hat{x}_C + \lambda_{LF}\hat{a}_{LF} + \lambda_{LC}\hat{a}_{LC}$$

$$\hat{T} = \lambda_{TF}\hat{x}_F + \lambda_{TC}\hat{x}_C + \lambda_{TF}\hat{a}_{TF} + \lambda_{TC}\hat{a}_{TC}$$

where $\lambda_{Li} = x_i a_{Li}/L$, $\lambda_{Ti} = x_i a_{Ti}/T$, $i = F, C$, denote the fraction of L and T employed in i; note that $\lambda_{LF} + \lambda_{LC} = 1$ and $\lambda_{TF} + \lambda_{TC} = 1$. Moreover, by (3.7),

$$\lambda = \lambda_{LF} - \lambda_{TF} > 0. \qquad (3.14)$$

Now, using (3.13) and (3.12), we have

$$\lambda_{LF}\hat{x}_F + \lambda_{LC}\hat{x}_C = \hat{L} + (\lambda_{LF}\theta_{TF}\sigma_F + \lambda_{LC}\theta_{TC}\sigma_C)\frac{1}{\theta}(\hat{p}_F - \hat{p}_C)$$

$$\lambda_{TF}\hat{x}_F + \lambda_{TC}\hat{x}_C = \hat{T} - (\lambda_{TF}\theta_{LF}\sigma_F + \lambda_{TC}\theta_{LC}\sigma_C)\frac{1}{\theta}(\hat{p}_F - \hat{p}_C)$$

so that

$$\hat{x}_F - \hat{x}_C = \frac{1}{\lambda}(\hat{L} - \hat{T}) +$$

$$+ \frac{1}{\theta\lambda}(\lambda_{LF}\theta_{TF}\sigma_F + \lambda_{LC}\theta_{TC}\sigma_C + \lambda_{TF}\theta_{LF}\sigma_F + \lambda_{TC}\theta_{LC}\sigma_C)(\hat{p}_F - \hat{p}_C)$$

$$= \frac{1}{\lambda}(\hat{L} - \hat{T}) + \sigma(\hat{p}_F - \hat{p}_C) \qquad \text{(say)}. \qquad (3.15)$$

Note that σ is positive, and (3.15) shows that (full-employment) outputs may be altered by either a change in the endowment structure or a change in the commodity prices. Since

$$\left.\frac{\hat{x}_F - \hat{x}_C}{\hat{p}_F - \hat{p}_C}\right|_{\bar{L}, \bar{T}} = \sigma,$$

we may interpret σ as the elasticity of substitution along the usual production possibility locus.

Thus, with substitution under constant returns to scale, the model of production may appear more flexible, but the entire set of results of the last section holds, given the labour intensiveness of the F-sector.

3.3   A Linear Activity Analysis Model of Production

The production model is next generalized one step further, while essentially
maintaining constant returns to scale. The generalization is in two directions.
First, we shall break out of the two-by-two structure, and second, we shall
allow joint products. We shall then consider a production unit; it may be the
economy as a whole, or it may be a firm with alternative processes. The
decision-maker controlling this unit will be called a *producer*. A producer has
under his control several processes which transform primary factors into
goods for final consumption; some goods may be produced only to be used in
producing other commodities; these are the *intermediate goods*. However, it
would be convenient to distinguish between only two classes of commodities;
one we shall call *final goods*, although some of them may be intermediate
goods; the other is *primary goods*, which are always inputs.

Typically, a production process would be written as a column vector:

$$a^j = \begin{pmatrix} a_{ij} \\ \vdots \\ a_{rj} \\ a_{r+1\,j} \\ \vdots \\ a_{nj} \end{pmatrix}$$

where the first r components refer to final goods and components $r+1$ to n
refer to the primary goods. A useful sign convention to distinguish between
inputs and outputs is as follows:

$a_{ij} > 0 \Rightarrow i$ is an output of the jth process.

$a_{ij} < 0 \Rightarrow i$ is an input of the jth process.

$a_{ij} = 0 \Rightarrow i$ is not involved in the jth process.

With this convention, for any j, $a_{ij} \leqslant 0$ for all $i \geqslant r+1$. If a^1, a^2 are processes
(or activities), then we shall assume that λa^1, λa^2 are activities too for any
scalar $\lambda > 0$; this is naturally the assumption of *constant returns to scale*. Also,
$a^1 + a^2 = a^3$ implies that a^3 is a possible process; this is *additivity* and
eliminates externalities in production. By a *basic activity* we shall mean an
activity a^1 such that there are no other activities $a^2, \ldots, a^k$ such that

$$a^1 = \sum_{i=2}^{k} \lambda_i a^i, \quad \lambda_i \geqslant 0.$$

The producer will be assumed to have under his control a finite number m of
basic activities:

$$A = \begin{pmatrix} \underline{a^1, \ldots, a^m} \\ a_{11}, \ldots, a_{1m} \\ \vdots \qquad \vdots \\ a_{r1}, \ldots, a_{rm} \\ a_{r+11} \cdots \cdots a_{r+1m} \\ \vdots \qquad \vdots \\ a_{n1}, \ldots, \quad a_{nm} \end{pmatrix} = \begin{pmatrix} A_F \\ A_P \end{pmatrix}.$$

The matrix of basic activities A (where each column is a basic activity) may be written in partitioned form as shown above: A_F is made up of the first r rows of A; A_P is made up of the remaining rows. Thus, A_F is $r \times m$ and A_P is $(n-r) \times m$.

Thus, from our sign convention, $-A_P \geqslant 0$. The columns $a^1, \ldots, a^m$ would be assumed to represent activities at their *unit level of operation*. The producer has to choose an activity level, i.e. a level of operation, for each activity. Suppose he chooses to operate the jth activity a^j at level $x_j \geqslant 0$; then the column

$$x = \begin{pmatrix} x_1 \\ \vdots \\ x_m \end{pmatrix}$$

will be called an activity vector. For any such activity vector, the aggregate inputs and outputs resulting from such levels of operation are given by the matrix product Ax. The kth component of this product is

$$d_k = \sum_{j=1}^{m} a_{kj} x_j.$$

For $k = r+1, \ldots, n$, $d_k \leqslant 0$. If $d_k > 0$ for $k \leqslant r$, then k is an output and d_k denotes the amount of net output produced. If $d_k = 0$, no net output is available; it may be the case that whatever k was produced was used up in other processes as inputs. On the other hand, if $d_k < 0$ for $k \leqslant r$, then the kth commodity is required as an overall input; however, since $k \leqslant r$ and the producer has only a stock of primary goods to begin with, such an activity vector cannot be implemented. An activity vector x is feasible only if $d_k \geqslant 0$ for $k \leqslant r$. Another requirement of feasibility is that, if b denotes the *positive vector*

$$\begin{pmatrix} b_{r+1} \\ \vdots \\ b_n \end{pmatrix},$$

where b_k is the amount of the kth primary commodity or resource available, then an activity vector x is feasible only if

$$-A_{\mathrm{P}}x \leqslant b.$$

The set X of feasible activity vectors is then defined by

$$X = \{x \in R^n_+ \mid A_{\mathrm{F}}x \geqslant 0, \quad -A_{\mathrm{P}}x \leqslant b\},$$

and the set of possible net outputs,

$$Y = \{y \in R^n_+ \mid y = A_{\mathrm{F}}x \quad \text{for some } x \in X\}.$$

For an interesting model of production, certain guarantees are required which would allow us to conclude that X and Y have some structure. These guarantees are often put together under the following 'axioms' for a productive model:

    I: There is $x^* \geqslant 0$ such that $A_{\mathrm{F}}x^* > 0$.
   II: For no $x \geqslant 0$ is it the case that $Ax \geqslant 0$.
  III: For no $x \geqslant 0$ is it the case that $Ax = 0$.

Axiom I ensures that $X \neq \varnothing$. It states that it is possible simultaneously to produce positive amounts of net outputs of all final goods. Thus there is x^* such that $A_{\mathrm{F}}x^* > 0$. Clearly, for some λ small,

$$-A_{\mathrm{P}}(\lambda x^*) \leqslant b, \quad \text{and so } \lambda x^* \in X.$$

Axiom II guarantees that one has to use inputs to produce output; thus $A_{\mathrm{P}}x^* \leqslant 0$ where x^* is as in Axiom I.

Axiom III is called the 'irreversibility of production'; i.e., it states that, if a^1 is an activity, then $-a^1$ cannot be an activity. Usually, such an axiom is introduced on the grounds that primary factors cannot be produced. Thus, in two dimensions, the basic activities a^1, a^2 must be as shown in Figure 3.8. The

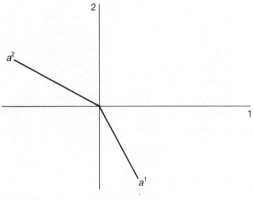

F$_{\mathrm{IG}}$. 3.8

producer, when informed of prices $p_1, \ldots, p_r$, seeks to solve

$$\max \sum_{i=1}^{r} p_r y_r = py$$

s.t. $y \in Y$

or

$$\max \quad pA_F x$$

s.t. $x \in X;$

i.e.,

$$\max \quad pA_F x$$

s.t. $-A_F x \leqslant 0$

$$-A_p x \leqslant b \qquad\qquad (M)$$

$$x \geqslant 0.$$

This is a standard maximal problem of linear programming, and there are known methods of computing the solution of (M), provided (M) is solvable. But what guarantees do we have that (M) *is* solvable? Some basic facts regarding linear programming are necessary for this purpose (see Section 8.6.3 below).

Consider the following pair of problems:

$$\left.\begin{array}{l} \max \quad cx \\ \text{s.t.} \quad Bx \leqslant s \\ \qquad x \geqslant 0 \end{array}\right\} \qquad (P)$$

$$\left.\begin{array}{l} \min \quad ys \\ \text{s.t.} \quad yB \geqslant c \\ \qquad y \geqslant 0 \end{array}\right\} \qquad (D)$$

for some c, B, and s. The two problems are related as follows.
 (i) (P) and (D) are solvable if and only if both are *feasible*, i.e. if there exist $x \geqslant 0$ and $y \geqslant 0$ such that $Bx \leqslant s$ and $yB \geqslant c$.
(ii) If x^* solves (P) and y^* solves (D), then $cx^* = y^*s$; moreover,

$$(Bx^*)_i < s_i \Rightarrow y_i^* = 0$$

$$(y^*B)_j > c_j \Rightarrow x_j^* = 0$$

where $(Bx^*)_i = \sum_j b_{ij} x_j^*$ and $(y^*B)_j = \sum_i y_i^* b_{ij}$.

The minimum problem (D) is said to be the *dual* of the maximum problem (P).

To apply these results, note that (M) is feasible whenever X, the set of feasible activity vectors, is non-empty, and hence, under Axiom I, (M) is feasible.

The dual to problem (M) may now be written:

$$\text{min} \quad z_1 \cdot 0 + \ldots + z_r \cdot 0 + z_{r+1} b_{r+1} + \ldots + z_n b_n$$

$$\left. \begin{array}{l} \text{s.t.} \quad -z \cdot \begin{pmatrix} A_F \\ A_P \end{pmatrix} \geqq p A_F \\[20pt] \qquad\quad z \geqq 0 \end{array} \right\} \qquad \text{(N)}$$

We need to guarantee that (N) is feasible. We shall show that, by virtue of Axioms II and III, Theorem SH (see Section 8.3.2) implies that (N) is feasible. Suppose that (N) is not feasible; then SH2 (Section 8.3.2) guarantees that there is an $x \geqq 0$ such that

$$\begin{pmatrix} A_F \\ A_P \end{pmatrix} x \geqq 0 \quad \text{and} \quad -p A_F x < 0;$$

i.e., there must exist $x \geqq 0$ such that $Ax \geqq 0$, which violates either Axiom II or Axiom III. Hence (N) is feasible; i.e., there is $z \geqq 0$ such that

$$zA \leqq -p A_F.$$

Thus, our Axioms I–III guarantee that problem (M) (and hence (N)) has a solution. Given p, therefore, the producer can choose $y \in Y$ which solves (M); one may think of the chosen y as the *supply*, given p.

The solution to (M) need not be unique. Nevertheless, this relationship between p and y which solves (M) has interesting properties. First of all, let p^*, $\hat{p}$ be two price vectors; let y^* be chosen at p^* and $\hat{y}$ at $\hat{p}$. From the definition,

$$p^* y^* \geqq p^* \hat{y}$$

and

$$\hat{p} \hat{y} \geqq \hat{p} y^*,$$

or

$$(\hat{p} - p^*)(\hat{y} - y^*) \geqq 0.$$

So if $p_j^* = \hat{p}_j \ \forall j \neq k$, then $(\hat{p}_k - p_k^*)(\hat{y}_k - y_k^*) \geqq 0$.

Thus, *with an increase in the price of commodity k, all other prices being held constant, the net output of k cannot decrease.*

It should be clear that the set of net outputs Y corresponds to the usual notion of a production possibility locus. There is another aspect of Y which is important; to introduce this, we require the notion of *efficiency*. $\hat{y} \in Y$ will be said to be *efficient* if there is no other $y \in Y$ such that $y - \hat{y} \geqq 0$.

We shall first show that, *if ŷ is chosen at some p̂ > 0, i.e. if ŷ solves (M) given p̂, then ŷ is efficient*. For if ŷ is not efficient, then there is $y \in Y$ and $y - \hat{y} \geq 0 \Rightarrow \hat{p}y > \hat{p}\hat{y}$ so that ŷ cannot solve (M). Hence ŷ is efficient.

The above result also has a converse: *if ŷ is efficient, then there is p̂ ⩾ 0 such that ŷ may be chosen at p̂.*

To see the above assertion, let $\varepsilon = (\varepsilon_1, 0, \ldots, 0)$, $\varepsilon_1 > 0$. Now, since y is efficient,

$$-A_F x \leqslant -(\hat{y} + \varepsilon)$$

$$-A_P x \leqslant b$$

$$x \geqslant 0$$

has no solution. Hence, by virtue of SH1 (see Section 8.3.2), there is $(p, q) \geqq 0$ such that

$$-pA_F - qA_P \geqq 0, \quad -p\hat{y} - p_1\varepsilon_1 + qb < 0$$

hold.

In particular, we may choose a solution $(p(\varepsilon), q(\varepsilon))$ such that

$$\| \{p(\varepsilon), \quad q(\varepsilon)\} \| = 1.$$

(For a definition of $\| \|$, see Section 8.4.)

Notice that as $\varepsilon_1 \to 0$, $(p(\varepsilon), q(\varepsilon))$ is a bounded sequence (see Section 8.4 below), and hence has a limit point $(\hat{p}, \hat{q})$ such that $\| (\hat{p}, \hat{q}) \| = 1$, $(\hat{p}, \hat{q}) \geqq 0$. Also,

$$-\hat{p}A_F - \hat{q}A_P \geqq 0 \quad \text{and} \quad -\hat{p}\hat{y} + \hat{q}b \leqslant 0.$$

Note that if $\hat{p} = 0$, then $0 \leqslant \hat{q}b \leqslant 0 \Rightarrow \hat{q} = 0$, which cannot be true. Therefore $\hat{p} \geqslant 0$.

Now consider any $y \in Y$; i.e., there is $x \geqq 0$ such that

$$A_F x \geqq y$$

$$-A_P x \leqslant b.$$

Therefore

$$-\hat{q}A_P x \geqq \hat{p}A_F x \geqq \hat{p}y,$$

or $\hat{q}b \geqq \hat{p}y$. But since

$$-\hat{p}\hat{y} + \hat{q}b \leqslant 0, \quad \hat{p}\hat{y} \geqq \hat{q}b \geqq \hat{p}y,$$

for any feasible y, so ŷ may be chosen at p̂.

Finally, what about the connection between commodity and factor prices established in the last section? Up to now, the prices were prices of the final goods. It turns out that, given a set of prices p^* for the final goods, a set of implicit prices for the factors becomes determined via problem (N), the dual to (M). To examine these prices, we return to the facts stated about linear programming problems.

Let x^* solve (M) given p^*; then there is z^* such that

$$p^* A_F x^* = z_{r+1}^* b_{r+1} + \ldots + z_n^* b_n.$$

Thus z_k^*, $k \geqslant r+1$, are in fact some prices—often called 'shadow-prices'—associated with the primary factors, since z_k^* denotes the maximum amount that the producer is willing to pay for an additional unit of the kth commodity ($k = 1, 2, \ldots, n$). Moreover,

$$-\sum_j a_{ij} x_j^* < 0, \qquad i = 1, 2, \ldots, r \Rightarrow z_i^* = 0;$$

$$-\sum_j a_{ij} x_j^* < b_i, \qquad i \geqslant r+1 \Rightarrow z_i^* = 0;$$

and

$$-\sum_{i=1}^{n} z_i^* a_{ij} > \sum_{i=1}^{r} p_i^* a_{ij}, \Rightarrow x_j^* = 0,$$

which follow from the facts stated about linear programming problems.

These have ready interpretation in the present context. First, if a commodity is produced in a positive amount after meeting all input requirements, the shadow price is zero; if a primary factor is not fully used up, its shadow price is zero; and finally, if for some activity the 'costs' exceed the 'revenue', then that process is not operated.

Before we turn to other models of production, it should be mentioned that a very special case of the above model of production has received a substantial amount of attention in the literature. This model is special in two ways. First, it is assumed that there is only a single primary factor; i.e., A_P consists of a single row. Secondly, each column of A_F has at most one positive entry; that is, each process produces a single good and hence no joint production is allowed. This is the well-known model of Leontief. An exhaustive analysis of the Leontief model is contained in the mathematical notes to this chapter.

3.4   Supply Functions and their Properties

In the above discussion of production, as indicated earlier, the decision-maker is best identified with the planner in an economy. In the present section, we move to a somewhat different scene, where a producer or a firm has many alternative methods of producing different goods. Thus, a firm has some technology, and to earn profits it buys factors and converts them into outputs according to the technology it possesses. If $a^1, a^2, \ldots, a^m$ of Section

3.3 are the basic activities for the producer, then writing A to be the matrix whose columns are a^j, the set of all possible input–output vectors, is given by

$$P = \{z : z = Ax, \quad x \geqslant 0\}.$$

P thus contains all possible (feasible) processes and is called the *production possibility set* for the firm. To distinguish inputs from outputs, we follow the earlier convention. Notice that, for the case considered in Section 3.3, P is a convex set—in fact, it is a convex *cone*; i.e., $x, y \in P \Rightarrow \lambda x \in p$ and $x + y \in P$ for all $\lambda > 0$. These assumptions have thus ruled out externalities in production and introduced constant returns to scale. Rather than begin with basic activities, the present section takes as given the set of all possible input–output vectors, with the production possibility set P as the starting point. Thus, the nature of P would be determined by the nature of the technology.

For producer J, the production possibility set would be denoted by P^J. We shall consider $P^J \subseteq R^n$. It is also customary to have some of the following restrictions imposed on P^J:

1 $0 \in P^J$; i.e., the firm J may not use any inputs and may produce no outputs; usually this is termed to be the possibility of inaction for J.
2 $P^J \cap R^n_+ = \{0\}$; i.e., to produce outputs, inputs are necessary.
3 $P^J \cap -P^J = \varnothing$; i.e., production is irreversible.
4 P^J is convex; i.e., $z^1, z^2 \in P^J \Rightarrow \lambda z^1 + (1 - \lambda) z^2 \in P^J$ for any $\lambda, 0 \leqslant \lambda \leqslant 1$, thus ruling out externalities in production.
5 P^J is bounded above; i.e., there is $M \in R^n$ such that $z \in P^J \Rightarrow z \leqslant M$.

It should be emphasized that assumption 5 rules out constant returns to scale; since resources are scarce, one may expect that the attainable production possibility set is bounded above. One may thus dispense with this assumption, but at the cost of introducing various technical complications. However, as it stands, assumption 5 guarantees that P^J is bounded above from technological considerations alone and therefore may be interpreted as some sort of capacity constraints on production. We shall also impose two further restrictions:

6 P^J is a closed subset of R^n.
7 $z \in P^J$ and $z' \leqslant z \Rightarrow z' \in P^J$ (free disposal).

In other words, if z is a possible input–output vector, then it is possible to produce *less* by using *more*. Technically, this allows us to conclude that R^n_- (the non-positive orthant) $\subseteq P^J$, so that P^J has full dimensionality. It would be also useful to strengthen assumption 4 to the following:

8 P^J is a strictly convex set.

Put another way, $z^1, z^2 \in P^J, z^1 \neq z^2 \Rightarrow \lambda z^1 + (1 - \lambda) z^2 \in$ relative interior of P^J.

'Relative interior of P^J' means the interior of P^J relative to the smallest linear subspace containing P^J; however in the face of assumption 7, one may replace 'relative interior' by 'interior', where by 'interior' we mean the following: $z \in$ interior of P^J if there exists a neighbourhood $N(z)$ of z such that $N(z) \subseteq P^J$.

Now we shall assume that the firm or producer is perfectly competitive, so that the producer wants to maximize profits when informed of prices. Notice that profits associated with any given input–output vector z at prices p is simply

$$pz = \sum_{i \ni z_i \geqslant 0} p_i z_i + \sum_{i \ni z_i < 0} p_i z_i = \text{revenue} - \text{costs},$$

given our sign convention. Thus the producer's problem is:

$$\max \quad py$$

$$\text{s.t.} \quad y \in P^J. \tag{P}$$

If y^* solves (P), then profits at prices p are given by $\pi^J(p) = py^*$.

Let $S^J(p) = \{y \in P^J : py = \pi^J(p)\}$, the profit-maximizing input–output vectors. First of all,

A: Given $p > 0$, (P) has a solution.

This follows from assumptions 5 and 6. Notice now that $\pi^J(p)$ is well defined for all $p > 0$. An important property of the profit function is as follows.

B: $\pi^J(p)$ is a convex function of p for all $p > 0$; i.e.,

$$p = \lambda p^1 + (1 - \lambda) p^2, \quad 0 \leqslant \lambda \leqslant 1$$

$$p^1, p^2 > 0 \Rightarrow \pi^J(p) \leqslant \lambda \pi^J(p^1) + (1 - \lambda) \pi^J(p^2).$$

To see this, let $\hat{z}$ solve the problem (P) with p defined as above; let z^1 solves (P) given p^1 and let z^2 solve (P) given p^2. Then $p\hat{z} \geqslant pz^i$, $i = 1, 2$; $p^i z^i \geqslant p^i \hat{z}$, $i = 1, 2$ from definition. Therefore

$$\pi^J(p) = p\hat{z} = \lambda p^1 \hat{z} + (1 - \lambda) p^2 \hat{z}$$

$$\leqslant \lambda p^1 z^1 + (1 - \lambda) p^2 z^2$$

$$= \lambda \pi^J(p^1) + (1 - \lambda) \pi^J(p^2),$$

as claimed.

C: $S^J(p)$ contains a unique element whenever $S^J(p) \neq \varnothing$, if assumption 8 holds.

For suppose that z^1, z^2, with $z^1 \neq z^2$, be such that $z^i \in S^J(p)$, $i = 1, 2$. Consider $z = \lambda z^1 + (1 - \lambda) z^2$, $0 < \lambda < 1$. Then $pz = pz^i = \pi^J(p)$; also by assumption 8, $z \in$ interior of P^J, which implies that there is $\tilde{z} \in P^J$ such that $p\tilde{z} > pz = \pi^J(p)$: a contradiction. Therefore z^1, $z^2 \in S^J(p) \Rightarrow z^1 = z^2$.

Given assumption 8, one may therefore speak of the *supply function*. Notice that this is defined only if $p>0$. If assumption 8 does not hold, then in general we have a *supply correspondence*. Also, if $p \ngtr 0$, neither $\pi^J(p)$ nor $S^J(p)$ may be well defined. This fact may be noted for future reference.

D: If $\hat{p}$ be such that $\hat{p}_i=0$ for some i, then $S^J(\hat{p})=\emptyset$, provided assumption 8 holds.

For suppose, to the contrary, that $z\in S^J(\hat{p})$; consider $\hat{z}$, $\hat{z}_j=z_j$ for all $j\neq i$, $\hat{z}_i<z_i$. Then $\hat{p}\hat{z}=\hat{p}z$, and so $\hat{z}\in S^J(p)$ and $\hat{z}\neq z$: a contradiction to property C.

Also, as one may expect, if relative prices do not alter, the suply function does not change. Thus, under assumptions 1–3, 5, and 8,

E: $S^J(\lambda p)=S^J(p)$ for all $\lambda>0$, $p>0$ (homogeneity of degree zero in the prices);
   (ii) $S^J(p)$ is a continuous function of p for all $p>0$.

To see the homogeneity property, note that, if

$$p\hat{z} \geqslant pz \quad \text{for all} \quad z\in P^J$$

then

$$\lambda p\hat{z} \geqslant \lambda pz \quad \text{for all} \quad z\in P^J \text{ for any } \lambda>0.$$

Next, let p^s be a sequence: $p^s \to \hat{p}>0$; $z^s=S^J(p^s)$. If possible, let $\|z^s\| \to +\infty$ with s. Since $z^s\in P^J$ and P^J is bounded above, then the only possibility is $z_k^s \to -\infty$ for some k; i.e., $p^s z^s \to -\infty$, and $\pi^J(p^s)<0$ for s large. However, by virtue of assumption 1, $\pi^J(p) \geqslant 0$ for all $p>0$; i.e., $z^s \neq S^J(p^s)$ for s large: a contradiction. Thus z^s must be bounded; i.e., there is a limit point $\hat{z}$. If $\hat{z}\notin S^J(\hat{p})$, there exists $\bar{z}\in P^J$ such that $\hat{p}\bar{z}>\hat{p}\hat{z}$, since $\hat{z}\in P^J$ by the closure assumption.

Let $z^{s_k} \to \hat{z}$; then $p^{s_k}\bar{z}>p^{s_k}z^{s_k}$ for all k large; i.e., $z^{s_k}\neq S^J(p^{s_k})$: a contradiction. Hence $\hat{z}=S^J(\hat{p})$. Since this is true for an arbitrary limit point $\hat{z}$, $z^s \to \hat{z}=S^J(\hat{p})$, which establishes part (ii).

The remaining properties have to do with derivatives of $S^J(p)$, whenever they exist. Hence these are to be interpreted as relating to the case when $S^J(p)$ is differentiable.

F:
$$\sum_j \hat{p}_j \frac{\partial S_j^J(\hat{p})}{\partial p_k}=0 \quad \text{for} \quad \hat{p}>0.$$

For p close to $\hat{p}, p>0$. By profit maximization,

$$\hat{p}S^J(\hat{p}) \geqslant \hat{p}S^J(p)$$

so that $\hat{p}S^J(p)$ is maximized at $p=\hat{p}$; the claim amounts to the necessary first-order condition (see Section 8.6.1 below).

G: If $\pi^J(\hat{p})$ is differentiable at $\hat{p} > 0$,

$$\frac{\partial \pi^J(\hat{p})}{\partial p_k} = S_k^J(\hat{p}) \quad \text{and} \quad \frac{\partial^2 \pi^J(\hat{p})}{\partial p_k \partial p_j} = \frac{\partial S_k^J(\hat{p})}{\partial p_j}.$$

Since $\pi^J(\hat{p}) = \sum_j \hat{p}_j \{ S_j^J(\hat{p}) \}$, the claim follows by virtue of F.

Moreover, by virtue of the convexity of $\pi^J(p)$ (see property B above), one may conclude (see Section 8.5.2) that

$$.\nabla^2 \pi(p) = \left\{ \frac{\partial^2 \pi^J(p)}{\partial p_k \partial p_j} \right\}$$

exists almost everywhere for $p > 0$, and that the matrix is positive semi-definite; i.e., $\nabla^2 \pi(p)$ is symmetric and

$$x' \nabla^2 \pi(p) x \geq 0 \quad \text{for all } x.$$

By virtue of property G, the above has the following implications:

$$\frac{\partial S_k^J(p)}{\partial p_j} = \frac{\partial S_j^J(p)}{\partial p_k}$$

$$\frac{\partial S_k^J}{\partial p_j} \quad \text{is positive semi-definite.}$$

$$\frac{\partial S_k^J}{\partial p_k} \geq 0 \quad \text{for all } k.$$

From the last condition, notice that, for k which is an input for the Jth producer, it follows that an increase in the price of the kth factor cannot increase demand for it. *The firm's demand curve for a factor is never upward-rising.* Also, for a commodity k which is an output for firm J, the same inequality implies that *the supply curve cannot be downward-sloping.* One may note the formal similarity between the results of this section and the results discussed in the mathematical notes to Chapter 2. In particular, the relationship between the profit function and the supply function is rather similar to the one between the expenditure function and the Hicksian demand function. The only difference obtains from the fact that, whereas profits are maximized, expenditure is minimized.

MATHEMATICAL NOTES

3.5 The Leontief Model

We return to a special case of the model of production discussed in Section 3.3. The specialization lies in first requiring that, in the basic activities' matrix, the portion A_P consists of only one row. In other words, there is only a single non-producible factor. Secondly, each activity has a single output; thus there is no joint production. So there are as many basic activities as there are produced commodities. We shall consider the case where there may be many basic activities for producing each commodity later.

Assume that there are n sectors of production. Each sector j produces only an output j by using as inputs the outputs of other sectors and a single non-produced factor traditionally identified with labour. For each sector, there is a unique method of producing its output. Let us suppose that (a_j, b_j) is required to produce *one unit of j*; here, a_j stands for the vector of produced commodities required as inputs and b_j, a scalar, represents the amount of labour required. Let A denote the matrix whose jth column is a_j; A is the Leontief Matrix; we take $a_j \geqslant 0$ and $b_j \geqslant 0$ for all j. In the terminology of Section 3.3, noting that each (a_j, b_j) produces 1 unit of j, we have

$$A_F = I - A$$

$$A_P = -b.$$

Recall the axioms introduced in Section 3.3; we reinterpret them as follows:

I′   There is $x \geqslant 0$ such that $(I - A)x > 0$.
II′   For no $x \geqslant 0$ is it the case that

$$\begin{pmatrix} I - A \\ -b \end{pmatrix} x \geqslant 0.$$

III′   For no $x \geqslant 0$ is it the case that

$$\begin{pmatrix} I - A \\ -b \end{pmatrix} x = 0.$$

Notice that II′ and III′ would be trivially true if we required

$$b > 0;$$

i.e., each basic activity requires a positive amount of labour; i.e., labour is indispensable for production. Given this, the only axiom is I′, which states that the production is *viable*.

The viability of the above system of production lies in its ability to produce a surplus (over and above its input requirements) of each commodity. Thus, A, is said to be *productive* if

$$(I - A)x > 0 \quad \text{for some} \quad x \geqslant 0. \tag{P1}$$

$x_j \geqslant 0$ is the activity level or, equivalently, the gross output for sector j. Ax then stands for the intersectoral input requirements to produce x, and so $x - Ax$ is the surplus. Note that $(I - A)$ is a B-matrix, and hence the results of Section 8.3.4, are applicable. We use these results to restate (P1) in several equivalent forms. (All references are to the equations and results of Section 8.3.4.)

A is productive

iff $(I-A)$ has a positive dominant diagonal (d.d.) (from (P1) and the definition of d.d.); (P2)

iff for any $c \geqslant 0$, $(I-A)x = c$ has a unique non-negative solution (this follows from (P2) and result 3 of Section 8.3.4); (P3)

iff $(I-A)^{-1} \geqslant 0$ (follows from (P3) and result 4 of Section 8.3.4); (P4)

iff $\pi_A^* < 1$ (follows from (P4) and result 9 of Section 8.3.4); (P5)

iff the Hawkins–Simon conditions hold (follows from (P2) and result 5 of Section 8.3.4; (P6)

iff for *some* $c > 0$, $(I-A)x = c$ has a unique non-negative solution; (P7)

iff *all* principal minors of $(I-A)$ have positive determinants. (P8)

Notice that $(P3) \Rightarrow (P7) \Rightarrow (P2) \Rightarrow (P3)$. Also, $(P8) \Rightarrow (P6)$; whereas $(P6) \Leftrightarrow (P2) \Rightarrow B^J$ has a positive d.d. for every J, where $B = (I-A)$, $J \subseteq \{1, 2, \ldots, n\}$, $B^J = (b_{ij})i, j \in J$, and hence $\det B^J > 0$ by result 5, Section 8.3.4 $\Rightarrow (P8)$.

One may also note the following conditions:

$$\left. \begin{array}{ll} (P1) \Rightarrow & \sum_i a_{ij} < 1 \qquad \text{for some } j \\[2ex] & \sum_i a_{ij} < 1 \qquad \text{for every } j \Rightarrow (P1), \end{array} \right\} \qquad (P9)$$

which is a trivial consequence of (P2).

Given that A satisfies (P1), notice that, for any scalar $w > 0$, there is $p > 0$ such that

$$p(I-A) = wb$$

or, alternatively, $p = wb(I-A)^{-1}$.

The price vector is defined to be the equilibrium price vector given a wage rate w. The rationale for such a price vector is clear, since, given such a p, and w, the entire model is able to pay for labour and other intermediate goods and exactly break even. We shall sometimes adopt $w = 1$, so that the prices are all relative to labour.

Finally, given a fixed amount of labour L, the model is capable of generating all net outputs c with the property that there is $x \geqslant 0$ such that $(I-A)x = c$ and $bx \leqslant L$; or, since $x = (I-A)^{-1}c$, we may write the set of attainable c's by

$$b(I-A)^{-1}c \leqslant L.$$

This expression therefore provides us with the production possibility locus for the Leontief model.

3.6   Non-Substitution Theorem

Each produced commodity j was assumed to be produced by means of a single process (a_j, b_j). Suppose now that for each j there is a set of such activities T_j. This then allows for some substitution among activities, and in principle one may expect that, for changes in levels of outputs, the producer switches to alternative activities. However, such an expectation cannot be supported by virtue of a result called the Non-Substitution Theorem, which states that, if a certain set of activities is used to produce a given net output configuration, then that set may be chosen to produce all net output configurations.

Consider the production model of the last section, except that, instead of the unique configuration of inputs (a_j, b_j) required to produce one unit of j, we now assume that there is a collection T_j of such processes for each j. We shall insist that

I: T_j is a closed subset of R^{n+1} and $(a_j, b_j) \in T_j \Rightarrow b_j > 0$.

When each sector chooses a process, say when j chooses $(\bar{a}_j, \bar{b}_j)$ from T_j, the $\bar{a}_j$'s form a Leontief matrix $\bar{A}$ whose jth column is $\bar{a}_j$. For each configuration of choice, a separate Leontief matrix becomes applicable. For the model to be viable, we shall also insist that

II: There is $(a_j^*, b_j^*) \in T_j$ such that $A^* = (a_j^*)$ is productive.

Let

$$p^*(I - A^*) = b^* \tag{3.16}$$

where $b^* = (b_j^*)$. Thus, we have normalized prices by taking the wage rate as unit. In this setup, it is meaningful to enquire into the question of choice of processes by each sector. Given that labour is the only primary factor, it is reasonable to expect that each sector minimizes its labour costs; and if there is a set of processes, one for each sector, that minimizes these costs, then this set of processes may be chosen regardless of what surplus has to be generated. So even though substitution possibilities exist, no substitution may occur: this, then, is the *non-substitution theorem*. Thus, our restriction of considering only one activity per commodity was not much of a restriction.

Let L denote the quantity of labour available; then, given

$$(a_j, b_j) \in T_j, \quad j = 1, 2, \ldots, n, \quad A = (a_j), b = (b_j),$$

let

$$U(A, b) = \{ y \geqslant 0 \colon y \leqslant (I - A)x, \, bx \leqslant L, \, x \geqslant 0 \}.$$

We shall write $(A, b) \in T$ whenever $A = (a_j)$, $b = (b_j)$, and $(a_j, b_j) \in T_j$ for each j. If there is $(\hat{A}, \hat{b}) \in T$ such that, for all $(A, b) \in T$, $U(A, b) \subseteq U(\hat{A}, \hat{b})$, then $(\hat{A}, \hat{b})$

has *the non-substitution property*. A direct demonstration for the existence of such an $(\hat{A}, \hat{b})$ is presented below; in the process, the crucial role of the productivity conditions (P1)–(P9) stand revealed.

We begin by observing that

A: If $(a_j^s, b_j^s) \in T_j$, $s = 1, 2, \ldots$, and $b_j^s \to 0$, then $a_{kj}^s \to +\infty$ for some k.

For if not, then (a_j^s, b_j^s) forms a bounded sequence and by (BW) (Section 8.4.1) must have a limit point $(\bar{a}_j, 0)$ in T_j: a contradiction. Let

$\mathscr{P} = \{p: \ 0 \leqslant p \leqslant p^*$ and for each p there is some $(A, b) \in T$ such that $p(I - A) = b\}$.

In the definition of $\mathscr{P}$, p^* is as in (3.16) above. Hence $p^* \in \mathscr{P}$. Thus $\mathscr{P}$ is non-empty and bounded. Let p^s, $s = 1, 2, \ldots$ be a sequence in $\mathscr{P}$; without any loss of generality, assume $p^s \to p^0$ as $s \to \infty$.

Since $p^s \in \mathscr{P}$ for all s, there exist $(A^s, b^s) \in T$ such that

$$p^s(I - A^s) = b^s.$$

Thus, by virtue of (P2), A^s is productive for all s. Moreover,

B: $a_{ij}^s \to +\infty$ for some $i, j \Rightarrow p_i^s \to 0$.

This is immediate, since

$$p_j^* \geqslant p_j^s = \sum_{k=1}^{n} p_k^s a_{kj}^s + b_j^s \geqslant b_j^s > 0. \tag{3.17}$$

C: $\mathscr{P}$ is compact.

This would be established by showing that $p^0 \in \mathscr{P}$. If possible, let $J = \{j: p_j^0 = 0\} \neq \varnothing$. Then, by virtue of (3.17), observation B, and observation A,

$$j \in J \Rightarrow b_j^s \to 0,$$
$$\Rightarrow a_{kj}^s \to +\infty \text{ for some } k,$$
$$\Rightarrow k \in J \quad (\because p_k^s \to 0),$$

or

$$j \in J \Rightarrow \sum_{i \in J} a_{ij}^s \to +\infty.$$

For s sufficiently large, therefore, $A_J^s = (a_{ij}^s)$, $i, j \in J$ cannot be productive (by (P9)): which would contradict the fact that A^s is productive for all s. Hence $J = \varnothing$ or $p^0 > 0$. Thus, by B, a_j^s is bounded for all j; b_j^s is bounded by (3.17), and hence (a_j^s, b_j^s) has a limit point $(a_j^0, b_j^0) \in T_j$. Since $p^s(I - A) = b^s$, $p^0(I - A^0) = b^0$; moreover, $0 \leqslant p^s \leqslant p^*$ implies that $0 \leqslant p^0 \leqslant p^*$ and so $p^0 \in \mathscr{P}$. Hence the claim. $\square$

By virtue of observation C, one may make the following assertion:

D: There exists $\hat{p} \in \mathscr{P}$ such that $\hat{p}$ solves

$$\min \quad \sum_i p_i$$

$$\text{s.t.} \quad p \in \mathscr{P}.$$

Since $\hat{p} \in \mathscr{P}$, there is $(\hat{A}, \hat{b}) \in T$ such that

$$\hat{p}(I - \hat{A}) = \hat{b},$$

and since $\hat{b} > 0$, this means that $\hat{A}$ is productive by (P2). For this $(\hat{A}, \hat{b})$ we may claim the following:

E: $(\hat{A}, \hat{b})$ has the non-substitution property.

Proof. For if not, then there is $(A, b) \in T$ with $y \in U(A, b)$ and $y \notin U(\hat{A}, \hat{b})$. Since $\hat{A}$ is productive, $\hat{b}(I - \hat{A})^{-1}y > L$. Moreover, there is $x \geqslant 0$, $bx \leqslant L$, and $(I - A)x \geqslant y$ so that $\hat{p}(I - A)x \geqslant \hat{p}y = \hat{b}(I - A)^{-1}y > L \geqslant bx$. Therefore $\{\hat{p}(I - A) - b\}x > 0$, and hence there is j_1 such that

$$\hat{p}_{j_1} - \hat{p}a_{j_1} - b_{j_1} > 0.$$

Define $(\tilde{A}, \tilde{b})$ by $\tilde{A} = (\tilde{a}_j)$, $\tilde{b} = (\tilde{b}_j)$ such that

$$\tilde{a}_j = \hat{a}_j, \qquad \tilde{b}_j = \hat{b}_j \qquad \text{for } j \neq j_1$$

$$\tilde{a}_{j_1} = a_{j_1}, \qquad \tilde{b}_{j_1} = b_{j_1} \qquad \text{otherwise.}$$

Also,

$$\hat{p}\tilde{a}_j + \tilde{b}_j = \hat{p}\hat{a}_j + \hat{b}_j = \hat{p}_j, \qquad j \neq j_1$$

$$= \hat{p}a_{j_1} + b_{j_1} < \hat{p}_{j_1}, \qquad j = j_1.$$

Thus $(\tilde{A}, \tilde{b}) \in T$; and $\hat{p}(I - \tilde{A}) \geqslant \tilde{b} > 0 \Rightarrow \tilde{A}$ is productive. So let $\tilde{p} = \tilde{b}(I - \tilde{A})^{-1}$. Now note that $\{\hat{p}(I - \tilde{A}) - \tilde{b}\}(I - \tilde{A})^{-1} \neq 0$. Therefore $\hat{p} \geqslant \tilde{p}$, and the inequality must be strict for at least one component, which is a contradiction, since $\tilde{p} \in \mathscr{P}$. Therefore no such $\tilde{p}$ exists and the claim follows. $\square$

There are two related observations which complete the characterization of $\hat{p}$ whose existence is asserted in D.

F: $\hat{p}$, whose existence is asserted in D, is unique.

Proof. Suppose $\bar{p}$, $\hat{p}$, $\bar{p} \neq \hat{p}$ both solve the problem in D. Then there exist $(\bar{A}, \bar{b}) \in T$ and $(\hat{A}, \hat{b}) \in T$ such that

$$\hat{p}(I - \hat{A}) = \hat{b} \quad \text{and} \quad \bar{p}(I - \bar{A}) = \bar{b}.$$

Also, $\Sigma \hat{p}_i = \Sigma \bar{p}_i$ and

$$\hat{p} \neq \bar{p} \Rightarrow J = \{j : \bar{p}_j > \hat{p}_j\} \neq \varnothing.$$

Define $\hat{p}^*$, $(\hat{A}^*, \hat{b}^*)$ by

$$\hat{p}_j^* = \hat{p}_j, \, j \in J, \; \hat{p}_j^* = \bar{p}_j, \, j \notin J;$$
$$(\hat{a}_j^*, \hat{b}_j^*) = (\hat{a}_j, \hat{b}_j), \, j \in J;$$
$$= (\bar{a}_j, \bar{b}_j), \quad j \notin J.$$

Then $(\hat{A}^*, \hat{b}^*) \in T$; and

$$\hat{p}^* \hat{a}_j^* + \hat{b}_j^* = \sum_{i \in J} \hat{p}_i^* \hat{a}_{ij}^* + \sum_{i \notin J} \hat{p}_i^* \hat{a}_{ij}^* + \hat{b}_j^*.$$

So for $j \in J$,

$$\hat{p}^* \hat{a}_j^* + \hat{b}_j^* < \Sigma \bar{p}_i \bar{a}_{ij} + \bar{b}_j = \bar{p}_j = \hat{p}_j^*,$$

and for $j \notin J$,

$$\hat{p}^* \hat{a}_j^* + \hat{b}_j^* \leqslant \Sigma \hat{p}_i \hat{a}_{ij} + \hat{b}_j = \hat{p}_j = \hat{p}_j^*.$$

Therefore $\hat{p}^*(I - \hat{A}^*) \geqslant \hat{b}^*$ so that $\hat{A}^*$ is productive, and hence $\hat{p}^* \geqslant \hat{b}^*(I - \hat{A})^{-1} = \tilde{p}$, say, as in the proof to observation E. Now $\tilde{p} \in \mathscr{P}$ and $\hat{p} \geqslant \tilde{p}$: a contradiction. So no such $\bar{p}$ exists. $\square$

And finally,

G: If $(A, b) \in T$ has the non-substitution property, then

$$b(I - A)^{-1} = \hat{p}.$$

Proof. Suppose $(A, b) \in T$ has the non-substitution property; then A must be productive. Let $p = b(I - A)^{-1}$. If $p \neq \hat{p}$, observation F implies that $\Sigma p_i > \Sigma \hat{p}_i$ provided $p \in \mathscr{P}$. Let $\hat{c}_i = L/\Sigma \hat{p}_i$ for all i. Then $\hat{p}\hat{c} = L > p\hat{c} \Rightarrow \hat{c} \in U(\hat{A}, \hat{b})$; but $\hat{c} \notin U(A, b)$: a contradiction. Therefore $p \notin \mathscr{P}$; i.e., $p_j > p_j^*$ for some j_1, say, is the only possibility, since $(A, b) \in T$.

Let

$$c_{j_1} = L/p_{j_1}^* \quad \text{and} \quad c_j = 0, \quad j \neq j_1.$$

Then

$$pc = p_{j_1}(L/p_{j_1}^*) > L; \text{ but } p^*c = L \Rightarrow c \in U(A^*, b^*)$$

and $c \notin U(A, b)$: a contradiction. Hence $p = \hat{p}$. $\square$

To sum up, even if each sector j (identified by its only output commodity j) possesses a set of activities T_j that satisfy requirements I and II, we may see the production sectors choosing $(\hat{a}_j, \hat{b}_j) \in T_j$ for all j, regardless of the level of net outputs that have to be generated. This result is of course very special, as it is crucially dependent on the assumptions of (a) single non-producible factor and (b) no joint products.

This chapter begins by looking at a simple structure of production where two commodities are produced by means of two factors. This leads to an analysis that is used particularly in the pure theory of international trade; see, for example, Jones (1965a, 1965b). In fact, the analytical apparatus and (Figure 3.2–3.3) are borrowed from these papers. Results such as the Factor Price Equalization Theorem, the Stolpe–Samuelson (1941) Theorem, and the Rybczynski (1955) Theorem are discussed. The text moves on to a discussion of more general production structures; linear activity analysis models and strictly convex production possibility sets are considered. The former grew out of the work of Koopmans (1951), Leontief (1951), and Dorfman, Samuelson, and Solow (1958). The latter, which grew out of an analysis involving production functions, cost functions, and profit functions, may be traced to the contributions of Samuelson (1947) and Shephard (1953). Analytically, the apparatus resembles the theory of duality referred to in the bibliographical notes to Chapter 2, and Diewert (1982) may be consulted for a comprehensive survey.

The mathematical notes to this chapter, together with the Mathematical Appendix, Section 8.3.4, are based on Mukherji (1985) and contain an unified analysis of static Leontief models—see Dorfman, Samuelson, and Solow (1958: chs. 9 and 10) for an elementary treatment. This analysis was mainly motivated by the contribution of McKenzie (1960a). Both in the text and in the mathematical notes, the Separating Hyperplane Theorem of Gale (1960) is exploited to yield the results connected with efficient outputs, productivity conditions, and the Non-Substitution Theorem (see Georgescu-Roegen 1951; Samuelson 1951; Johansen 1972; and Dasgupta 1974).

4 Existence, Uniqueness, and Stability of Competitive Equilibrium

The main objectives of this chapter are first to provide a simple general equilibrium model of an economy where firms and individuals coexist, and then to analyse some of the properties of the general equilibrium for such a model. In this connection, it may be worth recalling how we set up the equations defining a general competitive equilibrium in Chapter 2. There we defined a price configuration to be a competitive equilibrium if the excess demand for each commodity was zero. We shall retain this definition, and consequently we need to examine how excess demand may be defined if there are both firms and individuals.

To this end, we shall first of all consider an economy in which there are individuals of the type examined in Chapter 2 (Sections 2.3 and 2.4) and firms of the type analysed in Chapter 3 (Section 3.4). The former would yield the demand function $x^i(p)$ for individual i; the firm J would provide us with the supply function $S^J(p)$ and we would then define, excess demand as

$$Z(p) = \sum_i x^i(p) - \sum_J S^J(p) - \sum_i w^i$$

where w^i is the endowment of i.

There is another matter that we need to examine, and that is the distribution of profits from firms to households, since the firms of Section 3.4 may make positive profits. Having laid a basis for the excess demand function, we examine the following questions:

(a) Is there a p^* such that $Z(p^*) = 0$?
(b) If such a p^* exists, is it unique?
(c) How does the system of competitive markets arrive at p^*?
(d) How is p^* altered when the parameters for the economy are altered?

The first is the question of the *existence* of a competitive equilibrium. It may be recalled from our discussion in Chapter 1 that it is only at such a configuration that agents can carry out their plans. Hence the existence of such a p^* provides us with a check of the consistency of our various assumptions. The second question, that of *uniqueness*, is a natural one in the present context. The existence of multiple equilibria brings with it a separate set of problems, and we shall try to understand the conditions under which equilibrium is unique. Having seen that our assumptions are consistent or that an equilibrium exists, we need to provide some mechanism which allows the system of competitive markets to arrive at the equilibrium configuration. This is the *stability* question. And finally, we need to examine the relationship of the equilibrium configuration to the parameters of our economy—the *comparative-statics* properties of the equilibrium. We shall take up the above questions one by one in the sections that follow.

4.1 A Model of General Equilibrium

As mentioned above, we shall consider an economy where there are firms of the type studied in Section 3.4, and households or individuals of the type analysed in Chapter 2. The firms and consumers are assumed to be competitive in the sense that each accepts prices as parameters; given prices, firms maximize profits and consumers maximize utility subject to a budget constraint. To be more specific, let us use the index J for firms, $J = 1, 2, \ldots, M$, the index i for households $i = 1, 2, \ldots, H$, and the index j for commodities $j = 1, 2, \ldots, n$. In addition, households own the firms in the following sense: each household i receives a share θ_{iJ} of the Jth firm's profits, where $\theta_{iJ} \geqq 0$ and $\Sigma_i \theta_{iJ} = 1$ for each J. The shares θ_{iJ} are specified initially and are parameters of the system. Notice that such a scheme for the redistribution of profits has to be introduced, as the firms analysed earlier (Section 3.4), may make positive profits. With this provision for profit income, the budget constraint for household i becomes

$$px \leqq pw^i + \sum_J \theta_{iJ}\pi^J(p)$$

where w^i denotes the endowment of i and $\pi^J(p)$ denotes the profits of firm J.

Now, given that household i has an increasing and strictly quasi-concave utility function, the demands $x^i(p)$ are continuous functions of p for $p > 0$. We have just seen that the supply functions $S^J(p)$ are continuous functions of prices too, whenever $p > 0$. Let

$$X(p) = \sum_i x^i(p), \quad Y(p) = \sum_J S^J(p), \quad W = \sum_i w^i.$$

Then $Z(p) = X(p) - Y(p) - W$ is defined to be the *excess demand function* for the model. This function has the following properties:

(a) it is defined and is a continuous function of p for all $p > 0$;
(b) $Z(\lambda p) = Z(p)$ for $\lambda > 0$, $p > 0$;
(c) $p\{Z(p)\} = 0$ (Walras's Law).

Properties (a) and (b) follow from the corresponding properties of demand and supply functions to see (c), notice that

$$p\{Z(p)\} = \sum_i p\{x^i(p)\} - \sum_J p\{S^J(p)\} - \sum_i pw^i$$

$$= \sum_i p\{x^i(p) - w^i\} - \sum_J \pi^J(p)$$

$$= \sum_i \left[p\{x^i(p) - w^i\} - \sum_J \theta_{iJ}\pi^J(p) \right] \quad \left(\text{since } \sum_i \theta_{iJ} = 1\right)$$

$$= 0$$

from the budget constraint being exactly met at demands. p^* is defined to be an equilibrium if $Z(p^*) = 0$. We will see that there is such a p^*. Given property (b) of excess demand functions, prices will be normalized so that prices of·commodities can be considered relative to good 1; this is the numeraire, and so prices are restricted to

$$\mathscr{P} = \{p: p_1 = 1, p_j > 0, \quad \text{for all } j \neq 1\}.$$

Property (a) allows us to consider excess demand functions only on $\mathscr{P}$. Let $\mathscr{E} = \{p: p \in \mathscr{P} \text{ such that } Z(p) = 0\}$: the set of equilibrium prices. Our first goal is to show that $\mathscr{E} \neq \varnothing$. We need to show this because it is only at prices $p \in \mathscr{E}$ that all agents can simultaneously carry out their various objectives: households can carry out utility maximization and firms can carry out profit maximization; furthermore, the households get to consume what they want and firms to sell all they wish to. In other words, a model of the type spelled out above can be deemed consistent only if an equilibrium exists. I shall now present a formal argument which establishes the existence of an equilibrium.

4.2   Existence of a Competitive Equilibrium

This section relies heavily on Sections 8.4 and 8.5 below; the Kakutani Fixed-Point Theorem is our principal mathematical tool. Recall the definitions

$$\mathscr{P} = \{p: p_1 = 1, p_j > 0, j = 2, \ldots, n\}$$

and

$$\mathscr{E} = \{p \in \mathscr{P}: Z(p) = 0\}.$$

Given that we shall consider $p \in \mathscr{P}$, it would be more convenient to consider $\mathscr{P}_1 = \{p_{\sim 1} = (p_2, \ldots, p_n): (1, p_{\sim 1}) \in \mathscr{P}\}$. Thus, $Z(p)$ for $p \in \mathscr{P}$ may be considered to be $Z(p_{\sim 1})$ for $p_{\sim 1} \in \mathscr{P}_1$. I shall sometimes write q, r for $p_{\sim 1}$ whenever the context makes it clear that we are considering prices of goods 2 to n.

We wish to conclude that $\mathscr{E} \neq \varnothing$; we proceed, first of all, to construct a set $S \subseteq \mathscr{P}_1$ such that S is convex, bounded, and open (in R^{n-1}); further, if $p^* \in \mathscr{E}$, then $p^*_{\sim 1} \in S$, so that we may confine our attention to S. Now let

$$K = \left\{ p_{\sim 1} \in \mathscr{P}_1 : \sum_{j=1}^{n} Z_j(p_{\sim 1}) \leqslant 0 \right\};$$

then it is shown that K is a *non-empty compact* subset of S, and we may narrow our region of search from S to K. However, as the statement of the Fixed-Point Theorem should convince us, we need a *convex* and a *compact* domain. To obtain such a region, we proceed as follows. By virtue of Urysohn's Lemma, which guarantees that, whenever $A \subseteq B$ where A is compact and B is open, there is an open set D such that

$$A \subseteq D \quad \text{and} \quad \text{cl} D \subseteq B$$

where $\text{cl} D = $ closure of D, we can conclude that there is an open set V such that

$$K \subseteq V \quad \text{and} \quad \text{cl} V \subseteq S.$$

Clearly, $\text{cl} V$ is compact; consider the smallest convex set containing $\text{cl} V$, $\text{con}(\text{cl} V)$: the convex hull of $\text{cl} V$. Then, since S is convex, $\text{con}(\text{cl} V) \subseteq S$. Thus let $Q = \text{con}(\text{cl} V)$. We have then

$$K \subseteq V \subseteq \text{cl} V \subseteq Q \subseteq S,$$

and Q is the required domain, being both convex and compact. Moreover, K is contained in the *interior* of Q, a fact that will be of crucial importance. Finally, it should be made clear that the terms 'open' and 'interior' are with reference to R^{n-1}, within which we shall be working.

A map is now constructed of $\psi: Q \to Q$ which satisfies the conditions of the Kakutani Fixed-Point Theorem so that there is $p^*_{\sim 1} \in Q$ such that

$$p^*_{\sim 1} \in \psi(p^*_{\sim 1}).$$

We will see that $p^* = (1, p^*_{\sim 1}) \in \mathscr{E}$, and our demonstration would be complete. In the following paragraphs, details are provided of the above in a series of small steps.

1: If $p^s \in \mathscr{P}$ and $\|p^s\| \to +\infty$, then $\sum_j Z_j(p^s) \to +\infty$.

Consider

$$v^s = \frac{1}{\|p^s\|} p^s;$$

then $\|v^s\| = 1$ for all s; hence there is a sub-sequence (v^{s_k}) such that $v^{s_k} \to v^0$ as $k \to \infty$ where $\|v^0\| = 1$ but $v^0_j = 0$ for some j. By property D of Section 3.4, it follows that $\pi^J(v^0)$ is not defined for all J. In particular, this means that $\|y^J(v^{s_k})\| \to \infty$, since otherwise $y^J(v^{s_k})$ has a limit point $\hat{y}^J \in P^J$ and $v^0 \hat{y}^J \geqslant v^0 y^J$ for all $y^J \in P^J \Rightarrow \pi^J(v^0) = v^0 \hat{y}^J$: a contradiction. Since P^J is bounded above, this means that for each J there is some m such that $y_m^J(v^{s_k}) \to -\infty$; i.e.,

$$Y_m(v^{s_k}) = \sum_J y_m^J(v^{s_k}) \to -\infty$$

for some m, or $Z_m(v^{s_k}) \to +\infty$. Since all $Z_j(\cdot)$ are bounded below, the claim follows. Thus, for some N,

$$\|p^s\| > N \Rightarrow \sum_{j=1}^{n} Z_j(p^s) > 0.$$

Hence there is some $M > 0$ such that $p_{\sim 1} \in \mathscr{P}_1$ and $p_j > M$ for some $j \Rightarrow \sum_j Z_j(p) > 0$.

Let

$$S = \{p_{\sim 1} \in \mathscr{P}_1 : 0 < p_j < M + 1, j = 2, \ldots, n\};$$

then S is a convex, open, and bounded subset of $\mathscr{P}_1$. Let $K = \{p_{\sim 1} \in \mathscr{P}_1 : \sum_j Z_j(p_{\sim 1}) \leqslant 0\}$. We can now proceed to the next step.

2: K is a non-empty compact subset of S.

Consider $\tilde{p}_{\sim 1}$ with $p_j = 1$ for all j. Then $\tilde{p}_{\sim 1} \in \mathscr{P}_1$, and by Walras's Law

$$\sum_j \tilde{p}_j Z_j(\tilde{p}) = 0 \Rightarrow \sum_j Z_j(\tilde{p}) = 0 \Rightarrow \tilde{p}_{\sim 1} \in K.$$

Also, $p_{\sim 1} \in K \Rightarrow p_j \leqslant M$ for all $j \neq 1 \Rightarrow p_{\sim 1} \in S$. Thus, K is a bounded subset of S.

Let $p_{\sim 1}^s \in K$, a sequence, with $p_{\sim 1}^0$ as its limit. In case $p_{\sim 1}^0 > 0$,

$$\sum_{j=1}^{n} Z_j(p_{\sim 1}^s) \leqslant 0 \Rightarrow \sum_{j=1}^{n} Z_j(p_{\sim 1}^0) \leqslant 0$$

and $p_{\sim 1}^0 \in K$.

Suppose $p_k^0 = 0$ for some k. Then, as in the above demonstration, $\sum_j Z_j(p_{\sim 1}^s) \to +\infty$ so that $p_{\sim 1}^s \notin K$ for sufficiently large s. Hence $p_{\sim 1}^0 > 0$ and $p_{\sim 1}^0 \in K$. Thus K is a compact subset of an open bounded set S.

By Urysohn's Lemma, stated above, there is an open set V such that

$$K \subseteq V \quad \text{and} \quad \text{cl}\, V \subseteq S.$$

In fact, writing $Q = \text{con}(\text{cl}\, V)$ (the convex hull of the closure), we have

$$K \subseteq V \subseteq \text{cl}\, V \subseteq \text{con}(\text{cl}\, V) \subseteq S,$$

where the last step follows from the fact that S is convex and from the definition of convex hull. Thus, Q is compact and convex (see Section 8.4.2 below).

Consider $\psi: Q \to Q$:

$$\psi(p_{\sim 1}) = \left\{ q \in Q: \sum_{j=2}^{n} q_j Z_j(p_{\sim 1}) \geqslant \sum_{j=2}^{n} r_j Z_j(p_{\sim 1}) \text{ for all } r \in Q \right\}.$$

Then it is immediate that

(a) $\psi(q) \neq \varnothing$ for all $q \in Q$;
(b) $\psi(q)$ is convex for all $q \in Q$.

Moreover, if $q^s \in Q$, $q^s \to q^0 \in Q$, $r^s \in \psi(q^s)$ and $r^s \to r^0$, then $r^0 \in \psi(q^0)$.
If $r^0 \notin \psi(q^0)$, then there is $\hat{q} \in Q$ such that

$$\sum_{j=2}^{n} \hat{q}_j Z_j(q^0) > \sum_{j=2}^{n} r_j^0 Z_j(q^0).$$

Hence for all s large enough,

$$\sum_{j=2}^{n} \hat{q}_j Z_j(q^s) > \sum_{j=2}^{n} r_j^s Z_j(q^s).$$

Thus, $r^s \notin \psi(q^s)$. Hence $r^0 \in \psi(q^0)$ and the map $\psi: Q \to Q$ is closed at every $q \in Q$.

By Kakutani's Theorem (see Section 8.5.3), there is $q^* \in Q$ such that $q^* \in \psi(q^*)$.

We also need the following property of $\psi(\cdot)$:

3: If $Z(q) \neq 0$, then $r \in \psi(q) \Rightarrow r \notin \text{int } Q$.

For suppose $r \in \text{int } Q$; i.e., suppose there is $N(r) \subseteq Q$ where $N(r)$ is some open set containing r. Since $Z(q) \neq 0$, either $Z_k(q) > 0$ for some $k \neq 1$, or $Z_k(q) < 0$ for some $k \neq 1$. Accordingly, one may choose $q' \in N(r)$ such that

$$\sum_{j=2}^{n} q_j' Z_j(q) > \sum_{j=2}^{n} r_j Z_j(q):$$

hence the claim.

Returning to the fixed point q^* of ψ,

$$q^* \in \psi(q^*) \Rightarrow \sum_{j=2}^{n} q_j^* Z_j(q^*) \geqslant \sum_{j=2}^{n} q_j Z_j(q^*) \text{ for all } q \in Q;$$

i.e.,

$$\sum_{j=2}^{n} q_j^* Z_j(q^*) \geqslant \sum_{j=2}^{n} Z_j(q^*), \text{ since } (1, 1, \ldots, 1) \in K \subseteq Q$$

or

$$Z_1(q^*) + \sum_{j=2}^{n} q_j^* Z_j(q^*) \geqslant \sum_{j=1}^{n} Z_j(q^*)$$

or

$$0 \geqslant \sum_{j=1}^{n} Z_j(q^*) \Rightarrow q^* \in K.$$

Now $q^* \in V \subseteq Q$ where V is an open set, which implies that q^* is an interior point of $Q \Rightarrow Z(q^*) = 0$, by step 3.

Thus we have shown that

$$\mathscr{E} = \{p \in \mathscr{P} : Z(p) = 0\} \neq \varnothing.$$

For any $p^* \in \mathscr{E}$, define

$$K_{p*} = \{p \in \mathscr{P} : p^*[Z(p)] \leqslant 0\}.$$

As above, one may show that K_{p*} is compact. Also, $\mathscr{E} \subseteq K_{p*}$.

The following relationships may also be noted.

A: For any price vector $p \in \mathscr{P}$, $p^* \in \mathscr{E}$, $p \neq p^*$, and $Y(p) \neq Y(p^*)$
   $\Rightarrow p\{X(p) - X(p^*)\} > 0$.

Note that

$$p\{X(p)\} = p\{Y(p) + w\} \text{ by Walras's Law}$$

$$> p\{Y(p^*) + w\} \text{ from profit maximization}$$

$$= p\{X(p^*)\} \text{ since } p^* \in \mathscr{E}.$$

B: For any $p \in K_{p*}$, $p^*\{X(p) - X(p^*)\} < 0$ if $Y(p) \neq Y(p^*)$, since

$$p \in K_{p*}, \; p^* Z(p) \leqslant 0$$

or

$$p^* X(p) \leqslant p^* \{Y(p) + w\}$$

$$< p^* \{Y(p^*) + w\}$$

$$= p^* X(p^*).$$

Whenever $K_{p*} = \{p^*\}$, i.e. whenever $p \neq p^*$, $p \in \mathscr{P} \Rightarrow p^* Z(p) > 0$, we say that the *Weak Axiom of Revealed Preference* holds in the aggregate. (see Section 4.3 below for an application.)

4.3   Uniqueness of Equilibrium

In the last section, we saw that under our assumptions an equilibrium exists. Often it is necessary that there be a unique equilibrium configuration. The assumptions made above, however, are not enough to guarantee this, and we need to impose some additional conditions. To properly appreciate how stringent the requirement of uniqueness of equilibrium is, we shall present a characterization of uniqueness of equilibria.

Recall our definitions of $\mathscr{P}$ and $\mathscr{E}$ from the last section. For any $p \in \mathscr{P}$ and $q \in \mathscr{P}$, there is a λ such that $\lambda > 0$ and $\lambda p \geqq q$; in particular,

$$\lambda = \max_k q_k/p_k$$

would serve the purpose. Define $I(p, q) = \{k : \lambda p_k = q_k\}$.

CONDITION U : For $\hat{p} \in \mathscr{E}$, $q \in \mathscr{P}$, if, for some λ, $\lambda \hat{p} \geqq q$, $I(\hat{p}, q) \neq \varnothing$, and there exists $k \notin I(\hat{p}, q)$, then $Z_j(q) \neq 0$ for some j.

1: $\hat{p}, \bar{p} \in \mathscr{E} \Rightarrow \hat{p} = \bar{p}$ if and only if condition (U) holds.

To see the validity of this claim, note first of all that necessity is clear. For the sufficiency part of the argument, suppose $\hat{p} \in \mathscr{E}$, and condition U holds. Consider any $q \in \mathscr{P}$, $q \neq \hat{p}$. Define

$$\lambda = \max_k q_k/\hat{p}_k;$$

then $I(\hat{p}, q) \neq \varnothing$; also, $q \neq \hat{p}$ implies that, for some j, $j \notin I(\hat{p}, q)$. Hence $Z_i(q) \neq 0$ for some $i \Rightarrow q \notin \mathscr{E}$. Hence $\mathscr{E}$ consists of a single member.

The above characterization may not be particularly revealing; however, if one considers another similar result, the strength of our requirement will be appreciated.

CONDITION U* : For p, $q \in \mathscr{P}$, if, for some λ, $I(p, q) \neq \varnothing$ and there is $k \notin I(p, q)$, then for some index $j \in I(p, q)$, $Z_j(q) \neq Z_j(p)$.

Condition U* is stronger than U in two ways: first, $p \in \mathscr{P}$ (rather than $\mathscr{E}$); second, the index j for which $Z_j(q) \neq Z_j(p)$ must satisfy $j \in I(p, q)$. It turns out that, if Z_j are differentiable, condition U* implies that

$$\frac{\partial Z_j(p)}{\partial p_k} > 0 \forall \quad j \neq k \quad \text{for all } p \in \mathscr{P}. \tag{GS}$$

I shall not consider here a proof for the above assertion but refer readers to Iritani (1981). It may be noted that the assumption of gross substitutes i.e., (GS) is a very special assumption.

Let us first reinterpret (GS), as follows:

If $p, q \in R^n_{++}$ (strictly positive prices) and $p \geqq q$, $p \neq q$,

then for any j such that $p_j = q_j$, $Z_j(p) > Z_j(q)$.

2: Under the above condition, $\hat{p}, \bar{p} \in \mathscr{E} \Rightarrow \hat{p} = \bar{p}$.

For, suppose $\hat{p}, \bar{p} \in \mathscr{E}$; $\hat{p} \neq \bar{p}$; then define

$$\lambda = \max_i \hat{p}_i/\bar{p}_i \,{\dot{=}}\, \hat{p}_k/\bar{p}_k, \text{ say.}$$

Now

$$\lambda \bar{p} \geqslant \hat{p} \quad \text{and} \quad \lambda \bar{p}_k = \hat{p}_k \Rightarrow Z_k(\lambda \bar{p}) > Z_k(\hat{p}) = 0$$

or $Z_k(\bar{p}) > 0$; i.e., $\bar{p} \notin \mathscr{E}$: a contradiction.

Another type of restriction often used in this context is the *Aggregate Weak Axiom of Revealed Preference*, which guarantees that

$$p^* Z(p) > 0 \quad \text{for all } p \in \mathscr{P}, p^* \in \mathscr{E}. \tag{WARP}$$

It is known that $(GS) \Rightarrow (WARP)$.

(WARP) also follows if aggregate consumer demand $X(p)$ follows the same rules as those followed by individual demand; in other words, consider the situation when there is a single individual whose utility maximization yields $X(p)$. Under this situation, for any two different price vectors $\bar{p}, \hat{p}$, with $\bar{p} \neq \hat{p}$, the following revealed preference axiom should hold:

$$\text{If } \bar{p}\{X(\hat{p}) - X(\bar{p})\} \leqslant 0, \quad \text{then } \hat{p}\{X(\hat{p}) - X(\bar{p})\} < 0.$$

In other words, if at prices $\bar{p}$ the consumer chooses $X(\bar{p})$ when $X(\hat{p})$ is available, he shows his preference for the bundle $X(\bar{p})$ over $X(\hat{p})$. Consequently, in the situation when $X(\hat{p})$ is chosen, i.e. at $\hat{p}$, the bundle $X(\bar{p})$ must cost more.

Given the above explanation, and given conditions A and B of the last section,

$$p^* Z(p) \leqslant 0 \Rightarrow p^*\{X(p) - X(p^*)\} \leqslant 0 \quad \text{(see condition B of the last section)}$$

$$\Rightarrow p\{X(p) - X(p^*)\} < 0 \quad \text{by the above discussion,}$$

which contradicts condition A. Therefore $p^* Z(p) > 0$ for all $p \in \mathscr{P}$. This immediately allows us to conclude that

3: Under (WARP), $\mathscr{E} = \{\hat{p}\}$.

A far weaker condition has been seen to imply uniqueness of equilibrium by using advanced mathematical tools in situations when $Z(\cdot)$ is assumed differentiable. I shall state the condition without going into a demonstration of the result:

4: If $D\{-Z(p^*)\}$ has a positive determinant at all $p^* \in \mathscr{E}$, then equilibrium is unique.

Here,

$$D\{-Z(p^*)\} = \left\{-\frac{\partial Z_i(p^*)}{\partial p_j}\right\}, \quad i, j = 2, \dots, n.$$

Moreover, the result is true only if a boundary condition of the type $Z_i(p) > 0$ when $p_i = 0$ is met. However, given the nonexistence of $Z(p)$ when prices vanish, some care is necessary to employ a proper boundary restriction.

Using the definition of $Z(p)$, one may analyse result 4 a bit further:

$$D\{-Z(p^*)\} = D\{Y(p^*)\} - D\{X(p^*)\}.$$

Notice, from the properties of the supply function deduced in Section 3.4, that

$$D\{Y(p^*)\} = \left\{\frac{\partial Y_i(p^*)}{\partial P_j}\right\}, \quad i, j = 2, \ldots, n$$

is a principal minor of a positive semi-definite matrix and would thus possess a non-negative determinant:

$$D\{X(p^*)\} = \sum_i D\{x^i(p^*)\},$$

where $x^i(p^*)$ is the demand function of the ith individual.

Using the Slutsky decomposition introduced in Section 2.6.2 above,

$$\frac{\partial x_k^i(p^*)}{\partial p_j} = \left\{\frac{\partial x_k^i(p^*)}{\partial p_j}\right\}_{u^i \text{ const.}} - \left\{x_j^i(p^*) - w_j^i - \sum_J \theta_J^i Y_j^J(p^*)\right\}\frac{\partial x^i}{\partial I}$$

where some additional terms now enter into the income effects matrix to take into account the profit income of the ith individual.

The substitution matrix is negative semi-definite; hence the corresponding matrix that appears in the expression for $D\{-Z(p^*)\}$ would have a non-negative determinant; it can be taken to be positive, provided the substitution matrix has rank $(n-1)$ as shown in the mathematical notes to Chapter 2. Thus, $D\{-Z(p^*)\}$ has a positive determinant provided income effects are small: a not unexpected result, given our preliminary considerations of the two-good exchange case in Chapter 2.

4.4 The Stability of Competitive Equilibrium

The entire area of the stability of competitive equilibrium consists of a vast collection of results, each applicable in some special situation. It would be impossible to survey all of them here; however, I shall attempt to discuss some of the results that will indicate to readers the nature of the problem.

One of the major difficulties in this area lies in specification of the problem. Walras never defined the notion of stability of equilibrium in the context of multiple markets, although he devoted considerable time to distinguishing between positions of stable and unstable equilibrium in the context of two goods (see Chapter 2 in this connection). For the case of multiple markets, the problem was viewed a bit differently; after defining the market balance equations (i.e. our excess demand equal to zero equations), Walras poses the following question: how does the market solve these equations? The answer is provided by the notion of the *tatonnement*. If initially prices are such that demands do not equal supply, and if

(a) *no trade occurs* and

(b) *the price of a commodity in excess demand is raised, the price of a commodity in excess supply is lowered, and the price of commodity in equilibrium is left unchanged,*

then Walras concluded that prices would be revised until an equilibrium was ultimately reached.

This assertion was of course rather like a wishful conjecture. And we shall see whether we can settle the question. For this purpose, it would be convenient to introduce an adjustment on prices reflecting condition (b):

$$\left. \begin{aligned} \dot{p}_j &= f_j\{Z_j(p)\}, \quad j = 2, \ldots, n \\ p_1 &= 1 \end{aligned} \right\} \tag{T}$$

where $f_j(\cdot)$ is a sign-preserving function of excess demands; i.e., $f_j\{Z_j(p)\}Z_j(p) > 0$ if $Z_j(p) \neq 0$, otherwise $f_j\{Z_j(p)\} = 0$. Thus (b) is considered; (a) is implicit in our writing $Z_j(p)$; the initial endowment distribution $\{w^i\}$ is held constant and does not alter while the process described above is operating. The above is a system of differential equations, and specifying an initial price $p^0 \notin \mathscr{E}$ and assuming $f_j(p)$ to be a continuously differentiable function of prices imply that there is a unique solution $p(t) = \psi(t; p^0)$ of the above with the property $p(0) = \psi(0; p^0) = p^0$ and $\dot{p}$ satisfying the above. Henceforth, we shall assume that $f_j(p)$ and $Z_j(p)$ are continuously differentiable functions of prices for all $p > 0$.

If, for any arbitrary $p^0 \notin \mathscr{E}$, $p(t) \to p^* \in \mathscr{E}$ as $t \to \infty$, we shall say that the *process is stable and p* is globally stable*; naturally, this makes sense only if p^* is unique. In case $p(t)$ is such that all its limit points are in $\mathscr{E}$, we shall say that the process is *quasi-stable*. If, on the other hand, $p(t) \to p^*$ only if p^0 lies in some appropriate neighbourhood of p^*, we shall say that p^* is *locally stable*, under an adjustment (T).

Global stability is, of course, a very demanding requirement; I shall present two sets of arguments for a globally stable equilibrium under an adjustment such as (T). First, let us consider the case of gross substitutes introduced above; since I wish to present a diagrammatic exposition, let us consider, further, the case when there are only three goods (see Figure 4.1). By the assumption of (GS), $Z_2(p_2, p_3) = 0$ is upward-sloping; so too is $Z_3(p_2, p_3) = 0$; moreover, the only type of intersection possible is the one depicted; i.e., $Z_2(\cdot) = 0$ is steeper than $Z_3(\cdot) = 0$.

Also, in the four regions I, II, III, and IV in the figure, the sign pattern of excess demands, again by (GS), is:

I: $Z_2(p) > 0$, $Z_3(p) < 0$ III: $Z_2(p) < 0$, $Z_3(p) > 0$

II: $Z_2(p) > 0$, $Z_3(p) > 0$ IV: $Z_2(p) < 0$, $Z_3(p) < 0$.

The arrows represent the direction of price adjustment in each region. From

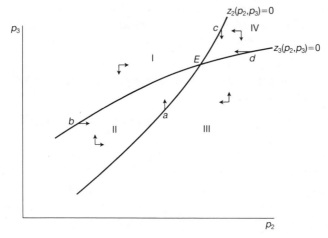

Fig. 4.1

any point in region I or III, an adjustment of type (T) would lead either to E (the equilibrium) or to points such as a, b, c, or d. In the latter cases, price adjustment would lead to a movement inside regions II or IV as the case may be. Moreover, if price revision leads to either II or IV, then (T) would never lead to prices outside these regions and they may only be revised towards E. The above 'phase diagram' method allows us to conclude that E is the globally stable equilibrium.

For an analytical argument covering the case of many goods, readers are referred to the mathematical notes at the end of the chapter.

Consider next the case of local stability of an equilibrium price p^*, under an adjustment such as (T). Consider a special case, $f_j(p) = k_j Z_j(p)$ with $k_j > 0$ for all j. Then, it has been customary to analyse a linear system:

$$\dot{p}_j = k_j \sum_k \left\{ \frac{\partial Z_j(p^*)}{\partial p_k} \right\} (p_k - p_k^*), \quad j = 2, \ldots, n$$

or

$$\dot{p} = K \left\{ \frac{\partial Z_j(p^*)}{\partial p_k} \right\} (p - p^*).$$

Given any p^0 sufficiently close to p^* for which the above is an approximation to (T), the aim is to study the solution of the linear system through p^0. The behaviour of the solution of the linear system is completely determined by the characteristic roots of the matrix

$$K \left\{ \frac{\partial Z_j(p^*)}{\partial p_k} \right\}.$$

It is known that the solution converges to $p*$ *if and only if all the characteristic roots have real parts which are negative.* (Such a matrix is called a *stable* matrix). In this connection, we have the following.

LIAPUNOV THEOREM: A real $n \times n$ matrix C is stable if and only if there is a symmetric positive definite matrix B such that $BC + C'B$ is negative definite.

For definitions of positive and negative definite matrices, see Section 8.3.3 below.

The following conclusions may now be drawn regarding local stability of an equilibrium $p*$ under an adjustment process of the type described above.

1 If income effects cancel out at $p*$, then $p*$ is locally stable. First, the discussion of Section 4.3 may be used to conclude that, if income effects cancel out, then $\{Z_{jk}(p*)\}$ is negative definite where

$$\{Z_{jk}(p*)\} = \left\{\frac{\partial Z_j(p*)}{\partial p_k}\right\}, \quad j, k = 2, \ldots, n.$$

Next, note that, since K is a diagonal matrix, it is symmetric too, and, on account of the symmetry of $\{Z_{jk}(p*)\}$ and K:

$$K\{Z_{jk}(p*)\} = \{Z_{jk}(p*)\}K.$$

Therefore the fact that

$$K^{-1}[K\{Z_{jk}(p*)\}] + [K\{Z_{jk}(p*)\}]K^{-1} = \{Z_{jk}(p*)\} + \{Z_{jk}(p*)\}$$

is negative definite and K^{-1} is positive definite ensures our claim via Liapunov's Theorem.

2 If $\{Z_{jk}(p*)\}$ has a dominant diagonal which is negative, then $p*$ is locally stable. In this case, one may directly show that $\{Z_{jk}(p*)\}$ is stable. (For a definition of dominant diagonal matrix and its properties, see Section 8.3.4).

Consider $\{Z_{jk}(p*) - \lambda I\} = B = (b_{ij})$, say. Notice that, if $\lambda = a + ib$ and $a \geqslant 0$, then $|b_{jj}| \geqslant |Z_{jj}(p*)|$ (where $|\alpha|$ is to be interpreted as the modulus of α if α is complex). Consequently B has a dominant diagonal and is hence non-singular; so λ cannot be a characteristic root of $\{Z_{jk}(p*)\}$. Hence if λ is a characteristic root of $\{Z_{jk}(p*)\}$, this implies that $\lambda = a + ib$ with $a < 0$.

3 If Z_j satisfy (GS) at $p*$, then $p*$ is locally stable.

$$Z_{jk}(p*) > 0, \quad j \neq k,$$

by (GS). Now

$$\sum_{j \neq 1} p_j Z_j(p) = -Z_1(p),$$

by Walras's Law; therefore

$$\sum_{j \neq 1} p_j \left\{ \frac{\partial Z_j(p)}{\partial p_k} \right\} + Z_k(p) = - \left\{ \frac{\partial Z_1(p)}{\partial p_k} \right\}, \quad k \neq 1.$$

Therefore at $p = p^*$,

$$p^* \left\{ \frac{\partial Z_j(p^*)}{\partial p_k} \right\} = - \left\{ \frac{\partial Z_1(p^*)}{\partial p_k} \right\} < 0, \text{ by (GS)}.$$

Also, because of (GS), if follows that $\{Z_{jk}(p^*)\}$ has a dominant diagonal which is negative. The claim now follows, by virtue of conclusion 2 above.

Thus, for both local stability and uniqueness, income effects have to be small or negligible. In fact, it turns out that, if all equilibria are locally stable, there can be only one equilibrium (see result 4 of the last section). The converse to this proposition is unfortunately false, i.e. that there may be a unique equilibrium that is globally unstable. Examples of such an equilibrium were produced by Scarf (1960) and Gale (1963).

A related question has also attracted some attention of late; suppose, in our restrictions on the nature of adjustment of prices in disequilibrium, that we are prepared to give up (b) and retain only (a), i.e. retain only the assumption that trade does not occur at disequilibrium prices: in such a case, are there adjustments on prices that would lead to equilibria? Affirmative answers to this question have been provided. References to such literature are contained in the bibliographical notes to this chapter.

4.5   Comparative Statics

We have seen how an equilibrium may be demonstrated to exist; we have also considered conditions under which such an equilibrium is unique. And we have seen how such an equilibrium may be attained, under some conditions, beginning with an initial disequilibrium price. This last exercise is of particular importance if one realizes that the equilibrium may be disturbed by shifts in certain environmental parameters such as tastes, technology, etc.

Let $p^* = (1, p_2^*, \ldots, p_n^*)$ be an equilibrium; suppose some parameters (tastes, for example) undergo a change; let $\hat{p}$ be the new equilibrium configuration. After the change, p^* would be a disequilibrium configuration, and so some adjustment would occur beginning from p^*. If, under the adjustment, the equilibrium $\hat{p}$ is stable, then prices generated by the adjustment would approach $\hat{p}$. Thus, if $\hat{p}_2 > p_2^*$, it would be meaningful to say that the price of commodity 2 increases because of a shift in the parameters *only if* the equilibrium $\hat{p}$ is stable. Thus, the comparison between $\hat{p}$ and p^* is meaningful only if equilibrium positions are stable. This, then, is the 'intimate connection', observed by Samuelson (1947: ch. IX), between theorems of comparative statics (wherein positions of equilibrium are compared) and the stability of equilibrium. Although stability of equilibrium is necessary for a comparative-statics exercise to be meaningful, whether stability is sufficient to yield determinate comparative-statics results is another matter. It is the nature of the 'intimate connection' that is the subject of this section.

First, we wish to establish the content of this 'intimate connection': the *'correspondence principle'* of Samuelson. Consider the basic model of this chapter—the economy specified by excess demand functions $Z_j(\cdot)$, $j = 1, 2, \ldots, n$, which are continuously differentiable functions of prices and a new variable α, the shift parameter. Thus, given $\alpha = \bar{\alpha}$,

$$Z_j(p; \bar{\alpha}) = 0, \quad j = 1, 2, \ldots, n \qquad (4.1)$$

defines the equilibrium prices $\bar{p}$. By the Implicit Function Theorem (see Section 8.5 below), whenever

$$\left\{ \frac{\partial Z_j(\bar{p}; \bar{\alpha})}{\partial p_k} \right\}, \quad j, k = 2, \ldots, n$$

does not vanish, we can express $\bar{p}$ as a function of α; e.g. $\bar{p} = g(\bar{\alpha})$; it is this function that we wish to analyse.

We consider a particularly simple parameter α, one that shifts tastes from the numeraire to good 2, leaving unaffected the excess demands of other goods. Totally differentiating (4.1), we write

$$\left\{ \frac{\partial Z_j(\bar{p}; \bar{\alpha})}{\partial p_k} \right\}, \quad j, k = 2, \ldots, n$$

as

$$A = (a_{jk}), \quad Z_{2\alpha} = \frac{\partial Z_2(\bar{p}: \bar{\alpha})}{\partial \alpha}.$$

For the sake of definiteness, let $Z_{2\alpha} > 0$. Then we have

$$A(p_{j\alpha}) = b \qquad (4.2)$$

where

$$p_{j\alpha} = \frac{\mathrm{d}\bar{p}_j}{\mathrm{d}\alpha}; \quad b' = (-Z_{2\alpha}, 0, \ldots; 0).$$

Thus, in case A^{-1} exists, as it should, for our analysis to be meaningful,

$$(p_{j\alpha}) = A^{-1}b.$$

Therefore $p_{j\alpha} = -Z_{2\alpha}C_{ji}$ if C_{j1} is the $(j-1)$th element of A^{-1}.

The rest of the section is devoted to solving (4.2), at least qualitatively, for the sign of the $p_{j\alpha}$ terms. As indicated at the outset, for meaningful comparative statics, we assume that $\bar{p}$ is at least locally stable under an adjustment of the type (T) defined in Section 4.4, where for simplicity we may assume that $k_j = 1$ for all j. Then the linear approximation process is

$$\dot{p} = A(p - \bar{p})$$

where A is as above. Given local stability would imply that A is stable. A^{-1}, hence, exists.

Given that A is stable, A^{-1} must be stable too, since the characteristic roots of A^{-1} are reciprocals of those of A. By virtue of the Liapunov Theorem mentioned in the last section, there must exist a positive definite B such that $BA^{-1} + (A^{-1})'B$ is negative definite. Thus from (4.2), $(p_{j\alpha}) = A^{-1}b$, we have

$$b'B(p_{j\alpha}) = b'(BA^{-1})b < 0$$

since

$$b'(BA^{-1})b = \tfrac{1}{2}b'\{BA^{-1} + (A^{-1})'B\}b.$$

Therefore $Z_{2\alpha}\sum_j B_{1j}p_{j\alpha} > 0$ or $\sum_j B_{1j}p_{j\alpha} > 0$ where (B_{1j}) is the first row of B. Thus,

1: A is stable implies that there is a positive definite matrix B such that, if there is a shift in demand from numeraire to good k $(k = 2, \ldots, n)$, then

$$B^k(p_{j\alpha}) > 0$$

where B^k denotes the $(k-1)$th row of B.

This is, of course, somewhat disappointing; one cannot, in general, even conclude that prices rise. All that we know about the rows B^k is that they constitute a positive definite matrix. To guarantee that prices rise, we need additional assumptions. For example, if we assume that the numeraire is a gross substitute for any other commodity (NGS), then, following the steps outlined in the demonstration of result 3 in the last section, we have

$$p^{*\prime}A < 0.$$

Thus, by the theorem of the separating hyperplane and its corrolaries, (see Section 8.3.2), $Ay \geqslant 0$ cannot have a semi-positive solution.

However, we know that $A \cdot A^{-1} = I$; hence each column of A^{-1} must have negative entries. In particular, $C_{j1} < 0$ for some j. Hence

2: If A is stable and NGS holds, then a *shift in demand from good 1 to good 2 will raise the price of some j*.

One cannot guarantee that $j = 2$, even. However, since A^{-1} is stable, some diagonal element of A^{-1} must be negative; i.e., $C_{jj} < 0$ for some j. Then

3: If A is stable, there is some j such that, if there is a shift in demand from good 1 to j, then price of j rises.

These three assertions seem to exhaust the content of the celebrated corre-spondence principle expounded by Samuelson (1947). Rather strong com-parative-statics results may be seen to follow if we have (GS). In fact, as opposed to local comparative-statics analysis of the type considered above, a 'global' analysis may now be carried out. It is convenient for this purpose to consider the case when there are only three goods—all gross substitutes of one another. Recall then the illustration used for the phase diagram method (see Figure 4.2). A shift in demand from numeraire to good 2 shifts the $Z_2(\cdot)$ $= 0$, as shown, with no effect on the $Z_3(\cdot) = 0$ line. The results are:

(a) $\hat{p}_2$ goes up;
(b) $\hat{p}_3$ goes up too;
(c) the increase in $\hat{p}_2$ is proportionately more than $\hat{p}_3$.

These three statements are sometimes called the three 'Hicksian Laws of Comparative Statics'. However, for the validity of these 'laws', we require some strong assumption such as (GS). Instead of pursuing (GS), we shall assume that we have the following restriction:

$$A \text{ has dominant negative diagonal.} \qquad \text{(DD)}$$

In other words, there are constants $d_j > 0, j = 2, \ldots, n, w_j > 0, j = 2, \ldots, n,$ such that

$$d_j |a_{jj}| > \sum_{i \neq j} d_i |a_{ij}|, \qquad j = 2, \ldots, n \qquad (4.3)$$

and

$$w_j |a_{jj}| > \sum_{i \neq j} w_i |a_{ji}|, \qquad j = 2, \ldots, n. \qquad (4.4)$$

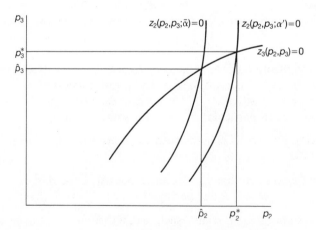

Fig. 4.2

Such a matrix is known to be Hicksian; i.e., a principal minor of order r has the sign of $(-1)^r$; consequently, diagonal elements of A^{-1} are negative. (See, for example, the results of Section 8.3.4 below.) Thus from (4.2),

    4: Under (DD), a shift in demand from good 1 to good 2 raises the price of good 2 (the first Hicksian Law).

Next, notice that $d'A < 0$ from (4.3). Let $-h' = d'A$, $h' > 0$. Then, from (4.2),

$$d'A(p_{j\alpha}) = d'b = -d_2 Z_{2\alpha}$$

or

$$h'(p_{j\alpha}) > 0$$

where $h > 0$. Hence

    5: Under (DD), a shift in demand to good 2 from the numeraire leads to an increase in a weighted sum of prices. (Positive weights are as defined above.)

We thus have a sort of generalization of the second and third Hicksian Laws. Note that, even if demand shifts from the numeraire to a group of goods, the above result holds. Thus, under (DD) prices will generally rise when there is a shift in the demand from the numeraire to some other good or group of goods.

    Finally, it should be pointed out that we have already carried out another set of comparative-statics exercises, in the mathematical notes to Chapter 2, where we looked at the effect of a change in the endowment pattern on equilibrium prices; such parameter changes are far more complicated than the simple binary changes analysed here.

4.6 A Résumé

We have defined an economy where there are firms and individuals, and one that allows us to define a well behaved excess demand function $Z(p)$ for all $p > 0$. The individuals of Sections 2.3. and 2.4 and the firms of Section 3.4, together with a profit-sharing rule described in Section 4.1, have allowed us to obtain $Z(p)$. In fact, it should be clear that our interest in $Z(p)$ forced the choice of the type of production structure we wanted; the aggregative constant-returns-to-scale production models would not lead to the notion of an excess demand function. For a treatment of such models in analysing the existence and uniqueness questions, readers should refer to the bibliographical notes of this chapter.

    A proof has been provided for the existence of a p^* such that

$$Z(p^*) = 0;$$

the main technical problem that we have had to overcome was the fact that our $Z(p)$ was defined only for $p > 0$; thus, we could not assume continuity when some prices were zero. Also, the prices for our economy were all relative to a given numeraire commodity at the outset. Having demonstrated that a p^* exists, we examined restrictions on $Z(\cdot)$ that would guarantee that p^* is unique; we found that if, roughly speaking, income effects are small, p^* will be unique.

The question of the stability and comparative statics of p^* were investigated by analysing some further restrictions on $Z(\cdot)$. It was also clear that these restrictions may not hold if income effects dominate. Since the existence of meaningful comparative statics is tied up with the property of stability and uniqueness, a condition is employed which provides not only uniqueness but also stability, and we saw what comparative-statics information flowed from this source.

Each of the topics covered above is of such complexity that a whole chapter could have been devoted to it alone. The results presented are therefore to be considered as a representative sample; for more details, the bibliographical notes for this chapter are to be consulted.

MATHEMATICAL NOTES

4.7   Global Stability: An Analytical Argument

Consider the definition of the set K_{p^*} in Section 4.2:

$$K_{p^*} = \{p \in \mathscr{P} : p^* Z(p) \leqslant 0\}$$

where

$$\mathscr{P} = \{p : p_1 = 1, p_j > 0, j \neq 1\}$$

and

$$p^* \in \mathscr{E} = \{p \in \mathscr{P} : Z(p) = 0\}.$$

Here, we shall assume that $\mathscr{E} = \{p^*\}$, i.e. that the equilibrium is unique, and $K_{p^*} = \{p^*\}$ so that $p \neq p^* \Rightarrow p^*\{Z(p)\} > 0$ (WARP). These two conditions follow if we have the gross substitute assumption, for example. Hereafter, we shall assume that

$$K_{p^*} = \{p^*\} = \mathscr{E}. \tag{4.5}$$

Price adjustment is governed by a system of differential equations which constitute a special case of (T):

$$\left.\begin{aligned}
\dot{p}_j &= k_j Z_j(p), \quad j = 2, \ldots, n \\
p_1 &= 1
\end{aligned}\right\} \tag{T$'$}$$

where we assume that $Z_j(p)$, the excess demand functions, are continuously differentiable functions of prices p for all $p \in \mathscr{P}$, Given any $p^0 \in \mathscr{P}$, there is a solution $p(t, p^0)$ to (T$'$) such that $p(0, p^0) = p^0$.

We shall next examine the behaviour of $p(t, p^0)$; in particular, we are interested in the question of convergence of $p(t, p^0)$ to p^* as $t \to \infty$. We shall investigate how (4.5) allows us to conclude that $p(t, p^0)$ does approach p^* as t becomes large.

However, before we approach the convergence question, we need to guarantee that $p(t, p^0) \in \mathscr{P}$ for all t. The above is not sufficient; we need an additional restriction.

BOUNDARY RESTRICTION (BR): There is $\varepsilon > 0$ such that $p \in \mathscr{P}$ and $p_i \leqslant \varepsilon$ for some $i \Rightarrow Z_i(p) > 0$.

Under BR, $p(t, p^0) > 0 \,\forall\, t$; thus prices remain positive along the solution.
Next, we need to construct a function $V\{p(t, p^0)\} = V(t)$ such that

(a) $V(t) \geqslant 0$ for all t, with a strict inequality whenever $p(t, p^0) \notin \mathscr{E}$;
(b) $V\{p(t, p^0)\}$ is a continuous and a strictly increasing function of p for all $p \in \mathscr{P}$;
(c) $\dot{V}\{p(t, p^0)\} < 0$ whenever $p(t, p^0) \notin \mathscr{E}$
$\qquad\qquad\qquad = 0$ when $p(t, p^0) \in \mathscr{E}$.

Such a function is called a *Liapunov function*. Now, if $p^0 \notin \mathscr{E}$, then (b) and (c) combine to guarantee that

$$V\{p(t, p^0)\} \leqslant V(p^0),$$

so that $p(t, p^0)$ belongs in some bounded sub-region of $\mathscr{P}$. Thus, by virtue of theorem BW (Section 8.4.1), one may conclude that the solution has a limit point $\hat{p}$; i.e., there is a sub-sequence (t_s) such that

$$p(t_s, p^0) \to \hat{p} \quad \text{as } s \to \infty.$$

Secondly, since $0 \leqslant V(t) \leqslant V(p^0)$, $\dot{V} \leqslant 0$, we have

$$\lim_{t \to \infty} V(t) \text{ exists and is, say, } V^*;$$

$$\therefore \quad V(\hat{p}) = V^*, \text{ given property (b).}$$

The next step uses a property of the solution $p(t, p^0)$; i.e., that it is continuous and unique with respect to the initial point p^0. Let $p(t, \hat{p})$ denote the solution to (T') beginning from $\hat{p}$; then

$$V^* = \lim_{s \to \infty} V\{p(t_s, p^0)\} = \lim_{s \to \infty} V\{p(t_s + t, p^0)\} \quad \text{for any fixed } t;$$

$$= \lim_{s \to \infty} V[p\{t, p(t_s, p^0)\}]$$

from the uniqueness property;

$$= V\{p(t, \hat{p})\} \quad \text{from the continuity property.}$$

Therefore along $p(t, \hat{p})$, $V(t)$ remains constant at V^*; hence by (c), $\hat{p} \in \mathscr{E}$.

Finally, by (4.5), $\hat{p} = p^*$; and since this is the fate of any arbitrary limit point, we must have

$$p(t, p^0) \rightarrow p^* \quad \text{as } t \rightarrow \infty,$$

which is the result that we seek.

Given the above, we need to show that it is possible to construct such a function $V\{p(t, p^0)\}$, given (4.5). Consider

$$V\{p(t, p^0)\} = \frac{1}{2} \sum_{j=2}^{n} \{p_j(t, p^0) - p_j^*\}^2 / k_j.$$

Properties (a) and (b) are self-evident So far as (c) is concerned, consider

$$\dot{V} = \sum_{j=2}^{n} \{p_j(t, p^0) - p_j^*\} Z_j\{p(t, p^0)\}, \qquad \text{by (T')}$$

$$= -Z_1\{p(t, p^0)\} - \sum_{j=2}^{n} p_j^* Z_j\{p(t, p^0)\}, \qquad \text{by Walras's Law}$$

$$= -\sum_{j=2}^{n} p_j^* Z_j\{p(t, p^0)\}$$

$$< 0 \quad \text{whenever } p(t, p^0) \notin \mathscr{E}: \text{ which is property (c)}.$$

Thus we have demonstrated that $p(t, p^0) \rightarrow p^*$ as $t \rightarrow \infty$, under (WARP) (or (GS), say).

Given other restrictions, we can construct other Liapunov functions. For details, consult the bibliograpical notes that follow.

BIBLIOGRAPHICAL NOTES

Chapter 4, technically the most demanding chapter, begins with a proof of the existence of competitive equilibrium. It may be noted that the existence of a competitive equilibrium is equivalent to the existence of a fixed point of a continuous function from a convex compact domain into itself. See Uzawa (1962) for an elegant demonstration of this relationship. The text looks at a model of competitive equilibrium where demand and supply are obtained as in Chapter 2 and Section 3.4. The proof provided is similar to the one in Neuefeind (1980). Two excellent surveys by Debreu (1982) and McKenzie (1981) are available for readers wishing to look at more general formalizations; in particular, for a general equilibrium model with an aggregative production side as analysed in Sections 3.1–3.3, see McKenzie (1981). Arrow and Hahn (1971: ch. 6), Koopmans (1957), and Arrow (1974) contain an exhaustive account. For Urysohn's Lemma, see Kelley (1955).

Uniqueness of competitive equilibrium was considered next; the characterization studied was due to Iritani (1981). For further reading, consult Arrow and Hahn (1971: ch. 9). For result 4 of Section 4.3, see Dierker (1972) and Varian (1975).

The section on stability of equilibrium utilizes some results from the theory of differential equations; see Coddington and Levinson (1955). Results on the stability of equilibrium are surveyed by Negishi (1962) and Hahn (1982); the need for additional and restrictive assumptions can be appreciated if one realizes that Walras's Law and homogeneity do not pin down the nature excess demand functions; see Shafer and Sonnenschein (1982) in this connection. The text provides a sample of global and local stability results; the former is illustrated by means of phase diagrams from Takayama (1974: ch. 3). These diagrams are useful in situations when there are two variables; see e.g. Patinkin (1965). A version of stability analysis due to Hicks (1946) is not taken up, attention being restricted to Samuelson's (1947) formulation. However, see McFadden (1968) for an interesting contribution. For generalizations of the gross substitute condition, see Mukherji (1972), Ohyama (1972), and Quirk (1974). Also on this topic, see Arrow and Hahn (1971: chs. 11 and 12) and Mukherji (1974a). For examples of unstable equilibrium, see Gale (1963) and Scarf (1960); for a peculiarity of the Gale example, see Mukherji (1973); on the Scarf example, see Hirota (1985) for an illuminating contribution. For an interesting result, see Yun (1979). By far the most general adjustment process studied has been the one in McKenzie (1960b); this process satisfies condition b of Section 4.4 but leads to equilibrium only under a weak gross substitute assumption. For examples of processes that may violate b, but always lead to an equilibrium, see Smale (1976a) and Scarf (1982).

The method of local comparative statics originates from the work of Samuelson (1947) and Hicks (1946). For such an analysis to be meaningful, not only must equilibrium be stable, it must also be unique. Most of the results sought here were based on qualitative information alone; but this is possible only in some particular cases, such as that of gross substitutes. The text investigates the kind of results that may be obtained when some quantitative information is also available; these results are based on Mukherji (1975). For an exhaustive account of qualitative comparative statics, see Quirk and Saposnik (1968). The global comparative-statics exercises uses a diagram from Hicks (1946) and Morishima (1964).

5 Welfare Economics

The interest in competitive equilibria developed and has been sustained mainly because of a belief that they are closely connected to optimal or efficient states. By an 'optimal state' we shall mean a feasible configuration of consumption and production such that the lot of an agent may be improved only at the cost of someone else's condition. The precise relationship between competitive equilibria and optimal states constitute the two Fundamental Theorems of Welfare Economics. The first of these states that any competitive equilibrium induces an optimal state. Thus, even though each agent is busy selfishly maximizing utility or profits, consumption and production are so organized that one individual may be made better off only at the expense of someone else. The second result is a sort of converse of the first, namely, that any optimal state may be realized at an appropriate competitive equilibrium. In the present chapter, we shall be concerned with a detailed examination of the equilibrium–optimum relationship.

First, I shall present a demonstration of these Fundamental Theorems. Next, I shall show how the relationship may be destroyed when we have situations of externalities or when one agent's action affects the other. Simple examples of externalities are investigated to show how and why the connection between equilibria and optima breaks down. The same examples are used to show how the matter may be set right. It turns out that, in the presence of externalities, the competitive markets fail to deliver the goods, and consequently we need to introduce our third type of agent, the planner or the government, into our setup.

One particular case of externality is studied in some detail. This is the case of public goods, or goods that can be jointly consumed. These goods are such that one person's consumption of them does not reduce the amount available for consumption by others. A standard example of such a good or service is national defence. The interesting and highly complex issues that such a good raises are examined.

We begin, as in earlier chapters, with a look at the Fundamental Theorems in a very simple model.

5.1 Equilibrium and the Optimum in a Simple Model

We shall assume that the economy is made up of two persons, A and B; thus, the analysis of Chapter 2 is available so far as the demand side is concerned;

two goods F and C are produced by means of two scarce factors T and L, so
that the production side is exactly like the production models considered in
the Sections 3.1 and 3.2. The assumptions made in Chapters 2 and 3 will be
invoked in the present chapter also.

It will be somewhat more convenient to rewrite the production relations in
the form of production functions:

$$x_F = h_F(L_F, T_F) \tag{5.1}$$

$$x_C = h_C(L_C, T_C), \tag{5.2}$$

where $h_F(\cdot)$ and $h_C(\cdot)$ satisfy *constant returns to scale* and the production
functions are *strictly concave*, and L_j, T_j denote the amount of L and T used
in the production of $j, j = F, C$. Let $\bar{L}, \bar{T}$ denote the total amounts of L and T
available for the economy. A *feasible state* for this simple economy is made up
of $\{x_{AF}, x_{AC}; x_{BF}, x_{BC}; x_F, x_C\}$, i.e. consumption of the two goods F and C by
A and B respectively and production levels of F and C such that

(a) $x_{AF} + x_{BF} = x_F$; $x_{AC} + x_{BC} = x_C$;   and
(b) x_F, x_C satisfy (5.1) and (5.2) for some L_F, T_F, L_C, T_C such that
(c) $\left.\begin{array}{l} L_F + L_C = \bar{L} \\ T_F + T_C = \bar{T}. \end{array}\right\}$ $\tag{5.3}$

Let $\{\bar{L}_A, \bar{T}_A; \bar{L}_B, \bar{T}_B\}$ be any distribution of $(\bar{L}, \bar{T})$ such that

$$\bar{L}_A + \bar{L}_B = \bar{L}$$

and

$$\bar{T}_A + \bar{T}_B = \bar{T}.$$

One may think of $(\bar{L}_i, \bar{T}_i)$ as the endowment for $i, i = A, B$; for any such
distribution, a feasible state $\{x_{AF}^*, x_{AC}^*; x_{BF}^*, x_{BC}^*; x_F^*, x_C^*\}$ together with a
configuration of prices $\{p_F^*, p_C^*, w^*, r^*\}$ constitute a *competitive equilibrium* if
the following holds:

(i) (x_{iF}^*, x_{iC}^*) solves

$$\max U_i(x_{iF}, x_{iC})$$
$$\text{s.t. } p_F^* x_{iF} + p_C^* x_{iC} \leqslant w^* \bar{L}_i + r^* \bar{T}_i, \quad i = A, B;$$

(ii) if (L_j^*, T_j^*) is associated with the given feasible state in accordance with
(b) and (c) above, then, (L_j^*, T_j^*) solves

$$\max \{p_j^* h_j(L_j, T_j) - w^* L_j - r^* T_j\} \quad \text{for each } j = F, C.$$

It should be straightforward to recognize that (i) implies utility maximization,
whereas (ii) ensures the maximization of profits. Since the conditions we
called 'market balance conditions' are subsumed in the definition of a feasible
state, the above definition of a competitive equilibrium is not different from
the one employed in Chapter 4.

A Pareto-optimal state is a feasible state $\{x_{AF}^*, x_{AC}^*; x_{BF}^*, x_{BC}^*; x_F^*, x_C^*\}$ such that there is no other feasible state $\{x_{AF}, x_{AC}; x_{BF}, x_{BC}; x_F, x_C\}$ satisfying

$$U_A(x_{AF}, x_{AC}) \geqslant U_A(x_{AF}^*, x_{AC}^*)$$

$$U_B(x_{BF}, x_{BC}) \geqslant U_B(x_{BF}^*, x_{BC}^*)$$

with strict inequality for at least one of the above.

In words, a state is optimal if the only way to make someone better off is to do so at someone else's expense. Thus, we may characterize an optimal state as the solution to the following, for some $\bar{U}_B$:

$$\max U_A(x_{AF}, x_{AC})$$

$$\text{s.t. } U_B(x_{BF}, x_{BC}) = \bar{U}_B$$

and conditions (a), (b), and (c).

We shall now investigate the relationship between the two concepts introduced above. Given a competitive equilibrium, we have a feasible state $\{x_{AF}^*, x_{AC}^*; x_{BF}^*, x_{BC}^*; x_F^*, x_C^*\}$ together with prices $\{p_F^*, p_C^*, w^*, r^*\}$ satisfying (i) and (ii). The First Fundamental Theorem claims that this feasible state must be Pareto-optimal; for if this is not so, then there must be an alternative feasible state $\{\bar{x}_{AF}, \bar{x}_{AC}; \bar{x}_{BF}, \bar{x}_{BC}; \bar{x}_F, \bar{x}_C\}$ such that

$$U_i(\bar{x}_{iF}, \bar{x}_{iC}) \geqslant U_i(x_{iF}^*, x_{iC}^*), \quad i = A, B,$$

and the inequality must be strict for some i. Given the property (i) of a competitive equilibrium, assuming interior maximum, we should have the state depicted in Figure 5.1.

Now $(\bar{x}_{iF}, \bar{x}_{iC})$ cannot be located in the budget set considered above; thus,

$$p_F^* \bar{x}_{iF} + p_C^* \bar{x}_{iC} > w^* \bar{L}_i + r^* \bar{T}_i.$$

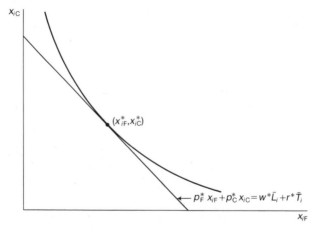

FIG. 5.1

Therefore

$$p_F^* \bar{x}_F + p_C^* \bar{x}_C > w^* \bar{L} + r^* \bar{T} = p_F^* x_F^* + p_C^* x_C^*,$$

where the inequality follows from adding the above inequalities for each i and the equality follows on account of constant returns to scale. So either $p_F^* \bar{x}_F > p_F^* x_F^*$, or $p_C^* \bar{x}_C > p_C^* x_C^*$; in any case, condition (ii) of the definition of a competitive equilibrium is violated. Hence no such state $\{\bar{x}_{AF}, \bar{x}_{AC}; \bar{x}_{BF}, \bar{x}_{BC}; \bar{x}_A, \bar{x}_C\}$ can exist.

For a more general demonstration of the above, readers are referred to Section 5.5.

Returning to the maximum problem implicit in the definition of an optimal state, the Lagrangean for this problem (see Section 8.6) is given by

$$L = U_A(x_{AF}, x_{AC}) + \lambda_1 \{\bar{U}_B - U_B(x_{BF}, x_{BC})\} + \lambda_2 \{x_{AF} + x_{BF}$$
$$- h_F(L_F, T_F)\} + \lambda_3 \{x_{AC} + x_{BC} - h_C(L_C, T_C)\}$$
$$+ \lambda_4 (L_F + L_C - \bar{L}) + \lambda_5 (T_F + T_C - \bar{T}).$$

If at a maximum all variables are positive, the following first-order conditions are implied:

$$\frac{\partial U_A^*}{\partial x_{AF}} + \lambda_2^* = 0 \qquad\qquad -\lambda_1^* \frac{\partial U_B^*}{\partial x_{BF}} + \lambda_2^* = 0$$

$$\frac{\partial U_A^*}{\partial x_{AC}} + \lambda_3^* = 0 \qquad\qquad -\lambda_1^* \frac{\partial U_B^*}{\partial x_{BC}} + \lambda_3^* = 0$$

$$-\lambda_2^* h_{FL}^* + \lambda_4^* = 0 \qquad\qquad -\lambda_3^* h_{CL}^* + \lambda_4^* = 0$$

$$-\lambda_2^* h_{FT}^* + \lambda_5^* = 0 \qquad\qquad -\lambda_3^* h_{CT}^* + \lambda_5^* = 0.$$

In addition, we have the constraints; the asterisk denotes the fact that the various partial derivatives have all been evaluated at the optimum; h_{iL}, h_{iT} denote the partial derivatives of $h_i(\cdot)$ with respect to j, $i = F, C, j = L, T$. Thus,

$$\frac{\partial U_A^*}{\partial x_{AF}} \bigg/ \frac{\partial U_A^*}{\partial x_{AC}} = \frac{\lambda_2^*}{\lambda_3} = \frac{\partial U_B^*}{\partial x_{BF}} \bigg/ \frac{\partial U_B^*}{\partial x_{BC}} \qquad\qquad \text{(I)}$$

$$h_{FL}^* / h_{FT}^* = \frac{\lambda_4^*}{\lambda_5^*} = h_{CL}^* / h_{CT}^* \qquad\qquad \text{(II)}$$

and

$$h_{CL}^* / h_{FL}^* = \frac{\lambda_2^*}{\lambda_3^*} = h_{CT}^* / h_{FT}^*$$

$$= \text{common value of terms in (I).} \qquad \text{(III)}$$

Thus at an optimum, (I) states that the marginal rate of substitution between the two commodities must be the same for the two persons; and (II) states that the marginal rate of transformation between L and T in the two lines of production must be the same.

Before we can interpret (III), some further algebraic work becomes necessary. Consider the slope of the transformation frontier at the optimal production levels:

$$\frac{dx_F^*}{dx_C} = \frac{h_{FL}^* dL_F + h_{FT}^* (dT_F)}{h_{CL}^* dL_C + h_{CT}^* (dT_C)}$$

$$= -\frac{h_{FT}^*}{h_{CT}^*} \frac{(h_{FL}^*/h_{FT}^*)dL_C + dT_C}{(h_{CL}^*/h_{CT}^*)dL_C + dT_C}, \text{ since } dL_F + dL_C = 0$$

$$\text{and } dT_F + dT_C = 0$$

$$= -\frac{h_{FT}^*}{h_{CT}^*}, \quad \text{by (II).}$$

Thus, (III) states that the common value of the marginal rates of substitution between the two commodities must be equal to the marginal rate of transformation.

These three conditions are perhaps the best known implications of an optimal state. Notice that these are *necessary* conditions; they are *sufficient*, where the utility functions are increasing and strictly quasi-concave and the production functions obey the restrictions mentioned at the outset (see Section 8.6 below).

We turn now to the Second Fundamental Theorem. Let $\{x_{AF}^*, x_{AC}^*; x_{BF}^*, x_{BC}^*; x_F^*, x_C^*\}$ denote a particular optimum; in other words, let $\{x_{AF}^*, x_{AC}^*; x_{BF}^*, x_{BC}^*; x_F^*, x_C^*\}$ solve the maximum problem defined above with some value of $\bar{U}_B$. Let λ_j^* denote the associated multipliers. Suppose, then, that we set

$$p_F^* = \lambda_2^*, \qquad p_C^* = \lambda_3^*$$

$$w^* = \lambda_4^*, \qquad r^* = \lambda_5^*$$

and allow individuals to maximize their satisfaction levels and firms to maximize profits, provided the initial resources $\bar{L}, \bar{T}$ are distributed among A and B so that

$$p_F^* x_{AF}^* + p_C^* x_{AC}^* = w^* L_A + r^* T_A$$

$$p_F^* x_{BF}^* + p_C^* x_{BC}^* = w^* L_B + r^* T_B$$

$$L_A + L_B = \bar{L}$$

$$T_A + T_B = \bar{T}.$$

Then individuals would choose (x^*_{AF}, x^*_{AC}) (x^*_{BF}, x^*_{BC}) as demands; the profit-maximizing full-employment outputs would be (x^*_F, x^*_C), and thus a competitive equilibrium would be acheived.

A word about the last four equations: notice that there are, in fact, three independent equations, since adding the first two gives

$$p^*_F(x^*_F + p^*_C x^*_C) = w^*(L_A + L_B) + r^*(T_A + T_B);$$

i.e.,

$$w^*\bar{L} + r^*\bar{T} = w^*(L_A + L_B) + r^*(T_A + T_B),$$

which follows, since $p^*_F x^*_F + p^*_C x_C = w^*\bar{L} + r^*\bar{T}$ under constant returns to scale. Thus, one may in fact have a degree of freedom in specifying the variables L_A, T_A, L_B, T_B to satisfy the above. Figure 5.2 may be helpful in understanding how prices can be chosen to allow a given optimal state to be attained as a competitive state. The Second Fundamental Theorem asserts that this can be done for any optimal state; i.e., any optimal state may be attained by agents following their selfish motives provided the right prices are used and provided the resources are correctly distributed.

Thus, in an economy where A and B own L and T and sell these resources to buy F and C, and where firms use L and T to produce F and C, a given optimal state may be attained provided A and B have enough income to be on the appropriate budget line. This aspect of the relationship is often summarized by the statement that an optimum may be decentralized via competitive markets. For a more general analysis, readers are referred to Section 5.5.

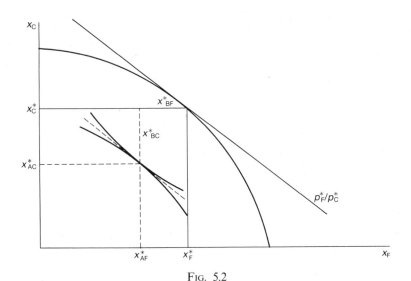

Fig. 5.2

5.2   The Choice among Optimal States

A state from which someone can be made better off while leaving no one worse off is of little interest. A movement to an optimal state from an inoptimal state can always be made and justified on the grounds that society's welfare surely could not have decreased. Problems arise whenever we wish to compare optimal states. It is on such comparisons that we shall focus our attention in this section.

An easy way out would be to consider some kind of social welfare function W which determines some ranking of the society over the various Pareto-optimal states; in that case, maximization of the social welfare function subject to the various feasibility constraints will enable us to pick a particular Pareto-optimal state as being the best for society as a whole. Then, if the conditions of the last section are met, the chosen optimal state may be decentralized by appropriately choosing prices and redistributing resources.

Thus, if the social welfare function $W(\cdot)$ has contours rather like indifference curves of the usual type, the problem may be cast in familiar terms: what is the highest indifference curve of $W(\cdot)$ that can be attained by society as a whole, subject to feasibility constraints? However, the problem is that such welfare contours may not exist; i.e., a property of individual indifference curves is that they do not intersect—thus, the higher the indifference curve, the better off the individual. But for society as a whole, a given aggregate (x_F, x_C) may correspond to various distributions, (x_{AF}, x_{AC}), (x_{BF}, x_{BC}), and consequently to various levels of social welfare. Thus, in the plane of aggregate consumption levels, there may be many values of social welfare attached to a given point (x_F, x_C). Some work has been carried out to determine the conditions under which social indifference curves exist, but unfortunately, these conditions reduce to the case of there being a single individual or, at most, to situations where individuals are identical.

Given that such social indifference curves do not exist, or exist at best under very restrictive conditions, what about defining a social welfare function as

$$W(U_A, U_B) = c_A U_A(x_{AF}, x_{AC}) + c_B U_B(x_{BF}, x_{BC})$$

where c_A, c_B are positive numbers? In the U_A–U_B plane, at least, any value of U_A, U_B fixes W uniquely; so the problem we faced earlier in defining $W(x_F, x_C)$ is removed. It is easy to see that

$$\max \ W(U_A, U_B)$$
$$\text{s.t.} \ \ x_{AF} + x_{BF} = h_F(L_F, T_F)$$
$$x_{AC} + x_{BC} = h_C(L_C, T_C)$$
$$L_F + L_C = \bar{L}$$
$$T_F + T_C = \bar{T}$$

has a solution $(x_{AF}^*, x_{AC}^*; x_{BF}^*, x_{BC}^*; x_F^*, x_C^*)$ which is a Pareto-optimal state, where $x_F^* = h_F(L_f^*, T_F^*)$, $x_C^* = h_C(L_C^*, T_C^*)$. If the state is not Pareto-optimal, one may use the definition of a Pareto-optimal state to show that a higher value of $W(\cdot)$ may be achieved.

Notice that a social welfare function of the form such as above has not really solved the problem: it has merely changed the nature of the problem. For now the question is, what weights (i.e. what numbers c) should one choose? Clearly, by varying the weights, different Pareto-optimal states may be generated; thus, there may be various methods of choosing among optimal states, but these choices are ultimately arbitrary in nature.

We turn next to a class of 'tests' that are all attempts to bypass the problems associated with the distribution of 'income' among consumers. These tests are the so-called *compensation tests*; they attempt to focus attention on the real income associated with each state and, on this basis, to rank each state. Let us represent a state (of feasible consumption and production) by X and let X' be another alternative state. Let X and X' be states such that, in going from X to X', someone will gain while someone else will lose; the question we must try to settle is whether the movement from X to X' is better for society.

A method suggested by Kaldor to resolve this question involves examining the gains made and losses incurred; *if, in going from X to X', the gainers from the change are able to compensate the losers and still retain a part of their gains, then X' should be judged to be socially better than X.* This is the *Kaldor criterion*. Notice that we are mentioning only the *ability* to compensate: compensations need not be actually paid. The *Hicks criterion*, related to Kaldor, would judge X' to be better than X for society if, in the movement from X' to X, the gainers from the change are unable to compensate the losers and retain a part of their gains.

To understand the nature of these compensation tests a bit more clearly, consider the notion of the 'efficiency locus'. In the context of a two-person model such as the one we have been looking at, the specification of a state X specifies a point in the U_A–U_B plane; let us designate the point by X (Figure 5.3). From the state X, other states are derivable by lump-sum transfers between the individuals; each such state would give rise to alternative utility distributions. The locus of all such utility distributions obtained from X by means of lump-sum transfers is called the efficiency locus through X, denoted by EE. Consider a state such as X', which gives rise to the point denoted by X'. B is better off at X' than at X; A is better off at X than at X'.

The Kaldor criterion in ranking X over X' looks at the efficiency locus through X; if X' lies below this locus, X is considered to be better for society. The Hicks criterion, on the other hand, judges X to be superior to X' if the efficiency locus through X' lies below X. Thus the two criteria are distinct, and the source of the problem with both stands revealed.

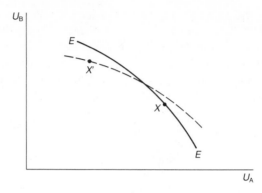

Fig. 5.3

Suppose then that the efficiency locus through X' is the broken line in the diagram. Now X is better than X' and X' is better than X: clearly a possible situation when one considers Figure 5.3. It was then suggested by Scitovsky that, *for X to be better than X', the efficiency locus through X' should lie below X and the efficiency locus through X should lie above X'*; in other words, both the Kaldor criterion and the Hicks criterion have to be met. This would clear up the problem mentioned above; however, what about the case when the loci do in fact intersect? It was suggested that in this situation society should be indifferent between the two states X and X'. This suggestion, which forces society to be indifferent between X and X', might lead to some other irrationality.

We shall consider, first, an example of a situation where the efficiency loci do in fact intersect.

	X'	X''
A	(2, 0)	(1, 0)
B	(0, 1)	(0, 2)

A's preferences: $(1, 1/2)$ $\mathscr{P}_A (2, 0)$ $\mathscr{P}_A (1\frac{1}{2}, 0)$ $\mathscr{P}_A (1, 0)$
B's preferences: $(\frac{1}{2}, 1)$ $\mathscr{P}_B (0, 2)$ $\mathscr{P}_B (0, 1\frac{1}{2})$ $\mathscr{P}_B (0, 1)$

In this example, states are defined by the distribution of the two goods among two individuals. A is better off, then, in state X'; B is better off in state X''.

By the Kaldor criterion, X' is better than X'', since A can give $\frac{1}{2}$ unit of the first good to B, which would leave both A and B better off when compared with their position in X''. But by the Kaldor criterion, once more, X'' is better than X', since B can give $\frac{1}{2}$ unit of the second good to A.

Thus there can be many quite otherwise sensible situations with efficiency loci intersecting. The problem of considering such states to be indifferent may be exposed by considering an example due to Arrow:

	A	B
X'	(2.0, 1.0)	(2.0, 1.0)
X''	(1.7, 1.3)	(1.8, 1.1)
X'''	(1.0, 2.0)	(1.0, 2.0)

A's preferences: $(2.1, 1.0)\mathscr{P}_A(1.0, 2.0)\mathscr{P}_A(2.4, 0.7)\mathscr{P}_A(1.7, 1.3)\mathscr{P}_A(2.0, 1.0)$; and the indifference curve through (1.0, 2.0) contains no bundle with less than 0.9 units of the second commodity.

B's preferences: $(1.4, 1.4)\mathscr{P}_B(1.0, 2.0)\mathscr{P}_B(1.6, 1.3)\mathscr{P}_B(1.8, 1.1)\mathscr{P}_B(2.0, 1.0)$; and the indifference curve through (1.0, 2.0) contains no bundle with less than 1.2 units of the second commodity.

Thus, as before, the three states X', X'', X''' are specified by the distribution of the two goods between two individuals. Consider, first, states X' and X''. Everyone is better off in X'' than in X', by virtue of their preferences; however, in state X' there are 4 units of good 1 and 2 units of good 2, which may be redistributed with (2.4, 0.7) going to A and (1.6, 1.3) to B; this would make both A and B better off when compared with X'. Thus, efficiency loci intersect, and one should have $X'\mathscr{I}_S X''$ (where $\mathscr{I}_S$ is the notation for indifference for society).

Next, consider X'' and X'''. Everyone is better off at X'', but there is a redistribution of the total (3.5, 2.4) in X'', namely, (2.1, 1.0) to A and (1.4, 1.4) to B, which would make both better off when compared with X'''. As above, $X''\mathscr{I}_S X'''$.

Finally, consider X' and X'''. Everyone is better off at X'''. There are (4, 2) units of commodities in X'; to redistribute these so as to make no one worse off when compared with state X''', we would require 2.1 units of good 2. Hence it is not possible to redistribute the totals in state X' so as to make them better off than at X'''. Thus $X'''\mathscr{P}_S X'$, and the indifference relation for the society is intransitive.

Thus, we find that an effort to extend the scope of the Pareto ranking has not been successful. The ability of the compensation tests to rank alternatives fails especially over those cases they were meant to cover. Actually, there are deeper reasons why such approaches are doomed, but since such considerations would take us far away from our present line of enquiry, readers are referred to the bibliographical notes at the end of this chapter.

5.3   Examples of Externalities and their Consequences

We return to examine the relationship between the equilibrium and the optimum, in the presence of externalities. We shall say that externalities exist when any agent — a firm or consumer — finds that his objectives (profits or utility) are affected by the behaviour of other agents. Such interdependence has been always ruled out; the presence of such externalities would result, as we shall show below, in a breakdown of the relations between equilibrium and the optimum. Indeed, the existence of equilibrium itself is in jeopardy. To appreciate properly the problems that may now appear, it may be worthwhile recalling the role played by the optimality conditions in the analysis in Section 5.1. It was shown there that, at an optimum, the common slope of the indifference curves must equal the slope of the transformation locus (see expression (III) in Section 5.1 and Figure 5.2). This, then, allowed us to choose this common slope as the relative price ratio, and hence such a price configuration will guarantee both utility maximization and profit maximization, provided resources are correctly distributed.

In the presence of interdependence either in consumption or production, the optimum may not require the equality of the common marginal rate of substitution to the marginal rate of transformation. In other words, the crucial condition (III) may not hold. Examples of such violations are presented below. Consequently, in our search for prices that would help decentralize a given optimum, our earlier method breaks down. In particular, we may now have prices at which profit maximization holds, or we may have prices at which utility maximization is satisfied; but we cannot have a single price configuration for both utility and profit maximization. Thus, the optimum cannot be decentralized. Further, if an equilibrium exists in the face of such interdependence, then it may not induce an optimal state; i.e., a redistribution of resources may make society better off. Thus, the links between the equilibrium and the optimum are completely destroyed.

The two examples that follow are designed to illustrate the above. The first considers a case of production externality while the second looks at the effects of the introduction of public goods. In both cases, we shall find that the failure of the market to generate an optimum may be amended by introducing the planner or the government into our setup. But the planner has no easy task, and there are some complex (and interesting) issues that need to be resolved before we can be confident of the planner achieving the optimum.

Example 1
Consider, first of all, an externality in production. To keep things really simple, consider the case of a single individual or a society with a welfare function $u(x_1, x_2, x_3)$ defined over consumption baskets containing three commodities. Let there be two firms; firm 1 produces good 1 by using good 3;

moreover, its output is affected by the level of operation of firm 2. Imagine firm 2 as a pollutant; firm 1's production function would then be written as

$$y_1 = f(x_{13}; y_2) \tag{5.4}$$

where x_{13} denotes the amount of 3 used in the production of 1; firm 2 produces 2 by means of 3 alone; its production function is taken as

$$y_2 = g(x_{23}) \tag{5.5}$$

The amount of the resource 3 that is available is given by w; if society were to consume x_3 units of it, then

$$x_{13} + x_{23} + x_3 = w \tag{5.6}$$

provides the sole feasibility constraint.

The optimum in such a simple environment may be obtained by solving the problem

$$\max u(x_1, x_2, x_3)$$

$$\text{s.t.} \quad x_1 = y_1; \ x_2 = y_2, \text{ and } (5.4)\text{--}(5.6).$$

Assuming an interior maximum, necessary conditions for $(x_1^*, x_2^*, x_3^*, x_{13}^*, x_{23}^*)$ to solve the above problem may be obtained by constructing the Lagrangean

$$L = u(x_1, x_2, x_3) + \lambda_1 \{x_1 - f(x_{13}; x_2)\} + \lambda_2 \{x_2 - g(x_{23})\}$$

$$+ \lambda_3 (w - x_{13} - x_{23} - x_3);$$

and, considering the partial derivatives at (x_1^*, x_2^*, x_3^*),

$$\frac{\partial u^*}{\partial x_1} + \lambda_1^* = 0; \quad \frac{\partial u^*}{\partial x_2} - \lambda_1^* f_2^* + \lambda_2^* = 0; \quad \frac{\partial u^*}{\partial x_3} - \lambda_3^* = 0;$$

$$-\lambda_1^* f_3^* - \lambda_3^* = 0; \quad -\lambda_2^* g_3^* - \lambda_3^* = 0.$$

These conditions together with the constraints, constitute the first-order conditions, we may restate them as follows:

$$\left.\begin{array}{c} \dfrac{\partial u^*}{\partial x_1} \Big/ \dfrac{\partial u^*}{\partial x_3} = -\dfrac{\lambda_1^*}{\lambda_3^*}; \quad \dfrac{\partial u^*}{\partial x_2} \Big/ \dfrac{\partial u^*}{\partial x_3} = -\dfrac{\lambda_2^*}{\lambda_3^*} + \dfrac{\lambda_1^*}{\lambda_3^*} f_2^* \\[2ex] \lambda_1^* f_3^* = -\lambda_3^* \\[1ex] \lambda_2^* g_3^* = -\lambda_3^* \end{array}\right\} \tag{A}$$

where $f_2 = \partial f / \partial y_2$, $f_3 = \partial f / \partial x_{13}$, and $g_3 = dg/dx_{23}$. These conditions must necessarily hold at an optimum. If we were to carry out an exercise similar to the one carried out earlier to check the validity of the Second Fundamental Theorem, then we would set

$$-\lambda_1^* = p_1^*, \quad -\lambda_2^* = p_2^*, \quad \lambda_3^* = p_3^*;$$

hence

$$
\left.
\begin{aligned}
\frac{\partial u^*}{\partial x_1} \Big/ \frac{\partial u^*}{\partial x_3} &= \frac{p_1^*}{p_3^*} \\[2ex]
\frac{\partial u^*}{\partial x_2} \Big/ \frac{\partial u^*}{\partial x_3} &= \frac{p_2^*}{p_3^*} - \frac{p_1^*}{p_3^*} f_2^* \\[2ex]
p_1^* f_3^* &= p_3^* \\[2ex]
p_2^* g_3^* &= p_3^*.
\end{aligned}
\right\} \qquad \text{(A')}
$$

But at an equilibrium, if there is one, we must have the marginal rates of substitution equal to the relative prices; so the above prices would not do. Thus the earlier method breaks down; but to show that there is a divergence between the optimum and equilibrium, we must show that there is no possibility of decentralization now.

Consider an equilibrium, if there is one, for the example at hand; then we must have a set of prices p_1, p_2, p_3, and consumption ($=$ production) x_1, x_2, x_3 and factor usages x_{13}, x_{23}, such that

$$
\frac{\partial u(x)}{\partial x_1} \Big/ \frac{\partial u(x)}{\partial x_3} = \frac{p_1}{p_3}; \quad \frac{\partial u(x)}{\partial x_2} \Big/ \frac{\partial u(x)}{\partial x_3} = \frac{p_2}{p_3}
$$

(i.e., utility maximization); and firms must be maximizing profits at production levels x_1, x_2 by using x_{13} and x_{23} units of good 3. In addition, $x_{13} + x_{23} + x_3 = w$. Let us try to spell out the profit-maximizing conditions; for firm 2, $\pi_2 = p_2 x_2 - p_3 x_{23}$; for this to be a maximum, it is necessary (and sufficient, given diminishing returns or the fact that $g(\cdot)$ is concave) that

$$
p_2 g_3 = p_3.
$$

For firm 1, $\pi_1 = p_1 x_1 - p_3 x_{13} = p_1 f(x_{13}; x_2) - p_3 x_{13}$; thus, the profits of firm 1 are influenced by the output of firm 2, and over this the firm has no control. Thus we have to be careful about defining profit maximization for firm 1; in fact, competitive equilibrium, as we have defined it in our earlier analysis, may become meaningless precisely because of this aspect of the profit function for firm 1.

However, suppose that firm 1 assumes that, since it has no control over the output of firm 2, it can maximize output taking as given the output of firm 2; this method, first introduced by Cournot, in the theory of duopoly, to cover essentially a similar problem, means that firm 1 considers

$$
\max \pi_1
$$

$$
\text{s.t. } x_2 = \text{const.}
$$

This would imply that, at the equilibrium (subject to the above modification),

$$
p_1 f_3 = p_3.
$$

Since, at the equilibrium, firm 2 would have no incentive to change its output level — since it is maximizing profits — firm 1's assumption is at least consistent at the equilibrium. Thus, at this equilibrium (properly called a *non-cooperative equilibrium* — see Section 8.7), we have

$$\left.\begin{array}{c} \dfrac{\partial u(x)}{\partial x_1} \bigg/ \dfrac{\partial u(x)}{\partial x_3} = \dfrac{p_1}{p_3}; \quad \dfrac{\partial u(x)}{\partial x_2} \bigg/ \dfrac{\partial u(x)}{\partial x_3} = \dfrac{p_2}{p_3} \\[2mm] p_1 f_3 = p_3 \\[2mm] p_2 g_3 = p_3 \end{array}\right\} \tag{B}$$

Comparing these with the conditions (A'), we notice a difference; to study this a bit more closely, suppose we take the prices that reflect the marginal rates of substitutions in (A); i.e., set

$$\frac{p_1}{p_3} = \frac{\partial u(x^*)}{\partial x_1} \bigg/ \frac{\partial u(x^*)}{\partial x_3}; \quad \frac{p_2}{p_3} = \frac{\partial u(x^*)}{\partial x_2} \bigg/ \frac{\partial u(x^*)}{\partial x_3}.$$

Then, using (A),

$$\frac{p_1}{p_3} = \frac{\lambda_1^*}{\lambda_3^*}$$

$$\frac{p_2}{p_3} = -\frac{\lambda_2^*}{\lambda_3^*} + \frac{\lambda_1^*}{\lambda_3^*} f_2^*$$

$$= -\frac{\lambda_2^*}{\lambda_3^*} - \frac{p_1}{p_3} f_2^*.$$

Therefore

$$f_3^* = -\frac{\lambda_3^*}{\lambda_1^*} \Rightarrow \frac{p_1}{p_3} f_3^* = 1$$

$$\frac{1}{g_3^*} = -\frac{\lambda_2^*}{\lambda_3^*} \Rightarrow \frac{1}{g_3^*} = \frac{p_2}{p_3} + \frac{p_1}{p_3} f_2^*$$

or

$$\frac{p_2}{p_3} g_3^* = 1 - \frac{p_1}{p_3} f_2^* g_3^*$$

$$= 1 - \frac{f_2^* g_3^*}{f_3^*}. \tag{E}$$

Thus with these prices, all but one condition in (B) are met; a profit maximization condition is violated. Thus, for any set of conditions in (B): either profit maximization conditions are met (A'), or utility maximization conditions hold (see above); but there are no set of prices for which both hold. The discrepancy between (A) and (B) is therefore clear.

To pinpoint the difference between an optimum and an equilibrium, assume for the sake of definiteness that $f_2 < 0$, e.g. that output 2 is a pollutant. Suppose also that we are at the equilibrium state defined by (B). Consider a change that involves a small shifting of the resource 3 from firm 2 to firm 1:

$$x_{13} + t, \quad x_{23} - t, \quad t \text{ small and positive.}$$

Then

$$x_1 + \Delta x_1 = f(x_{13} + t; \; x_2 + \Delta x_2)$$

$$x_2 + \Delta x_2 = g(x_{23} - t)$$

$$\approx g(x_{23}) - tg_3;$$

so that $\Delta x_2 \approx tg_3$.

The above approximation is obtained by the use of the mean value theorem (see Section 8.3.1). Using similar approximations, we have,

$$u(x_1 + \Delta x_1, \; x_2 + \Delta x_2, \; x_3) \approx u(x_1, \; x_2, \; x_3) + \Delta x_1 \left(\frac{\partial u}{\partial x_1} \right) + \Delta x_2 \left(\frac{\partial u}{\partial x_2} \right)$$

$$= u(x_1, \; x_2, \; x_3) + \frac{\partial u}{\partial x_3} (p_1 \Delta x_1 + p_2 \Delta x_2) \frac{1}{p_3}.$$

Now

$$p_1 \Delta x_1 + p_2 \Delta x_2 \approx p_1 (tf_3 + \Delta x_2 f_2) - p_2 tg_3$$

$$= t + p_1 \Delta x_2 f_2 - t$$

$$\approx -t(p_1 f_2 g_3) > 0.$$

Such a change, which does not violate any feasibility constraint, would therefore increase the level of well-being of the society. So the equilibrium would end up misallocating resources; it would cause *too much* of the pollutant to be produced at the equilibrium. Similarly, had f_2 been positive, i.e. had firm 2's output been beneficial to firm 1, then, with t small and negative, we could show that shifting the resource from firm 1 to firm 2 would cause u to increase.

Thus, at an equilibrium the production of the good causing the externality is not appropriate, when compared with the optimum. Having located the nature of the problem, we can turn next to the possibilities for a cure.

As a first step, we shall consider a merger involving firms 1 and 2, so that there is a single firm producing two outputs. Then aggregate profits π for the 'firm' are

$$\pi = p_1 x_1 + p_2 x_2 - p_3 (x_{13} + x_{23})$$

$$= p_1 f\{x_{13}; \; g(x_{23})\} + p_2 g(x_{23}) - p_3 (x_{13} + x_{23}).$$

And profit maximization entails

$$p_1 f_3 - p_3 = 0 \quad \text{or} \quad p_1/p_3 = 1/f_3$$

and

$$p_1 f_2(g_3) + p_2 g_3 - p_3 = 0$$

or

$$\frac{p_2}{p_3} g_3 = 1 - \frac{p_1}{p_3} f_2 g_3$$

$$= 1 - \frac{f_2 g_3}{f_3},$$

which is precisely (E): hence the difference between conditions (B) and (A) disappears. This process is known as 'internalizing the externality', and if it can be done, the relationship between the equilibrium and optimum is restored.

Yet another 'cure' would be to examine the source and consequence of the externality. The problem is that firm 1 has no control over the output of firm 2. Suppose however that there is a market for the service (or disservice) that firm 2 performs for firm 1. Assuming for the sake of definiteness that firm 2 provides a service for firm 1, i.e. that $f_2 > 0$, there is a price (p_4) per unit that firm 1 will have to pay firm 2 for the use of this service. Then the profit for firm 1 is

$$\pi_1 = p_1 x_1 - p_3 x_{13} - p_4 x_2.$$

Then profit maximization implies the following conditions:

$$p_1 f_3 = p_3;$$

$$p_1 f_2 = p_4.$$

So far as firm 2 is concerned, its profit function may now be written in the form

$$\pi_2 = (p_2 + p_4) x_2 - p_3 x_{13}$$

and profit maximization would imply that

$$(p_2 + p_1 f_2) g_3 = p_3$$

or

$$p_2 \frac{g_3}{p_3} = 1 - \frac{p_1}{p_3} f_2 g_3$$

which is (E), again.

Of course, the problem with this cure is that it assumes that a market can exist where none can, since firm 2 is unable to exclude firm 1 from using the service, and, whether firm 1 pays p_4 per unit or not, it enjoys the benefits of firm 2's output.

Yet another method often suggested is to introduce subsidies (taxes) for firm 2, whose output is the source of the external economy (diseconomy). For example, if firm 2 is a source of an external economy, i.e. if its output is beneficial for firm 1, it receives a subsidy at the rate τ per unit of output produced; then its profits may be written as

$$\pi_2 = (p_2 + \tau)x_2 - p_3 x_{23},$$

so that profit maximization implies

$$(p_2 + \tau)g_3 = p_3$$

or

$$\frac{p_2}{p_3}g_3 = 1 - \frac{\tau}{p_3}g_3.$$

So if $\tau = p_1 f_2$, we have obtained condition (E) once more. However, the problem is not completely solved; for clearly, we have to state the source of the subsidy. In the simple example we have considered so far, one of the sources of raising the amount of the subsidy is the consumer; an income tax on the consumer, say of the amount τx_2, would amount to the consumer's budget constraint being altered to

$$p_1 x_2 + p_2 x_2 + p_3 x_3 = p_3 w - \tau x_2.$$

But this would distort the consumer's choice between commodities, for now

$$\frac{\partial u}{\partial x_2} \bigg/ \frac{\partial u}{\partial x_3} = \frac{p_2 + \tau}{p_3},$$

so the income tax must be independent of the consumer's decisions. This feature of the tax-cum-subsidy scheme makes it a difficult one to implement; it is not even clear that such a scheme exists in principle.

Alternatively, one could have raised the amount of the subsidy from firm 1; firm 1 may be assumed to pay a tax at the rate τ proportional to its 'use' of firm 2's output; thus its profit function would be

$$\pi_1 = p_1 x_1 - p_3 x_{13} - \tau x_2$$
$$= p_1 f(x_{13}; x_2) - p_3 x_{13} - \tau x_2,$$

so that profit maximization implies that

$$p_1 f_3 = p_3$$

and

$$p_1 f_2 = \tau.$$

Notice that this would fit in exactly with our earlier requirement of what τ, the rate of subsidy, should be to firm 2. Also note that what we are formally doing is creating a 'market' for the service that firm 2 performs for firm 1; only, because the market does not exist, an outside agent—the government— is required to tax one firm and subsidize the other.

It should also be pointed out that we have assumed that an equilibrium would exist in all the cases considered above. This, of course, is a major assumption. Given that an equilibrium does exist, we have tried to locate the differences between the equilibrium and the optimum and to determine how these differences may be removed. The general problem with externalities is not discussed here (see, however, the bibliographical notes at the end of this chapter), but it is hoped that the problems will be better appreciated within the context of such simple examples.

Example 2
Consider next an example where the type of externality is different from the one above. This example is introduced to focus attention on the effects of a particular type of commodity, namely a public good. A public good (or service) is a commodity (or service) that is available for joint consumption; for example, the amount of national defence a country provides for is available for consumption by all the citizens of the country, and any one individual's consumption does not reduce the amount available for others. Thus, whatever is produced is available for joint consumption.

To see what the presence of such a good means for the theory, consider a simple example involving two individuals A and B and two goods x and y, where y is a public good. Let $G(x, y) = 0$ denote the transformation locus—the production possibility curve. We assume the utility functions to be strictly quasi-concave and $G(\cdot)$ to be concave.

A diagrammatic device introduced by Samuelson (1954) may be used to study the nature of an optimum in the present context (Figures 5.4–5.6). To

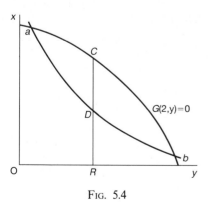

FIG. 5.4

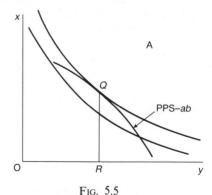

FIG. 5.5

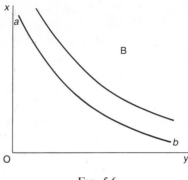

Fɪɢ. 5.6

locate an optimum, let us keep B at some fixed level of satisfaction, say the one denoted by *ab*; drawing this in the production possibility schedule (PPS) (Figure 5.4) allows us to infer how much of good x can be produced. The PPS–*ab* curve, obtained by displacing PPS vertically by the amounts required for being on *ab*, is drawn into the indifference map for A (Figure 5.5). The highest point (for A) on this curve is given by *Q*; thus, *OR* units of the public good is produced, and both A and B consume this; whereas *RD* units of x is consumed by B and $DC(=RQ)$ units of x is consumed by A. At *Q*, writing the marginal rates of substitution as MRS_i, $i = A$, B, and MRT as the marginal rate of transformation, we have

$$MRS_A = MRT - MRS_B$$

or

$$MRS_A + MRS_B = MRT.$$

Thus, at an optimum, the two marginal rate of substitutions ought to add up to the marginal rate of transformation. (See, in contrast, condition (III) of Section 5.1.) What we have done is to consider the problem

$$\max u_A(x_A, y)$$

$$\text{s.t.} \quad u_B(x_B, y) = \bar{u}_B$$

$$x_A + x_B = x$$

$$G(x, y) = 0.$$

If (x^*, y^*, x_A^*, x_B^*) solve this problem, and if these quantities are all positive, then the following necessary conditions must hold. Let

$$L = u_A(x_A, y) + \lambda_1 \{\bar{u}_B - u_B(x_B, y)\} + \lambda_2(x - x_A - x_B) + \lambda_3 G(x, y);$$

then

$$\frac{\partial u_A}{\partial x}(x_A^*, y^*) - \lambda_2^* = 0; \quad -\lambda_1^*\frac{\partial u_B}{\partial x_B}(x_B^*, y^*) - \lambda_2^* = 0$$

$$\frac{\partial u_A}{\partial y}(x_A^*, y^*) - \lambda_1^*\frac{\partial u_B}{\partial y}(x_B^*, y) + \lambda_3^*\frac{\partial G}{\partial y}(x^*, y^*) = 0$$

$$\lambda_2^* + \lambda_3^*\frac{\partial G}{\partial x}(x^*, y^*) = 0.$$

Thus

$$-\lambda_3^*\frac{\partial G}{\partial y}(x^*, y^*) = \frac{\partial u_A}{\partial y}(x_A^*, y^*) - \lambda_1^*\frac{\partial u_B}{\partial y}(x_B^*, y^*).$$

Dividing by $-\lambda_3^*(\partial G/\partial x)(x^*, y^*)$ on the left and λ_2^* on the right, and using the earlier expressions for λ_2^*,

$$MRT = MRS_A + MRS_B. \tag{5.7}$$

Notice that condition (5.7), at a configuration (x_A^*, x_B^*, x^*, y^*) where $G(x^*, y^*) = 0$, is sufficient for an optimal configuration given our restrictions on $u_A(\cdot)$, $u_B(\cdot)$, and $G(\cdot)$; for then, one may construct λ_1^*, λ_2^*, and λ_3^* such that the above necessary conditions hold (see Section 8.6 below on sufficiency of the first-order conditions).

Given the above condition, let us see whether decentralization is still possible. Notice now that, if we are to use any prices, say p (of y relative to x), utility maximization will entail

$$MRS_A = p$$

$$MRS_B = p$$

whereas profit maximization will imply $MRT = p$; thus, at any equilibrium, (5.7) cannot hold. So to decentralize, one cannot use the same price ratio for the two individuals. Suppose, then, that we find a p^A and p^B such that $p = p^A + p^B$; let individual A demand goods on the basis of p^A and let B demand on the basis of p^B, and let production occur according to p. Moreover, suppose that demands match supply. Can such a situation exist? Some such sets of price ratios may exist, but if we let individuals react to prices, each will reason that it is best not to report their correct demands for the public good since they will get to enjoy the benefits of the public good anyway, once it is produced. Thus, any such scheme is bound to lead to an underprovision of the public good at an equilibrium. Consequently, an individual's contribution towards the provision of public goods has to be extracted in some form of taxation.

To see what equilibrium results when agents are by themselves, and do not collude, we explore the following example. Let each agent have an identical utility function:

$$u_i(y, x) = \log y + \log x_i, \quad i = 1, 2$$

where y stands for the public good and x, the other good. Each agent has 1 unit of x as an endowment. The production side is kept particularly simple by assuming that

$$y = cx$$

as the production possibility locus with $c > 0$, a constant. Each individual has to decide on a subscription s_i towards the provision of the public good, with s_i being measured in the units of the x-good. So we may interpret the situation as a *game* (Section 8.7) where each individual i has to choose a strategy, s_i, from the set $0 \leqslant s_i \leqslant 1$. Once the s_i are chosen, consumption (y, x_i) results with a pay-off $u_i(y, x_i)$ to i; here, $y = c(s_1 + s_2)$ and $x_i = 1 - s_i$.

The restrictions on the strategy sets and pay-off functions satisfy the assumptions for the existence of a non-cooperative equilibrium. To compute this equilibrium, consider the first consumer's problem:

$$\max \log y + \log x_1$$

$$\text{s.t.} \quad x_1 = 1 - s_1$$

$$y = c(s_1 + \bar{s}_2).$$

The Lagrangean is

$$L = \log y + \log x_1 + \lambda_1 \{ x - (1 - s_1) \} + \mu_1 \{ y - c(s_1 + \bar{s}_2) \}.$$

Therefore

$$1/y^* + \mu_1^* = 0$$

$$1/x_1^* + \lambda_1^* = 0$$

$$\lambda_1^* - \mu_1^* c = 0$$

must necessarily hold at an interior maximum (x_1^*, y^*, s_1^*); or

$$x_1^*/y^* = \mu_1^*/\lambda_1^* = 1/c; \quad \text{or} \quad y^* = cx_1^*.$$

Therefore $cx_1^* = c(s_1^* + \bar{s}_2)$; i.e., $s_1^* + \bar{s}_2 = x_1^* = 1 - s_1^*$; i.e., $s_1^* = (1 - \bar{s}_2)/2$. A similar exercise for the agent 2 leads to $s_2^* = (1 - \bar{s}_1)/2$, so that a (non-cooperative) equilibrium leads to

$$2s_1^* = 1 - s_2^* = 1 - \tfrac{1}{2}(1 - s_1^*); \text{ or } \tfrac{3}{2}s_1^* = \tfrac{1}{2}; \text{ or } s_1^* = \tfrac{1}{3}.$$

Similarly, $s_2^* = 1/3$.

So at the non-cooperative equilibrium, each agent consumes 2/3 units of x good and $c(1/3+1/3)=2c/3$ units of the public good. A symmetric Pareto-optimal state may be obtained by considering

$$\max\ 2\log y + \log x_1 + \log x_2$$

$$\text{s.t.}\quad y = cx$$

$$x_1 + x_2 + x = 2$$

$$L = 2\log y + \log x_1 + \log x_2 + \lambda_1(y-cx) + \lambda_2(2-x_1-x_2-x),$$

so that, assuming an interior maximum, the first-order conditions are

$$2/y^* + \lambda_1^* = 0$$

$$1/x_1^* - \lambda_2^* = 0$$

$$1/x_2^* - \lambda_2^* = 0$$

$$(\lambda_1^* c + \lambda_2^*) = 0; \quad \text{i.e.,}\ \lambda_2^* = -\lambda_1^* c$$

$$\therefore\quad 2/y^* = -\lambda_1^* = \lambda_2^*/c = 1/cx_1^* = 1/cx_2^*$$

$$\therefore\quad x_1^* + x_2^* + x^* = 2 \Rightarrow 2x_1^* + 2x_1^* = 2;\ \text{or}\ x_1^* = 1/2$$

$$x_2^* = 1/2$$

$$y^* = c.$$

That the first-order conditions are sufficient follows from the nature of the objective function (strict concavity); so each individual has a utility of $\log(1/2) + \log c = \log(c/2)$; whereas at the non-cooperative equilibrium each agent has a utility of $\log(2c/3) + \log(2/3) = \log(4c/9) < \log(c/2)$.

Thus, although the optimum demands a production of c units of y, only $2c/3$ units of y are produced at the non-cooperative equilibrium. Had there been no public goods, the agents, left to themselves, would have attained an optimum. But the essential difference in the public good case is that, although each pays for $c/3$ units of y, each consumes $2c/3$ units of y.

5.4   Planning Approach to the Provision of Public Goods

Given the difficulties mentioned and discussed in the last section arising from the presence of public goods and the failure of the market forces to attain an optimum, we wish to consider here a process whereby an optimum may be established. This process is essentially an iterative one involving the exchange of information between the representatives of various consumers and a central planning authority or, say, the planner, whose objective is to guide the economy to an *optimal* configuration. This task is made difficult by allowing the planner to possess information about production conditions only. The information on individual preferences has to be sought from the consumers themselves.

Instead of considering the problem in its greatest generality, we shall take an example (similar to Example 2 of the previous section) and work our way through it. Some alternative processes will be considered in an effort to highlight several aspects of the problem. Our analysis will be based on the contribution made by Malinvaud (1971). Two individuals, $i = 1$, 2, have utility functions $u^i(x_i, y)$ defined over bundles (x_i, y), where y is the public good. The feasibility constraints may be written

$$x_i \geqslant 0, \ y \geqslant 0 \tag{5.8}$$

$$x_1 + x_2 + y = w \tag{5.9}$$

where w is some fixed constant. Expression (5.9) represents the production possibility schedule. Any triplet (x_1, x_2, y) satisfying (5.8) and (5.9) is said to be a feasible plan. Each individual has an income m_i, and a part $t_i y$ of m_i is raised as a tax on collective consumption. The disposable income $m_i - t_i y$ is spent on the x-good; i.e.,

$$x_i + t_i y = m_i \tag{5.10}$$

or, summing over i,

$$x_1 + x_2 + (t_1 + t_2)y = m_1 + m_2.$$

Since t_i simply reflects i's share in the total tax bill, $t_1 + t_2 = 1$; hence, by (5.9),

$$m_1 + m_2 = w. \tag{5.11}$$

In order to consider an equilibrium in such a context, Lindahl (1919) considered the demand for public good by i, i.e. the amount y_i of the public good that i would choose, given t_i and m_i. This would follow from the maximization of $u_i(x_i, y_i)$ subject to (5.10) (y being replaced by y_i). Thus, y_i may be considered a function of t_i, given m_i.

Figure 5.7 is almost self-explanatory. D_i denotes the 'demand curve' for y_i as a function of t_i; $OO' = 1$; the equilibrium occurs at E; $y_1 = y_2 = y^*$; and t_1^*, t_2^* are the shares of each consumer as shown. Now instead of this traditional diagram, consider an equilateral triangle of height w; any point in this triangle has the property that its distances from the three sides add up to w. (Figures 5.8 and 5.9). Indifference curves of individual 1 are drawn with AB, BC as axes; individual 2's indifference curves are drawn with AC, CB as axes. The coordinates of a typical point D are shown and they satisfy (5.9); so the equilateral triangle diagram is rather like the Edgeworth Box diagram in Chapter 2, the difference arising from the fact that good y is jointly consumed. Budget lines may also be drawn; they would be straight lines (such as FH) and would represent the budget line for both individuals 1 and 2 so long as $t_1 + t_2 = 1$ and (5.11) holds.

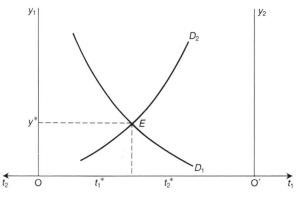

Fɪɢ. 5.7

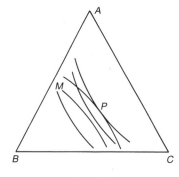

Fɪɢ. 5.8

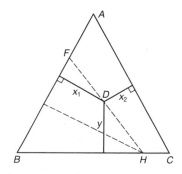

Fɪɢ. 5.9

To see this, notice that

$$x_1 + t_1 y - m_1 = (w - y - x_2) + (1 - t_2)y - (w - \dot{m}_2)$$

$$= -x_2 - t_2 y + m_2.$$

The budget line intersects AB to the left of A if $t_1 > m_1/w$; it passes through A if $t_1 = m_1/w$ and to the right if $t_1 < m_1/w$.

So much for the positioning of budget lines in the triangle; consider now a plan such as M in Figure 5.8. This point can be readily improved upon by reducing the quantity of public good associated with it and moving to a point such as P. What we wish to study are the processes that would allow for such improvements.

Recall that the central authority (or planner) has no information on tastes; so it has to devise a scheme of information exchange that would allow it to revise plans. The exchange of information occurs at successive stages $s = 1$,

2, . . . ; at stage s, the planners issue '*indicators*' to which agents or consumers respond by issuing '*proposals*'. On the basis of the proposals, the indicators are *revised* and the process goes on until, at the last stage, the planner chooses a programme that is to be implemented. The nature of the indicators and proposals and the method of revision of the indicators define a process.

We first consider the *Lindahl* solution; the indicators are the tax shares t_i such that $t_1 + t_2 = 1$, $t_i \geqslant 0$. The proposals are (x_i, y_i) which maximize $u_i(x_i, y_i)$ subject to $x_i + t_i y_i = m_i$ where m_i are fixed incomes. The process would be defined once we know how t_i are revised and then how the plan is chosen. Lindahl's solution is defined by the following steps.

(a) If $y_1^s = y_2^s$, there is no revision, and the plan is implemented.
(b) If y_i^s do not coincide, t_i should be raised for the individual requesting the higher quantity of the public good; since $t_1 + t_2 = 1$, t_i must be necessarily lowered for the other individual.
(c) The individual that sees his rate being increased will agree so long as the lowering of the rate for the other will induce from the latter a demand that he himself considers to be an improvement.
(d) If individuals do not agree, collective consumption will be fixed at the minimum of the two demands.

To understand the implication of the above steps, suppose that, initially, $t_1 = t_2 = 1/2$; also suppose that $m_1 = m_2 = w/2$. Notice then that consumer 1 demands more public good, so t_1 is increased; since m_1 and m_2 are fixed, the budget line in Figure 5.10 would rotate about H to $A'H$; then consumer 1 would agree to this so long as D_2' is preferred by 1 to D_2. If 1 did not agree, then step (d) would choose D_2; hence it is in 1's interest to agree to the tax rise.

However, such a process will not lead to an optimum, since at some stage D_2' (the demand by consumer 2 after his tax rate has been lowered) lies on a

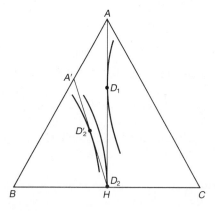

F_{IG}. 5.10

lower indifference curve for 1 than D_2, and 1 would refuse the tax rise. And this happens necessarily near an optimum (Figure 5.11).

Thus, the only way to attain an optimum is to change (c) above so that individual 1 must be required to report his demands under increasing tax shares even beyond the point where he benefits from 2's revision of demand. In this sense, Lindahl's solution is unfair for the person who needs collective consumption the most.

The next process we shall consider is aimed at removing some of the problems noted above; it has been called *a procedure with mutual concessions*. First of all, indicators and proposals remain as before; the differences are at the revision stage and at the stage when individuals do not agree. Suppose, as before, that individual i wants D_i, $i = 1, 2$; when revision occurs (Figure 5.12), *the budget line is rotated around P* (the average of D_1 and D_2) *instead of H*; if individuals do not agree, then P will be the chosen plan.

To find out the implications of such a rotation of the budget line, note that t_i must change *and* incomes m_i must be revised. Let the components of P be (y, x); then

$$y = \tfrac{1}{2}(y_1 + y_2); \quad x = \tfrac{1}{2}(x_1 + x_2).$$

Also, $x - x_i = -t_i(y_i - y)$, since (y, x) lies on the budget line. Since consumer 1 demands more collective consumption, it is natural to expect that t_1 would be made more than t_2; thus, for i such that $y_i > y$, t_i would be increased; or

$$t_i^{s+1} - t_i^s = b(y_i^s - y^s), \quad s = 1, 2, \ldots, \tag{5.12}$$

where $b > 0$ is some constant.

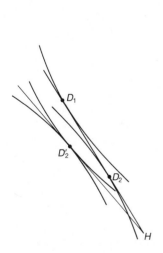

FIG. 5.11

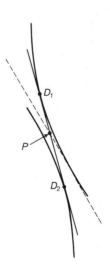

FIG. 5.12

Also, given the rotation of the budget line around P, a transfer of incomes must be imposed among the individuals; writing the net transfer received as $m_i - T_i$ (tax paid by i being $t_i y_i + T_i$), where initially $T_1 = T_2 = 0$; note that, since $m_1 + m_2 = w$ has to be preserved, $T_1 + T_2 = 0$ must be maintained. To find out what T_i should be, note that the budget line

$$x_i + t_i^{s+1} y_i = m_i - T_i^{s+1}$$

should contain the point P both before and after revision. Hence

$$x + t_i^s y = m_i - T_i^s$$

and

$$x + t_i^{s+1} y = m_i - T_i^{s+1}.$$

Therefore

$$(t_i^s - t_i^{s+1}) y = T_i^{s+1} - T_i^s. \tag{5.13}$$

Thus the transfer should lead to an increase in income for the individual who wishes to consume more of the public good and thus has to accept a higher burden. It is in this sense that the procedure is one with mutual concessions.

Notice that, if revisions are made in sufficiently small steps, (5.12) and (5.13) may be represented by the following system of differential equations:

$$\left. \begin{array}{l} \dot{t}_i = b(y_i - y) \\ \dot{T}_i = -\dot{t}_i y \end{array} \right\} \quad i = 1, 2.$$

Beginning with an arbitrary t_1^0, t_2^0, $T_1^0 = T_2^0 = 0$, the above system would generate a solution through the initial point (see Section 4.4 in this connection), and the question is whether the generated $t_i(s)$, $T_i(s)$ lead to an optimal plan. ($\dot{t}_i$, $\dot{T}_i$ are to be interpreted as dt_i/ds, dT_i/ds.) At an optimal plan, $y_i = y$ for $i = 1, 2$; hence $\dot{t}_i = 0$ and therefore $\dot{T}_i = 0$. Thus the enquiry is entirely analogus to the enquiry made in Section 4.4. Notice that

$$\dot{u}_i(x_i, y_i) = \frac{\partial u_i}{\partial x_i} \dot{x}_i + \frac{\partial u_i}{\partial y_i} \dot{y}_i$$

$$= \frac{\partial u_i}{\partial x_i} (\dot{x}_i + t_i \dot{y}_i)$$

$$= \frac{\partial u_i}{\partial x_i} \{-(\dot{T}_i + y_i \dot{t}_i)\}$$

$$= \frac{\partial u_i}{\partial x_i} \{\dot{t}_i(y - y_i)\} = -\frac{\partial u_i}{\partial x_i} b(y - y_i)^2 < 0$$

unless $y = y_i$.

Thus, each individual shares the burden of improving the consistency of his demands; on a technical level, we also have our Liapunov function (see

Chapter 4). We may use this to conclude that the plan $(x(s), y(s))$ (the coordinates of P at each stage s) approaches the line of Pareto optima as s increases, or, to put it somewhat differently, that the revision continues until an agreement is reached on the plans and tax rates.

A final procedure (*the MDP process*) examines a process where the indicators are quantities (instead of tax shares) and the proposals are 'prices' (instead of quantities). At each state s, the board or the planner chooses (x_1^s, x_2^s, y^s) from the equilateral triangle (i.e. a feasible plan). Each individual is then asked how much he would contribute at most, by restricting his consumption of x_i^s, to seeing collective consumption y^s increase by one unit—in other words, the consumers are asked to report the demand price for the public good, which is given by the quantity

$$\pi_i^s = \frac{\partial u^i}{\partial y} \bigg/ \frac{\partial u^i}{\partial x_i},$$

evaluated at (x_i^s, y^s). On receiving π_1^s, π_2^s the board decides to increase y if $\pi_1^s + \pi_2^s > 1$ and to lower y if $\pi_1^s + \pi_2^s < 1$. (Recall that the marginal rate of transformation of the public good for the private good is 1.) Thus,

$$y^{s+1} - y^s = b(\pi_1^s + \pi_2^s - 1), \quad b > 0.$$

The revision of x-good consumption must be such that each individual will not contribute more than proportionately to his marginal willingness to pay; i.e.,

$$x_1^{s+1} - x_1^s = \tfrac{1}{2}(\pi_2^s - \pi_1^s - 1)(y^{s+1} - y^s)$$
$$x_2^{s+1} - x_2^s = \tfrac{1}{2}(\pi_1^s - \pi_2^s - 1)(y^{s+1} - y^s).$$

So, if, say, $y^{s+1} - y^s > 0$, then $\pi_1^s + \pi_2^s > 1$; and

$$\tfrac{1}{2}(\pi_2^s - \pi_1^s - 1) > -\pi_1^s,$$

so that

$$x_1^{s+1} - x_1^s > -\pi_1^s(y^{s+1} - y^s).$$

In other words, the reduction in the consumption of the x-good can never be larger than the one the consumer was ready to accept. Conversely, if the public good is reduced, then the increase in the consumption of the x-good will always compensate the individual for the reduction in the production of the public good. Also, note that

$$x_1^{s+1} + x_2^{s+1} - (x_1^s + x_2^s) = -(y^{s+1} - y^s)$$

or

$$x_1^{s+1} + x_2^{s+1} + y^{s+1} = x_1^s + x_2^s + y^s;$$

i.e., feasibility is always maintained.

Thus, the individuals benefit from the plan revision. And if the revision is carried out in small steps, the process will converge to an optimum. Figure 5.13 shows the effect of revision of a plan such as P^s; the process aims to formulate a plan such as P^{s+1}; that such processes will lead to an optimum will be established in the mathematical notes to this chapter.

The rest of this section will be devoted to an important question regarding processes such as these. This has to do with the truthful revelation of the information sought from the agents. Recall that, while discussing the above iterative processes, we implicitly assumed that consumers do reveal the information sought from them. However, in the public good context, we saw that there is an incentive for under-reporting demand. The only suitable context within which such questions may be discussed is that of an N-person game. We shall look into this aspect of the matter in the mathematical notes to the chapter. For the present, let us examine whether it is in the interest of consumers to reveal their preferences.

Let us consider the first solution, the Lindahl solution. Suppose an individual knows not only his own tastes but the other's tastes too. Then to determine what is best for him, consumer 1 would determine consumer 2's behaviour line or *reaction function*. This is the locus of tangency points between the rotating budget line and indifference curves of consumer 2—say, line R_2 in Figure 5.14—and the consumer would choose the best (for himself) there: a point such as N_2. Again by virtue of our earlier discussion, it is also at N_2 that consumer 1 stops accepting higher burdens of the tax. Thus, with the revision of the tax shares, 1 would report his own demand for collective consumption as if his reaction curve (R_1) passed through N_2. Similarly, if consumer 2 assumes that 1 correctly reports along his reaction curve R_1, then 2 will aim at achieving N_1 and so will lower his demand for collective consumption. Thus, the under-reporting noted in the last section will be present here too. If an individual does not know the other's tastes, each will

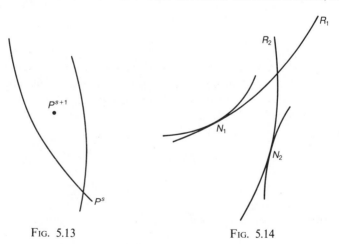

FIG. 5.13   FIG. 5.14

try to extrapolate the other's reaction curve and the same features will be present. The process with mutual concessions is somewhat more complicated, in that the budget line rotates around a point in the middle so that there are two parameters that change: t_i and T_i. Returning to Figure 5.12, if consumer 1 were to report a demand much greater than D_1, this would cause P to be placed higher. Thus consumer 1 would seek to impose on consumer 2 a larger concession than 2 would otherwise make. Similarly, consumer 2 would want a P situated as low as possible and would report a demand much lower than D_2. Such a distortion of preferences would lead to an exaggeration of their differences.

Finally, consider the MDP scheme with quantity indicators. Note that no one can lose if he reports correctly (assuming small revisions); this follows since, if π_i^s is the true marginal rate of substitution, then (x_i^{s+1}, y^{s+1}) is preferred to (x_i^s, y^s); choosing a false π_i^s might lead to loss for i, if other participants happen to pick a proposal that is particularly unfavourable to him. So reporting true marginal rates of substitution is a *minimax* strategy: it is a strategy (or a choice) that ensures that losses are kept to a minimum.

This need not imply, however, that consumer i will in fact reveal the true rates. He may, for example, try to misrepresent so as to obtain a particularly favourable outcome. Some results are presented in this connection in the mathematical notes that follow. The bibliographical notes contain additional references to this difficult and interesting area.

MATHEMATICAL NOTES

5.5 Fundamental Theorems of Welfare Economics

5.5.1 *The First Fundamental Theorem*

Consider a model of the economy described in Chapter 4; i.e., there are households h, $h = 1, \ldots, N$, and firms J, $J = 1, \ldots, m$; there are n goods j, $j = 1, 2, \ldots, n$. Each household h has a consumption possibility set $S_h \subseteq R^n$, each firm J has a production possibility set $P^J \subseteq R^n$, and W denotes the vector of resources available to the economy. All conventions regarding signs introduced in Chapters 2–4 still apply.

In such a setup, the array $\{x^h, y^J, h = 1, \ldots, N, J = 1, \ldots, m\}$ is said to constitute a *feasible state* for the economy if

(a) $x^h \in S_h$ (consumption is feasible);

(b) $y^J \in P^J$ (production is feasible);

(c) $\sum_h x^h \leqq \sum_J y^J + W$ (aggregate consumption is feasible, given aggregate production and initial resources).

Now suppose that on S_h, household h has a complete, reflexive, and transitive relation $\mathcal{R}_h$ (refer to the mathematical notes to Chapter 2 for definitions) which is the 'at-least-as-good-as' relation. By a *Pareto-optimal state* $\{x^{h*}, y^{J*}\}$, we shall mean that

(i) $\{x^{h*}, y^{J*}\}$ is a feasible state;
(ii) there is no other feasible state $\{x^h, y^J\}$ such that $x^h \mathcal{R}_h x^{h*}$ for all h with *not* $x^{h*} \mathcal{R}_h x^h$ for some h.

More simply, $\{x^{h*}, y^{J*}\}$ is a Pareto-optimal state if there is no other feasible state where no one is worse off and someone is better off.

Given a distribution of W among h, denoted by w^h, $\sum_h w^h = W$, and given $n-1$ markets for exchange of the $n-1$ goods with good 1, as the numeraire at prices $p = (1, p_2, \ldots, p_n)$, and also having specified profit shares $\theta_{hJ} \geqslant 0$, $\sum_h \theta_{hJ} = 1$ for each J, we are set to define a competitive equilibrium as a price $p^* = (1, p_2^*, \ldots, p_n^*)$ and a feasible state (x^{h*}, y^{J*}) such that

A: $x^{h*} \mathcal{R}_h x^h$ for all $x^h \in S_h$ satisfying $p^* x^h \leqslant p^* w^h + \sum_j \theta_{hJ} p^* y^{J*}$ for all h;

B: $p^* y^{J*} \geqslant p^* y^J$ for all $y^J \in P^J$, for all J.

Notice that condition A guarantees that x^{h*} belongs to the demand correspondence (see mathematical notes to Chapter 2), while B guarantees that y^{J*} belongs to the supply correspondence. Alternatively, condition A guarantees utility maximization while B sees to the maximization of profits. The match of demand and supply in each market is covered by the requirement that (x^{h*}, y^{J*}) be a feasible state (condition (c) noted above).

> ASSUMPTION 1: $\mathcal{R}_h$ is locally non-satiated if, for any $x \in S_h$ and for any neighbourhood $N_\delta(x)$ of x, there $x' \in N_\delta(x) \cap S_h$ such that $x' \mathcal{R}_h x$ and *not* $x \mathcal{R}_h x'$.

In other words, there are always strictly preferred bundles arbitrarily close to any given bundle. In our analysis of demand relationships, we saw that such an assumption implies that all income must be exhausted in obtaining the best bundle. The implication of Assumption 1 would be again invoked to provide the validity of the *First Fundamental Theorem*:

> THEOREM 1: Under Assumption 1, any competitive equilibrium $\{p^*, (x^{h*}, y^{J*})\}$ defines a Pareto-optimal state (x^{h*}, y^{J*}).

Proof: Suppose, to the contrary, that (x^{h*}, y^{J*}) is not Pareto-optimal; then there is a feasible state (x^h, y^J) such that

$$x^h \mathcal{R}_h x^{h*} \text{ for all } h \text{ and } not \ x^{h*} \mathcal{R}_h x^h \text{ for some } h, \text{ say } h_1.$$

$$\because x^{h_1} \mathcal{R}_{h_1} x^{h_1*} \text{ and } not \ x^{h_1*} \mathcal{R}_{h_1} x^{h_1};$$

it follows that $p^* x^{h_1} > p^* x^{h_1*}$, from condition A.

Now suppose that, for any other h, $p^*x^h < p^*x^{h*}$; then, by Assumption 1, there is $y \in S_h$, y arbitrarily close to x^h, and $y \mathscr{R}_h x^h$ with *not* $x^h \mathscr{R}_h y$. Therefore $y \mathscr{R}_h x^{h*}$ and *not* $x^{h*} \mathscr{R}_h y$ from the transitivity of $\mathscr{R}_h$.

Hence, on the one hand, $p^*y > p^*x^{h*}$ from condition A, and on the other, since y is arbitrarily close to x^h, $p^*y \leqslant p^*x^{h*}$, so that we arrive at a contradiction. Hence for all h, $p^*x^h \geqslant p^*x^{h*}$.

$$\therefore \sum_h p^*x^h > \sum_h p^*x^{h*}, \qquad \text{on account of the strict inequality for } h_1;$$

$$\therefore p^*\sum_J y^J + p^*\sum_h w^h \geqslant \sum_h p^*x^h, \qquad \text{from feasibility of } (x^h, y^J);$$

$$> \sum_h p^*x^{h*}, \qquad \text{deduced above;}$$

$$= \sum_h (p^*w^h + \sum_J \theta_{hJ}p^*y^{J*}), \qquad \text{on account of Assumption 1;}$$

$$= p^*\sum_h w^h + p^*\sum_J y^{J*}, \qquad \text{since } \sum_h \theta_{hJ} = 1 \text{ for each } J.$$

Therefore $p^*y^J > p^*y^{J*}$ for some J: a violation of B, since $y^J \in P^J$. Therefore (x^{h*}, y^{J*}) is a Pareto-optimal state. $\square$

It should be emphasized that in the above demonstration, only the local non-satiation of $\mathscr{R}_h$ was used. No other assumption was involved; in particular, *no assumption of convexity has been invoked*. Assumption 1 would be satisfied if individual preferences satisfy the condition that 'more' is always 'better', given that commodities are divisible—an assumption that we have always used.

5.5.2 *The Second Fundamental Theorem*

We move on to a consideration of a result that may be considered a converse to the above. However, it is a valid result only under special conditions, and we introduce them first.

ASSUMPTION 2: S_h is a convex subset of R^n for each h; further, $\mathscr{R}_h$ is a convex and strictly monotone ordering for each h.

Here $\mathscr{R}_h$ is a convex ordering if $x^1, x^2 \in S_h$ and $x^1 \mathscr{R}_h x^2$; then

$$\lambda x^1 + (1-\lambda)x^2 \mathscr{R}_h x^2 \text{ for all } \lambda, 0 \leqslant \lambda \leqslant 1.$$

Let $x \mathscr{P}_h y$ be defined by $x \mathscr{R}_h y$ and *not* $y \mathscr{R}_h x$. Then we must also have

$$x^1 \mathscr{P}_h x^2 \Rightarrow \lambda x^1 + (1-\lambda)x^2 \mathscr{P}_h x^2 \text{ for any } \lambda, 0 < \lambda \leqslant 1.$$

$\mathscr{R}_h$ is strictly monotone if $x^1 \geqslant x^2$ (i.e. if $x_j^1 \geqslant x_j^2$ with strict inequality for some j) implies that $x^1 \mathscr{P}_h x^2$.

ASSUMPTION 3: $P = \sum_J P^J$ is convex.

Note that $P = \{y : y = \sum_J y^J \text{ for some } y^J \in P^J\}$.

ASSUMPTION 4: For any $x \in S_h$, the set $\{y \in S_h : y \mathscr{P}_h x\}$ is an open subset of S_h.

ASSUMPTION 5: For $x \in S_h$, given p, there is $x' \in S_h$ such that $px' < px$.

In our analysis of demand functions, we used a somewhat stronger version of Assumption 2; Assumptions 4 and 5 also played a role in that analysis. In our analysis of supply functions, we used the strict convexity of P^J; now Assumption 3 guarantees that the set sum P is convex, not that each P^J is convex. So various forms of these restrictions have been employed in the past chapters, and they play a major role now.

We shall establish the Second Fundamental Theorem in two steps. First,

THEOREM 2: Under Assumptions 2 and 3, if $\{x^{h*}, y^{J*}\}$ is a Pareto-optimal state, then there is $p^* \geqslant 0$ (i.e., $p_j^* \geqslant 0$ for all j, with a strict inequality for some j) such that

(a) $p^* x^{h*} \leqslant p^* x$ for all $x \in \{y \in S_h : y \mathscr{R}_h x^{h*}\}$ for all h;
(b) $p^* y^{J*} \geqslant p^* y^J$ for all $y^J \in P^J$ for all J.

Proof: Let $C^h(x) = \{y \in S_h : y \mathscr{P}_h x\}$. Define $C^* = \sum_h C^h(x^{*h})$; i.e., $y \in C^*$ if and only if $y = \sum_h y^h$ for some collection $\{y^h\}$ such that $y^h \in C^h(x^{*h})$. By virtue of Assumption 2, C^* is convex and non-empty.

Let $Z = \{z : z \leqslant y + W \text{ where } y \in P \text{ and } W \text{ is the aggregate resource vector}\}$. By virtue of Assumption 3, Z is convex and non-empty.

Since (x^{h*}, y^{J*}) is Pareto-optimal, $Z \cap C^* = \varnothing$. Hence by the Separation Theorem (see Section 8.4.1) there is $p^* \neq 0$ and a number α such that

$$p^* z \leqslant \alpha \text{ for all } z \in Z$$

$$p^* x \geqslant \alpha \text{ for all } x \in C^*.$$

Since (x^{h*}, y^{J*}) is feasible, $\sum_h x^{h*} \leqslant \sum_J y^{J*} + W$.

Now let $x^* = \sum_h x^{h*}$. Since $y^* = \sum_J y^{J*} \in P$, $x^* \in Z$. Therefore $p^* x^* \leqslant \alpha$. Let $\varepsilon_i = (\varepsilon_{ij})$ where $\varepsilon_{ik} = 0$, $k \neq i$;

$$= \varepsilon, \; k = i, \; \varepsilon > 0.$$

Now $x^* + \varepsilon_i \in C^*$ for any i and for any $\varepsilon > 0$. Therefore

$$p^* (x^* + \varepsilon_i) \geqslant \alpha \geqslant p^* x^* \Rightarrow p_i^* \geqslant 0 \text{ for all } i.$$

Since $p^* \neq 0$, $p^* \geqslant 0$.

Next, consider $y^h \in \{y \in S_h : y \mathscr{R}_h x^{h*}\}$; for some h, say h_1, $p^* y^{h_1} < p^* x^{h_1*}$. Consider $y^{h_1} + \lambda_{h_1} \varepsilon_i$ for some i and $x^{h*} + \lambda_h \varepsilon_i$ for $h \neq h_1$ where $\lambda_h > 0$ for all h and is so chosen that

$$\alpha = \sum_h p^* x^{h*} > p^* y^{h_1} + \sum_{h \neq h_1} p^* x^{h*} + p_i^* \sum_h \lambda_h \varepsilon_i$$

or

$$p^* x^{h_1 *} > p^* y^{h_1} + p_i^* \Sigma \lambda_h \varepsilon_i$$

or

$$\sum_h \lambda_h < (p^* x^{h_1 *} - p^* y^{h_1}) / \varepsilon_i p_i^*, \text{ provided } p_i^* \neq 0.$$

Hence we can choose i and λ_h for each h appropriately, since $p^* x^{h_1 *} > p^* y^{h_1}$. But

$$(y^h + \lambda_{h_1} \varepsilon_i) + \sum_{h \neq h_1} (x^{h*} + \lambda_h \varepsilon_i) \in C^*,$$

so that

$$p^* y^{h_1} + \sum_{h \neq h_1} p^* x^{h*} + \varepsilon_i p_i^* \sum_h \lambda_h \geqslant \alpha:$$

a contradiction. Hence no such y^{h_1} exists and part (a) of the theorem is established.

Again, since for any i, $p^*(x^* + \varepsilon_i) \geqslant \alpha$ for any $\varepsilon_i > 0$, we have

$$p^* x^* = \alpha.$$

Therefore

$$p^* z \leqslant p^* x^* \text{ for any } z \in Z.$$

Next, if for some J, say J_1, there is $y^1 \in P^{J_1}$ such that $p^* y^1 > p^* y^{J_1 *}$, then since

$$y^1 + \sum_{J \neq J_1} y^{J*} + W \in Z,$$

$$p^* x^* \geqslant p^* y^1 + \sum_{J \neq J_1} p^* y^{J*} + p^* W > \sum_J p^* y^{J*} + p^* W$$

$$\geqslant \sum_h p^* x^{h*} = p^* x^*:$$

a contradiction, where the last inequality in the chain follows on account of feasibility. Hence no such y^1 exists, and part (b) of Theorem 2 is established. $\square$

Note also that, under Assumption 2, (x^{h*}, y^{J*}) is Pareto-optimal, which implies that

$$\sum_h x^{h*} = \sum_J y^{J*} + W.$$

This is because, since (x^{h*}, y^{J*}) is given to be Pareto-optimal, it must be feasible so that

$$\sum_h x^{h*} \leqslant W + \sum_J y^{J*}.$$

Suppose that a strict inequality holds for some component, say the first. Then

$$\sum_h x_1^{h*} < W_1 + \sum_J y_1^{J*}.$$

Define

$$\bar{x}^h = x^{h*} \text{ for all } h \neq N$$

$$\bar{x}_j^N = x_j^{N*} \text{ for all } j \neq 1$$

$$\bar{x}_1^N = x_1^{N*} + \left(\sum_J y_1^{J*} + W_1 - \sum_h x_1^{h*} \right) > x_1^{N*}.$$

Notice that $\bar{x}^h \, \mathcal{R}_h \, x^{h*}$ for all h and $\bar{x}^N \, \mathcal{P}_h \, x^{h*}$ by Assumption 2; and, further, that

$$\sum_h \bar{x}^h \leqslant W + \sum_J y^{J*},$$

so that $(\bar{x}^h, y^{J*})$ is a feasible state; i.e., (x^{h*}, y^{J*}) cannot be Pareto-optimal. Therefore, we must have

$$\sum_h x^{h*} = W + \sum_J y^{J*}$$

if (x^{h*}, y^{J*}) is Pareto-optimal and Assumption 2 holds.

With the aid of the above, we are now in a position to demonstrate the validity of the next theorem.

THEOREM 3: Suppose that Assumptions 2–4 hold. Let $\{x^{h*}, y^{J*}\}$ be a Pareto-optimal configuration, and let p^* be the price vector satisfying conditions (a) and (b) of Theorem 2. Let Assumption 5 hold at each x^{h*} and p^*. Then there exists a distribution of the aggregate resources $\{w^{h*}\}$ and a distribution of profit shares θ_{hJ} such that condition A in the definition of a competitive equilibrium is met by x^{h*}, given p^*, for all h.

Proof: We have, from part (a) of Theorem 2, that

$$p^*x \geqslant p^*x^{h*} \text{ for all } x \in \{y \in S_h \colon y \, \mathcal{R}_h \, x^{h*}\} = \bar{C}^h(x^{h*}), \text{ say.}$$

If possible, let there be $\bar{x} \in C^h(x^{h*})$ (i.e., $\bar{x} \, \mathcal{P}_h \, x^{h*}$) and $p^*\bar{x} = p^*x^{h*}$ for some h.

By virtue of Assumption 5 at x^{h*}, p^*, there is $x' \in S_h$ such that $p^*x' < p^*x^{h*}$. Consequently,

$$\lambda \bar{x} + (1 - \lambda)x' \in S_h \text{ for all } \lambda, \quad 0 \leqslant \lambda \leqslant 1$$

and

$$p^*\{\lambda \bar{x} + (1 - \lambda)x'\} < p^*x^{h*} \text{ for all } \lambda, \quad 0 \leqslant \lambda \leqslant 1.$$

Again by virtue of Assumption 4, $C^h(x^{h*})$ being an open set,

$$\lambda \bar{x} + (1 - \lambda)x' \in C^h(x^{h*}) \text{ for } \lambda \text{ arbitrarily close to } 1;$$

but then, by virtue of part (a) of Theorem 2,

$$p^*\{\lambda \bar{x} + (1 - \lambda)x'\} \geqslant p^*x^{h*}:$$

a contradiction, so no such $\bar{x}$ exists. Therefore, if

$$y \in \{x \in S_h: p^*x \leqslant p^*x^{h*}\},$$

then $y \notin C^h(x^{h*})$ or *not* $y \mathscr{P}_h x^{h*}$; i.e., $x^{h*} \mathscr{R}_h y$.
  Define w^{h*}, θ_{hJ} such that

$$w^{h*} \geqslant 0, \quad \theta_{hJ} \geqslant 0,$$

$$\sum_h w^{h*} = W, \quad \sum_h \theta_{hJ} = 1 \text{ for each } J,$$

and

$$p^*w^{h*} + \sum_J \theta_{hJ}p^*y^{J*} = p^*x^{h*}.$$

That this is possible is borne out by the fact that summing the left-hand side over all h yields

$$p^*W + \sum_J p^*y^{J*},$$

whereas summing the right-hand side over all h yields

$$\sum_h p^*x^{h*},$$

and the two are equal, as noted above.
  For such a distribution, w^{h*}, θ_{hJ}, x^{h*} satisfies condition A of the definition of the competitive equilibrium. $\square$

  The conclusions of Theorems 2 and 3 may be summed up in the following statement of the *Second Fundamental Theorem* of welfare economics:

Under Assumptions 2–5, given any Pareto-optimal state $\{x^{h*}, y^{J*}\}$, there is a price vector $p^* \geqslant 0$, a distribution of resources, $\{w^{h*}\}$, and a distribution of profits $\{\theta_{hJ}\}$ such that $\{x^{h*}, y^{J*}\}$ and p^* constitute a competitive equilibrium.

5.6 The MDP Process

5.6.1 *Properties*

We return to the analysis of the process of Section 5.4, where the indicators are quantities and the proposals are prices (or marginal rates of substitutions). Such processes are known as 'MDP processes' (M for Malinvaud, D for Dreze, and P for de la Vallee Poussin—see the bibliographical notes that follow).

Consider an economy with m public goods, $y_1, y_2, \ldots, y_m$, and one other good denoted by x. There are also N households, indexed by $h = 1, 2, \ldots, N$. There is also a planner, whose objective is to guide the economy to an optimal configuration. The planner has access to data relating to production but has no information on households' tastes. This latter bit of information has to be obtained from the households themselves, and, as we have seen above, households may not come forward with the correct information. We shall consider this problem, and we shall also discuss the attainment of an optimum if households reveal the information sought from them.

The production possibilities for the economy are contained in the transformation locus

$$G(x, y) = 0 \tag{5.14}$$

where $y = (y_1, \ldots, y_m)$.

It is assumed that the function $G(x, y)$ is concave and differentiable; also that the set (x, y) satisfying (5.14) forms a compact subset of R^{m+1}; further, that

$$\frac{\partial G(x, y)}{\partial x} > 0, \qquad \frac{\partial G(x, y)}{\partial y_k} \geq 0$$

for all k and for all (x, y) satisfying (5.14), so that the ratio

$$\gamma_k(x, y) = \frac{\partial G(x, y)}{\partial y_k} \bigg/ \frac{\partial G(x, y)}{\partial x}$$

is well defined on (5.14). It is assumed that the planner knows these γ_k.

The household h is assumed to possess a utility function $u_h(x_h, y)$ defined for all $(x_h, y) \in R_+^{m+1}$ where $u_h(\cdot)$ is a strictly quasi-concave function which is differentiable with

$$\frac{\partial u_h(x_h, y)}{\partial x_h} > 0 \quad \text{and} \quad \frac{\partial u_h(x_h, y)}{\partial y_k} \geq 0$$

for all $(x_h, y) \geq 0$. Thus the ratio

$$\pi_k^h(x_h, y) = \frac{\partial u_h(x, y)}{\partial y_k} \bigg/ \frac{\partial u_h(x_h, y)}{\partial x_h}$$

is well defined. The planner does not possess any knowledge regarding these π_k^h, and, as we shall soon see, these are the 'prices' that are sought from households.

First, let us note from the analysis earlier in this chapter that $(\bar{x}_1, \bar{x}_2, \ldots, \bar{x}_n, \bar{y}_1, \ldots, \bar{y}_m)$, satisfying

$$\bar{x} = \Sigma \bar{x}_h, \quad G(\bar{x}, \bar{y}) = 0, \quad \bar{x}_h > 0, \quad \bar{y}_k > 0 \quad \text{for all } h, k,$$

is an optimal configuration if and only if

$$\sum_h \pi_k^h(\bar{x}_h, \bar{y}) = \gamma_k(\bar{x}, \bar{y}) \text{ for all } k. \tag{5.15}$$

We saw a derivation of this result for the case $m = 1$, $N = 2$, but the extension is routine. It should also be clear that, with $\bar{x}_h \geqq 0$, $\bar{y}_k \geqq 0$, the above condition reduces to

$$\left. \begin{array}{ll} \sum_h \pi_k^h(\bar{x}_h, \bar{y}) \lessgtr \gamma_k(\bar{x}, \bar{y}) & \text{for all } k \\ \left\{ \sum_h \pi_k^h(\bar{x}_h, \bar{y}) - \gamma_k(\bar{x}, \bar{y}) \right\} \bar{y}_k = 0 & \text{for all } k. \end{array} \right\} \tag{P}$$

(To see the above conditions, refer to the Section 8.6 below.) We shall use conditions (P) below while locating optimal configurations, and it should be noted that (P) reduces to (5.15) whenever $\bar{y}_k > 0$. With conditions (P) in mind, consider the following scheme:

Indicators: (x_h, x, y_k), $h = 1, \ldots, N$; $k = 1, \ldots, m$, such that (x, y) satisfies (5.14) where $x = \sum_h x_h$.

Proposals: $\pi_k^h(x_h, y)$ for all h, k.

Before we introduce the method of revision of indicators, we should state that, for any variable w, $\dot{w} = dw/dt$, and the derivative should be interpreted as the derivative on the right; i.e.,

$$\dot{w} = \lim_{h \to 0+} \frac{w(t+h) - w(t)}{h}.$$

Revision of indicators: Recall that we have to indicate how x_h, x, and y_k are revised for all h and k. We have, first,

(i)
$$\left. \begin{array}{l} \dot{y}_k = \sum_h \pi_k^h - \gamma_k \quad \text{if} \quad y_k > 0 \\ = \max\left(0, \sum_h \pi_k^h - \gamma_k \right) \quad \text{if} \quad y_k = 0, \qquad k = 1, \ldots, m. \end{array} \right\} \tag{5.16}$$

(ii) Given (5.16), since revised indicators must also satisfy (5.14), we must have

$$\frac{\partial G}{\partial x}\dot{x} + \sum_k \frac{\partial G}{\partial y_k}\dot{y}_k = 0$$

or

$$\dot{x} = -\sum_k \gamma_k \dot{y}_k. \tag{5.17}$$

(iii) $\dot{x}_h$ is defined given (5.17), so $\sum_h \dot{x}_h = \dot{x}$; in particular, note that, from (5.17),

$$\dot{x} = \left\{ \sum_k \left(\sum_h \pi_k^h - \gamma_k \right) - \sum_h \pi_k^h \right\} \dot{y}_k$$

$$= \sum_k \dot{y}_k^2 - \sum_k \sum_h \pi_k^h \dot{y}_k, \text{ from (5.16).} \tag{5.18}$$

Also,

$$\dot{u}_h = \frac{\partial u_h}{\partial x_h}\dot{x}_h + \sum_k \frac{\partial u_h}{\partial y_k}\dot{y}_k = \frac{\partial u_h}{\partial x_h}\left(\dot{x}_h + \sum_k \pi_k^h \dot{y}_k \right) \geqq 0$$

if and only if $\dot{x}_h + \sum_k \pi_k^h \dot{y}_k \geqq 0$; so, using (5.18), define, for all $h = 1, 2, \ldots, N$,

$$\left. \begin{aligned} \dot{x}_h = \delta_h \sum_k \dot{y}_k^2 - \sum_k \pi_k^h \dot{y}_k \quad \text{where} \quad \delta_h \geqq 0, \\ \sum_h \delta_h = 1. \end{aligned} \right\} \tag{5.19}$$

Notice that $\sum_h \dot{x}_h = \dot{x}$ and $\dot{u}_h \geqq 0$ for all h. Thus our process is defined by the equations (5.16), (5.17), and (5.19).

It should be pointed out that a particular case of the above process has been discussed in the text. Thus, (5.16) ensures that, if for some public good k,

$$\sum_h \pi_k^h > \gamma_k,$$

that is, if marginal value exceeds (falls short of) the marginal cost, then the output of k should be increased (decreased). The second part of (5.16) guarantees that we never generate negative output levels. Notice that, given (5.16), we need to guarantee feasibility (i.e. that (5.14) holds), so (5.17) is naturally suggested. Thus, the output of x is adjusted according to (5.17), and we have only to work out how x_h is to be adjusted for each h. Since $\Sigma x_h = x$, $\Sigma \dot{x}_h = \dot{x}$. (5.19) satisfies this condition and may be interpreted as follows. The adjustment of x_h, $\dot{x}_h$, is made up of two terms: a positive term $\delta_h \sum_k \dot{y}_k^2$, and the term $-\sum_k \pi_k^h \dot{y}_k$, whose sign depends on the magnitudes of the term $\dot{y}_k$. The first term may be thought of as a share in the surplus left over after all compensations are settled; whereas the second term may be regarded as a compensation paid for adjusting the output level of public goods, with the adjustments being evaluated by prices revealed by the households. And incidentally, such an adjustment guarantees that the revised basket of (x_h, y) is no less attractive to h.

Just as we have guarded against generating negative output levels of y_k, so too we must ensure that x_h remains non-negative for all h. But this is difficult to do, simply because, given (5.16), (5.17) and (5.19) are locked in, and we have no room for manipulating the adjustment of x_h independently. Problems may arise if $x_h = 0$, and yet,

$$\delta_h \sum_k \dot{y}_k^2 - \sum_k \pi_k^h \dot{y}_k < 0;$$

but this can come about only if $\pi_k^h > 0$. It is this that we rule out in the following assumption.

ASSUMPTION A: If $x_h = 0$ and $y \geqslant 0$, $\pi_k^h = 0$ for all k.
   Thus, in some sense, if x_h becomes very small, $(\partial u^h/\partial x_h)\, (x_h,\ y)$ becomes very large, or else no household would go bankrupt to consume more public goods. Finally, from (5.16), $\dot{y}_k = 0$ for all k if and only if conditions (P) hold.

With these preliminaries out of the way, one may assert the following theorem.

THEOREM 4: Under our assumptions, the process (5.16), (5.17), (5.19) has a solution $\{x_h(t), x(t), y_k(t)\}$ given any (x_h^0, x^0, y_k^0) satisfying (5.14) such that $\{x_h(t), x(t), y_k(t)\} \rightarrow (x_h^*, x^*, y_k^*)$, an optimal configuration.

Proof: Let z denote (x_h, x, y_k), $h = 1, \ldots, N$, $k = 1, \ldots, m$. By a result of Henry (1972), there is a continuous solution $z(t)$ of the system (5.16), (5.17), (5.19) for all $t \geqslant 0$, given any z^0 such that $z(0) = z^0$; further, if $g(z)$ denotes the right-hand side of the system (5.16), (5.17), (5.19), then $g\{z(t)\}$ denotes the derivative on the right of $z(t)$.

Next, note that $z(t)$ belongs to a compact set in R^{m+N+1}. In fact, by construction, $\{x(t), y_k(t)\}$ satisfies $G\{x(t), y_k(t)\} = 0$ for all t, and hence, by our assumption on $G(\cdot)$, $\{x(t), y_k(t)\}$ belongs to a compact set Q of R^{m+1}. Furthermore, by construction, $\sum_h x_h(t) = x(t)$ for all t, and by virtue of assumption A, $x_h(t) \geqslant 0$ for all h and t so that

$$\{x_1(t), x_2(t), \ldots, x_n(t)\} \in Y = \Big\{(x_1, \ldots, x_N)\colon x_h \geqslant 0 \quad \text{all } h,$$

$$\sum_h x_h = x \text{ such that there is } y \text{ and } (x, y) \in Q \Big\};$$

and hence

$$z(t) = \{x_h(t),\, x(t),\, y_k(t)\} \in \theta = \{z = (x_h,\, x,\, y_k) \colon (x,\, y_k) \in Q \text{ and } (x_h) \in Y\},$$

a compact subset of R^{m+N+1}.

Next, for any h, say $h = N$ such that $\delta^N > 0$, $u^N(x, y)$ attains a maximum on θ, say $\bar{u}^N$. Consider

$$V\{z(t)\} = \bar{u}^N - u^N\{x_N(t),\, y(t)\} \geqslant 0.$$

From our earlier considerations, $\dot{V}\{z(t)\} \leqslant 0$. Therefore

$$0 \leqslant V\{z(t)\} \leqslant V\{z(0)\} \Rightarrow V\{z(t)\} \to V^* \text{ as } t \to \infty.$$

Also by virtue of this, $\dot{V}\{z(t)\}$ cannot be bounded away from zero; hence there is a sub-sequence t_s, such that

$$\dot{V}\{z(t_s)\} \to 0 \quad \text{as} \quad s \to \infty.$$

Let z^* be a limit point for the sub-sequence $z(t_s)$. (Being bounded, such limit points exist.) Consequently, from the continuity of $\dot{V}(z)$,

$$\dot{V}(z^*) = 0;$$

i.e., if $z^* = (x_h^*,\, x^*,\, y_k^*)$, then

$$\frac{\partial u^N(x_N^*,\, y^*)}{\partial x_N}\, \delta^N\left(\sum_j \dot{y}_j^2\right) = 0 \quad \text{at} \quad z^*,$$

so that

$$z^* \text{ satisfies conditions (P).}$$

Let $\bar{z}$ be any other limit point of $z(t)$, $\bar{z} = (\bar{x}_h,\, \bar{x},\, \bar{y}_k)$:

$$\because\ V^* = \bar{u}^N - u^N(\bar{x}_N,\, \bar{y}) = \bar{u}_N - u^N(x_N^*,\, y^*);$$

strict quasi-concavity of $u^h(\cdot)$ implies that

$$u^N\{\tfrac{1}{2}(\bar{x}_N,\, \bar{y}) + \tfrac{1}{2}(x_N^*,\, y^*)\} > u^N(x_N^*,\, y^*).$$

But, given that z^* is optimal, for some h,

$$u^h\{\tfrac{1}{2}(\bar{x}_h,\, \bar{y}) + \tfrac{1}{2}(x_h^*,\, y^*)\} < u^h(x_h^*,\, y^*),$$

and hence, for this h,

$$u^h(\bar{x}_h,\, \bar{y}) < u^h(x_h^*,\, y^*).$$

Let $z(t_r) \to \bar{z}$ and $z(t_k) \to z^*$; then, given the above inequality, there would be t_r and t_k for some r and k such that

$$t_r > t_k$$

$$u^h\{x_h(t_r),\, y(t_r)\} < u^h\{x_h(t_k),\, y(t_k)\}.$$

But this violates the monotonicity of $u^h(\cdot)$ (recall that $\dot{u}_h \geqq 0$ for all h); hence no other limit point $\bar{z}$ can exist, and the assertion follows. $\square$

5.6.2 *Truthful Revelation of Preferences*

We turn next to the question of whether households h have any incentive to reveal their true π_k^h. The only context within which such issues may be analysed is within the context of a *game*. (See Section 8.7 below for definitions and concepts.) Our process (5.16), (5.17), (5.19) may be thought of as defining an N-person game where, at each period t, player h has to announce a vector $\psi^h(t)$. With everyone announcing such a vector ψ^h, payoffs result in the shape of consumption vectors (x_h, y) for each h. Ideally, then, can we expect that $\psi_k^h = \pi_k^h$ for all h and k? To answer such a question, we need to specify the game further; but here issues become somewhat complicated. In general, $\psi_k^h(t)$ chosen by h at t may be depend not only on t, but on the past history from 0 to t. Such time-dependent choice of strategy may vitiate the convergence of the path, for one thing. However, some general points can be made without having to spell out the nature of the game further.

In the first place, our system (5.16), (5.17), (5.19) needs to be reformulated as

$$\dot{y}_k = \sum_h \psi_k^h - \gamma_k, \quad y_k > 0$$

$$= \max\left(0, \sum_h \psi_k^h - \gamma_k\right), \quad y_k = 0, \quad k = 1, \ldots, m. \tag{5.16'}$$

(5.17) remains as before, with $\dot{y}_k$ being interpreted by (5.16'). And instead of (5.19), we now have

$$\dot{x}_h = \delta_h \sum_k \dot{y}_k^2 - \sum_k \psi_k^h \dot{y}_k. \tag{5.19'}$$

In this situation, consider

$$\dot{u}_h = \frac{\partial u_h}{\partial x_h}\left(\dot{x}_h + \sum_k \pi_k^h \dot{y}_k\right)$$

$$= \frac{\partial u_h}{\partial x_h}\left\{\delta_h \sum_k \dot{y}_k^2 + \sum_k (\pi_k^h - \psi_k^h)\dot{y}_k\right\}. \tag{5.20}$$

Now consider the most unfavourable revisions of y_k as far as h is concerned. The expression for $\dot{u}_h$ is minimized if

$$\dot{y}_k = (\psi_k^h - \pi_k^h)/2\delta_h \quad \text{if either } y_k > 0 \text{ or } \psi_k^h \geqq \pi_k^h$$

$$= 0 \quad \text{otherwise.}$$

For such an adjustment,

$$\dot{u}_h = -\frac{\partial u_h}{\partial x_h} \left\{ \frac{1}{4\delta_h} \sum_{k \in I} (\psi_k^h - \pi_k^h)^2 - \frac{1}{2\delta_h} \sum_{k \in I} (\psi_k^h - \pi_k^h)^2 \right\}$$

$$= -\frac{\partial u_h}{\partial x_h} \frac{1}{4\delta_h} \sum_{k \in I} (\psi_k^h - \pi_k^h)^2 \leqslant 0$$

where $I = \{k$: either $y_k > 0$ or $\psi_k^h \geqslant \pi_k^h\}$; and this is the worst that can happen to h when a particular choice ψ_k^h is made.

It is also clear that, by choosing different ψ_k^h, the worst situation may be altered, and the best among the worst is guaranteed, when

$$\psi_k^h = \pi_k^h \text{ for all } k \in I;$$

for then $\dot{u}_h = 0$.

So, by revealing the true and desired information, h can guarantee that the worst that can happen is $\dot{u}_h = 0$; hence h cannot lose by being truthful. For $k \notin I$, however, $\psi_k^h \leqslant \pi_k^h$, and any such ψ_k^h rules out losses. For with $k \notin I$, $y_k = 0$ and y_k cannot be reduced further, so understating has no effect.

The above discussion allows us to conclude as follows.

THEOREM 5: Correct revelation of preferences is *a* minimax strategy; in the case of positively produced goods, it is *the only* minimax strategy.

Thus, any individual can guarantee for himself an outcome that is no worse than the initial position. But no coalition J, other than the full coalition, can guarantee an outcome; for members not in J can always enforce $\dot{y}_k = 0$ for all k, with

$$\sum_{i \notin J} \psi_k^i(t) \leqslant \gamma_k(t) - \sum_{i \in J} \psi_k^i(t),$$

with equality whenever $y_k(t) > 0$, so the initial position is maintained. If we confine attention to the equilibrium for the process (5.16′), (5.17), (5.19′), we can provide some other results. By an 'equilibrium of the process' is meant a configuration (x_h, x, y_k, ψ_k^h) that $\dot{y}_k = 0$ for all k; i.e., by virtue of (5.16′),

$$\sum_h \psi_k^h - \gamma_k \leqslant 0 \text{ with equality if } y_k > 0. \tag{E}$$

Notice that at (E), conditions (P) may not hold. But does condition (E) characterize an equilibrium of the game?

We shall use the concepts of Nash equilibrium and strong equilibrium to answer the above question. (See Section 8.7 below.) Given a configuration (x_h^*, x^*, y_k^*) and strategies (ψ_k^{h*}), we shall say that they constitute

(i) a Nash equilibrium of the game, provided that
(E) holds, and for all $h = 1, \ldots, N$, $\psi_k^h = \psi_k^{h*}$ for all $h \neq i$ implies that $\dot{u}^i \leqslant 0$ for any choice of ψ_k^i;

(ii) a strong equilibrium of the game, provided that
(E) holds, and for any coalition J, $\psi_k^h = \psi_k^{h*}$ for all $h \notin J$ implies that, for any choice $(\psi_k^i, i \in J)$, either $\dot{u}^i = 0$ for all $i \in J$ or $\dot{u}^i < 0$ for some $i \in J$.

These two concepts of equilibria will be used below. Notice that a strong equilibrium is a Nash equilibrium but the converse is not necessarily true. From the definition, it is clear that, in order to qualify as an equilibrium for the game, it must satisfy the equilibrium condition for the process. Moreover, at a Nash equilibrium, no h has an incentive to change his strategy if no one else changes strategies. And for a strong equilibrium, no coalition has an incentive to change choices so long as others keep their strategies fixed. A characterization of a strong equilibrium follows.

THEOREM 6: Let (x_h^*, x^*, y_k^*) and announced strategies (ψ_k^{h*}) satisfy (E). Then it is a strong equilibrium if and only if

$$\sum_{h \in J} \pi_k^{h*} \leqslant \gamma_k^* - \sum_{h \notin J} \psi_k^{h*} \quad \text{and} \quad y_k^* \sum_{h \in J} (\pi_k^{h*} - \psi_k^{h*}) = 0 \qquad \text{(S)}$$

for all coalitions J and for all k.

Proof: For the necessity, if (S) does not hold, then there is a coalition J and k_1 such that either

$$\sum_{h \in J} \pi_{k_1}^{h*} > \gamma_{k_1}^* - \sum_{h \notin J} \psi_{k_1}^{h*}$$

or

$$y_{k_1}^* \sum_{h \in J} (\pi_{k_1}^{h*} - \psi_{k_1}^{h*}) \neq 0. \qquad (\sim S)$$

In any case,

$$\sum_{h \in J} (\pi_{k_1}^{h*} - \psi_{k_1}^{h*}) \neq 0.$$

Let

$$\psi_k^h = \pi_k^{h*} \quad \text{for} \quad k = k_1 \quad \text{and} \quad h \in J$$

$$= \psi_k^{h*} \quad \text{otherwise.}$$

Then

$$\dot{y}_k = 0 \quad \text{for} \quad k \neq k_1, \text{ by (E)},$$

and

$$\dot{y}_{k_1} = \sum_{h \notin J} \psi_{k_1}^{h*} + \sum_{h \in J} \pi_{k_1}^{h*} - \gamma_{k_1}^*.$$

Therefore either

$$\dot{y}_{k_1} > 0, \text{ or } y_{k_1}^* > 0 \text{ and } \dot{y}_{k_1} = \sum_{h \in J} (\pi_{k_1}^{h*} - \psi_k^{h*}) \neq 0.$$

Hence

$$\dot{x}_h = -\pi_{k_1}^{h*} \dot{y}_{k_1} + \delta_h \dot{y}_{k_1}^2,$$

so that $\dot{u}_h > 0$ for all $h \in J$, so that $(\sim S)$ implies we cannot have a strong equilibrium.

Next for the sufficiency part: let J be any arbitrary coalition; let $\psi_k^h = \psi_k^{h*}$ for all $h \notin J$ and all k; consider any arbitrary ψ_k^h for all $h \notin J$. Let

$$I = \{k : y_k^* > 0\},$$

$$II = \left\{ k : y_k^* = 0 \quad \text{and} \quad \sum_{h \in J} \psi_k^h + \sum_{h \notin J} \psi_k^{h*} - \gamma_k^* > 0 \right\}.$$

Then

$$\dot{y}_k = \sum_{h \in J} \psi_k^h + \sum_{h \notin J} \psi_k^{h*} - \gamma_k^*, \quad k \in I \cup II$$

$$= 0 \qquad\qquad\qquad \text{otherwise.}$$

So we have

$$\dot{y}_k = \sum_{h \in J} (\psi_k^h - \psi_k^{h*}) \quad \text{for } k \in I \text{ using (E)}$$

and

$$\dot{y}_k > 0 \qquad\qquad \text{for } k \in II.$$

Again,

$$\dot{x}_h = -\sum_k \psi_k^h \dot{y}_k + \delta_h \sum_k \dot{y}_k^2, \quad \text{by (5.19').}$$

But $\dot{u}_h \geq 0$ if and only if $\dot{x}_h + \sum_k \pi_k^h \dot{y}_k \geq 0$. Hence if, for all $h \in J$, $\dot{u}_h \geq 0$, then

$$0 \leq \sum_{h \in J} \left\{ \sum_k (\pi_k^h - \psi_k^h) \dot{y}_k + \delta_h \sum_k \dot{y}_k^2 \right\}$$

$$= \sum_{h \in J} \sum_{k \in I} \{ (\pi_k^h - \psi_k^h) \dot{y}_k + \delta_h \dot{y}_k^2 \} + \sum_{h \in J} \sum_{k \in II} \{ (\pi_k^h - \psi_k^h) \dot{y}_k + \delta_h \dot{y}_k^2 \}$$

$$= \sum_{k \in I} \sum_{h \in J} \left\{ (\pi_k^h - \psi_k^h) + \delta_h \sum_{h \in J} (\psi_k^h - \psi_k^{h*}) \right\} \sum_{h \in J} (\psi_k^h - \psi_k^{h*})$$

$$+ \sum_{k \in II} \sum_{h \in J} \left\{ (\pi_k^h - \psi_k^h) + \delta_h \left(\sum_{h \in J} \psi_k^h + \sum_{h \notin J} \psi_k^{h*} - \gamma_k^* \right) \right\}$$

$$\times \left(\sum_{h \in J} \psi_k^h + \sum_{h \notin J} \psi_k^{h*} - \gamma_k^* \right)$$

$$= \sum_{k \in I} \left(\sum_{h \in J} \delta_h - 1 \right) \left(\sum_{h \in J} \psi_k^h - \psi_k^{h*} \right)^2 + \sum_{k \in II} \left(\sum_{h \in J} \delta_h - 1 \right) \dot{y}_k^2$$

$$+ \sum_{k \in II} \dot{y}_k \left(\sum_{h \notin J} \psi_k^{h*} - \gamma_h^* + \sum_{h \in J} \pi_k^h \right)$$

$$\leqq 0.$$

$$\because \quad \sum_{h \in J} \delta_h \leqq 1 \text{ and } \dot{y}_k > 0 \text{ for } k \in II \text{ and (S)}.$$

Therefore $\dot{u}_h \geqq 0$ for all $h \in J \Rightarrow \dot{u}_h = 0$ for all $h \in J$. Hence either $\dot{u}_h < 0$ for some $h \in J$, or $\dot{u}_h = 0$ for all $h \in J$, as was to be shown. Since J is an arbitrary coalition, the result follows. $\square$

There are two immediate implications of the above.

1: If $(x_h^*, x^*, y_k^*$ and strategies ψ_k^{h*} satisfy (E), then (x_h^*, x^*, y_k^*), (ψ_k^{h*}) constitute a Nash equilibrium of the game if and only if

$$\pi_k^{h*} \leqq \gamma_k^* - \sum_{i \neq h} \psi_k^{i*}$$

and

$$y_k^*(\psi_k^{h*} - \pi_k^{h*}) = 0 \text{ for all } h \text{ and } k. \left.\vphantom{\sum}\right\} \quad \text{(NE)}$$

By considering coalitions J made up of a single household, the above follows.

2: Every strong equilibrium of the game is optimal; so is every Nash equilibrium in which $y_k^* > 0$ for all k.

Consider conditions (S) and (E) at (x_h^*, x^*, y_k^*) and (ψ_k^{h*}); i.e.,

$$\sum_h \psi_k^{h*} - \gamma_k^* \leqq 0; \quad y_k^* \left(\sum_h \psi_k^{h*} - \gamma_k^* \right) = 0;$$

$$\sum_{h \in J} \pi_k^{h*} + \sum_{h \notin J} \psi_k^{h*} - \gamma_k^* \leqq 0,$$

$$y_h^* \left\{ \sum_{h \in J} (\pi_k^{h*} - \psi_k^{h*}) \right\} = 0 \left.\vphantom{\sum_{h \in J}}\right\} \quad \text{for any coalition } J;$$

$$y_k^* \gamma_k^* = y_k^* \sum_h \psi_k^{h*} = y_k^* \left(\sum_{h \in J} \psi_k^{h*} + \sum_{h \notin J} \psi_k^{h*} \right)$$

$$= y_k^* \left(\sum_{h \in J} \pi_k^{h*} + \sum_{h \notin J} \pi_k^{h*} \right);$$

or

$$y_k^* \left(\sum_h \pi_k^{h*} - \gamma_k^* \right) = 0. \tag{i}$$

Next, suppose that $\sum_h \pi_k^{h*} - \gamma_k^* > 0$ \qquad for some k.

Then

$$\sum_{h \in J} \pi_k^{h*} + \sum_{h \notin J} \pi_k^{h*} - \gamma_k^* > 0 \qquad \text{for any coalition } J$$

or

$$0 < \sum_{h \notin J} (\pi_k^{h*} - \psi_k^{h*}), \quad \text{using (S).} \tag{ii}$$

Again, by (ii),

$$\gamma_k^* - \sum_{h \in J} \psi_k^{h*} \gtrless \sum_{h \notin J} \pi_k^{h*} > \sum_{h \notin J} \psi_k^{h*},$$

or

$$\gamma_k^* - \sum_h \psi_k^{h*} > 0 \text{: a violation of (E).}$$

Hence

$$\sum_k \pi_k^{h*} - \gamma_k^* \leqslant 0 \text{ for all } k. \tag{iii}$$

But conditions (i) and (iii) are exactly the required conditions (P). At a Nash equilibrium, $y_k^* > 0$ for all $k \Rightarrow 0 \ \psi_k^{h*} = \pi_k^{h*}$ for all k, so (E) reduces to (P).

At an equilibrium of the process (i.e. (E)), which is also a Nash equilibrium for the game, households h have an incentive to reveal their true preferences for positively produced public goods. If a public good is not being produced and preferences are being under-reported, revelation of true preferences by a single household is unlikely to bring about a positive output; so no positive gain may be expected unless many act simultaneously. But once a positive output is reached, incentives for the revelation of true preferences exist for all consumers.

To conclude: in general, reporting correctly avoids loss. So if you prefer to play safe, then speak the truth! Moreover, *if* the process (i.e. the system (5.16'),

(5.17), (5.19′) with arbitrary choices of ψ_k^h) converges, it must converge to an optimal configuration if the game is to be in strong equilibrium. Thus, if strategy choices do not disturb convergence, they will not disturb optimality either—but the particular optimal configuration arrived at would depend on the choices made.

BIBLIOGRAPHICAL NOTES

Welfare economics is such a vast and complex area that even an entire book devoted to it might not be able to do it justice. However, for a more detailed discussion on some of the topics covered in this chapter, see Feldman (1980). The topics can be classified into two broad themes: (1) the Classical (or Fundamental) Theorems of Welfare Economics, and (2) the effects of externalities. Some other areas of welfare economics may be pursued from the modest beginnings made here, as I shall indicate.

The discussion begins with the notion of a Pareto-optimal state and its relationship with a competitive equilibrium. This relationship is embodied in the classical theorems of welfare economics; an elementary discussion is presented in the text and, at a more general level, in the mathematical notes above. For such an analysis, Bator (1957), Arrow (1950, 1974), Arrow and Hahn (1971: ch. 4), Koopmans (1957: ch. 1), and Debreu (1954, 1959) constitute an exhaustive set of readings.

A movement from an inoptimal to an optimal state involves an increase in social welfare, but comparison among optimal states is a different matter. The latter type of comparison can be made only if there is a social welfare function—see Bergson (1938) and Samuelson (1947: ch. VIII). Such social welfare functions allow one to compensate A's loss by B's gain. Attempts to get rid of interpersonal comparisons led to the development of compensation tests—see Graaff (1967) and Arrow (1951) in this connection; see also the papers in Part V of Arrow and Scitovsky (1969). None of this led to any significant advances, owing to a major difficulty—the Arrow Impossibility Theorem. The area of social choice, which grew out of Arrow's pioneering contribution (1951), is not discussed here at all; see Sen (1970) or Sen (1984) for an updated lucid and exhaustive account. For elementary discussions of this and other related topics, see Feldman (1980).

The presence of externalities leads to market failures, or to a breakdown of the classical theorems of welfare economics. The text looks at examples of externalities in production and consumption and tries to demonstrate how or why markets may fail to attain an optimum. The examples considered are similar to the ones considered in Malinvaud (1972: ch. 9) and Dasgupta and Heal (1979: ch. 3). Again within the context of such examples, various corrective taxes and subsidies are considered. For a recent general treatment of externalities, see Greenwald and Stiglitz (1986); also see papers in Part III of Arrow and Scitovsky (1969).

For the case of public goods, the Samuelson (1954) optimality conditions are discussed and the problem of provision of public goods is considered within a planning type model due to Malinvaud (1971), which is closely followed; see also Feldman (1980). For a more recent discussion on this topic, see Heal (1984). In the mathematical notes to this chapter, the contribution of Dreze and de la Vallee Poussin

(1971) is presented with a comprehensive analysis of the MDP process. There is some discussion in the text on the important question of revelation of preferences. Such questions may be analysed only within the context of an N-person game. An analysis of this sort is provided in the mathematical notes while reporting the Dreze–de la Vallee Poussin (1971) contribution. See Hurwicz (1984) for a more recent discussion of such issues.

Among several topics we have not discussed, two deserve special mention. It may be recalled that discussion in the text led us to the conclusion that the maximization of social welfare or the achievement of an optimum cannot be left to market forces. In many situations, we have to introduce another agent, the government or the planner, whose objective is to guide the economy to an optimal state. Consequently, the policies that should be followed by such agents need to be carefully examined; see Mirrlees (1986) for a recent survey of results in this connection. A related topic of great interest is pricing the output of public firms. If public firms are charged with the maximization of social welfare, then they ought to charge a price that is equal to marginal cost. But this may not be possible, for a variety of reasons. For an analysis of such questions see Sheshinski (1986).

6   Non-Walrasian Equilibria

6.1   Introduction

One of the fundamental assumptions of the earlier chapters has been that transactions occur at equilibrium configurations. This is why we have concerned ourselves only with the equilibrium, where by an 'equilibrium' we mean a configuration such that demand and supply match in each market. It is this matter that we shall seek to relax in the present chapter. Given that prices may move in disequilibrium in such a manner that an equilibrium may not be attained, it is important to consider whether transactions can occur at non-market-clearing prices; and if such transactions occur, then we need to examine the nature of these transactions. To keep matters simple, we shall assume that all prices are completely fixed and that at this price configuration markets do not clear. Further, we shall return to the world of Chapter 2, namely, to one of exchange. In this situation, we shall first try to characterize the set of possible transactions by beginning with certain desirable features of such transactions. Then we shall see how these may result from alternative scenarios.

6.2   Transactions at Fixed Prices

In situations of price rigidity, markets may not clear. Thus, if some transactions occur, there is likely to be a deviation between *actual transactions* (purchases and sales) and *desired transactions* (excess demands and excess supplies). Consider, first of all, a rather simple situation where there are only two goods, $j = 1, 2$. An individual i maximizes his utility function $U^i(x_1, x_2)$ subject to a budget constraint

$$px_1 + x_2 = pw_1^i + w_2^i \tag{6.1}$$

where p denotes the price of good 1 relative to 2 and $w^i = (w_1^i, w_2^i)$ is the initial endowment that i possesses. Such a situation was analysed earlier, and hence we may claim that, under standard assumptions, we have demands

$$x^i(p, w^i);$$

hence the *desired transactions* are given by

$$z^i(p, w^i) = x^i(p, w^i) - w^i.$$

Let $z(p, w^i) = \sum_i z^i(p, w^i)$: the market excess demand. Let us denote by t^i the actual transactions that i makes; then

$$z(p, \ldots) = 0 \Rightarrow t^i = z^i(p, w^i). \tag{6.2}$$

But suppose $z(p, \ldots) \neq 0$: what are the possible configurations of $\{t^i\}$? First of all, for the sake of feasibility, t^i is a feasible configuration of transactions if all púrchases equal all sales for each commodity, or

$$\sum_i t^i = 0. \tag{6.3}$$

Then again, since we are studying voluntary transactions, and since after the transactions are made the individual is left with $w^i + t^i$, we must have

$$U^i(w^i + t^i) \geqslant U^i(w^i); \tag{6.4}$$

and from the budget constraint, since transactions occur at prices p,

$$pt_1^i + t_2^i = 0 \tag{6.5}$$

must hold for each i.

To provide an example of such a configuration of $\{t^i\}$, it would be instructive to divide the set of individuals into the following two groups:

$$S(p, \{w^i\}) = \{i : z_1^i(p, w^i) z_1(p, w^i) \leqslant 0\}:$$

the short side of the market, and

$$L(p, \{w^i\}) = \{i : i \notin S(p, \{w^i\})\}:$$

the long side of the market; since $z(p, \ldots) \neq 0$, there is $i \in L(p, \{w^i\})$, but $S(p, \{w^i\}) = \emptyset$ may be possible. In case of the latter eventuality,

$$z_1^i(p, \ldots) z_1(p, \ldots) > 0 \text{ for all } i,$$

so that all individuals wish to buy the same good and sell the other. In such a situation, short of forcing individuals to act contrary to their desires, the only alternative is that

$$t^i = 0 \quad \text{for all } i.$$

In cae $S(p, \{w^i\}) \neq \emptyset$, consider the following:

$$t^i = z^i(p, w^i) \quad \text{for} \quad i \in S(p, \{w^i\})$$
$$= \delta_i z^i(p, w^i), \quad i \in L(p, \{w^i\}) \tag{6.6}$$

where $0 \leqslant \delta_i \leqslant 1$ for each i, such that (6.3) holds. Thus, if i is on the short side, he is able to make his desired trade; those on the long side try to get as close as possible to their x^i.

Notice that such a configuration is not unique; choosing an alternative configuration of δ_i keeping (6.3) satisfied alters the possible t^i. Moreover, if

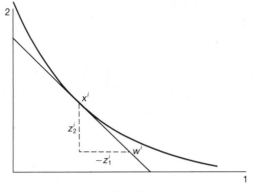

FIG. 6.1

$i \in S(p, \{w^i\}) \Rightarrow z^i(p, \ldots) = 0$, then $\{t^i\}$ defined by (6.6) also satisfies $t^i = 0$ for all i. However, if, for some $i \in S(p, \{w^i\})$, $z^i(p, \ldots) \neq 0$, then $\{t^i\}$ defined by (6.6) satisfies $t^i \neq 0$ for some i.

Note, further, that

$$i \in S(p, \{w^i + t^i\}) \Rightarrow z^i(p, w^i + t^i) = 0,$$

so that no further transactions occur after trade according to (6.6) is completed. Finally, the t^i defined by (6.6) satisfy (6.4) and (6.5); moreover, no individual is able to increase his utility by trading less (i.e. buying less and selling less) than the amount specified by (6.6): this follows, since movement from w^i to x^i along the budget line (see Figure 6.1) leads to a monotonic increase in utility given the usual properties. We shall now try to extend these ideas to consider the case of n goods, where $n > 2$.

The first problem encountered in the general case is that the division of individuals into the short side and the long side of *the* market is no longer possible, simply because there is more than one market. Thus, given n goods, there are $n-1$ markets; in the jth market, commodity j is bought or sold against the numeraire—say commodity 1. So, an individual who is on the short side of the kth market may be on the long side of the jth (in the two-good case—this problem never arose above since there was only one market). Additionally, although an individual on the short side of a market can in fact carry out his desired transaction in that market, it is not clear that he should do so. For desired transactions in each market are contingent on desired transactions in other markets. So if a person is on the long side of some market, then the desired transaction may not be achieved there; consequently, his desired transactions in other markets may alter. Put another way, suppose that an individual is on the short side of the jth market (say, he wants to sell commodity j and buy k) but on the long side of the kth market.

Whether he sells j depends, then, on whether he is able to purchase k. The upshot of this discussion is that scheme (6.6) would be unacceptable in the multi-market situation. But what about the properties of possible transactions? Surely properties such as (6.3), (6.4), and (6.5) should hold?

To enable us to answer the above question, let us consider the following notion of a 'Non-Walrasian' Younes equilibrium. A configuration of trades, t^{i*} is said to constitute a *Younes equilibrium* at a given $[p, \{w^i\}]$ if

Y1: $\sum_i t^{i*} = 0.$

Y2: $x^{i*} = w^i + t^{i*}$ solves the problem

$$\max U^i(x)$$

$$\text{s.t.} \quad px \leqslant pw^i$$

$$\min (0, t_j^{i*}) \leqslant x_j - w_j^i \leqslant \max (0, t_j^{i*}) \quad \text{for all } j \neq 1$$

$$x \geqslant 0.$$

Y3: There does not exist a pair of consumers (i, h), a commodity j, and a real number $\varepsilon > 0$ such that

$$U^i(w^i + t^{i*}) < U^i(w^i + t^{i*} + \varepsilon a^j)$$

$$U^h(w^h + t^{h*}) < U^h(w^h + t^{h*} - \varepsilon a^j)$$

with $w^i + t^{i*} + \varepsilon a^j \geqslant 0$ and $w^h + t^{h*} - \varepsilon a^j \geqslant 0$, where

$$a_k^j = 0, \qquad k \neq j, 1$$

$$= -p_j, \quad k = 1$$

$$= 1, \qquad k = j.$$

(The vector a^j shows how the endowment is altered when 1 unit of j is purchased.)

(Y1) is clearly (6.3), i.e. *feasibility* of transactions; (Y2) guarantees (6.4) and (6.5); it also guarantees that no one can improve his welfare by trading less; thus, (Y2) ensures that transactions are *voluntary*. Finally, (Y3) guarantees that, after the transactions $\{t^{i*}\}$ are completed, no further mutually advantageous bilateral trades can occur. This aspect is often described by the statement that markets are *frictionless*. Recall that these were the properties we had obtained in our discussion of the transactions specified by (6.6). It may be shown that there will always exist such a Younes equilibrium. Instead of a direct demonstration of this proposition, however, we shall see next how such an equilibrium may be generated; moreover, it can be demonstrated that such constructions are always possible. In the process, an alternative route to the demonstration of the existence of a Younes equilibrium will be provided.

6.3 Rationing (Dreze) Equilibria

Consider, once more, the exchange economy of the last section; there is a distribution of the n goods among the N individuals ($i=1, 2, \ldots, N$), where each i possesses w^i; a price configuration $p=(1, p_2, \ldots, p_n)$ with $p_j > 0$ for all j; finally, each i ranks alternatives by means of an *increasing, continuously differentiable, strictly quasi-concave* utility function $U^i(\cdot)$. We have seen that in general, since $z(p, \ldots) \neq 0$, $t^i = z^i(p, w^i)$ cannot be feasible (since (6.3) would be violated), so the question is whether constraints can be devised on purchases and sales (i.e. ration purchases and sales quotas) such that the constrained demands balance.

Let $C^i_j, c^i_j, j=2, \ldots, n; i=1, 2, \ldots, N$, be such that

D1: $\qquad\qquad c^i_j \leqslant 0 \leqslant C^i_j \quad$ for all i and $j=2, \ldots, n$;

D2: $\qquad\qquad \sum_i x^i(c^i, C^i, p, w^i) = \sum_i w^i$

$\qquad\qquad$ where $x^i(c^i, C^i, p, w^i)$ solves the problem

$\qquad\qquad$ max $U^i(\cdot)$

$\qquad\qquad$ s.t. $\quad px \leqslant pw^i$

$\qquad\qquad\qquad\quad c^i_j \leqslant x_j - w^i_j \leqslant C^i_j, \quad j=2, \ldots, n$

$\qquad\qquad\qquad\quad x \geqslant 0.$

D3: (i) If, for $j=j_1$, there is i_0 such that

$$x^{i_0}_{j_1}(c^{i_0}, C^{i_0}, p, w^{i_0}) = c^{i_0}_{j_1},$$

$\qquad$ then $x^i_{j_1}(c^i, C^i, p, w^i) < C^i_{j_1}$ for all i.

$\quad$ (ii) If, for $j=j_0$ there is i_1 such that

$$x^{i_1}_{j_0}(c^{i_1}, C^{i_1}, p, w^{i_1}) = C^{i_1}_{j_0},$$

$\qquad$ then $x^i_{j_0}(c^i, C^i, p, w^i) > c^i_{j_0}$ for all i.

For such a configuration, let

$$\bar{t}^i = x^i(c^i, C^i, p, w^i) - w^i$$

denote *Dreze transactions* and $\{c^i, C^i\}$ a *Dreze equilibrium* at $[p, \{w^i\}]$.

From the definition, it should be clear that $\{c^i, C^i\}$ denote constraints on i's sales and purchases, respectively, of goods $j \neq 1$; by D2, $\sum_i \bar{t}^i = 0$; also,

$$U^i\{x^i(c^i, C^i, \ldots)\} = U^i(w^i + \bar{t}^i) \geqslant U^i(w^i) \quad \text{for all } i,$$

and by trading less, individuals cannot increase their level of satisfaction. Next, D3 guarantees that the *constraints can be binding on one side of any market at most*. Thus, constraints such as (c^i, C^i) at a given (p, w^i) may generate transactions of the type specified above in Y1–Y3; the interest in such (c^i, C^i) would be greater provided such a configuration always exists. It may be shown that this indeed is the case.

For any $p > 0$, $\{w^i\}$, $w^i \geq 0$, $w_1^i \neq 0$, for all i, there exist $\{c^i, C^i\}$ satisfying (D1)–(D3).

A proof of this proposition is contained in the mathematical notes to this chapter.

To analyse the nature of the Dreze equilibrium further, recall that the transactions $\bar{t}^i$ for each i at a Dreze equilibrium solve the problem

$$\left.\begin{array}{ll} \max & U^i(w^i + t) \\ \text{s.t.} & pt \leq 0 \\ & c_j^i \leq t_j \leq C_j^i, \quad j \neq 1 \\ & w^i + t \geq 0. \end{array}\right\} \tag{D}$$

Using the strict quasi-concavity and differentiability of $U^i(\cdot)$ and noting that the constraints are all linear, we may appeal to the results of Section 8.6 to conclude that if $\bar{t}^i$ solves (D), then there are non-negative numbers $\lambda^{i*}, \mu_{ij}^*, \delta_{ij}^*, \theta_{ij}^*$ satisfying the Kuhn–Tucker conditions:

$$\frac{\partial \bar{U}^i}{\partial x_1} - \lambda^{i*} + \theta_{i1}^* = 0; \tag{i}$$

$$\frac{\partial \bar{U}^i}{\partial x_j} - \lambda^{i*} p_j + \mu_{ij}^* - \delta_{ij}^* + \theta_{ij}^* = 0; \tag{ii}$$

$$\lambda^{i*} p\bar{t}^i = 0 \tag{iii}$$

$$\theta_{ij}^*(w_j^i + \bar{t}_j^i) = 0 \qquad \text{for all } j; \tag{iv}$$

$$\mu_{ij}^*(\bar{t}_j^i - c_j^i) = 0 \qquad \text{for all } j \neq 1 \tag{v}$$

$$\delta_{ij}^*(C_j^i - \bar{t}_j^i) = 0 \qquad \text{for all } j \neq 1 \tag{vi}$$

The bar over a partial derivative represents the fact that these derivatives are all evaluated at $w^i + \bar{t}^i$. Assume that $w_1^i + \bar{t}_1^i > 0$; then $\theta_{i1}^* = 0$ and

$$\frac{\partial \bar{U}^i}{\partial x_1} = \lambda^{i*},$$

and, by virtue of the fact that the U^i are strictly increasing, $\lambda^{i*} > 0$. Now define

$$s_j^i(x^i) = \frac{\partial U^i(x)}{\partial x_j} \bigg/ \frac{\partial U^i(x)}{\partial x_1} \qquad \text{for all } i \text{ and } j.$$

Then

$$\text{(ii)} \Rightarrow \bar{s}_j^i = p_j + \{(\delta_{ij}^* - \mu_{ij}^* - \theta_{ij}^*)/\lambda^{i*}\} \quad \text{for all } j \neq 1. \tag{vii}$$

By virtue of D3,

$$\delta_{ij}^* > 0 \text{ for some } i \Rightarrow \mu_{ij}^* = 0 \text{ for all } i$$

and

$$\mu_{ij}^* > 0 \text{ for some } i \Rightarrow \delta_{ij}^* = 0 \text{ for all } i.$$

Note that at a Dreze equilibrium, for any market $j \neq 1$, there are three possibilities:

(a) there is i such that $c_j^i = \bar{t}_j^i$, i.e. the market is sales-constrained;

(b) there is i such that $C_j^i = \bar{t}_j^i$, i.e. the market is purchase-constrained;

(c) for every i, $c_j^i < \bar{t}_j^i < C_j^i$, i.e. the market is unconstrained.

In case (c), (v) and (vi) $\Rightarrow \mu_{ij}^* = \delta_{ij}^* = 0$, so that

$$\text{(vii)} \Rightarrow \bar{s}_j^i \leqslant p_j \quad \text{for all } i \text{ with equality if } w_j^i + \bar{t}_j^i > 0. \tag{viii}$$

In case (b), $c_j^h < \bar{t}_j^h$ for all h, so that $\mu_{hj}^* = 0$ for all h and

$$\text{(vii)} \Rightarrow \bar{s}_j^i \leqslant p_j + \delta_{ij}^*/\lambda^{i*} \quad \text{for all } i \text{ with equality if } w_j^i + \bar{t}_j^i > 0. \tag{ix}$$

In case (a), $C_j^h > \bar{t}_j^h$ for all h, so that $\delta_{hj}^* = 0$ for all h and

$$\text{(vii)} \Rightarrow \bar{s}_j^i \leqslant p_j - \mu_{ij}^*/\lambda^{i*} \quad \text{for all } i \text{ with equality if } w_j^i + \bar{t}_j^i > 0. \tag{x}$$

Thus, in a sales-constrained market,

$$\left. \begin{array}{l} \bar{s}_j^i \leqslant p_j \quad \text{for all } i, \\[8pt] \text{whereas in a purchase-constrained market} \\[8pt] \bar{s}_j^i \geqslant p_j \quad \text{for all } i \text{ such that } w_j^{i*} + \bar{t}_j^i > 0. \end{array} \right\} \tag{α}$$

These two implications will be used below and we shall refer to them frequently. Finally, we may not have $\bar{t}^i \neq 0$ for some i at a Dreze equilibrium. But (α) tells us that, if $\{w^i\}$ and p are such that

$$s_j^{i_1}(w^{i_1}) > p_j > s_j^{i_2}(w^{i_2}) \tag{T}$$

for some i_1, i_2 and j where $w_j^{i_2} > 0$, then at a Dreze equilibrium some trade will occur; i.e., $\bar{t}^i \neq 0$ for some i.

We shall now consider whether the transactions $\{\bar{t}^i\}$ can be thought of as a Younes equilibrium; first, notice that $\{\bar{t}^i\}$ must satisfy Y1 and Y2, by definition. Thus the question is whether $\{\bar{t}^i\}$ satisfies Y3; the violation of Y3 implies the existence of a pair (i, h), a commodity j, and a number $\varepsilon > 0$ such that we have the following:

$$U^i(w^i + \bar{t}^i + \lambda \varepsilon a^j) > U^i(w^i + \bar{t}^i)$$
$$U^h(w^h + \bar{t}^h - \lambda \varepsilon a^j) > U^h(w^h + \bar{t}^h) \quad \text{for all } \lambda,$$

$0 < \lambda < 1$, using the strict quasi-concavity of U^i for all i. But as $\{\bar{t}^i\}$ satisfies D2, writing the constraint set of the problem in D2 as $B^i(D)$, it follows that

$$w^i + \bar{t}^i + \lambda \varepsilon a^j \notin B^i(D) \quad \text{for all } \lambda, \qquad 0 < \lambda < 1$$

$$w^h + \bar{t}^h - \lambda \varepsilon a^j \notin B^h(D) \quad \text{for all } \lambda, \qquad 0 < \lambda < 1.$$

Therefore $w_j^i + \bar{t}_j^i = C_j^i$ and $w_j^h + \bar{t}_j^h = c_j^h$: a violation of D3. Hence Y3 must hold. Thus, we may note that

> *Transactions $\{\bar{t}^i\}$ associated with a Dreze equilibrium constitute a Younes equilibrium.*

For the above proposition to hold, it should be emphasized that all U^i should be *strictly quasi-concave*. Without some such assumption, the proposition would not be true. In what follows, differentiability of $U^i(\cdot)$ will play a crucial role. Given our earlier assertion regarding the existence of a Dreze equilibrium, we see now that a Younes equilibrium exists also.

Conversely, it may be shown that,

> *Given any Younes equilibrium $\{t^{i*}\}$ satisfying Y1–Y3 and $w_1^i + t_1^{i*} > 0$ for all i, one may construct (c^i, C^i) such that we have a Dreze equilibrium with $\{t^{i*}\}$ as the Dreze transactions.*

While comparing the requirements Y1–Y3 with D1–D3, one might be led to suppose that the above proposition may be trivially demonstrated by defining

$$c_j^i = \min(0, t_j^{i*}),$$

$$C_j^i = \max(0, t_j^{i*}) \quad \text{for all } i \text{ and for all } j \neq 1.$$

Such a definition would satisfy D1 and D2, but D3 may not hold. These considerations are taken into account and an appropriate set of constraints are provided in the Section 6.7 below.

We have now seen one particular method of generating transactions satisfying Y1–Y3; that is, by defining appropriate constraints on sales and purchases, one may define constrained demands and supplies that balance. In particular, the transactions so defined satisfy Y1–Y3. We turn now to a more comprehensive scheme wherein the constraints on purchases and sales are endogenized.

6.4   Perceived Constraints, Effective Demands, and Rationing

We consider here a rather comprehensive notion of transactions at a non-Walrasian equilibrium. Before proceeding with formal definitions, it may be more revealing to consider things at an intuitive level. We shall be concerned with three types of quantity variables:

(a) perceived constraints, denoted $(\underline{z}^i, \bar{z}^i)$;
(b) effective demands, denoted $(\tilde{z}^i)$;
(c) trades or transactions, denoted (z^{i*}).

In addition, there are two rules:

(A) the Rationing Rule,
(B) the Constraint Perception Rule.

The manner in which these variables and rules are tied up is perhaps best explained by means of the schematic diagram in Figure 6.2. At a given $\{p, w^i\}$, each agent i has some idea regarding the constraints that he is likely to face in each market. Let $\underline{z}^i$ denote the constraints on sales and $\bar{z}^i$ the constraints on purchases; these are constraints that the individual expects to face. Based on these expectations, the individual i expresses certain (effective) demands. (We shall postpone the discussion of how effective demands are formed for the present.) Given effective demands $\tilde{z}^i$, in general, $\sum_i \tilde{z}^i \neq 0$, i.e., the effective demands may not be compatible. The task of the Rationing Rule is to associate with a given array of effective demands $\{\tilde{z}^i\}$ an array of trades $\{z^{i*}\}$ such that $\sum_i z^{i*} = 0$. Given that z^{i*} may be different from $\tilde{z}^i$, agent i would revise his perceptions of the constraints (the Constraint Perception Rule serves this purpose) and express different effective demands. An equilibrium of this system—a *Benassy equilibrium*—is a configuration such that no agent has any reason to alter his perception of the constraints; the transactions z^{i*} that an agent can make in such a situation supports the perception $(\underline{z}^i, \bar{z}^i)$ that an agent had at the outset. Alternatively, if one views the formation of expectations regarding constraints as a recursive process, a Benassy equilibrium is attained when the process comes to a halt.

We need next to examine how effective demands $\{\tilde{z}^i\}$ are formed. First, notice that $\tilde{z}^i$ are actually effective *excess* demands; i.e., these are the desired

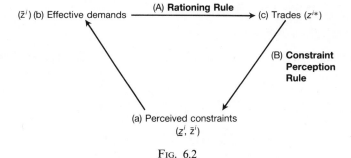

FIG. 6.2

trades in a sense to be made explicit soon. Given $(\underline{z}^i, \bar{z}^i)$, consider the following problem:

$$
\begin{array}{rl}
\max & U^i(x) \\
\text{s.t.} & x = w^i + z \\
& pz \leqslant 0 \\
& \underline{z}^i_j \leqslant z_j \leqslant \bar{z}^i_j, \quad j \neq 1, h.
\end{array}
\quad\quad (\mathrm{P}^i_h)
$$

Let γ^i_h denote the constraint set of the problem (P^i_h); an examination of the constraints indicates that the agent takes into account the constraints he is likely to encounter in all markets except the hth. (As before, 1 is the numeraire.) Let $z^i(h)$ solve the above problem; assuming strict quasi-concavity of $U^i(\cdot)$ would guarantee that $z^i(h)$ is unique. The effective demand for commodity h is then defined to be

$$
\tilde{z}^i_h = z^i_h(h).
$$

Thus, by solving problems $\mathrm{P}^i_2, \mathrm{P}^i_3, \ldots, \mathrm{P}^i_n$ where the constraint sets are, respectively, $\gamma^i_2, \gamma^i_3, \ldots, \gamma^i_n$, an array of vectors $z^i(2), z^i(3), \ldots, z^i(n)$ is determined. The effective demand vector $\tilde{z}^i$ is now defined by

$$
\tilde{z}^i_j = z^i_j(j), \quad\quad j = 2, \ldots, n
$$

and

$$
\tilde{z}^i_1 = - \sum_{j=2}^n p_j \tilde{z}^i_j.
$$

Given the manner in which $\tilde{z}^i$ are formed, it is clear that

$$
\underline{z}^i_j \leqslant \tilde{z}^i_j \leqslant \bar{z}^i_j, \quad\quad j \neq 1,
$$

need not hold; neither will the vector of effective demands $\tilde{z}^i$ maximize utility subject to some constraints. But we shall show below how, at a Benassy equilibrium, the transactions z^{i*} have some such rationality, provided the U^i are strictly quasi-concave.

Given the array of effective demands $\tilde{z}^i$, *the rationing rule* $F(\cdot)$ associates a transaction z^{i*} for each i: i.e.,

$$
F: (\tilde{z}^1, \ldots, \tilde{z}^N) \to (z^{1*}, z^{2*}, \ldots, z^{N*}),
$$

and we shall write $z^{i*} = F^i(\tilde{z})$ where $\tilde{z} = (\tilde{z}^{1'}, \ldots, \tilde{z}^N)$. It is also required that

$$
\sum_i F^i(\tilde{z}) = 0 \quad\quad\quad\quad (\text{R1})
$$

$$
\tilde{z}^i_j F^i_j(\tilde{z}) \geqslant 0, \quad |\tilde{z}^i_j| \geqslant |F^i_j(\tilde{z})| \quad \text{for all } i, j \quad\quad (\text{R2})
$$

$$
\tilde{z}^i_j \sum_i \tilde{z}^i_j \leqslant 0 \Rightarrow F^i_j(\tilde{z}) = \tilde{z}^i_j \quad \text{for all } i, j \quad\quad (\text{R3})
$$

$$
F^i(\cdot) \text{ is a continuous function for each } i. \quad\quad (\text{R4})
$$

From our earlier discussions, it is easy to see what the above conditions mean. (R1) is the basic feasibility condition; (R2) guarantees that the transactions are voluntary, i.e. that no one is forced to trade in a direction opposite to his desired trade or to trade more than he desires. (R3), of course, is the short-side rule, used to define trades in the two-good context, redefined to fit the present general context.

Having been allowed to trade $z^{i*} = F^i(\tilde{z})$, each agent considers the constraints he perceives in each market. There is a rule whereby such perceptions are revised; this is called the *Constraint Perception Rule* for i and encompasses a pair of functions $\{\underline{G}^i, \bar{G}^i\}$ such that

$$\left.\begin{array}{c} \{\underline{G}^i, \bar{G}^i\} \text{ are continuous functions:} \\ \underline{G}^i: R^{(n-1)N} \to R^{n-1}_- \\ \bar{G}^i: R^{(n-1)N} \to R^{n-1}_+ \end{array}\right\} \quad \text{(PC1)}$$

$$\underline{G}^i_j \leqslant F^i_j(\tilde{z}) \leqslant \bar{G}^i_j \quad \text{(PC2)}$$

$$\tilde{z}^i_j > F^i_j(\tilde{z}) \Rightarrow \bar{G}^i_j = F^i_j(\tilde{z}); \; \tilde{z}^i_j < F^i_j(\tilde{z}) \Rightarrow \underline{G}^i_j = F^i_j(\tilde{z}). \quad \text{(PC3)}$$

Note that a constraint perception rule $G^i = \{\underline{G}^i, \bar{G}^i\}$ is defined given a rationing rule $F(\cdot)$.

With these definitions, we are now in a position formally to define a *Benassy equilibrium*.

A rationing rule $F = (F^i)$, a constraint perception rule $G = (\underline{G}^i, \bar{G}^i)$, and transactions $\{z^{i*}\}$ constitute a Benassy equilibrium at a given $\{p, w^i\}$ if there exists $\tilde{z} = (\tilde{z}^i)$ such that

$$z^{i*}_j = F^i_j(\tilde{z}); \quad \text{(E1)}$$

$\tilde{z}^i_j$ is the jth component of the vector maximizing $U^i(x)$ subject to $pz \leqslant 0$, and $\bar{G}^i_h(\tilde{z}) \geqslant z_h \geqslant \underline{G}^i_h(\tilde{z})$ for all $h \neq 1, j$; \quad (E2)

$$z^{i*}_1 = -\sum_{j=2}^n p_j z^{i*}_j. \quad \text{(E3)}$$

(E2) thus guarantees that agents do not have any reason to change their effective demands $\tilde{z}^i$ given the transactions z^{i*}. But before we accept this as a meaningful equilibrium, we need to consider whether transactions z^{i*} are voluntary. In answer to such a query, the following may be demonstrated (assuming U^i are strictly quasi-concave):

z^{i*} appearing in (E1)–(E3) solves the following problem:

$$\left.\begin{array}{l} \max \quad U^i(w^i + z) \\ \text{s.t.} \quad pz \leqslant 0 \\ \quad \underline{G}^i_j(\tilde{z}) \leqslant z_j \leqslant \bar{G}^i_j(\tilde{z}), \quad j \neq 1 \end{array}\right\} \quad \text{(B}^i\text{)}$$

For a proof of the above assertion, let $\hat{z}^i$ solve (B^i). Consider $h \neq 1$ and define the problem (B$_h^i$) by

$$\text{max} \quad U^i(w^i + z)$$

$$\left.\begin{array}{l} \text{s.t.} \quad pz \leqq 0 \\[2mm] \underline{G}_j^i(\tilde{z}) \leqq z_j \leqq \bar{G}_j^i(\tilde{z}), \qquad j \neq 1, h. \end{array}\right\} \qquad \text{(B}_h^i\text{)}$$

Suppose $\hat{z}^i$ does not solve (B$_h^i$); then

$$\tilde{z}_h^i \notin (\underline{G}_j^i, \bar{G}_h^i).$$

Now if $\tilde{z}_h^i > \bar{G}_h^i$, then $\hat{z}_h^i = \bar{G}_h^i$; for if not, then $\hat{z}_h^i < \bar{G}_h^i$. Let $z(h)$ solve (B$_h^i$) where $z_h(h) = \tilde{z}_h^i$ so that

$$U^i\{w^i + z(h)\} > U^i(w^i + \hat{z}^i) \Rightarrow U^i\{w^i + \lambda z(h) + (1 - \lambda)\hat{z}^i\}$$

$$> U^i(w^i + \hat{z}^i) \qquad \text{for all } \lambda, \quad 0 < \lambda < 1;$$

Then, since

$$\lambda z_h(h) + (1 - \lambda)\hat{z}_h^i \leqq \bar{G}_h^i \text{ for } \lambda \text{ appropriate,}$$

we arrive at a contradiction.

Again, $\tilde{z}_h^i > \bar{G}_h^i(\tilde{z}) \Rightarrow z_h^{i*} = \bar{G}_j^i(\tilde{z})$, so that $\hat{z}_h^i = z_h^{i*}$. Next, let $\hat{z}^i$ solve (B$_h^i$): hence $\hat{z}_h^i = \tilde{z}_h^i \in (\underline{G}_h^i, \bar{G}_h^i)$. Therefore

$$z_h^{*i} = \tilde{z}_h^i = \hat{z}_h^i.$$

Thus, in any case, $\hat{z}_h^i = z_h^{*i}$ for all $h \neq 1$; hence $z_1^{*i} = \hat{z}_1^i$ and the assertion follows.

It can now be seen that the transactions $\{z^{i*}\}$ at a Benassy equilibrium are voluntary. In fact, these transactions satisfy conditions (Y1)–(Y3) as well. In other words, one may assert:

> *Given strict quasi-concavity of $U^i(\cdot)$, if $\{z^{i*}\}$ constitute a Benassy equilibrium for some F, G at a given $(p, \{w^i\})$, then $\{z^{i*}\}$ constitutes a Younes equilibrium.*

First, note that, by virtue of the rationalization of $\{z^{i*}\}$ presented above, $\{z^{i*}\}$ solves the problem

$$\text{max} \quad U^i(w^i + z)$$

$$\text{s.t.} \quad pz \leqq 0$$

$$\text{min} \quad (0, z_j^{i*}) \leqq z_j \leqq \text{max}(0, z_j^{i*}), \qquad j \neq 1,$$

so that conditions (Y1) and (Y2) are immediately seen to hold. Suppose that (Y3) is violated; i.e., suppose there are individuals i, h, a number $\varepsilon > 0$, and a good j such that

$$U^i(w^i + z^{i*} + \varepsilon a^j) > U^i(w^i + z^{i*}) \tag{xi}$$

$$U^h(w^h + z^{h*} - \varepsilon a^j) > U^h(w^h + z^{h*}). \tag{xii}$$

Recall that $\tilde{z}_j^i z_j^{i*} \geqslant 0$ and $|z_j^{i*}| \leqslant |\tilde{z}_j^i|$, by condition (R2). By (xi) and (xii),

$$\tilde{z}_j^i > z_j^{i*}, \tilde{z}_j^h < z_j^{h*},$$

and

$$z_j^{i*} + \varepsilon \notin (\underline{G}_j^i, \bar{G}_j^i), z_j^{h*} - \varepsilon \notin (\underline{G}_j^h, \bar{G}_j^h),$$

so that $z_j^{i*} + \varepsilon > \bar{G}_j^i$ and $z_j^{h*} - \varepsilon < \underline{G}_j^h$. Since (xi) and (xii) would hold if ε were replaced by $\lambda\varepsilon$ for all λ, $0 < \lambda \leqslant 1$, we conclude that $z_j^{i*} = \bar{G}_j^i$ and $z_j^{h*} = \underline{G}_j^h$. Therefore

$$\tilde{z}_j^i > z_j^{i*} \geqslant 0 \quad \text{and} \quad \tilde{z}_j^h < z_j^{h*} \leqslant 0. \tag{xiii}$$

Now if $\sum_k \tilde{z}_j^k \leqslant 0$,

$$\tilde{z}_j^i \sum_k \tilde{z}_j^k \leqslant 0 \Rightarrow z_j^i = z_j^{i*}:$$

which is a contradiction to (xiii). Therefore $\sum_k \tilde{z}_j^k > 0$; but then,

$$\tilde{z}_j^h \sum \tilde{z}_j^k < 0 \Rightarrow \tilde{z}_j^h = z_j^{h*},$$

which also leads to a contradiction to (xiii). Hence no such individuals i, h exist. Thus (Y3) holds as well, and our assertion is seen to be valid.

Combining the above result with the result of the last section, it follows that

> If $\{z^{i*}\}$ is a Benassy equilibrium for some (F, G) at $[p, \{w^i\}]$, then there exists (c^i, C^i) such that (c^i, C^i) constitute a Dreze equilibrium with $\{z^{i*}\}$ as the associated transactions.

And finally, to complete the chain:

> Given a Dreze equilibrium (c^i, C^i) with associated transactions $\{z^{i*}\}$ at (p, w^i), there exists a rationing rule F satisfying (R1)–(R4) such that $\{z^{i*}\}$ is a Benassy equilibrium with respect to (F, G) for all G satisfying (PC1)–(PC3).

As the construction of the rationing rule $F(\cdot)$ is somewhat involved, we shall not go into it; see the bibliographical notes at the end of the chapter for a reference to such a construction.

The general problem we set out to consider (i.e., what transactions may occur at a price configuration that does not clear markets) has been investigated at length. The general properties of such transactions are contained in the characterization Y1–Y3. Such transactions may be induced either within the framework of a Dreze equilibrium or within the setup of a Benassy equilibrium. We turn next to the question of how this apparatus may be used to provide an analysis of how prices are formed, a topic on which Walrasian equilibrium theory did not shed much light.

6.5 Disequilibrium Dynamics

Consider, first of all, the simple case of two goods with transactions at $(p, \{w^i\})$ as described in Section 6.2. It may not be possible for any one individual agent to find out that such prices are not right, i.e. that they do not clear markets. The disequilibrium (in the Walrasian sense) would manifest itself to an agent only when the agent failed to make the desired trade. Thus, for example, individuals on the short side would fail to distinguish the situation from one of equilibrium since they would have made their desired trades: it is individuals on the long side who would realize that prices were not market-clearing. Given this situation, one may assume that the individuals on the long side would try to bid the price up if there were an excess demand and to lower the price if there were an excess supply; individuals on the short side who were satisfied at the earlier price situation would find the prices changing and might decide to participate in the market once more.

Before we formalize the above process of bidding by individuals, we have to consider what bids may be made. Figures 6.3 and 6.4 may be of some help. Let us say that individual i has attained $w^i + t^i \neq x^i$ (the Walrasian demand). His s^i denotes the marginal rate of substitution (MRS); also, as long as i is interested in selling good 1, s^i will be the lowest price at which he is prepared to sell it; i.e., he would not bid the price lower than s^i. Similarly, if i is on the long side and has attained $w^i + t^i \neq x^i$ and now wishes to buy more of good 1, he will bid the price up, but not higher than s^i. So these are the natural limits for the bidding process; in the circumstances, the new price can be

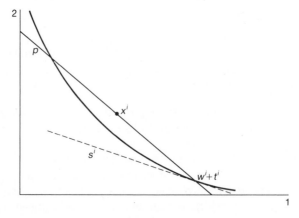

FIG. 6.3

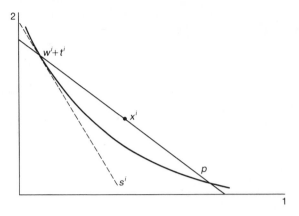

FIG. 6.4

thought of as a convex combination between the highest s^i and the lowest s^i in the market. At the new price configuration, the entire process of transactions and subsequent price change is repeated. The objective then is to study the sequence of prices so generated.

We move on to a setting of the above problem in a multi-market situation. Let there be n commodities indexed $j = 1, 2, \ldots, n$ with 1 as the numeraire; suppose also that there are N individuals indexed by $i = 1, 2, \ldots, N$; each i has an endowment $w^i \geqslant 0$. Any price vector is represented by $p = (1, p_2, \ldots, p_n) > 0$. Given a configuration $\{p, (w^i)\}$ such that markets do not clear, it is possible to define a Dreze equilibrium $\{c^i, C^i\}$ with associated Dreze transactions $\{E^i\}$.

Thus, if, at stage k, $\{p(k), w^i(k)\}$, trade occurs according to some Dreze transactions $E^i(k)$, endowments alter to

$$w^i(k + 1) = w^i(k) + E^i(k) \quad \text{for all } i. \tag{6.7}$$

After trade has occurred as above, recall that in each market there are either only unsuccessful buyers or only unsuccessful sellers. Then, as in the preliminary discussion of this section, we assume that

$$p_j(k + 1) = \alpha_j(k + 1)\max_i s_j^i\{w^i(k + 1)\} +$$

$$\{1 - \alpha_j(k + 1)\} \min_{i \in I(j, k + 1)} s_j^i\{w^i(k + 1)\} \quad \text{for all } j \neq 1 \tag{6.8}$$

where $0 < \sigma_j < \alpha_j(k) < 1 - \eta_j < 1$ for some constants σ_j and η_j, and $I(j, k) = \{i: w_j^i(k) > 0\}$.

In Section 6.3 above, we saw that, after trade according to a Dreze equilibrium is carried out, condition (α) holds. So if at stage k the market j is sales-constrained, then

$$s_j^i\{w^i(k+1)\} \leqslant p_j(k) \qquad \text{for all } i;$$

thus (6.8) implies that in such a market, price is bid down. Similarly, if the market j is purchase-constrained, then

$$\min_{i \in I(j, k+1)} s_j^i\{w^i(k+1)\} \geqslant p_j(k);$$

so (6.8) implies that in such a market the price is bid up. Finally, in an unconstrained market, prices are not revised at all. This much follows from (6.8) and conditions (α).

When individuals are bidding prices up or down, what prices do they use as bids? So long as a constrained purchaser never bids the price beyond his s_j^i and an unsuccessful seller (i.e. one who wishes to sell more) never bids the price below his s_j^i, the new price may be described by an equation such as (6.8). It should be emphasized that individuals do not need to reveal their s_j^i; if they follow the limits described above, then (6.8) will be an adequate description. How the new price is actually set up need not be specified beyond requiring that it lies between the largest and lowest bid where bids themselves are subjected to limits stated above.

Thus, beginning with an arbitrary $[p^0, \{w^{i0}\}]$, a sequence $[p(k), \{w^i(k)\}]$ is generated. Under assumptions to be made precise in the mathematical notes to this chapter, it may be shown that

$[p(k), \{w^i(k)\}]$ *converges to a no-trade Walrasian equilibrium.*

Before attempting to interpret it, it should be noted that the major assumption required for this result is that $w_1^i(k) > 0$ for all i and for all k; i.e., everyone must possess some numeraire at each stage. If an individual runs out of 'cash', some transactions may not be feasible and the process may get stuck at some non-Walrasian configuration.

We shall use the results of the last section to interpret the above processes (6.7) and (6.8) in a more interesting way. Consider an exchange economy with some rationing rule $F(\cdot)$; an agent, when informed of prices, has certain expectations of the constraints he is likely to face in each market; on the basis of these expectations, the agent expresses effective demands and the rationing rule translates these effective demands into transactions that each agent may make. At a Benassy equilibrium, these transactions will confirm the expectations of the agents. Thus, if at each $[p(k), \{w^i(k)\}]$ a Benassy equilibrium obtains with transactions $\{E^i(k)\}$, then at each stage agents learn about the effective quantity constraints by entering into the transactions $E^i(k)$. After transactions are complete, the agents bid up the price of a purchase-constrained commodity and bid down the price of a sales-constrained commodity subject to the bounds discussed above. Since $\{E^i(k)\}$ are the transactions associated with a Benassy equilibrium, we know also that there will be some $\{c^i(k), C^i(k)\}$ forming a Dreze equilibrium for which $\{E^i(k)\}$ will be the Dreze transactions; thus the convergence result mentioned above is applicable. Essentially, then, participating in disequilibrium transactions is a method whereby an agent obtains information regarding effective quantity constraints.

This interpretation has one problem, however—it requires an infinite round of meetings between each pair of agents to establish a Benassy equilibrium. What I have suggested is that this sequence of meetings happens quickly—in fact, instantaneously. Relaxation of this aspect is possible without disturbing the convergence claimed earlier. For details of such an analysis, a reference is provided in the bibliographical notes to this chapter.

To sum up, agents participate in transactions to find out the nature of effective quantity constraints; once this information is obtained, prices are bid up or down; in any case, the marginal rate of substitution is taken to be a bound for these bids. Thus, a sequence of $[p(k), \{w^i(k)\}]$ is generated. At each stage k, we have transactions associated with a non-Walrasian equilibrium. Ultimately, a no-trade Walrasian equilibrium configuration is reached. This means that $\{w^i(k)\}$ approaches a Pareto-optimal distribution $\{w^{i*}\}$ and prices $p(k)$ approach p^*, which support the distribution $\{w^{i*}\}$.

MATHEMATICAL NOTES

6.6   Existence and Continuity of Dreze Equilibria

Consider the problem

$$
\left.
\begin{aligned}
\max \quad & U(x) \\
\text{s.t.} \quad & px \leqslant pw \\
& C_j \geqslant x_j - w_j \geqslant c_j, \qquad j = 2, \ldots, n \\
& x \geqslant 0
\end{aligned}
\right\}
\tag{D}
$$

where $p_j > 0$ for all j, $w \geqslant 0$, and $c_j \leqslant 0 \leqslant C_j$, $j = 2, \ldots, n$. Under the assumption that U is strictly quasi-concave, the above problem has a unique solution $x^* = x(c, C, p, w)$. Let $U(\cdot)$ be a continuously differentiable function; i.e., $U_j(x) = \partial U(x)/\partial x_j$ exist and are continuous functions of x. We shall see that this solution varies continuously with (c, C, p, w), and as such the argument would be identical to the one that established continuity of the demand functions (see mathematical notes to Chapter 2). Let the constraint set of (D) be written as $\gamma(c, C, p, w)$; recall that the crucial property to establish is that $\gamma: R_-^{n-1} \times R_-^{n-1} \times R^n \times R_+^n \to R_+^n$ is lower hemi-continuous (l.h.c.) (see Section 8.5.3). ($R_-^n = \{x \in R^n : x \leqslant 0\}$).

To prove this, we first establish

1: Let $\sigma(c, C, w) = \{x : x \geqslant 0, c_j \leqslant x_j - w_j \leqslant C_j, j = 2, \ldots, n\}$. Then $\sigma: R_-^{n-1} \times R_-^{n-1} \times R_+^n \to R_+^n$ is l.h.c. at all (c, C, w) such that $w \geqslant 0$, $w \neq 0$, $c_j \leqslant 0 \leqslant C_j$.

Proof: Consider any arbitrary configuration (c^0, C^0, w^0) satisfying the conditions mentioned. Notice that $\sigma(c^0, C^0, w^0) \neq \varnothing$ and choose $x^0 \in \sigma(c^0, C^0, w^0)$.

Define

$$J_1 = \{j : C_j^0 = x_j^0 - w_j^0 = c_j^0\}; \qquad J_2 = \{j : C_j^0 > x_j^0 - w_j^0 = c_j^0\}$$
$$J_3 = \{j : C_j^0 = x_j^0 - w_j^0 > c_j^0\}; \qquad J_4 = \{j : j \notin J_1 \cup J_2 \cup J_3\}.$$

Consider then a sequence $(c^s, C^s, w^s) \to (c^0, C^0, w^0)$ where $c_j^s \leqslant 0 \leqslant C_j^s$, $w^s \geqslant 0$.

Define

$$\begin{aligned}
x_j^s &= x_j^0, \quad j \in J_4 \\
&= w_j^s, \quad j \in J_1 \\
&= C_j^s + w_j^s, \quad j \in J_3 \\
&= t_j^s(c_j^s + w_j^s) + (1 - t_j^s)(C_j^s + w_j^s), \quad j \in J_2
\end{aligned}$$

where

$$t_j^s = \max_{(0, 1)} t \text{ such that } x_j^s \geqslant 0.$$

By construction, $x^s \in \sigma(c^s, C^s, w^s)$ for all s sufficiently large. Moreover, $x_j^s \to x_j^0$ for all $j \in J_1 \cup J_3 \cup J_4$. For $j \in J_2$, since t_j^s is bounded, it has a limit point, $\bar{t}_j$ say, so let $\bar{t}_j < 1$, if possible. Hence $x_j^s, j \in J_2$ has a limit point

$$\begin{aligned}
\bar{x}_j &= \bar{t}_j(c_j^0 + w_j^0) + (1 - \bar{t}_j)(C_j^0 + w_j^0) \\
&= x_j^0 + (1 - \bar{t}_j)(C_j^0 - c_j^0) > 0;
\end{aligned}$$

i.e., $x_j^s, j \in J_2$ has a sub-sequence $x_j^{s_r} \to \bar{x}_j$ and $x_j^{s_r} > 0$ for all r large. But then $t_j^{s_r} = 1$ for all r large; i.e., $\bar{t} = 1$: a contradiction. Hence $t_j^s \to 1$ and

$$x_j^s \to c_j^0 + w_j^0 = x_j^0 \text{ for } j \in J_2.$$

This establishes the claim. $\square$

The above enables us to demonstrate

2: $\gamma(c, C, p, w)$ is l.h.c. at all (c, C, p, w) such that $c_j \leqslant 0 \leqslant C_j, j \neq 1, p_j > 0$ for all j, and $w \geqslant 0$.

Proof: Consider (c^0, C^0, p^0, w^0) and let $x^0 \in \gamma(c^0, C^0, p^0, w^0)$ and $(c^s, C^s, p^s, w^s) \to (c^0, C^0, p^0, w^0)$.

If $w_1^0 = 0$ and for every j such that $w_j^0 > 0$, $c_j^0 = 0$, then $x^0 = w^0$; consequently, choose $x^s = w^s \in \gamma(c^s, C^s, p^s, w^s)$ and $x^s \to x^0$.

Consider then the case when either $w_1^0 > 0$ or, for some j such that $w_j^0 > 0$, $c_j^0 < 0$: then there is $\bar{x} \in \gamma(c^0, C^0, p^0, w^0)$ such that $p^0\bar{x} < p^0 w^0$.

Since $\bar{x} \in \sigma(c^0, C^0, w^0)$, there is $x^s \in \sigma(c^s, C^s, w^s)$, $x^s \to x^0$, by claim 1. Moreover, $x^0 \in \sigma(c^0, C^0, w^0)$, hence there is $x^{s_0} \in \sigma(c^s, C^s, w^s)$ and $x^{s_0} \to x^0$.

Define $x^s = t^s x^{s_0} + (1 - t^s)x^s$ where t^s is defined by

$$\max_{(0,1)} t$$

such that $p^s x^s \leqslant p^s w^s$. The proof is completed by showing $t^s \to 1$, as in the proof of claim 1. $\square$

Using these results, it is easy to see that

3: $x(c, C, p, w)$ (the solution to (D)) is a continuous function of (c, C, p, w) at all (c, C, p, w) such that $p_j > 0$ for all j, $w \geqslant 0$, and $c_j \leqslant 0 \leqslant C_j, j \neq 1$.

Proof: This follows the proof of continuity of demand functions provided in the mathematical notes to Chapter 2. $\square$

The above claims allow us to conclude that

$$z(c, C, p, w) = x(c, C, p, w) - w$$

is a continuous function of (c, C, p, w), and this would be of crucial importance in establishing the validity of the following proposition.

PROPOSITION I: Given any $\{p, (w^i)\}$ such that $p_j > 0$ for all j, $w^i \geqslant 0$ with $w_1^i > 0$ for all i, there exists (c^i, C^i) satisfying

D1: $c_j^i \leqslant 0 \leqslant C_j^i$, $\quad j = 2, \ldots, n$ for all i

D2: $\sum_i x^i(c^i, C^i, p, w^i) = \sum_i w^i$

where $x^i(c^i, C^i, p, w^i)$ solves the problem

$$\max U^i(x)$$
$$\text{s.t.} \quad px \leqslant pw^i$$
$$c_j^i \leqslant x_j - w_j^i \leqslant C_j^i, \quad j \neq 1$$
$$x \geqslant 0$$

and

D3: (i) $x_j^i(c^i, C^i, p, w^i) - w_j^i = c_j^i$ for some i and j

      $\Rightarrow x_j^h(c^h, C^h, p, w^h) - w_j^h < C_j^h$ for all h;

   (ii) $x_j^i(c^i, C^i, p, w^i) - w_j^i = C_j^i$ for some i and j

      $\Rightarrow x_j^h(c^h, C^h, p, w^h) - w_j^h > c_j^h$ for all h.

Proof: Let

$$w_j^* = \max_i w_j^i; \qquad M_j^i = \sum_r p_r w_r^i / p_j; \qquad \varepsilon > 0.$$

$$V_j = w_j^* + \max_i M_j^i + \varepsilon$$

$$I_{j_1} = [-V_j, 0]; \quad I_1 = \mathop{\times}_{j=2}^{n} I_{j_1}$$

$$I_{j_2} = [0, V_j]; \quad I_2 = \mathop{\times}_{j=2}^{n} I_{j_2}$$

$$c^i \in I_1, \quad C^i \in I_2, \quad (c^i, C^i) \in I_1 \times I_2 = I.$$

Thus,

$$\{(c^1, C^1), (c^2, C^2), \ldots, (c^N, C^N)\} \in I^N.$$

Define

$$I^* = [\{(c^i, C^i)\}: \{(c^i, C^i)\} \in I^N \quad \text{and} \quad C_j^i - c_j^k \geqq V_j \text{ for all } i, k$$

$$\text{and all } j = 2, \ldots, n]$$

Now I^* is non-empty, compact and convex and for each $\{(c^i, C^i)\} \in I^*$; define $Q(\{(c^i, C^i)\}) = \{(c^{i'}, C^{i'})\}$ by

$$c_j^{i'} = \frac{c_j^i}{1 + |z_j(c^i, C^i)|} \qquad \text{if } z_j(c^i, C^i) \leqq 0;$$

$$= \frac{c_j^i - V_j |z_j(c^i, C^i)|}{1 + |z_j(c^i, C^i)|} \qquad \text{otherwise};$$

$$C_j^{i'} = \frac{C_j^i + V_j |z_j(c^i, C^i)|}{1 + |z_j(c^i, C^i)|} \qquad \text{if } z_j(c^i, C^i) \leqq 0;$$

$$= \frac{C_j^i}{1 + |z_j(c^i, C^i)|} \qquad \text{otherwise},$$

where

$$z_j(c^i, C^i) = \sum_i x^i(c^i, C^i, p, w^i) - \sum_i w^i.$$

Notice that $\{(c^{i'}, C^{i'})\} \in I^N$, and

$$C_j^{i'} - c_j^{k'} = \frac{C_j^i - c_j^k + V_j|z_j(c^i, C^i)|}{1 + |z_j(c^i, C^i)|}$$

$$\geqslant V_j \quad \text{if } \{(c^i, C^i)\} \in I^*.$$

Thus $Q: I^* \to I^*$; moreover, the continuity of $z_j(\cdot)$ established by virtue of claims 1, 2, and 3 implies that Q is a continuous function from I^* to itself. Hence by virtue of Brouwer's Fixed-Point Theorem (see Section 8.5.3), there is $\{(c^{i*}, C^{i*})\} \in I^*$ such that

$$Q[\{(c^{i*}, C^{i*})\}] = \{(c^{i*}, C^{i*})\}.$$

Suppose now that $z_j(c^{i*}, C^{i*}) < 0$ for some $j \neq 1$. Then

$$c_j^{i*} = c_j^{i*}/[1 + |z_j(\cdot)|] \Rightarrow c_j^{i*} = 0 \Rightarrow z_j(\cdot) \geqslant 0:$$

a contradiction. Hence $z_j(c^{i*}, C^{i*}) \geqslant 0$ for all $j \neq 1$. Suppose that the strict inequality holds for some j. Then

$$C_j^{i*} = C_j^{i*}/[1 + |z_j(\cdot)|] \Rightarrow C_j^{i*} = 0 \Rightarrow z_j(\cdot) \leqslant 0:$$

a contradiction once again. Hence $z_j(c^{i*}, C^{i*}) = 0$ for all $j \neq 1$; so $z_1(c^{i*}, C^{i*}) = 0$. Thus, conditions D1 and D2 hold at $\{(c^{i*}, C^{i*})\}$.

Finally, suppose that for some j there exist i, k such that

$$x_j^i(c^{i*}, C^{i*}, p, w^i) - w_j^i = C_j^{i*}$$

and

$$x_j^k(c^{k*}, C^{k*}, p, w^k) - w_j^k = c_j^{k*}.$$

Then

$$x_j^i(\cdot) = w_j^i + C_j^{i*} \leqslant M_j^i + w_j^k + c_j^{k*} \quad \text{since } w_j^k + c_j^k \geqslant 0.$$

Therefore

$$M_j^i + w_j^k \geqslant C_j^{i*} - c_j^{k*} + w_j^i \geqslant V_j + w_j^i$$

or

$$0 \geqslant V_j - M_j^i - w_j^k + w_j^i \geqslant \varepsilon + w_j^i > 0:$$

a contradiction. Hence D3 must hold at $\{(c^{i*}, C^{i*})\}$. This completes the proof of the proposition. $\square$

We shall also require the following continuity property of Dreze equilibria:

PROPOSITION II: Let $(c^{ir}, C^{ir}, p^r, w^{ir})$ be a sequence of Dreze equilibria, and let $x^{ir} = x(c^{ir}, C^{ir}, p^r, w^{ir})$. Let $(c^{ir}, C^{ir}, p^r, w^{ir})$
$\rightarrow (c^{i*}, C^{i*}, p^*, w^{i*})$ where $p_j^* > 0$ for all j and $w^{i*} \geqq 0$, for all i;
assume also that $x^{ir} \rightarrow x^{i*}$ where $x_1^{i*} > 0$ for all i. Then

(i) $\sum_i x^{i*} = \sum_i w^{i*}$ and $x^{i*} = x^i(c^{i*}, C^{i*}, p^*, w^{i*})$;

(ii) for any $j \neq 1$, either $s_j^{i*} \leqq p_j^*$ for all i, or $s_j^{i*} \geqq p_j^*$ for all i such that
$x_j^{i*} > 0$.

Proof: Part (i) follows by virtue of the continuity of the constrained demand
established in claim 3. For part (ii), notice that, at $(c^{ir}, C^{ir}, p^r, w^{ir})$,

$$x^{ir} = x(c^{ir}, C^{ir}, p^r, w^{ir}) \Rightarrow x^{ir} \text{ solves the following problem:}$$

$$\max U^i(x)$$
$$\text{s.t.} \quad p^r x \leqq p^r w^{ir}$$
$$c_j^{ir} \leqq x_j - w_j^{ir} \leqq C_j^{ir}, \quad j \neq 1$$
$$x \geqq 0.$$

It follows therefore that for such r there exist non-negative $\lambda^{ir*}, \mu_j^{ir*}, \delta_j^{ir*},$
$j = 2, \ldots, n$ (see Section 8.6), such that

$$\frac{\partial U^i(x^{ir})}{\partial x_1} - \lambda^{ir*} \leqq 0 \quad \text{with equality if } x_1^{ir} > 0;$$

$$\frac{\partial U^i(x^{ir})}{\partial x_j} - \lambda^{ir*} p_j - \delta_j^{ir*} + \mu_j^{ir*} \leqq 0 \quad \text{with equality if } x_j^{ir} > 0.$$

Moreover,

$$C_j^{ir} > (x_j^{ir} - w_j^{ir}) \Rightarrow \delta_j^{ir*} = 0$$
$$c_j^{ir} < (x_j^{ir} - w_j^{ir}) \Rightarrow \mu_j^{ir*} = 0.$$

Since $x_1^{i*} > 0$, it follows that $x_1^{ir} > 0$ for all r large, so that

$$\frac{\partial U^i(x^{ir})}{\partial x_1} = \lambda^{ir*} \quad \text{for all } r \text{ large.}$$

Assuming strictly increasing utility functions, $\lambda^{ir*} > 0$. Therefore

$$\frac{\partial U^i(x^{ir})}{\partial x_j} \bigg/ \frac{\partial U^i(x^{ir})}{\partial x_1} \leqq p_j^r + (\delta_j^{ir*} - \mu_j^{ir*})/\lambda^{ir*}$$

so that

$$s_j^i(x^{ir}) \lessgtr p_j^r + (\lambda_j^{ir*} - \mu_j^{ir*})/\lambda^{ir*}$$

where

$$s_j^i(x) = \frac{\partial U^i(x)}{\partial x_j} \bigg/ \frac{\partial U^i(x)}{\partial x_1}.$$

Using property 3 of a Dreze equilibrium D3, it follows that either $\delta_j^{ir*} = 0$ for all i, or $\mu_j^{ir*} = 0$ for all i; i.e.,

either $\quad s_j^i(x^{ir}) \leqslant p_j^r$ for all i

or $\qquad s_j^i(x^{ir}) \geqslant p_j^r$ for all i such that $x_j^{ir} > 0.$ $\Bigg\}$ $\qquad$ (α)

Now claim (ii) follows; for if possible, let there exist j and i_1 and i_2 such that

$$s_j^{ir}(x^{ir*}) > p_j^* > s_j^{i_2}(x^{i_2*})$$

where $x_j^{i_2*} > 0.$ Then notice that (α) must be violated for large r. $\square$

6.7 Dreze Constraints at Younes Equilibria

At a Younes equilibrium, t^{i*}, for a given configuration $\{p, (w^i)\}$, each t^{i*} solves

$$\begin{array}{ll} \max & U^i(w^i + t) \\ \text{s.t.} & pt \leqslant 0 \\ & \min(0, t_j^{i*}) \leqslant t_j \leqslant \max(0, t_j^{i*}) \\ & w^i + t \geqslant 0. \end{array} \Bigg\} \qquad \text{(Y)}$$

Given the similarity of problem (Y) to problem (D) in Section (6.3), it is easy to see that

$$t_j^{i*} < 0 \Rightarrow s_j^{i*} \leqslant p_j \qquad \text{(xiv)}$$

and that

$$t_j^{i*} > 0 \Rightarrow s_j^{i*} \geqslant p_j. \qquad \text{(xv)}$$

These follow from the Kuhn–Tucker conditions applicable to (Y); alternatively, recall conditions (α) of Section 6.3 above.

Now note that $t_j^{i*} < 0$ applies in the current context to a sales-constrained situation, whereas $t_j^{i*} > 0$ is a purchase-constrained situation together with $w_j^i + t_j^{i*} > 0$. Hence (xiv) and (xv) follow.

Next, we have assumed that $U^i(\cdot)$ is strictly quasi-concave; as a reference to Section 8.5.2 will tell us, this means that

$$U^i(x) > U^i(y) \Rightarrow \nabla U^i(y)(x - y) \geqslant 0.$$

However, we shall use a somewhat stricter requirement now:

$$U^i(x) > U^i(y) \Rightarrow \nabla U^i(y)(x - y) > 0. \tag{xvi}$$

This would follow if $U^i(\cdot)$ happened to be concave, for example. (Again, see Section 8.5.2.)

Now define, for all i and $j \neq 1$,

$$\varepsilon_{ij} = 0 \qquad \text{if } s_j^{i*} > p_j$$
$$= \varepsilon > 0 \qquad \text{otherwise;}$$
$$\delta_{ij} = 0 \qquad \text{if } s_j^{i*} < p_j$$
$$= \delta > 0 \qquad \text{otherwise;}$$
$$\gamma_{ij} = 0 \qquad \text{if } w_j^i + t_j^{i*} > 0$$
$$= \gamma > 0 \qquad \text{otherwise.}$$

$$c_j^i = \min(0, t_j^{i*}) - \delta_{ij} - \gamma_{ij}; \quad C_j^i = \max(0, t_j^{i*}) + \varepsilon_{ij}.$$

We claim: $\{(c^i, C^i)\}$ constitutes a Dreze equilibrium at $[p, (w^i)]$ with (t^{i*}) as the Dreze transactions. Note that D1 is met by construction.

Also, since $\sum_i t_j^{i*} = 0$ for all j, by virtue of Y1, we need only check whether t^{i*} solves

$$\left. \begin{array}{l} \max \ U^i(w^i + t) \\ \text{s.t.} \quad pt \leqslant 0 \\ \qquad c_j^i \leqslant t_j \leqslant C_j^i \\ \qquad w^i + t \geqslant 0. \end{array} \right\} \tag{D}$$

First of all, t^{i*} is feasible. If t^{i*} does not solve (D), let $\hat{t}^i$ solve (D). Hence

$$U^i(w^i + \hat{t}^i) > U^i(w^i + t^{i*}),$$

and by virtue of (xvi), we have

$$\nabla U^i(w^i + t^{i*})(\hat{t}^i - t^{i*}) > 0$$

or

$$s^{i*}(\hat{t}^i - t^{i*}) > 0.$$

Again, $pt^i = 0 = pt^{i*}$, since U^i is strictly monotonic; we have then

$$(s^{i*} - p)(\hat{t}^i - t^{i*}) > 0;$$

so there is j such that

$$(s_j^{i*} - p_j)(\hat{t}_j^i - t_j^{i*}) > 0.$$

If $s_j^{i*} > p_j$, $t_j^i > t_j^{i*}$; or

$$C_j^i = \max(0, t_j^{i*}) \geq t_j^i > t_j^{i*} \Rightarrow t_j^{i*} < 0 \Rightarrow s_j^{i*} \leq p_j:$$

a contradiction. If $s_j^{i*} < p_j$, $\hat{t}_j^i < \hat{t}_j^{i*}$; or, since $\hat{t}^i$ is feasible,

$$c_j^i = \min(0, t_j^{i*}) \leq \hat{t}_j^i < t_j^{i*} \Rightarrow t_j^{i*} > 0 \Rightarrow s^{i*} \geq p_j,$$

which is a contradiction, too. Thus, no such $\hat{t}^i$ exists and t^{i*} solves (D). Thus D2 is met.

Finally, suppose there are i_2, i_1, and j such that

$$c_j^{i_1} = t_j^{i_1*}, \quad C_j^{i_2} = t_j^{i_2*},$$

in violation of D3. Hence $t_j^{i_1*} \leq 0$; also, $s_j^{i_1*} < p_j$, and $w_j^{i_1*} + t_j^{i_1*} > 0$. Further, $t_j^{i_2*} \geq 0$ and $s_j^{i_2*} > p_j$.

Now suppose that i_1 sells $\lambda > 0$ units of j to i_2, where λ is small. Then

$$U^{i_1}(w^i + t^{i_1*} - \lambda a^j) \approx U^{i_1}(w^{i_1} + t^{i_1*})$$

$$-(-p_j + s_j^{i_1*})\frac{\partial U^{i_1}}{\partial x_1}(w^{i_1} + t^{i_1*})$$

$$> U^{i_1}(w^{i_1} + t^{i_1*}).$$

Similarly,

$$U^{i_2}(w^{i_2} + t^{i_2*} + \lambda a^j) > U^{i_2}(w^{i_2} + t^{i_2*}).$$

But this violates Y3. Hence D3 holds. This completes the demonstration. $\square$

6.8 Disequilibrium Dynamics and the Convergence to a Walrasian Configuration

In this section, the validity of the convergence result claimed in the text will be demonstrated. First, we shall make use of the following assumptions concerning the utility functions:

A: $U^i(x)$ is strictly quasi-concave, increasing, and continuously differentiable on $X = \{x: x \geq 0, x_1 > 0\}$.

B:

$$s_j^i(x) = \frac{\partial U^i(x)}{\partial x_j} \Big/ \frac{\partial U^i(x)}{\partial x_1} > 0 \quad \text{for all } i, j \text{ on } X;$$

moreover, $s_j^i(x) \to 0 \Rightarrow x_j \to \infty$ for any i, for all $j \neq 1$.

Now consider

$$G = \{x = (x^1, \ldots, x^N): x^i \geq 0, \; \sum_i x_j^i = \tilde{w}_j' \quad \text{for all } j,$$

$$U^i(x^i) \geq U^i(w^i) \quad \text{for all } i\}$$

where w^i is the initial endowment of i and $\tilde{w}_j = \sum_i w^i_j$. The final requirement is

C: $x \in G \Rightarrow x = (x^i)$ such that $x^i_1 > 0$ for all i.

Recall that, at each stage k, $\{c^i(k), C^i(k), p(k), w^i(k)\}$ constitute a Dreze equilibrium with $E^i(k)$ as the associated transactions, and that in Section 6.5 we defined

$$w^i(k + 1) = w^i(k) + E^i(k)   \text{for all } i. \tag{6.7}$$

Moreover,

$$p_j(k + 1) = \alpha_j(k + 1) \max_i s^i_j\{w^i(k + 1)\}$$

$$+ \{1 - \alpha_j(k + 1)\} \min_{i \in I(j, k + 1)} s^i_j\{w^i(k + 1)\}   \text{for all } j \neq 1 \tag{6.8}$$

where $0 < \sigma_j < \alpha_j(k) < 1 - \eta_j < 1$ for some positive constants σ_j, η_j; also, $I(j, k) = \{i: w^i_j(k) > 0\}$. The adjustment coefficients $\alpha_j(k)$ may vary from commodity to commodity and from stage to stage—no restrictions need be placed on them apart from the ones stated.

Let us now introduce the following notation:

$$a_j(k) = \max_i s^i_j\{w^i(k)\}$$

$$b_j(k) = \min_{i \in I(j, k)} s^i_j\{w^i(k)\}$$

$$D_j(k) = a_j(k) - b_j(k).$$

Thus,

$$a_j(k) - p_j(k) = \{1 - \alpha_j(k)\} D_j(k) \geqq \eta_j D_j(k) \tag{6.9}$$

and

$$p_j(k) - b_j(k) = \alpha_j(k) D_j(k) \geqq \sigma_j D_j(k). \tag{6.10}$$

Beginning with an arbitrary $\{p^0, w^{i0}\}$, (6.7) and (6.8) generate a sequence $\{p(k), w^i(k)\}$. Our objective is to analyse the behaviour of this sequence. Note, first of all, that

4: If, at some stage $\bar{k} > 1$, no trade occur; i.e., if

$$w^i(\bar{k} + 1) = w^i(\bar{k})   \text{for all } i,$$

then $\{p(\bar{k}), w^i(\bar{k})\}$ is a no-trade Walrasian equilibrium. In other words, for every j,

$$s^i_j\{w^i(\bar{k})\} \leqq p_j(\bar{k})   \text{for all } i,$$

with equality if $i \in I(j, \bar{k})$.

Proof: For any $j \neq 1$, either

$$a_j(\bar{k} + 1) \lessgtr p_j(\bar{k}) \qquad \text{(xviii)}$$

or

$$b_j(\bar{k} + 1) \gtrless p_j(\bar{k}). \qquad \text{(xix)}$$

(See, for example, the derivation of (α) in the proof of Proposition II.) But since no trade occurred, $a_j(\bar{k} + 1) = a_j(\bar{k})$ and $b_j(\bar{k} + 1) = b_j(\bar{k})$. Thus,

$$\text{(xviii)} \Rightarrow a_j(\bar{k}) - p_j(\bar{k}) \lessgtr 0 \Rightarrow D_j(\bar{k}) = 0,$$

$$\text{(xix)} \Rightarrow p_j(\bar{k}) - b_j(\bar{k}) \lessgtr 0 \Rightarrow D_j(\bar{k}) = 0,$$

and the claim follows. $\square$

Thus, unless the process comes to a halt at a Walrasian equilibrium with no trade, trade occurs at each stage k.

Notice next that

5: The sequence $\{c^i(k), C^i(k), E^i(k), p(k), w^i(k)\}$ is bounded and hence has limit points $\{\bar{c}^i, \bar{C}^i, \bar{E}^i, \bar{p}, \bar{w}^i\}$, say.

In particular, $\{w^i(k)\} \in G$: a compact set. Hence $s_j^i(k)$, being continuous, attains a maximum, $\hat{s}_j$, and a minimum, $\bar{s}_j > 0$, on G. Thus, by virtue of (6.8), $p_j(k)$ is bounded on G and is bounded away from zero, since $\bar{s}_j > 0$.

Since $\{w^i(k)\} \in G$, $U^i\{w^i(k)\} \leqslant U^i\{w^i(k + 1)\}$, it follows that $U^i(k)$ converges to $\bar{U}^i$, say. Now let $\{c^i(k), C^i(k), p(k), w^i(k)\}$ be generated by the process (6.7) and (6.8); i.e., given $\{p(k), w^i(k)\}$, $\{c^i(k), C^i(k)\}$ constitute a Dreze equilibrium. Notice that

$$-\tilde{w} \leqslant c^i(k) \leqslant 0$$

and

$$0 \leqslant C_j^i(k) \leqslant \frac{\max_k p(k)\tilde{w}}{\min_k p_j(k)} \quad \text{for all } i, j.$$

Since prices are bounded, and are bounded away from zero, $\{c^i(k), C^i(k)\}$ is bounded too. Let $E^i(k)$ denote the associated transactions. Since $\{w^i(k)\} \in G$: a compact set, $\{E^i(k)\}$ remain bounded too.

Thus, $\{c^i(k), C^i(k), E^i(k), p(k), w^i(k)\}$ remains bounded for all k, and has limit points $(\bar{c}^i, \bar{C}^i, \bar{E}^i, \bar{p}, \bar{w}^i)$, where $\bar{w}^i \in G$ and hence $\bar{w}_1^i > 0$ for all i. $\square$

Let k_r be a sub-sequence such that

$$\{c^i(k_r), C^i(k_r), E^i(k_r), p(k_r), w^i(k_r)\} \rightarrow \{\bar{c}^i, \bar{C}^i, \bar{E}^i, \bar{p}, \bar{w}^i\} \text{ as } r \rightarrow \infty.$$

6: $E^i(k) \rightarrow 0$ as $k \rightarrow \infty$ for all i.

Proof: In the sub-sequence k_r defined above, let

$$x^i(k_r) = w^i(k_r) + E^i(k_r)(= w^i(k_r + 1)).$$

Then $x^i(k_r) \to \bar{w}^i + \bar{E}^i$.

Also, since $U^i\{w^i(k)\} \to \bar{U}^i$ for all i, it follows that $U^i\{w^i(k_r)\} \to \bar{U}^i$ and $U^i\{w^i(k_r + 1)\} \to \bar{U}^i$, so that

$$U^i(\bar{w}^i) = U^i(\bar{w}^i + \bar{E}^i) = \bar{U}^i \text{ for all } i.$$

By virtue of Proposition II(i), $\bar{w}^i + \bar{E}^i$ solves the problem

$$\max U^i(x)$$

$$\text{s.t.} \quad \bar{p}x \leqslant \bar{p}\bar{w}^i$$

$$\bar{c}^i_j \leqslant x_j - \bar{w}^i_j \leqslant \bar{C}^i_j, \quad j \neq 1.$$

But since $U^i(\bar{w}^i + \bar{E}^i) = U^i(\bar{w}^i)$, $U^i(\bar{w}^i + \lambda\bar{E}^i) > U^i(\bar{w}^i)$ if $\bar{E}^i \neq 0$ for any λ, $0 < \lambda < 1$, by virtue of strict quasi-concavity and $\bar{w}^i + \bar{E}^i$ feasible: a contradiction. Hence $\bar{E}^i = 0$ for all i.

As this was established for an arbitrary limit point, the claim follows. $\square$

Thus the transactions diminish as k increases. As a consequence, we note that

7: $w^i(k + 1) - w^i(k) \to 0$ as $k \to \infty$; hence $w^i(k + t) - w^i(k) \to 0$ for any fixed t as $k \to \infty$.

Next, it follows that

8: If k_s is a sub-sequence such that, given some j, for each s, there is some i satisfying

$$c^i_j(k_s) = w^i_j(k_s + 1) - w^i_j(k_s) < C^i_j(k_s),$$

then $D_j(k_s) \to 0$ as $s \to \infty$. Further, $D_j(k_s + 1) \to 0$ as $s \to \infty$.

Proof: By the condition specified,

$$s^i_j(k_s + 1) \leqslant p_j(k_s) \text{ for all } i$$

(see condition (α) above). Therefore

$$a_j(k_s + 1) \leqslant p_j(k_s) \leqslant a_j(k_s) \text{ for all } s.$$

Since $a_j(k_s) - a_j(k_s + 1) \to 0$, by claim 7,

$$a_j(k_s) - p_j(k_s) = \{1 - \alpha_j(k_s)\} D_j(k_s) \geqslant \eta_j D_j(k_s) \geqslant 0$$

$$\Rightarrow D_j(k_s) \to 0 \quad \text{as } s \to \infty.$$

To show that $D_j(k_s + 1) \to 0$, too, assume that there is some sub-sequence $\{k_{s_t} + 1\}$ and that

$$D_j(k_{s_t} + 1) \geqslant \delta > 0$$

for $t > T$, say. Now we have, for $t > T$,

$$\delta \leqq D_j(k_{s_t} + 1) = a_j(k_{s_t} + 1) - b_j(k_{s_t} + 1)$$
$$= \{(a_j(k_{s_t} + 1) - a_j(k_{s_t}))$$
$$+ a_j(k_{s_t}) - b_j(k_{s_t})\}$$
$$+ \{b_j(k_{s_t}) - b_j(k_{s_t} + 1)\}.$$

The first term tends to zero, by virtue of claim 7 and since $D_j(k_s) \to 0$. Hence for t large enough, say $t > T_1$,

$$b_j(k_{s_t}) - b_j(k_{s_t} + 1) > \delta/2.$$

Let

$$i_1 \in I(j, k_{s_t} + 1) \quad \text{and} \quad s_j^{i_1}(k_{s_t} + 1) = b_j(k_{s_t} + 1).$$

Then for $t > T_1$, $i_1 \in I(j, k_{s_t})$ too; for otherwise,

$$w_j^{i_1}(k_{s_t}) = 0 < w_j^{i_1}(k_{s_t} + 1);$$

that is,

$$c_j^{i_1}(k_{s_t}) < w_j^{i_1}(k_{s_t} + 1) - w_j^{i_1}(k_{s_t}),$$

so that

$$b_j(k_{s_t} + 1) = s_j^{i_1}(k_{s_t} + 1) \geqq p_j(k_{s_t}) > b_j(k_{s_t}),$$

which is a contradiction. Hence

$$D_j(k_{s_t}) = a_j(k_{s_t}) - b_j(k_{s_t}) \geqq s_j^{i_1}(k_{s_t}) - b_j(k_{s_t}) \geqq 0.$$

Thus, for $t > T_1$,

$$\delta/2 < \left| b_j(k_{s_t}) - b_j(k_{s_t} + 1) \right|$$
$$\leqq \left| b_j(k_{s_t}) - s_j^{i_1}(k_{s_t}) \right| + \left| s_j^{i_1}(k_{s_t}) - s_j^{i_1}(k_{s_t} + 1) \right|,$$

and the last two terms on the right are both going to zero with t: the first because $D_j(k_s) \to 0$, and the second owing to claim 7.

So no such sub-sequence k_{s_t} can exist, and the claim follows. $\square$

We use the above to characterize the limiting configurations $\{\bar{p}, \bar{w}^i\}$. Now at any such limiting configuration, Proposition II guarantees that there are three possibilities at any j:

(a) $\bar{a}_j \leqq \bar{p}_j$;
(b) $\bar{b}_j \geqq \bar{p}_j$;
(c) $\bar{a}_j = \bar{b}_j = \bar{p}_j$;

where

$$\bar{a}_j = \max_i \bar{s}^i_j, \ \bar{b}_j = \min_{i \in I(j, \, \mathbf{w})} \bar{s}^i_j, \qquad \bar{s}^i_j = s^i_j(\bar{w}^i), \text{ and } I(j, \bar{w}) = \{i : \bar{w}^i_j > 0\}.$$

Let $\bar{D}_j = \bar{a}_j - \bar{b}_j$. Then

9: (a) $\Rightarrow$ (c).

Proof: Let

$$\{c^i(k_r), C^i(k_r), p(k_r), w^i(k_r)\} \rightarrow \{\bar{c}^i, \bar{C}^i, \bar{p}, \bar{w}^i\} \text{ as } r \rightarrow \infty.$$

Since $p_j(k_r) \leqslant a_j(k_r)$ for all r, (a) $\Rightarrow \bar{p}_j = \bar{a}_j$. But then, by (6.9),

$$a_j(k_r) - p_j(k_r) \geqslant \eta_j D_j(k_r),$$

so that $D_j(k_r) \rightarrow 0$ as $r \rightarrow \infty$.

Now note that $I(j, \bar{w}) \subseteq I(j, k_r)$ for r large enough, so that

$$a_j(k_r) \geqslant \min_{i \in I(j, \, \mathbf{w})} s^i_j(k_r) \geqslant b_j(k_r)$$

and

$$D_j(k_r) \rightarrow 0 \Rightarrow \bar{D}_j = 0.$$

Therefore condition (c) is satisfied. $\square$

10: (b) $\Rightarrow \bar{D}_j = 0$.

Proof: Suppose $\bar{D}_j = \delta > 0$ and $\bar{a}_j > \bar{b}_j \geqslant \bar{p}_j$, so that, for some i_1,

$$\bar{s}^{i_1}_j > \bar{p}_j.$$

As before, let

$$\{c^i(k_r), C^i(k_r), p(k_r), w^i(k_r)\} \rightarrow \{\bar{c}^i, \bar{C}^i, \bar{p}, \bar{w}^i\} \text{ as } r \rightarrow \infty.$$

Since $w^i(k_r + 1) \rightarrow \bar{w}^i$, by claim 7, $s^i_j(k_r + 1) \rightarrow \bar{s}^i_j$, for all i. Hence, for r large enough,

$$s^{i_1}_j(k_r + 1) > p_j(k_r).$$

Therefore

$$b_j(k_r + 1) \geqslant p_j(k_r) \qquad \text{for all } r \text{ large enough,}$$

so that

$$p_j(k_r + 1) - p_j(k_r) \geqslant p_j(k_r + 1) - b_j(k_r + 1)$$

$$\geqslant \sigma_j D_j(k_r + 1).$$

Therefore

$$\liminf_{r \rightarrow \infty} p_j(k_r + 1) \geqslant \bar{p}_j + \sigma_j \bar{D}_j,$$

since

$$\liminf_{r \to \infty} D_j(k_r + 1) \geqslant \bar{D}_j, \qquad \text{by claim 7.}$$

Repeating the above argument, and using claim 7, we may conclude that, for any fixed t,

$$\liminf_{r \to \infty} p_j(k_r + t) \geqslant \liminf_{r \to \infty} p_j(k_r + t - 1) + \sigma_j \bar{D}_j$$

$$\geqslant \bar{p}_j + t\sigma_j \bar{D}_j$$

$$\geqslant \bar{a}_j \qquad \text{for } t \text{ chosen appropriately.}$$

Therefore there is a sub-sequence $\{k_r + t\}$ with limit points $\{\hat{p}, \bar{w}^i\}$ where $\hat{p}_j \geqslant \bar{a}_j$ or (a) holds; i.e., by claim 9, $\bar{D}_j = 0$: a contradiction. So $\bar{D}_j = 0$. $\square$

Thus, at any limiting configuration $\{\bar{w}^i\}$, $\bar{D}_j = 0$ for all j; i.e.,

$$\bar{a}_j = \bar{b}_j,$$

or $\{\bar{w}^i\}$ is Pareto-optimal (see Chapter 5). Now suppose there is another limiting configuration $\{\hat{w}^i\}$, where $\bar{w}^i \neq \hat{w}^i$; then $\{\hat{w}^i\}$, too, is Pareto-optimal.

Again, recall the convergence of $U^i\{w^i(k)\}$ to $\bar{U}^i$ noted at the beginning; therefore, for each i, $U^i(\hat{w}^i) = U^i(\bar{w}^i) = \bar{U}^i$. Now strict quasi-concavity of $U^i(\cdot)$ implies that

$$U^i(\tfrac{1}{2}\hat{w}^i + \tfrac{1}{2}\bar{w}^i) > \bar{U}^i$$

for all i; moreover, $\{\tfrac{1}{2}\hat{w}^i + \tfrac{1}{2}\bar{w}^i\} \in G$, too: a contradiction to the Pareto optimality of $\{\bar{w}^i\}$ and $\{\hat{w}^i\}$.

Hence there cannot be two distinct limiting configurations. In otherwords,

11: $w^i(k) \to w^{i*}$ as $k \to \infty$ where $\{w^{i*}\}$ is Pareto-optimal.

We now conclude with an argument regarding the price sequence $p(k)$.

12: $p(k) \to p^*$ as $k \to \infty$ where $\{p^*, w^{i*}\}$ constitute a no-trade Walrasian equilibrium; i.e., for each i, w^{i*} solves

$$\max U^i(x)$$

$$\text{s.t.} \quad p^* x \leqslant p^* w^{i*}$$

$$x \geqslant 0.$$

Proof: We show first that

$$\limsup_{k \to \infty} p_j(k) = p_j^* = a_j^* = b_j^*.$$

Notice that $p_j(k) \leqslant a_j(k)$ for all k; hence

$$\limsup_{k \to \infty} p_j(k) \leqslant a_j^*.$$

First, suppose there is a sequence k_s such that at every stage there is some i satisfying

$$c_j^i(k_s) = w_j^i(k_s + 1) - w_j^i(k_s).$$

Then $s_j^i(k_s + 1) \leqslant p_j(k_s)$ for all i, for all s, so that

$$a_j(k_s + 1) \leqslant p_j(k_s)$$

and since

$$D_j(k_s) \to 0 \text{ (see claim 8)}, \ p_j(k_s) \to p_j^* = a_j^* = b_j^*.$$

If no such sequence exists, then $p_j(k + 1) - p_j(k) \geqslant 0$ for all k and, given the boundedness of prices,

$$\lim_{k \to \infty} p_j(k) = p_j^*$$

exists.

Again, since

$$p_j(k + 1) - p_j(k) \geqslant p_j(k + 1) - b_j(k + 1) \geqslant \sigma_j D_j(k + 1),$$

where the first inequality follows from the fact that

$$p_j(k) \leqslant b_j(k + 1) \qquad \text{for all } k,$$

we have $D_j(k) \to 0$ as $k \to \infty$. Hence $p_j^* = a_j^* = b_j^*$. Thus,

$$\limsup_{k \to \infty} p_j(k) = p_j^* = a_j^* = b_j^*.$$

If possible, let

$$\liminf_{k \to \infty} p_j(k) = \tilde{p}_j < a_j^*.$$

Then there is some $\varepsilon > 0$ and a sub-sequence (k_r) such that

$$p_j(k_r) \in (a_j^* - \varepsilon, \ a_j^* + \varepsilon)$$

$$p_j(k_r + 1) \notin (a_j^* - \varepsilon, \ a_j^* + \varepsilon).$$

Since

$$\limsup_{k \to \infty} p_j(k) = a_j^*, \qquad \text{for } r \text{ large enough,}$$

$$p_j(k_r + 1) \leqslant a_j^* - \varepsilon < p_j(k_r).$$

Therefore

$$\min_{i \in I(j, \, k_r + 1)} s_j^i(k_r + 1) < p_j(k_r + 1)$$

$$< \max_i s_j^i(k_r + 1) \leqslant p_j(k_r).$$

But by claim 8, $D_j(k_r + 1) \to 0$, so that

$$p_j(k_r + 1) \to a_j^*:$$

a contradiction. So no such sub-sequence can exist and our claim is established. $\square$

Collecting the above steps together, we have shown that:

The sequence $\{p(k), w^i(k)\}$ generated by (6.7) and (6.8), given conditions A, B, and C, converges to a no-trade Walrasian configuration $\{p^*, w^{i*}\}$.

BIBLIOGRAPHICAL NOTES

When compared with the topics discussed in earlier chapters, the study of non-Walrasian equilibria is of more recent vintage. Some of the most important contributions to this area appeared simultaneously, i.e. Benassy (1975), Dreze (1975), Hahn (1978), and Younes (1975). The basic point of departure is that trades may occur at non-market-clearing prices; as such, the *non-tâtonnement* processes considered by Hahn and Negishi (1962) and Uzawa (1962) are the forerunners to this area; the former contributed the short-side rule, i.e. that agents on the short side achieve their desired transactions, while the Uzawa paper contributed the property that no one should lose through trading since trading must be voluntary.

It is these two aspects that have been combined with certain other attributes to characterize the transactions that should occur at a non-Walrasian equilibrium. The text looks at these conditions as laid down by Dreze, Younes, and Benassy; the existence of a Dreze equilibrium is demonstrated in the mathematical notes to the chapter. In Sections 6.3, 6.4, and 6.7, the contribution of Silvestre (1982) is utilized to examine the interconnections between the different definitions of non-Walrasian equilibria, and it turns out that a given set of transactions may be interpreted as being obtained at either a Dreze equilibrium or a Benassy equilibrium or a Younes equilibrium. The result relating a Dreze equilibrium to a Benassy equilibrium referred to in the text may be found in Silvestre (1982); see also the paper by Grandmont (1982) in this connection. For a discussion of non-Walrasian equilibria, see the papers by Malinvaud and Younes (1977) and Grandmont and Laroque (1976).

Two topics were not discussed in this chapter. The first is the efficiency of non-Walrasian equilibrium. On this, see Hahn (1978), Dreze and Muller (1980), and Nayak (1980). The second is an explanation of why prices may turn out to be rigid. Two types of answers to this question have been provided: Negishi (1979) argues in favour of a setup involving imperfect competition with kinked demand curves, while Hahn (1978) considers the notion of a conjectural equilibrium wherein the conjectures of agents play a role to fix the prices.

Apart from the existence of a Dreze equilibrium, the mathematical notes to the chapter contain an attempt to explain how prices may be formed. This is based on an unpublished paper by Anjan Mukherji entitled 'Disequilibrium Dynamics and the Ultimate Equilibrium' (Cornell University Department of Economics, Discussion Paper no. 294). Related *non-tâtonnement* processes are contained in Hahn (1962) and

Smale (1976b). Utility-improving trades, together with price adjustment according to the level of excess demand, lead to a no-trade Walrasian configuration, together with a price system supporting it; this was shown in Mukherji (1974b). The result in the mathematical notes is similar, but there are two major differences; first, the process is discrete; second, price adjustment and transactions are related so that, in a market with constrained buyers, price is bid up, whereas in a market with constrained sellers, price is bid down. For a somewhat different point of view, see Laroque (1978).

7 Unemployment Equilibria in
an Aggregative Model

7.1 Introduction

In this chapter, we shall consider an application of the concept of a non-Walrasian equilibrium, developed in the last chapter. It is obvious that a competitive equilibrium or a Walrasian equilibrium is incapable of explaining why imbalances may appear and how such imbalances may be removed. An imbalance that is particularly difficult to analyse is that which occurs in the labour market, i.e. the phenomenon of unemployment. Now the Walrasian equilibrium denies the very existence of such a situation; it is assumed that prices are flexible and hence that they should adjust in such a manner that demand and supply match. This was the general view of unemployment: that (real) wages must be too high to sustain full employment, and that all that is required is a reduction in real wages. It was against such a view that Keynes (1936) argued.

I do not intend here to present a complete analysis of the contribution of Keynes, or indeed to provide a comprehensive account of unemployment. Instead, I shall formulate and describe a simple aggregative model and show how rigidities in prices may allow a situation of unemployment to arise. We shall then try to analyse how this unemployment may be reduced. It will turn out that the nature of unemployment depends very crucially on the kind of binding constraints in the other markets when all prices are rigid. Thus, with price rigidity, one may have a situation of unemployment that cannot be cured by the classical prescription of a reduction in real wages — in fact, this might make the situation worse — whereas the Keynesian prescription of an increase in autonomous demand will reduce unemployment through a process like the multiplier. One may label such a configuration 'Keynesian', because the Keynesian policy works. But within the context of the same model there may be another type of unemployment, arising under a different configuration of binding constraints, which may be reduced by the classical policy alone. Such a configuration would be termed 'classical'.

We shall also analyse situations where prices are flexible but the money wage rate is not. The type of unemployment that may now appear will be studied; it turns out that the Keynesian prescription is always effective, whereas the classical policy need not always succeed.

Models such as the one considered below form part of the literature that has been directed towards establishing a micro-foundation of macroeconomics. A joint product of our analysis of unemployment turns out to be an exhaustive study of the 'consumption function' (if one uses a term common in macroeconomics) or the 'effective demand for goods' (if we stick to the terminology of the last chapter). Additionally, within the context of this simple model I shall introduce the notion of a temporary equilibrium. This becomes necessary because we shall be dealing with a model where consumers worry not only about their fate today but also about their fate tomorrow. And because tomorrow's world is uncertain, individuals may wish to hold something today for which there is no immediate need but which may be used tomorrow to purchase goods. Such a commodity is 'money'.

Until now, the only aspect of money that we have been able to model is the role that the numeraire has played in earlier chapters, i.e. as a medium of exchange. But there is another aspect of money that we shall try to incorporate now, and that is as a store of value. Such an attempt would not have succeeded in our earlier context of a Walrasian equilibrium, and even here, the treatment is not quite satisfactory; the items noted in the bibliographical notes to the chapter may be consulted in this connection. Finally, this two-period model forces us to introduce the consumer's expectations regarding tomorrow, on the basis of which the consumer must act today. Thus, some quite complex issues are introduced.

7.2   The Model

We shall consider a model with three types of agents: consumers, firms, and a government. There are three commodities: output, labour, and money. Thus there are two (current) markets: one in which output is exchanged against money at a price p, and the other in which labour is exchanged against money at the wage rate w. When these prices do not clear their respective markets, we rely on the discussion of the last chapter to pin down what transactions occur. Given our discussion in Section 6.2, and also recalling the short-side rule, we may expect that transactions should be the minimum of supply and demand. Where do these supplies and demands originate? In the labour market, the supply comes from consumers and the demand from firms. In the output market, the supply is from firms, and the demand is from consumers and the government.

Before spelling out the behavioural hypothesis governing the agents, it should be pointed out that, typically, consumers maximize a utility function that depends on current consumption and future consumption subject to two sequential budget constraints: one the current period, and the other relating to the future. In the latter, expected prices and income play a role. Such an exercise is carried out in the mathematical notes to this chapter. Here we should note simply that the only commodity that individuals can store for the future is money. Output cannot be stored; thus, firms do not carry any inventories. With these remarks, we are ready to conduct a detailed examination of each agent's behaviour.

7.2.1 *The Firms*

Firms use labour to produce the output under a technology specified by the production function

$$y = f(z)$$

where y stands for output and z is amount of labour employed. $f(\cdot)$ satisfies $f'(z) > 0, f''(z) < 0$, for all z; also,

$$f(0) = 0; \quad \lim_{z \to 0} f'(z) = +\infty, \quad \lim_{z \to \infty} f'(z) = 0.$$

Given a money wage w and a price of output p, firms carry out the following maximization exercise:

$$\max \quad py - wz$$

$$\text{s.t.} \quad y \lessgtr f(z)$$

$$y \lessgtr \bar{y}$$

where $\bar{y}$ is the demand for output. Hence the *effective demand* for labour may be obtained as

$$z = \min \{h(w/p), f^{-1}(\bar{y})\} \tag{7.1}$$

where $h(w/p) = f'^{-1}(w/p)$ and $h'(\cdot) < 0$.

Thus $z = h(w/p)$ denotes the unconstrained demand for labour (the profit-maximizing response), whereas $z = f^{-1}(\bar{y})$ is the constrained demand for labour. The former is the level of employment that the firm would like to attain given w and p: in no circumstances would the firm employ more. The latter is the level of employment that the firm would make if it were constrained by the amount of output it can sell. The effective demand for labour is the minimum of these two.

Correspondingly,

$$y = \min [f\{h(w/p)\}, \bar{y}] \tag{7.2}$$

denotes the constrained supply of firms.

7.2.2 *The Consumers*

There are N identical consumers. Each has a maximum supply of labour b, which he is prepared to offer at any wage rate w. Aggregate supply of labour at any wage rate w is Nb, and is hence perfectly inelastic. In situations of unemployment, the demand for labour z is less than Nb. Define the variable

$$e = z/Nb \qquad \text{if } z < Nb$$
$$= 1 \qquad \text{otherwise.}$$

Then $e \leqslant 1$. When $e < 1$, we assume that there is uniform rationing of all households in the labour market in the sense that such households supply be (the constrained supply), and this fact is taken into consideration in determining the effective demand for output. Apart from wages wbe, each individual has an initial stock of money, m^0, and these amounts together limit the purchases of each consumer in the current markets. Regarding consumers' tastes, we postulate a utility function of the form

$$V(c_1, c_2) = v_1(c_1) + v_2(c_2)$$

where c_1 is current consumption and c_2 is future consumption. This is maximized subject to the budget constraints

$$p_1 c_1 + m = w_1 be_1 + m^0$$
$$p_2 c_2 = w_2 be_2 + m$$

where variables with subscript 2 refer to the future prices, consumption, and wages, etc. Money is the only commodity that can be stored, and the amount of money to be held depends on the household's expectations regarding the future. Given the current price p_1, the household expects a future price p_2, where $p_2 = \phi(p_1)$; moreover, given w_1, e_1, the expected future real wages is given by

$$\frac{w_2}{p_2} be_2 = \psi(w_1, p_1, e_1).$$

Thus, based on current values of w_1, p_1, and e_1, the household expects a certain level of real wages in the future; however, the expected price is completely determined by p_1. We do not require any further restriction on $\phi(\cdot)$ and $\psi(\cdot)$ for the present.

Thus, from the second budget constraint,

$$c_2 = (w_2 be_2 + m)/p_2 = \frac{\psi(w_1, e_1, p_1) + m}{\phi(p_1)}.$$

So future consumption is determined completely by current prices, the unemployment level, wages, and the current choice of money stock. Consequently,

$$V(c_1, c_2) = v_1(c_1) + v_2 \left\{ \frac{\psi(w_1, e_1, p_1) + m}{\phi(p_1)} \right\}$$

$$= u(c_1, m; p_1, w_1, e_1),$$

and thus, given p_1, w_1, e_1, the consumer chooses (c_1, m) so as to maximize the above subject to the current budget constraint

$$p_1 c_1 + m = w_1 be_1 + m^0.$$

This gives rise to a consumption function of the form

$$c_1(p_1, w_1, e_1, m^0).$$

Note that this level of consumption is based on the household being able to supply only be_1, and hence denotes the effective demand for output. We shall assume that the above consumption function has the following properties:

$$\frac{\partial c_1}{\partial p_1} < 0, \qquad \frac{\partial c_1}{\partial w_1} > 0, \qquad \frac{\partial c_1}{\partial e_1} > 0, \qquad \frac{\partial c_1}{\partial m^0} > 0.$$

The derivation of a consumption function with the above properties requires some restriction on the nature of the expectations; for the details of such an analysis, see the mathematical notes at the end of this chapter.

Aggregate consumption is now defined by

$$C_1(p_1, w_1, e_1, m^0) = N c_1(p_1, w_1, e_1, m^0), \qquad (7.3)$$

and so the above sign restrictions on partial derivatives hold for the aggregate as well.

7.2.3 The Government

The government has an autonomous demand g for output which must be met. The government buys output in exchange for money. (We could have introduced the financing of government purchases partly by taxation and partly by the creation of money without really altering any of the conclusions.) To understand more clearly the financing of government purchases, let us look at the current social accounts for this model.

Writing Y as output, C as consumption, G as autonomous demand, and W as total wages (all in money terms), we have

$$Y = C + G.$$

Define T by

$$W = C + T$$

so that $T = N(m - m^0)$: savings by the consumers. Also, the excess of Y over W, in the producers' current accounts, amounts to an increase in their money holding. Thus, total savings amount to $(Y - W) + T$, which is just sufficient to finance G or, alternatively, to absorb the change in the money supply, $\dot{M}$.

7.3   The Walrasian Temporary Equilibrium

When p_1, w_1 are fully flexible, we expect that, given the expectation functions $\phi(\cdot)$ and $\psi(\cdot)$, markets in the current period should equilibrate; i.e.,

$$g + C_1(p_1, w_1, 1, m^0) = f\{h(w_1/p_1)\} \qquad (7.4)$$

$$Nb = h(w_1/p_1). \qquad (7.5)$$

(7.4) guarantees equilibrium in the current output market and (7.5) guarantees equilibrium in the current labour market. (See the derivation of the unconstrained demand and supply in the Section 7.2.) Thus, (p_1^*, w_1^*) solving (7.4) and (7.5) constitute an equilibrium in current markets, given the expectations regarding the future. This is called a *temporary Walrasian equilibrium*. We are interested, first of all, in the question of whether such a configuration exists.

   Given the boundary condition on the production function $f(\cdot)$ there is a unique real wage r^* which satisfies (7.5) (Figure 7.1); at this real wage, the output $= y^* = f(Nb)$ is the full-employment output. Consider then the locus of (w_1, p_1) satisfying

$$C_1(w_1, p_1, 1, m^0) = y^* - g. \qquad (7.4')$$

Since $\partial C_1/\partial p_1 < 0$, $\partial C_1/\partial w_1 > 0$, assuming that

$$C_1(w_1, p_1, 1, m^0) \to 0 \quad \text{as} \quad p_1 \to \infty \text{ for any fixed } w_1$$

and

$$C_1(w_1, p_1, 1, m^0) \to \infty \quad \text{as} \quad p_1 \to 0 \text{ for any fixed } w_1,$$

we have the family of curves of $C_1(\bar{w}_1, p_1, 1, m^0)$ shown in Figure 7.2. Along each curve of the family, w_1, m^0 are both constant; as w_1 is changed, the curve shifts, and hence we generate a family of (w_1, p_1) satisfying (7.4').

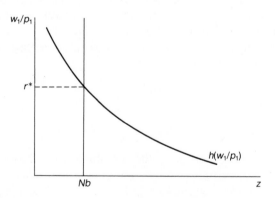

Fig. 7.1

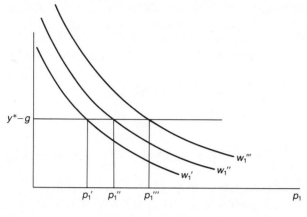

FIG. 7.2

Solving (7.4) and (7.5) amounts to locating a pair (w_1, p_1) in this family such that $w_1/p_1 = r^*$.

Notice that, when $w_1 = 0$, the (current period) budget constraint reduces to $p_1 c_1 + m = m^0$; and assuming $m^0 > 0$, there is a p_1 such that

$$C_1(p_1, 0, 1, m^0) = y^* - g,$$

provided $g < y^*$. Taking this fact into consideration, we can draw a diagram in the (w_1, p_1) plane (Figure 7.3). The r^*-ray is self-explanatory; the locus

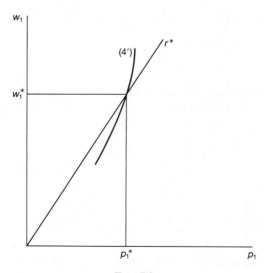

FIG. 7.3

(7.4') begins below the r^*-ray on account of considerations mentioned above. But we are still not sure of an intersection; if however $w_1/p_1 \to \bar{r} > r^*$ as $p \to \infty$, then we have an intersection as shown above. But if an intersection exists, it must be one where the slope of (7.4') is greater than r^*, i.e. where

$$-\frac{\partial C_1}{\partial p_1}(w_1^*, p_1^*, 1, m^0) > r^* \frac{\partial C_1}{\partial w_1}(w_1^*, p_1^*, 1, m^0)$$

or

$$\frac{\partial C_1}{\partial p_1}(w_1^*, p_1^*, 1, m^0) + r^* \frac{\partial C_1}{\partial w_1}(w_1^*, p_1^*, 1, m^0) < 0. \tag{7.6}$$

To understand the implications of (7.6) more clearly, we return to the question of flexibility of (w_1, p_1). This means that implicit in our analysis is an adjustment of prices in disequilibrium. In the light of our discussion in Chapter 4, we introduce the two adjustment equations:

$$\dot{p}_1 = \alpha[C_1(w_1, p_1, 1, m^0) + g - f\{h(w_1/p_1)\}],$$
$$\dot{w}_1 = \beta\{h(w_1/p_1) - Nb\},$$

where α, β are increasing, continuously differentiable, and sign-preserving functions of their arguments. Linearizing the above in a neighbourhood of (w_1^*, p_1^*), again as discussed in Chapter 4, we have

$$\dot{w}_1 = \beta'\left\{h'\frac{1}{p_1}(w_1 - w_1^*) + h'\left(\frac{-1}{p^2}\right)w_1(p_1 - p_1^*)\right\}$$

$$\dot{p}_1 = \alpha'\left\{\left(\frac{\partial C_1}{\partial w_1} - f'h'\frac{1}{p_1}\right)(w_1 - w_1^*)\right\}$$

$$+ \left(\frac{\partial C_1}{\partial p_1} + f'h'\frac{w_1}{p^2}\right)(p_1 - p_1^*)$$

where all derivatives are evaluated at (w_1^*, p_1^*). Necessary and sufficient conditions for local stability are that

$$h'\frac{1}{p_1} + \frac{\partial C_1}{\partial p_1} + f'h'\frac{w_1}{p_1^2} < 0$$

and

$$h'\frac{1}{p_1}\left(\frac{\partial C_1}{\partial p_1} + f'h'\frac{w_1}{p_1^2}\right) + h'\frac{w_1}{p_1^2}\left\{\left(\frac{\partial C_1}{\partial w_1}\right) - f'h'\frac{1}{p_1}\right\} > 0.$$

The first condition is satisfied (each term being negative), whereas the second condition reduces to

$$h' \frac{1}{p_1} \left(\frac{\partial C_1}{\partial p_1} + r^* \frac{\partial C_1}{\partial w_1} \right) > 0,$$

which is (7.6), given that $h'(\cdot) < 0$.

Thus, (7.6) is a condition for local stability, and the above analysis demonstrates that, *if a configuration* (w_1^*, p_1^*) *exists, then there must be one that is locally stable.* We shall have an opportunity to return to a condition similar to (7.6) in our discussion below.

7.4 Rigid Prices and Alternative Regimes

Consider, next, the polar opposite case where both price and money wage rate are fixed in the current markets. Thus, the markets may not clear, and we have to use our theory of Chapter 6 to pin down transactions in each market. There were three properties of such transactions, as we saw in the last chapter: (1) feasibility, (2) voluntariness, and (3) that the markets must be frictionless or, alternatively, that only one side of the market should be constrained. Thus, in any market, either only purchasers are constrained or only sellers fail to realize their desired transactions. In the present context of two markets—labour and output—we also know which agents are buyers and which are sellers. In the former market, firms are buyers and households are sellers; in the output market, on the other hand, firms are sellers and households are buyers.

Also by virtue of our earlier discussion, the pattern of effective demands and supplies are as shown in Table 7.1, where y is the amount of output sold and z the level of employment, with $e_1 = \min(1, z/Nb)$. Also, recalling that no participant can be forced to trade at more than his desired level (i.e. that trade must be voluntary), and that markets must be frictionless, realized transactions must satisfy

$$z^* = \min[(Nb), \quad \min\{f^{-1}(y^*), h(\bar{w}_1/\bar{p}_1)\}]$$
$$y^* = \min\{f(z^*), g + C_1(\bar{w}_1, \bar{p}_1, e_1^*, m^0)\}$$

where $e_1^* = \min(1, z^*/Nb)$.

The feasibility of these transactions is guaranteed by y^* and z^* being related in the manner indicated; a given y^* determines a z^* and hence e_1^*.

TABLE 7.1

	Effective supply	Effective demand
Labour market	Nb	$\min\{f^{-1}(y), h(w_1/p_1)\}$
Output market	$f(z)$	$C_1(w_1, p_1, e_1, m^0) + g$

Now z^* and e_1^* must imply the level of y^* we began with. Thus, our investigations of the last chapter play a role in determining what the logical possibilities are.

Given that there are two markets and each market may be either demand-constrained or supply-constrained by virtue of our requirement that markets be frictionless, there are four possibilities, as can be seen in Table 7.2. Notice, first of all, that the transactions in each case would be different. To see what these transactions are, consider first situation K. Here both labour and goods markets are demand-constrained. If y^*, z^* denote the transaction in each market, then our earlier discussion tells us that

$$C_1(\bar{w}_1, \bar{p}_1, e_1, m^0) + g = y^*: \quad \text{demand-constrained output market} \quad (7.7)$$

$$Nbe_1 = z^* = f^{-1}(y^*): \quad \text{demand-constrained labour market} \quad (7.8)$$

(7.7) and (7.8) together determine e_1^*, y_1^* and hence z^*. Let us rewrite (7.7) as

$$g + C_1\left(\bar{w}_1, \bar{p}_1, \frac{1}{Nb} f^{-1}(y^*), m^0\right) = y^*, \quad (7.7')$$

by using (7.8). Then we can consider Figure 7.4. Since for $y = 0$, $g + C_1(\bar{w}_1, \bar{p}_1, 0, m^0) > 0$, and since the maximum value of the left-hand side is $g + C(\bar{w}_1, \bar{p}_1, 1, m^0)$, there is the possibility of an intersection of the type drawn with $y^k \lessgtr y^f$ where y^k solves (7.7') and $y^f = f(Nb)$: the full-employment output. However, if $y^k < y^f$, unemployment appears, since then $e_1^* = (1/Nb)f^{-1}(y^k) < 1$.

Thus, at this configuration,

$$y^* = y^k = g + C_1\left(\bar{w}_1, \bar{p}_1, \frac{1}{Nb} f^{-1}(y^k), m^0\right)$$

and

$$z^* = Nbe_1^* = f^{-1}(y^k).$$

If the intersection occurs at $y^k > y^f$ (Figure 7.5), notice that no equilibrium

TABLE 7.2

	Labour market	
Output market	Demand-constrained	Supply-constrained
Demand-constrained	K	Q
Supply-constrained	C	R

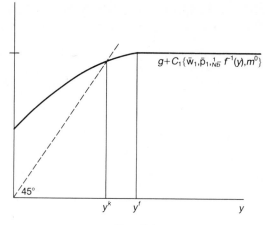

$$g + C_1\{\bar{w}_1, \bar{p}_1, \tfrac{1}{N\bar{b}} f^{-1}(y), m^0\}$$

$$45°$$

$$y^k \qquad y^f \qquad\qquad\qquad\qquad y$$

FIG. 7.4

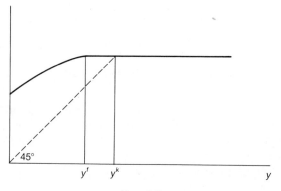

$$45°$$

$$y^f \quad y^k \qquad\qquad\qquad\qquad\qquad y$$

FIG. 7.5

exists for the system (7.7)–(7.8); i.e., g is too large to be met. Thus, the condition for there being an equilibrium is

$$g + C_1(\bar{w}_1, \bar{p}_1, 1, m^0) < y^f. \tag{7.9}$$

The border-line case when $y^k = y^f$ is not considered, since that is the Walrasian case, considered in detail in Section 7.3.

Suppose we have an equilibrium with unemployment, i.e. $y^k < y^f$; then what measures would lead to an increase in employment? Note that in Figure 7.4 an increase in g shifts the

$$g + C_1\left(\bar{w}_1, \bar{p}_1, \frac{1}{Nb}f^{-1}(y), m^0\right)$$

curve upwards and hence shifts y^k to the right—thus leading to an increase in employment. Alternatively, since

$$y^k = C_1\left(\bar{w}_1, \bar{p}_1, \frac{1}{Nb}f^{-1}(y^k), m^0\right) + g,$$

we have

$$\frac{\partial y^k}{\partial g} = \frac{\partial C_1}{\partial e_1}\left(\frac{1}{Nb}\right)\left(\frac{1}{f'(y^k)}\right)\left(\frac{\partial y^k}{\partial g}\right) + 1$$

so that, collecting terms,

$$\frac{\partial y^k}{\partial g} = 1 \bigg/ \left[1 - \frac{1}{Nb}\left(\frac{\partial C_1}{\partial e_1}\right)\left\{\frac{1}{f'(y^k)}\right\}\right]. \tag{7.10}$$

Notice that at y^k the slope of

$$g + C_1\left(\bar{w}_1, \bar{p}_1, \frac{1}{Nb}f^{-1}(y), m^0\right) > 1:$$

this follows from our discussion of the nature of the curve

$$g + C_1\left(\bar{w}_1, \bar{p}_1, \frac{1}{Nb}f^{-1}(y), m^0\right).$$

But this means that the denominator in the right-hand side of (7.10) is positive and less than unity. We can now see that (7.10) contains the well-known multiplier formula. *An increase in g leads to a magnified increase in output; and, employment is also increased.*

Consider, next, a cut in money wages as a possible measure to increase employment. Again,

$$y^k = g + C_1\left(\bar{w}_1, \bar{p}_1, \frac{1}{Nb}f^{-1}(y^k), m^0\right),$$

so that

$$\frac{\partial y^k}{\partial w_1} = \frac{\partial C_1(\cdot)}{\partial w_1} + \frac{\partial C_1(\cdot)}{\partial e_1}\left(\frac{1}{Nb}\right)\left(\frac{1}{f'(y^k)}\right)\left(\frac{\partial y^k}{\partial w_1}\right),$$

and hence

$$\frac{\partial y^k}{\partial w_1} = \frac{\partial C_1(\cdot)/\partial w_1}{1 - \frac{1}{Nb}\left\{\frac{1}{f'(y^k)}\right\}\left\{\frac{\partial C_1(\cdot)}{\partial e_1}\right\}} > 0, \tag{7.11}$$

so that a cut in money wages reduces y^k, and hence employment is reduced. Thus, hoping to reduce real wages (by a cut in $\bar{w}_1$), and so increase employment, does not work when transactions are demand-constrained. This is the situation where the Keynesian prescriptions work completely; hence the label 'K'—for Keynesian—for such cases.

Finally, it may be noted that

$$\frac{\partial C_1}{\partial y}\left(\bar{w}_1, \bar{p}_1, \frac{1}{Nb} f^{-1}(y^k), m^0\right) = \frac{1}{Nb}\left\{\frac{1}{f'(Nbe_1)}\right\}\left\{\frac{\partial C_1(\cdot)}{\partial e_1}\right\},$$

so that equation (7.10) may be represented in the more traditional form:

$$\frac{\partial y^k}{\partial g} = 1 \bigg/ \left\{1 - \frac{\partial C_1(\cdot)}{\partial y}\right\}.$$

Consider next the situation labelled 'C'; here the output market is supply-constrained and the labour market is demand-constrained. The transactions are then defined by

$$y^* = f\{h(\bar{w}_1/\bar{p}_1)\} \qquad (\leqslant g + C_1(\bar{w}_1, \bar{p}_1, e_1^*, m^0)) \qquad (7.12)$$

$$z^* = Nbe_1^* = h(\bar{w}_1/\bar{p}_1) \qquad (\leqslant Nb). \qquad (7.13)$$

It is clear that, with the presence of unemployment,

$$e^* < 1,$$

so that

$$z^* = h(\bar{w}_1/\bar{p}_1) < Nb.$$

Again, since the firms are carrying out their unconstrained profit-maximizing plans given $(\bar{w}_1, \bar{p}_1)$, changing g (the Keynesian prescription) would have no effect. The only way to reduce unemployment is to lower the real wages; in other words, the so-called 'classical' prescription will eliminate unemployment. Hence the label 'C' for the situation when the labour market is demand-constrained and the goods market is supply-constrained.

Situation R is the one where both the labour market and the goods market are supply-constrained. Thus transactions are

$$z^* = Nb \qquad (\leqslant h(\bar{w}_1/\bar{p}_1)) \qquad (7.14)$$

and

$$y^* = y^f = f(Nb) \qquad (\leqslant g + C_1(\bar{w}_1, \bar{p}_1, 1, m^0)). \qquad (7.15)$$

There is no unemployment, and firms are constrained on both markets in the sense that, had there been a larger labour supply, the firms would have produced more and sold more. Notice that the realized consumption is

$$C_1^* = \max(y^f - g, 0).$$

Given that there is a latent or hidden demand for output in such situations, there is a tendency for the price to rise if it is allowed to. In the literature, such a configuration has been called one of repressed inflation, hence the letter 'R'.

Finally, consider Q, where the labour market is supply-constrained and the goods market is demand-constrained. To see what this means, note that in such a situation transactions should be

$$z^* = Nb \qquad (\leqslant h(\bar{w}_1/\bar{p}_1)) \qquad (7.16)$$

and

$$y^* = C_1(\bar{w}_1, \bar{p}_1, 1, m^0) + g \quad (\leqslant f\{h(\bar{w}_1/\bar{p}_1)\}). \qquad (7.17)$$

But then, since $z^* = Nb$, this implies that

$$y^* = f(Nb) = y^f = C_1(\bar{w}_1, \bar{p}_1, 1, m^0) + g$$

and may appear only in very special circumstances. It cannot be possible, for example, if (7.9) holds.

Both R and Q (if it exists) have one thing in common, and that is that there can be no unemployment in such situations. In addition, comparing conditions (7.14), (7.15), (7.16), and (7.17) with (7.4) and (7.5), one may note that R and Q degenerate to the Walrasian configuration. Since we wish to focus attention on equilibria with unemployment, we shall concentrate on the other two cases. In both configurations, labelled 'K' and 'C', there is unemployment. But the nature of unemployment in K is quite distinct from the nature of unemployment in C. In situation K firms are rationed in the output market, encountering a demand constraint there, whereas in C, firms are not rationed at all: they attain their profit-maximizing transactions in both markets. The difference in policy prescriptions in the two cases has usually been attributed to the difference in the status of firms noted above. The Keynesian prescription works in K because there is not enough demand, and so increasing the autonomous component of demand leads to increased output and employment. In C, on the other hand, real wages are too high, so a cut in money wages serves to stimulate output and employment. Therefore it would seem that, in order to model an unemployment equilibrium that may be cured by Keynesian prescriptions, one needs to have firms constrained. But this predominant view is not quite accurate, as we shall see in the next section.

The alternative regimes have been conveniently exhibited in terms of Figure 7.6. The r^*-ray denotes the unique real wage at which there is full employment. W denotes the *unique* Walrasian equilibrium (Section 7.3). The upward-sloping curve from W denotes the locus of (w_1, p_1) such that

$$g + C\left(w_1, p_1, \frac{1}{Nb} h(w_1/p_1), m^0\right) = f\{h(w_1/p_1)\}. \qquad (7.18)$$

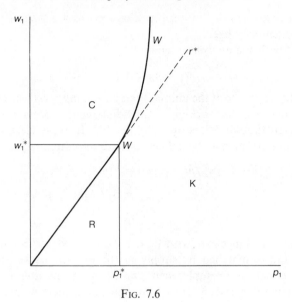

FIG. 7.6

For such a classification of the (w_1, p_1) space to be valid, there are some implicit assumptions:

(i) the slope of the locus (7.16), to equilibrate the goods market, a higher p_1 should be associated with a higher w_1 (if and when such equilibria exist). This aspect is discussed in the mathematical notes to this chapter.

(ii) W, the Walrasian configuration, is unique; in the absence of uniqueness, the neat division of the w_1–p_1 space into regions C, K, etc., disappear.

7.5 Flexible Prices and Rigid Wages

In contrast to the earlier two sections—both extremes—we shall consider here an intermediate situation where prices are flexible but money wages are not. There is ample evidence in Keynes (1936) to support the view that he considered such a situation. In fact, Keynesians would argue that there is no rigidity at all in Keynes's framework. In the light of our earlier discussion of the configurations C and K in the preceding section, we wish now to investigate whether the rationing of firms is crucial for an unemployment equilibrium to be Keynesian in nature. In fact, we shall see below that, even if firms are not rationed, there may be an unemployment configuration that is Keynesian; i.e., unemployment may be reduced by an increase in autonomous demand, and a cut in money wages need not generate employment. We shall carry out our investigations in a setup where prices are flexible but money wages are exogenously fixed.

To proceed with the analysis, assume that

$$w_1 = \bar{w}_1 > w_1^*$$

where w_1^* is the wage rate at the unique Walrasian configuration. This may be enough to jeopardize the working of the adjustment process referred to in Section 7.3, even though prices are fully flexible. In these circumstances, a 'temporary equilibrium' may be defined as a configuration $(\bar{p}_1, \bar{e}_1)$ satisfying

$$g + C_1(\bar{w}_1, \bar{p}_1, \bar{e}_1, m^0) = f\{h(\bar{w}_1/\bar{p}_1)\}, \qquad (7.19)$$

$$\bar{e}_1 = (1/Nb)h(\bar{w}_1/\bar{p}_1), \qquad (7.20)$$

$$\bar{e}_1 \lessgtr 1. \qquad (7.20a)$$

If such a configuration exists with $\bar{e}_1 < 1$, then (7.19) assures us that the effective demand is matched by supply in the output market, and in the labour market there is unemployment, with firms being able to hire their profit-maximizing demand. At such a configuration, there would be

(a) no rationing of firms;
(b) a rationing of households' supply of labour ($\bar{e}_1 b$ instead of b), although their constrained demands for output would be met.

To understand the nature of the unemployment equilibrium, let us examine Figure 7.7. The curve ABC depicts $e_1 = \min\{h(\bar{w}_1/p_1), 1\}$; on the AB portion, both (7.20) and (7.20a) are met so that

$$\left.\frac{de_1}{dp_1}\right|_{AB} = -\frac{1}{Nb}h'(\cdot)\frac{\bar{w}_1}{p_1^2} > 0.$$

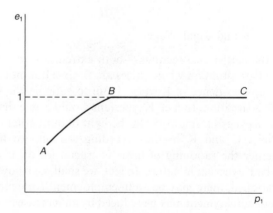

Fig. 7.7

Rewriting (7.19) as

$$\gamma_g(p_1, e_1) = C_1(\bar{w}_1, p_1, e_1, m^0) + g - f\{h(\bar{w}_1/p_1)\} = 0,$$

we have, along $\gamma_g(\cdot) = 0$, writing C_{1p} for $\partial C_1/\partial p_1$ and C_{1e} for $\partial C_1/\partial e_1$,

$$\left.\frac{de_1}{dp_1}\right|_{\gamma_g=0} = -\frac{C_{1p} + f'h'(\bar{w}_1/p_1^2)}{C_{1e}} > 0,$$

from the restrictions on slopes in Section 7.2. Thus $\gamma_g(\cdot) = 0$ is upward-rising too, and it may intersect ABC at

(a) a point below B: an unemployment equilibrium;
(b) the point B: even with rigidity in w_1, price flexibility guarantees that (7.4) and (7.5) hold (see Section 7.3): the Walrasian configuration;
(c) between B and C: (7.19) and (7.20a) are satisfied, and in particular (7.20a) holds with an equality, i.e. no unemployment, but firms are constrained to sell the full employment output; or, finally,
(d) no point at all; i.e., $\gamma_g(\cdot) = 0$ lies wholly above or below ABC.

We shall neglect cases (b) and (c), noting them as logical possibilities, and confine our attention to cases (a) and (d). For this purpose, let us write (7.19) as

$$X(p_1, e_1) = g \qquad (7.21)$$

where

$$X(p_1, e_1) = f\{h(\bar{w}_1/p_1)\} - C_1(\bar{w}_1, p_1, e_1, m^0).$$

Note that

$$\frac{\partial X(\cdot)}{\partial p_1} > 0, \quad \frac{\partial X(\cdot)}{\partial e_1} < 0,$$

and, for any given $\bar{e}_1$, $X(p_1, \bar{e}_1) \to \infty$ as $p_1 \to \infty$;

$$X(p_1, \bar{e}_1) \lessgtr g \,\forall\, p_1 \lessgtr \tilde{p}_1$$

where $\tilde{p}_1$ satisfies $f\{h(\bar{w}_1/\tilde{p}_1)\} = g$.

Thus, for any $\bar{e}_1$, there is a unique p_1, $p_1(\bar{e}_1)$ satisfying (7.21). By varying $\bar{e}_1$, we generate the locus $\{p_1(e_1), e_1\}$ which is the locus $\gamma_g(\cdot) = 0$. Also, there is $p_1^0 > 0$ such that

$$X(p_1^0, 0) = g$$

where $p_1^0 \gtrless \tilde{p}_1$. Moreover, along AB, $e_1 \to 0 \Rightarrow p_1 \to 0$, it follows that $\gamma_g(\cdot) = 0$ must lie below AB for small e_1; i.e., in case (d), the only possibility is given in Figure 7.8.

Consider then an employment level, e_1; for this to be sustained in the labour market, p_1 is required, whereas in order to clear the output market,

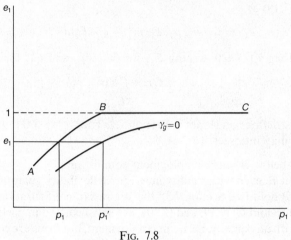

Fig. 7.8

$p_1'(>p_1)$ is required. Thus, at (p_1, e_1), the effective demand is $g - X(p_1, e_1) > 0$, and this is true for every (p_1, e_1) on AB.

We specified at the beginning that prices are flexible; but to explain what this means, we need an adjustment on prices. It is natural, in such circumstances, to use the effective excess demand to define

$$\dot{p}_1 = \theta\{g - X(p_1, e_1)\} \qquad (7.22)$$

where

$$e_1 = \min\left\{1, \frac{1}{Nb}h(\bar{w}_1, p_1)\right\}$$

and $\theta(\cdot)$ is an increasing sign-preserving function of its argument. Additionally, we are assuming that (7.22) is such that p_1 adjusts instantaneously whenever there is excess demand. In situations such as that depicted in Figure 7.8, p_1 rises without limit; e_1, of course, reaches 1 and no unemployment exhibits itself.

Alternatively, case (d) may be analysed as follows. At B in Figure 7.8, let us say that $e_1 = 1$, $p_1 = \hat{p}_1$, and

$$y = f\{h(\bar{w}_1/\hat{p}_1)\} = y^f,$$

the full-employment output. Moreover, from the figure we must have

$$g > y^f - C_1(\bar{w}_1, \hat{p}_1, 1, m^0),$$

so that one may consider g to be too large. Consequently, so long as

$$0 < g < y^f - C_1(\bar{w}_1, \hat{p}_1, 1, m^0), \qquad (7.23)$$

we are assured of an unemployment equilibrium $(\bar{p}_1, \bar{e}_1)$. Hence (7.23) is sufficient to imply that case (a) prevails; i.e., we have an unemployment equilibrium $(\bar{p}_1, \bar{e}_1)$ such that

$$\text{slope of } \gamma_g(\cdot) = 0|_{\text{at } (\bar{p}_1, \bar{e}_1)} > \text{slope of } AB|_{\text{at } (\bar{p}_1, \bar{e}_1)};$$

i.e.,

$$-\left.\frac{C_{1p} + f'h'\bar{w}_1/\bar{p}_1^2}{C_{1e}}\right|_{\text{at } (\bar{p}_1, \bar{e}_1)} > -\frac{1}{Nb}h'\frac{\bar{w}_1}{\bar{p}_1}\left(\frac{\bar{w}_1}{\bar{p}_1^2}\right)$$

or

$$h'(\cdot)\frac{\bar{w}_1}{\bar{p}_1^2}\left\{\frac{1}{Nb}C_{1e}(\cdot) - \frac{\bar{w}_1}{\bar{p}_1}\right\} - C_{1p}(\cdot)\Big|_{\text{at } (\bar{p}_1, \bar{e}_1)} > 0 \qquad (7.24)$$

This slope condition is guaranteed if an unemployment equilibrium exists because $\gamma_g(\cdot) = 0$ is below AB when e_1 is small. We may check that (7.24) guarantees the local stability of (7.22) by linearizing $\theta(\cdot)$ in a neighbourhood of $(\bar{p}_1, \bar{e}_1)$.

Given that we have established conditions under which an unemployment equilibrium exists, we now wish to determine how shifts in parameters g and $\bar{w}_1$ change the configuration $(\bar{p}_1, \bar{e}_1)$. First of all, we consider

Variations in g
At $(\bar{p}_1, \bar{e}_1)$ we have, from (7.19) and (7.20),

$$\bar{e}_1 = \frac{1}{Nb}h\left(\frac{\bar{w}_1}{\bar{p}_1}\right)$$

and

$$g + C_1(\bar{w}_1, \bar{p}_1, \bar{e}_1, m^0) = f\{h(\bar{w}_1/\bar{p}_1)\}.$$

From the above, we have

$$\frac{\partial e_1}{\partial g} = -\frac{1}{Nb}h'(\cdot)\frac{\bar{w}_1}{\bar{p}_1^2}\left(\frac{\partial p_1}{\partial g}\right)$$

and

$$1 + \frac{\partial C_1}{\partial p_1}\left(\frac{\partial p_1}{\partial g}\right) + \frac{\partial C_1}{\partial e_1}\left(\frac{\partial e_1}{\partial g}\right) = -f'h'\frac{\bar{w}_1}{\bar{p}_1^2}\left(\frac{\partial p_1}{\partial g}\right),$$

where all partial derivatives are evaluated at $(\bar{p}_1, \bar{e}_1)$. Thus, substituting and collecting terms,

$$\frac{\partial p_1}{\partial g} = 1\Big/\left[h'(\cdot)\frac{\bar{w}_1}{\bar{p}_1^2}\left\{\frac{1}{Nb}C_{1e}(\cdot) - \frac{\bar{w}_1}{\bar{p}_1}\right\} - C_{1p}(\cdot)\right] > 0 \qquad (7.25)$$

by virtue of (7.24). Hence $\partial e_1/\partial g > 0$ too, and since $\bar{y}_1 = f\{h(\bar{w}_1/\bar{p}_1)\}$, we have

$$\frac{\partial y_1}{\partial g} = \frac{-f'h'(\bar{w}_1/\bar{p}_1^2)}{-f'h'(\bar{w}_1/\bar{p}^2) - \{C_{1p} - h'(\cdot)(\bar{w}_1/\bar{p}_1^2)(1/Nb)C_{1e}\}} > 0,$$

$$= 1/(1-\eta), \text{ say, where}$$

$$\eta = \frac{\{C_{1p} - h'(\bar{w}_1/\bar{p}_1^2)(1/Nb)C_{1e}\}}{-f'h'(\bar{w}_1/\bar{p}_1^2)},$$

which yields a multiplier-type formula adjusted for price increase, since $0 < \eta < 1$ from (7.24).

Next, we consider

Variations in w_1

From (7.20), we have

$$\frac{\partial e_1}{\partial w_1} = \frac{1}{Nb} h'(\cdot)\frac{1}{\bar{p}_1^2}\left(\bar{p}_1 - \bar{w}_1 \frac{\partial p_1}{\partial w_1}\right),$$

and from (7.19),

$$\frac{\partial C_1(\cdot)}{\partial p_1}\left(\frac{\partial p_1}{\partial w_1}\right) + \frac{\partial C_1(\cdot)}{\partial w_1} + \frac{\partial C_1(\cdot)}{\partial e_1}\left(\frac{\partial e_1}{\partial w_1}\right) = f'h'(\cdot)\frac{1}{\bar{p}_1^2}\left(\bar{p}_1 - \bar{w}_1 \frac{\partial p_1}{\partial w_1}\right),$$

where, as before, all derivatives are evaluated at $(\bar{p}_1, \bar{e}_1, \bar{w}_1, m^0)$. Substituting for $\partial e_1/\partial w_1$, we obtain

$$\frac{\partial p_1}{\partial w_1} = \frac{\dfrac{\partial C_1(\cdot)}{\partial w_1} + \dfrac{h'(\cdot)}{\bar{p}_1}\left\{\dfrac{\partial C_1(\cdot)}{\partial e_1}\left(\dfrac{1}{Nb}\right) - \dfrac{\bar{w}_1}{\bar{p}_1}\right\}}{h'(\cdot)\dfrac{\bar{w}_1}{\bar{p}_1^2}\left\{\dfrac{\partial C_1(\cdot)}{\partial e_1}\left(\dfrac{1}{Nb}\right) - \dfrac{\bar{w}_1}{\bar{p}_1}\right\} - \dfrac{\partial C_1(\cdot)}{\partial p_1}},$$

where the denominator is positive, by virtue of (7.24). Thus, $\partial p_1/\partial w_1 > 0$ if and only if

$$\frac{\partial C_1(\cdot)}{\partial w_1} + \frac{h'(\cdot)}{\bar{p}_1}\left\{\frac{\partial C_1(\cdot)}{\partial e_1}\left(\frac{1}{Nb}\right) - \frac{\bar{w}_1}{\bar{p}_1}\right\} > 0. \tag{7.26}$$

Regarding (7.26), note that

$$\frac{\partial C_1(\cdot)}{\partial e_1}\left(\frac{1}{Nb}\right) - \frac{\bar{w}_1}{\bar{p}_1} = \frac{\bar{w}_1}{\bar{p}_1}\left\{\frac{\partial C_1(\cdot)}{\partial e_1}\left(\frac{1}{Nb}\right)\left(\frac{1}{f'(Nbe_1)}\right) - 1\right\}$$

$$= \frac{\bar{w}_1}{\bar{p}_1}\left\{\frac{\partial C_1(\cdot)}{\partial y_1} - 1\right\},$$

as noted in Section 7.4. Thus

$$0 < \frac{\partial C_1(\cdot)}{\partial y_1} < 1$$

is sufficient for (7.26) to hold. But even if it holds, the sign of $\partial e_1 / \partial w_1$ is not determined, since $\partial e_1 / \partial w_1 < 0$ if and only if

$$\bar{p}_1 - \bar{w}_1 \, (\partial p_1 / \partial w_1) > 0,$$

since $h'(\cdot) < 0$; i.e.,

$$1 > \frac{\bar{w}_1}{\bar{p}_1} \left(\frac{\partial p_1}{\partial w_1} \right).$$

From the expression for $\partial p_1 / \partial w_1$, note that

$$\frac{\bar{w}_1}{\bar{p}_1} \left(\frac{\partial p_1}{\partial w_1} \right) = \frac{C_{1w} + \dfrac{h'(\cdot)}{\bar{p}_1} \left(\dfrac{1}{Nb} C_{1e} - \dfrac{\bar{w}_1}{\bar{p}_1} \right)}{-C_{1p} \dfrac{\bar{p}_1}{\bar{w}_1} + \dfrac{h'(\cdot)}{\bar{p}_1} \left(\dfrac{1}{Nb} C_{1e} - \dfrac{\bar{w}_1}{\bar{p}_1} \right)},$$

So that, given (7.26),

$$1 > \frac{\bar{w}_1}{\bar{p}_1} \left(\frac{\partial p_1}{\partial w_1} \right) \Leftrightarrow C_{1w} < - C_{1p} \left(\frac{\bar{p}_1}{\bar{w}_1} \right)$$

or

$$\bar{w}_1 C_{1w}(\bar{w}_1, \bar{p}_1, \bar{e}_1, m^0) + \bar{p}_1 C_{1p}(\bar{w}_1, \bar{p}_1, \bar{e}_1, m^0) < 0. \tag{7.27}$$

We can see that (7.27) is very much like condition (7.6) derived in Section 7.3; that was a similar expression, evaluated at a Walrasian configuration (w_1^*, p_1^*); but (7.27) is, as indicated, at the unemployment equilibrium $(\bar{w}_1, \bar{p}_1)$ where $\bar{e}_1 < 1$. Again, whereas we could demonstrate the validity of (7.6), we cannot, in general, demonstrate the validity of (7.27).

We can therefore conclude that

(a) *an increase in g raises the output through a multiplier type process and hence reduces unemployment;* and
(b) *a cut in $\bar{w}_1$ may not succeed in reducing unemployment.*

Thus, even in a situation where firms are not rationed, an unemployment equilibrium may be possible. Moreover, this unemployment may be reduced by an increase in the autonomous demand; a cut in money wages need not be effective in curbing unemployment.

Before passing on to other things, let us briefly consider a situation where (7.27) holds. As is discussed in the mathematical notes to this chapter, under a certain extreme form of expectation, $\psi(w_1, p_1, e_1) = 0$ and $\varphi(p_1) = p_1$, the consumer's utility function reduces to $u(c_1, m/p_1)$. These expectations are extreme because, regardless of what happens in the current period, the consumer expects to be unemployed the next period and also expects the same price to rule. Thus the consumer's problem reduces to

$$\max \quad u(c_1, m/p_1)$$

$$\text{s.t.} \quad c_1 + m/p_1 = m^0/p_1 + (w_1 be_1)/p_1.$$

Dropping the subscripts 1 for the present, note that, if $c(w, p, e, m^0)$ solves the above, then at any e, changing m^0, p, and w in the same proportion does not alter the budget line; hence at any e,

$$c_w w + c_p w + c_p p + c_{m^0} m^0 = 0$$

for all (w, p, m^0). It is also clear that increasing m^0 with everything else fixed enlarges the budget set, so that, assuming that the consumption good is non-inferior, we have

$$c_{m^0} > 0.$$

Consequently,

$$c_w w + c_p p < 0$$

at any (w, p, e, m^0), which implies (7.27).

That our assertions regarding the budget line are correct may be seen from the budget line drawn in Figure 7.9. Thus the relative price between c and real balances is always fixed at unity. Note that

$$\frac{m^0}{p} + \frac{w}{p} be$$

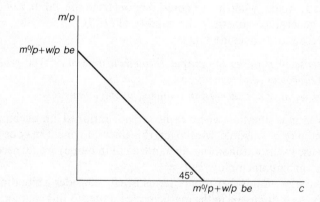

FIG. 7.9

is homogeneous of degree zero in (w, p, m^0), given any e. Moreover, increasing m^0 shifts the budget line out with the same slope.

7.6   An Alternative Formulation

In this section, we wish to make one change from our assumptions of Section 7.5. This has to do with the distribution of profits. In Section 7.2, where the model is described, it was seen that profits are not distributed to households; in fact, we assumed that all profits are saved. Thus it is as if there were two types of income-earners—wage-earners and profit-earners—and the latter do not consume. We now make the assumption that all profits are distributed, so that income in the current period for households (at the aggregate level) amounts to wages plus profits; i.e.,

$$w(Nbe_1) + \{py - w(Nbe_1)\} = py.$$

So, using the identical consumers' argument, we may consider the aggregate problem as

$$\max \quad U(C_1, m, p_1, y_1)$$

$$\text{s.t.} \quad p_1 C_1 + m = m^0 + p_1 y_1$$

where y_1 is current production. Such a problem yields the function $C_1(p_1, y_1, m^0)$; the details of such a derivation and the properties of such a function are contained in the mathematical notes to this chapter.

It may be tempting to claim that

$$C_{1p} < 0. \tag{7.28}$$

However, as we show in the mathematical notes, this term is, in general, of ambiguous sign, so that (7.28) takes on a special restrictive significance. To examine the implications of (7.28), the equilibrium with rigid wages is now given by

$$C_1(p_1, y_1, m^0) + g = y_1 \tag{7.29}$$

$$y_1 = f\{h(\bar{w}_1/p_1)\}. \tag{7.30}$$

Under (7.28), there may be an unemployment equilibrium $(\bar{p}_1, \bar{y}_1)$ with $\bar{y}_1 < y^f$, as shown in Figure 7.10. The nature of the curves in the figure follows, since

$$\left.\frac{dy_1}{dp_1}\right|_{\text{along (7.29)}} = \frac{C_{1p}}{1 - C_{1y}} < 0, \quad \text{under (7.28)}$$

and

$$\left.\frac{dy_1}{dp_1}\right|_{\text{along (7.30)}} = f'h'(\cdot)\frac{-\bar{w}_1}{p_1^2} > 0.$$

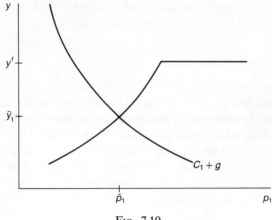

F<small>IG</small>. 7.10

However, given that (7.28) may not hold, in general, it could be that, at the solution $(\bar{p}_1, \bar{y}_1)$ of (7.29) and (7.30), $C_{1p}(\cdot) > 0$. Then the diagram would change to that of Figure 7.11.

To understand why the intersection should be as depicted in Figure 7.11, we return to the question of price flexibility. This should be interpreted to mean that price adjusts rapidly, so that (7.29) is guaranteed. To explain how prices adjust when there is disequilibrium in the output market, we choose, as before, the simple

$$\dot{p}_1 = \alpha[C_1\{p_1, s(p_1); m^0\} - s(p_1) + g]$$

where $s(p_1) = f\{h(\bar{w}_1/p_1)\}$ and $\alpha(\cdot)$ is some increasing sign-preserving func-

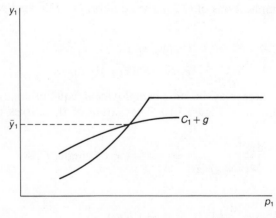

F<small>IG</small>. 7.11

tion. If there is an equilibrium $\bar{p}_1$ such that $s(\bar{p}_1) < y^f$, we have, on linearizing the above in a neighbourhood of $\bar{p}_1$,

$$\dot{p}_1 = \alpha'[C_{1p}(\cdot) + C_{1y}(\cdot)f'\{h'(\cdot)\}(-\bar{w}_1/p_1^2)$$
$$- f'h'(\cdot)(-\bar{w}_1/p_1^2)](p_1 - \bar{p}_1),$$

so that, for stability, we require

$$C_{1p}(\cdot) + f'h'(\cdot)(\bar{w}_1/\bar{p}_1^2)\{1 - C_{1y}(\cdot)\} < 0 \qquad (7.31)$$

where all derivatives are evaluated at $(\bar{p}_1, \bar{y}_1)$.

Notice that $(7.28) \Rightarrow (7.31)$ holds since the term in braces is positive and $h'(\cdot) < 0$; when (7.28) is violated, we note that

$$(7.31) \Rightarrow \frac{C_{1p}(\cdot)}{1 - C_{1y}(\cdot)} < -f'h'(\cdot)(\bar{w}_1/\bar{p}_1^2),$$

which implies that the relative positions of the two curves should be as depicted in Figure 7.11. Thus, whether (7.28) holds or not, (7.31) *should hold at* $(\bar{p}_1, \bar{y}_1)$.

Returning to (7.29) and (7.30), investigating the effects on $(\bar{p}_1, \bar{y}_1)$ of a variation in $\bar{w}_1$, we have

$$C_{1p}\frac{\partial p_1}{\partial \bar{w}_1} + C_{1y}\frac{\partial y_1}{\partial \bar{w}_1} = \frac{\partial y_1}{\partial \bar{w}_1}$$

and

$$\frac{\partial y_1}{\partial \bar{w}_1} = f'h'\frac{1}{\bar{p}_1^2}\left(\bar{p}_1 - \bar{w}_1\frac{\partial p_1}{\partial \bar{w}_1}\right)$$

where all derivatives are evaluated at $(\bar{p}_1, \bar{y}_1)$.

We may now note that

$$\frac{\partial y_1}{\partial \bar{w}_1} = C_{1p}\frac{f'h'(1/\bar{p}_1)}{C_{1p} + f'h'(\bar{w}_1/\bar{p}_1^2)(1 - C_{1y})}$$
$$= C_{1p} \text{ (a positive term)},$$

by virtue of (7.31) and since $f'h' < 0$. And since $C_{1p}(\cdot)$ is of ambiguous sign, so too is $\partial y_1/\partial \bar{w}_1$. Consequently, there is no guarantee that a cut in money wages will work to reduce unemployment.

Note that (7.28) guarantees that a cut in money wages will have an expansionary effect.

Considering the effect on unemployment of a variation in g, we have, from (7.29) and (7.30),

$$C_{1p}\frac{\partial p_1}{\partial g} + C_{1y}\frac{\partial y_1}{\partial g} + 1 = \frac{\partial y_1}{\partial g}$$

and

$$\frac{\partial y_1}{\partial g} = -f'h'\frac{\bar{w}_1}{\bar{p}_1^2}\left(\frac{\partial p_1}{\partial g}\right).$$

Hence, from the two expressions, we have

$$\frac{\partial y_1}{\partial g}\left\{1 - C_{1y} + \frac{C_{1p}}{f'h'(\bar{w}_1/\bar{p}_1^2)}\right\} = 1$$

or

$$\frac{\partial y_1}{\partial g} = \frac{1}{(1 - C_{1y}) + \dfrac{C_{1p}}{f'h'(\bar{w}_1/\bar{p}_1^2)}} = \frac{f'h'\bar{w}_1/\bar{p}_1^2}{(1 - C_{1y})f'h'(\bar{w}_1/\bar{p}_1^2) + C_{1p}} > 0$$

by virtue of (7.31), and since $f'h' < 0$. In fact, we have a multiplier-type formula which is adjusted for price change; an increase in g, therefore, would raise output y_1 and hence employment.

Thus the results of Section 7.5 carry over to the present formulation as well. In conclusion, we may sum up as follows.

(a) With rigidity of price and money wages, two types of unemployment equilibria may emerge. In one type, firms may be constrained. This situation of unemployment may be tackled by raising the level of autonomous demand g; reducing money wages makes the situation worse. In the other type of unemployment equilibrium, reducing money wages reduces unemployment, an increase in g has no effect.
(b) With money wage rigid and prices flexible, there is only one possible type of unemployment equilibrium: to increase employment, a sure method is an increase in g. A cut in money wages leads to ambiguous results.

MATHEMATICAL NOTES

7.7　Properties of the Consumption Function

Consider the following problem:

$$\max \quad V(c_1, c_2) = v_1(c_1) + v_2(c_2)$$
$$\text{s.t.} \quad p_1c_1 + m = w_1be_1 + m^0$$
$$p_2c_2 = w_2be_2 + m$$

where c_1 = present consumption
c_2 = future consumption
p_1 = present price
p_2 = future price

w_1 = present wage rate
w_2 = future wage rate
e_1 = present level of employment
e_2 = future level of employment
m^0 = initial stock of money
m = stock of money at the end of the present period

$\phi : (w_1, p_1, e_1) \to (w_2, p_2, e_2)$, the expectations function, generates, for any configuration of (w_1, p_1, e_1), an expectation regarding the future value of these parameters; thus,

$$w_2 = \phi_1(w_1, p_1, e_1)$$

$$p_2 = \phi_2(w_1, p_1, e_1)$$

$$e_2 = \phi_3(w_1, p_1, e_1),$$

and we shall assume that $\phi_i(\cdot)$ are differentiable functions. Specific assumptions regarding signs of derivatives will be introduced later. Regarding the utility functions, we shall assume $v_i' > 0$, $v_i'' < 0$, $i = 1, 2$. Thus,

$$c_2 = \frac{w_2 b e_2 + m}{p_2}$$

$$= \frac{\phi_1(\cdot) b \phi_3(\cdot) + m}{\phi_2(\cdot)} = \frac{\psi(\cdot) + m}{\phi_2(\cdot)}$$

where $\psi(w_1, p_1, e_1) = \phi_1(w_1, p_1, e_1)$. $\phi_3(w_1, p_1, e_1) = b w_2 e_2$: the expected wage income. Thus

$$V(c_1, c_2) = v_1(c_1) + v_2 \left(\frac{\psi(\cdot) + m}{\phi_2(\cdot)} \right)$$

$$= U(c_1, m; w_1, p_1, e_1),$$

which depends on current-period quantities alone. So the problem reduces to

$$\max \quad U(c_1, m; w_1, p_1, e_1)$$

$$\text{s.t.} \quad p_1 c_1 + m = w_1 b e_1 + m^0.$$

Given p_1, e_1, m^0, and w_1, if c_1^*, m^* provide an interior solution to the above problem, there is λ^* such that

$$\left. \begin{array}{l} \dfrac{\partial U^*}{\partial c_1} = U_c^* = \lambda^* p_1, \\[2ex] \dfrac{\partial U^*}{\partial m} = U_m^* = \lambda^*, \\[2ex] p_1 c_1^* + m^* = w_1 b e_1 + m^0. \end{array} \right\} \qquad (7.32)$$

and

The asterisks denote that all partial derivatives are evaluated at (c_1^*, m^*). If (c_1^*, m^*) and λ^* satisfy (7.32), and in addition if

$$\det \begin{pmatrix} U_{cc}^* & U_{cm}^* & -p_1 \\ U_{mc}^* & U_{mm}^* & -1 \\ -p_1 & -1 & 0 \end{pmatrix} > 0, \tag{7.33}$$

where $U_{cc}^* = \partial^2 U^*/\partial c_1^2$, $U_{mc}^* = U_{cm}^* = \partial^2 U^*/\partial m \partial c_1$, and $U_{mm}^* = \partial^2 U^*/\partial m^2$, then (c_1^*, m^*) solves the problem. We shall assume that both (7.32) and (7.33) hold. Thus, we have the functions

$$\left. \begin{aligned} c_1^* &= c_1(w_1, p_1, e_1, m^0) \\ m^* &= (w_1, p_1, e_1, m^0), \end{aligned} \right\} \tag{7.34}$$

and we wish to determine signs of the partial derivatives of the former function: the consumption function. To obtain this information, differentiate (7.32) to obtain

$$\begin{pmatrix} U_{cc}^* & U_{cm}^* & -p_1 \\ U_{mc}^* & U_{mm}^* & -1 \\ -p_1 & -1 & 0 \end{pmatrix} \begin{pmatrix} dc_1 \\ dm \\ d\lambda \end{pmatrix} = \begin{pmatrix} (\lambda^* - U_{cp}^*)dp_1 - U_{cw}^* dw_1 - U_{ce}^* de_1 \\ -U_{mp}^* dp_1 - U_{mw}^* dw_1 - U_{me}^* de_1 \\ c_1^* dp_1 - e_1 b\, dw_1 - w_1 b\, de_1 - dm^0 \end{pmatrix}.$$

Thus, (7.33) in effect guarantees that the partial derivatives of the functions in (7.34) exist. Before computing these, note that

$$U_c^* = v_1'(c_1^*); \quad U_{cm}^* = U_{cw}^* = U_{ce}^* = U_{cp}^* = 0;$$

$$U_m^* = v_2'(c_2^*)\frac{1}{\phi_2(\cdot)}$$

where

$$c_2^* = \frac{\psi(\cdot) + m^*}{\phi_2(\cdot)};$$

$$U_{mp}^* = \frac{-\phi_{2p}}{\phi_2^2}v_2'(c_2^*) + v_2''(c_2^*)\frac{1}{\phi_2}\left[\frac{\{\phi_2(\cdot)\psi_p\} - \{\psi(\cdot) + m^*\}\phi_{2p}}{\phi_2^2}\right];$$

$$U_{mm}^* = v_2''(c_2^*)\frac{1}{\phi_2^2};$$

$$U_{me}^* = v_2''(c_2^*)\frac{1}{\phi_2}\left[\frac{\phi_2(\cdot)\psi_e - \{\psi(\cdot) + m^*\}\phi_{2e}}{\phi_2^2}\right] - v_2'(c_2^*)\frac{\phi_{2e}}{\phi_2^2}$$

$$U_{mw}^* = v_2''(c_2^*)\frac{1}{\phi_2}\left[\frac{\phi_2(\cdot)\psi_w - \{\psi(\cdot) + m^*\}\phi_{2w}}{\phi_2^2}\right] - v_2'(c_2^*)\frac{\phi_{2w}}{\phi_2^2}.$$

Notice, before we proceed further, that we need some structure on the expectation functions. We can make some simplifications by assuming that

$$\left. \begin{array}{llll} \phi_{2p} > 0; & \phi_{2e} = 0, & \phi_{2w} = 0; \\ \psi_p = 0; & \psi_e \geqslant 0, & \psi_w \geqslant 0; \end{array} \right\} \tag{E}$$

i.e., the expectation regarding future prices does not depend on the current wage rate and employment rate; further, a higher current price implies that a higher future price is expected. Similarly, the expected wage income depends only on current wage and employment rates. Under these assumptions,

$$U_{mp}^* = -\frac{\phi_{2p}}{\phi_2^2} v_2'(c_2^*) + v_2''(c_2^*) - \frac{c_2^* \phi_{2p}}{\phi_2^2};$$

$$U_{me}^* = v_2''(c_2^*) \frac{\psi_e}{\phi_2^2};$$

$$U_{mw}^* = v_2''(c_2^*) \frac{\psi_w(\cdot)}{\phi_2^2}.$$

Now, writing the determinant in (7.33) as Δ, we have

$$\frac{\partial c_1}{\partial p_1} \Delta = -\lambda^* - p_1 U_{mp}^* + c_1^* p_1 U_{mm}^*$$

$$= -v_2'(c_2^*) \frac{1}{\phi_2} + p_1 v_2' \frac{\phi_{2p}}{\phi_2^2} + v_2'' \frac{1}{\phi_2^2} p_1 c_2^* \phi_{2p} + p_1 c_1^* v_2'' \frac{1}{\phi_2^2}$$

$$= -v_2'(c_2^*) \frac{1}{\phi_2} \left(1 - \frac{p_1 \phi_{2p}}{\phi_2} \right) + v_2''(\cdot) \frac{1}{\phi_2^2} (c_1^* + c_2^* \phi_{2p}) p_1$$

$$\frac{\partial c_1}{\partial m^0} \Delta = -p_1 U_{mm}^* > 0$$

$$\frac{\partial c_1}{\partial w_1} \Delta = -U_{mw}^* p_1 - be_1 U_{mm}^* p_1 > 0$$

$$\frac{\partial c_1}{\partial e_1} \Delta = -U_{me}^* p_1 - bw_1 U_{mm}^* p_1 > 0.$$

Since (7.33) guarantees that $\Delta > 0$, we have immediately

$$\frac{\partial c_1}{\partial m^0} > 0, \quad \frac{\partial c_1}{\partial w_1} > 0, \quad \frac{\partial c_1}{\partial e_1} > 0.$$

If, in addition to conditions (E), we have

$$p_1(\phi_{2p}/\phi_2) \lessgtr 1, \tag{7.35}$$

then $\partial c_1/\partial p_1 < 0$.

Thus we have obtained a set of conditions on the expectations ((E) and (7.35)) under which the consumption functions has the properties assumed in the text.

Finally, let us check whether condition (7.27) of Section 7.5 holds. To do this, we evaluate

$$
\left(\frac{\partial c_1}{\partial p_1} p_1 + \frac{\partial c_1}{\partial w_1} w_1 \right) \Delta = -v_2'(c_2^*) \frac{p_1}{\phi_2} \left(1 - \frac{p_1 \phi_{2p}}{\phi_2} \right) + v_2''(\cdot) \frac{p_1^2}{\phi_2^2} (c_1^* + c_2^* \phi_{2p_1})
$$
$$
- \left\{ p_1 w_1 v_2''(c_2^*) \frac{\psi_w(\cdot)}{\phi_2^2} + b e_1 w_1 p_1 \frac{1}{\phi_2^2} v_2''(\cdot) \right\}
$$
$$
= -v_2'(c_2^*) \frac{p_1}{\phi_2} \left(1 - \frac{p_1 \phi_{2p}}{\phi_2} \right)
$$
$$
+ \frac{v_2''(\cdot)}{\phi_2^2} p_1 (p_1 c_1^* - b_1 e_1 w_1 + p_1 c_2^* \phi_{2p} - w_1 \psi_w)
$$
$$
= -v_2'(c_2^*) \frac{p_1}{\phi_2} \left(1 - \frac{p_1 \phi_{2p}}{\phi_2} \right) + \frac{p_1 v_2''(\cdot)}{\phi_2^2}
$$
$$
\times \left[m^0 - m + p_1 \left\{ \frac{\psi(\cdot) + m}{\phi_2} \right\} \phi_{2p} - w_1 \psi_w \right]
$$
$$
= -v_2'(c_2^*) \frac{p_1}{\phi_2} \left(1 - \frac{p_1 \phi_{2p}}{\phi_2} \right)
$$
$$
+ p_1 v_2''(\cdot) \phi_2^2 \left[m^0 - m \left(1 - \frac{p_1 \phi_{2p}}{\phi_2} \right) \right. \tag{7.36}
$$
$$
\left. + \psi(\cdot) \left\{ \frac{p_1 \phi_{2p}}{\phi_2} - \frac{w_1 \psi_w}{\psi(\cdot)} \right\} \right],
$$

which, under the assumptions made so far, is of ambiguous sign since the first term is less than or equal to 0, whereas the expression within square brackets in the second term is of ambiguous sign.

However, if expectations regarding price are static, i.e. if

$$
\phi_2(w_1, p_1, e_1) = p_1,
$$

and if those regarding wage income are extremely pessimistic, i.e. if

$$
\psi(w_1, p_1, e_1) = 0,
$$

then we have, from (7.36),

$$
\Delta \left(\frac{\partial c_1}{\partial p_1} p_1 + \frac{\partial c_1}{\partial w_1} w_1 \right) = \frac{v_2''}{p_1} m^0 < 0.
$$

Moreover, under these assumptions,

$$c_2^* = m/p_1,$$

so that the individual maximizes

$$U(c_1, m/p_1)$$

subject to

$$c_1 + \frac{m_1}{p} = \frac{w_1 b e_1}{p_1} + \frac{m^0}{p_1},$$

which was analysed in Section 7.5 of the text.

There is another point worth noting regarding the classification of the various regimes attempted in Figure 7.6 above (p. 185). The curve WW, it may be recalled, is the locus of (w_1, p_1) such that

$$g + C_1\left(w_1, p_1, \frac{1}{Nb} h\left(\frac{w_1}{p_1}\right), m^0\right) = f\left\{h\left(\frac{w_1}{p_1}\right)\right\},$$

which is a condition that ensures that the goods market is in equilibrium.

The equilibria studied in Section 7.5 are precisely those located on the locus WW. For WW to be upward-rising, it must be the case that

$$\left.\frac{\partial p_1}{\partial w_1}\right|_{WW} > 0;$$

i.e., returning to (7.26), writing C_{1w} for $\partial C_1/\partial w_1$ and C_{1e} for $\partial C_1/\partial e_1$,

$$C_{1w} + \frac{h'(\cdot)}{p_1}\left\{C_{1e}\frac{1}{Nb} - \frac{w_1}{p_1}\right\} > 0.$$

A sufficient condition for the above is that

$$C_{1e}\frac{1}{Nb} - \frac{w_1}{p_1} < 0,$$

or, recalling that $Nc(\cdot) = C(\cdot)$,

$$c_{1e}\frac{1}{b} - w_1/p_1 < 0.$$

Considering the expression for C_{1e} derived earlier, note that

$$c_{1e} = \frac{-p_1 U_{me}^* - w_1 p_1 b U_{mm}^*}{-U_{cc}^* - p_1^2 U_{mm}^*}$$

$$= \frac{-p_1^2 U_{mm}^*}{-U_{cc}^* - p_1^2 U_{mm}^*} b\frac{w_1}{p_1} \quad \text{if } \psi_{e_1} = 0.$$

Notice that, now, $(1/b)c_{1e} < w_1/p_1$, so that (7.26) holds.

Thus, a sufficient condition for the locus WW to be upward-sloping is

$$\psi_e(\cdot) = 0. \tag{7.37}$$

Of course, this doesn't say whether, along WW, w_1/p_1 is increasing or decreasing. For that, (7.27) needs to hold. We know that at W the Walrasian configuration (7.27) holds; thus, for equilibria with a rigid wage and flexible prices close to W, (7.27) should also hold. Beyond this, there doesn't seem to be very much to add.

7.8   An Alternative Budget Constraint

In the above, profit incomes have played no role in determining the nature of the consumption function. Here, we shall examine whether allowing consumption out of profits alters our conclusions.

As described in Section 7.6, consider the problem

$$\max V(c_1, c_2)$$
$$\text{s.t.} \quad p_1 c_1 + m = p_1 y_1 + m^0$$
$$p_2 c_2 = p_2 y_2 + m.$$

Note that

$$c_2 = (y_2 + m)p_2 = \{\psi(p_1, y_1) + m\}/\{\phi(p_1, y_1)\}$$

where $\psi(\cdot)$ and $\phi(\cdot)$ are expectations regarding future output and prices given today's configuration. Thus, we can say that

$$V(c_1, c_2) = v_1(c_1) + v_2(\{\psi(p_1, y_1) + m\}/\{\phi(p_1, y_1)\})$$
$$= U(c_1, m; p_1, y_1),$$

and the two-period problem can be reduced to the following one-period one:

$$\max U(c_1, m; p_1, y_1)$$
$$\text{s.t.} \quad p_1 c_1 + m = p_1 y_1 + m^0.$$

We may now carry out an analysis similar to the one in Section 7.7 to determine the sign of the partial derivatives of the function $c_1(p_1, y_1, m^0)$. The first-order conditions are

$$\left.\begin{array}{r} U_c^* = \lambda^* p_1 \\ U_m^* = \lambda^* \\ p_1 c_1^* + m^* = p_1 y_1 + m^0, \end{array}\right\} \tag{7.38}$$

and the second-order coditions, which together with (7.38) constitute sufficient conditions, are

$$\det \begin{pmatrix} U_{cc}^* & U_{cm}^* & -p_1 \\ U_{mc}^* & U_{mm}^* & -1 \\ -p_1 & -1 & 0 \end{pmatrix} > 0. \tag{7.39}$$

To facilitate further calculations, note that, given the form of $U(\cdot)$, we have

$$U_{cc}^* = v_1''(c_1^*); \quad U_{cm}^* = U_{cp}^* = U_{mc}^* = 0$$

$$U_m^* = v_2'(c_2^*)(1/\phi)$$

$$U_{mm}^* = v_2''(c_2^*)(1/\phi^2)$$

$$U_{mp}^* = \frac{1}{\phi} v_2''(c_2^*)\left(\psi_p - \frac{m}{\phi^2}\phi_p\right) - v_2'(c_2^*)\frac{1}{\phi^2}\phi_p.$$

We have, then,

$$\begin{pmatrix} U_{cc}^* & 0 & -p_1 \\ 0 & U_{mm}^* & -1 \\ -p_1 & -1 & 0 \end{pmatrix} \begin{pmatrix} dc_1 \\ dm \\ d\lambda \end{pmatrix} = \begin{pmatrix} \lambda^* dp_1 \\ -U_{mp}^* dp_1 \\ (c_1^* - y_1)dp_1 - p_1 dy_1 - dm^0 \end{pmatrix};$$

and, writing the determinant in (7.39) as Δ',

$$\frac{\partial c_1}{\partial p_1}\Delta' = -v_2'(c_2^*)\frac{1}{\phi} + \frac{p_1\phi_p}{\phi^2}v_2'(c_2^*) - \frac{p_1 v_2''(c_2^*)}{\phi}\left(\psi_p - \frac{m^*}{\phi^2}\phi_p\right)$$

$$= -v_2'(c_2^*)\frac{1}{\phi}\left(1 - \frac{p_1\phi_p}{\phi}\right) - \frac{p_1 v_2''(c_2^*)}{\phi}\left(\psi_p - \frac{m^*}{\phi^2}\phi_p\right). \tag{7.40}$$

Even if we assume, as before, that price expectations are inelastic,

$$p_1\phi_p/\phi \lessgtr 1, \tag{7.41}$$

which is the counterpart of (7.35) in the present situation, the expression in (7.40) remains unsigned. It is in this sense that c_{1p} is of ambiguous sign. If (7.41) holds with an equality and $\psi_p = 0$, then (7.40) reduces to

$$\frac{\partial c_1}{\partial p_1} = +v_2''(c_2^*)\frac{m^*}{\phi^2} < 0.$$

Thus it is only under very special configurations of expectations that one may obtain (7.28) in Section 7.6.

Finally, note that

$$\frac{\partial c_1}{\partial y_1}\Delta' = -p_1^2 U_{mm}^* > 0,$$

$$\frac{\partial c_1}{\partial m_0}\Delta' = -p_1 U_{mm}^* > 0,$$

so that, given (7.39), one may conclude that

$$\frac{\partial c_1}{\partial y_1} > 0; \quad \frac{\partial c_1}{\partial m^0} > 0;$$

and since

$$\Delta' = -U_{cc}^* - p_1^2 U_{mm}^*,$$

it follows that

$$\frac{\partial c_1}{\partial y_1} < 1.$$

BIBLIOGRAPHICAL NOTES

The literature on micro-foundations of macroeconomics began with the pioneering contributions of Clower (1965) and Barro and Grossman (1971). The model that was considered and analysed in this chapter follows from the contributions of Malinvaud (1977) and Benassy (1982). The temporary equilibrium approach leading to an indirect utility for money is from the latter contribution; see, in particular, Benassy (1982: chs. 8, 11, 13). The classification of equilibria into different regimes and the diagrams in the w–p plane depicting such alternative regimes appeared in Malinvaud (1977); on these issues, Bhaduri (1983) and Hildenbrand and Hildenbrand (1978) provide interesting views. The latter part of the chapter (Sections 7.5, 7.6, and the mathematical notes) is based on Mukherji and Sanyal (1986). For Keynes's own position regarding the efficacy of a money wage cut, see Keynes (1936: ch. 19)

For a general introduction to temporary equilibrium—a concept that may be traced to Hicks (1946)—see the excellent survey by Grandmont (1982). Also, for a treatment of money in a general equilibrium context, see Grandmont (1983), and Gale (1982, 1983).

8 A Mathematical Appendix

8.1 Sets and Relations

A *set S* of elements is a collection of elements, for example the set N of positive integers, $N = \{1, 2, 3, \ldots\}$; the set $\bar{R}$ of positive rational numbers, $\bar{R} = \{r: r = p/q, q \neq 0, p, q$ are integers with the same sign$\}$. Thus, in the definition of $\bar{R}$, it is shown how positive rational numbers may be constructed. When we wish to say that x is an element of S, we shall write $x \in S$, Thus, $3/1 \in \bar{R}$. Given a set S, let $x, y \in S$; $x = y$ would denote that x and y are identical; $x \neq y$ would denote that x and y are distinct. Let $\mathscr{P}$ be a property that an element $x \in S$ may or may not have; then $T = \{x \in S | x$ has property $\mathscr{P}\}$ denotes all those elements of S that have property $\mathscr{P}$; such a sub-collection from a given set S constitutes a *subset* of S, and is denoted by $T \subseteq S$. Clearly, $N \subseteq \bar{R}$. If $T \subseteq S$ and $S \subseteq T$, then $S = T$; i.e., S and T are identical. Consider S and $T \subseteq S$; by the complement of T in S is meant the collection of elements of S that are not in T and is denoted by $S - T$; when S is the universal set, $S - T$ is written T^C. By the 'universal set', we shall mean the entire collection of objects being discussed. We shall use the notation $\varnothing$ for the *empty set*—or one with no elements. Thus, if $S = T$, $S - T = \varnothing$.

Given sets S, T one may form their *union* $S \cup T$, their *intersection* $S \cap T$, and their *product* $S \times T$, according to the following rules:

$$S \cup T = \{x: x \in S \text{ or } x \in T\};$$

$$S \cap T = \{x: x \in S \text{ and } x \in T\};$$

$$S \times T = \{(x, y): x \in S, y \in T\}.$$

Thus, the union consists of elements that belong to at least one of S and T, and the intersection of elements that are common to both S and T. It is easy to see that $S \cap T = T \cap S$ and $S \cup T = T \cup S$; i.e., $\cup$ and $\cap$ are *commutative*. They satisfy the following *associative* and *distributive* rules:

$S \cup (T \cup C) = (S \cup T) \cup C$; $S \cap (T \cap C) = (S \cap T) \cap C$ (Associative)

$S \cup (T \cap C) = (S \cup T) \cap (S \cup C)$; $S \cap (T \cup C) = (S \cap T) \cup (S \cap C)$ (Distributive).

However, $S \times T \neq T \times S$. Notice that $S \times T$ consists of ordered pairs of elements—the first from S, the second from T. Sometimes, $S \times S = S^2$,

$$S \times S \times \ldots \times S \ (n \text{ times}) = S^n,$$

and so on. S^n thus consists of ordered n-tuples of elements from S.

By a *binary relation* $\mathcal{R}$ defined on a set S we shall mean a set of ordered pairs of elements in S. Thus the usual $\geqq$ (at least as large as) is a binary relation on N. For a pair $(x, y) \in \mathcal{R}$, we say $\mathcal{R}$ holds for (x, y), and we shall write $x \mathcal{R} y$, just as one may write $4 \geqq 3$. If for a pair (x, y), $\mathcal{R}$ does not hold, then we shall write $\sim x \mathcal{R} y$ (or *not* $x \mathcal{R} y$).

We shall use the following terms in connection with a binary relation $\mathcal{R}$ defined on S:

$\mathcal{R}$ is *complete* on S if, for every pair $(x, y) \in S \times S$, either $x \mathcal{R} y$ or $y \mathcal{R} x$.
$\mathcal{R}$ is *reflexive* on S if $x \mathcal{R} x$ for all $x \in S$.
$\mathcal{R}$ is *transitive* on S if $x, y, z \in S$ and $x \mathcal{R} y, y \mathcal{R} z \Rightarrow x \mathcal{R} z$.

Given $\mathcal{R}$, a binary relation on S, we may sometimes use the following two binary relations defined with the help of $\mathcal{R}$:

$$x \mathcal{P} y \text{ if } x \mathcal{R} y \text{ and } \sim y \mathcal{R} x; \qquad x \mathcal{I} y \text{ if } x \mathcal{R} y \text{ and } y \mathcal{R} x.$$

If $S = N$ and $\mathcal{R}$ is $\geqq$, then $\mathcal{P}$ is $>$ and $\mathcal{I}$ stands for $=$. A complete relfexive and transitive relation $\mathcal{R}$ on S will be called an *ordering*.

8.2   Real Numbers

The set R of real numbers is a collection of elements having the following properties, which it is assumed that readers are familiar with (except perhaps the last).

There are two operations, $+$ (sum) and $\cdot$ (product), and a binary relation, $\geqq$ on R, such that $x + y, x \cdot y \in R$, and

1. $x + y = y + x; x \cdot y = y \cdot x.$ Commutative Laws

2. $x + (y + z) = (x + y) + z; (x \cdot y) \cdot z = x \cdot (y \cdot z).$ Associative Laws

3. $x \cdot (y + z) = x \cdot y + x \cdot z.$ Distributive Law

4. For any $x, y \in R$, there is $z \in R$ such that

$$x + z = y.$$

This z is denoted $y - x$. The number $x - x$ is denoted 0 and is independent of x. $0 - x$ is denoted $-x$.

5. There is at least one $x \in R$, $x \neq 0$. If $x, y \in R$, $x \neq 0$, then there is $z \in R$ such that $x \cdot z = y$; z is written y/x; x/x is written 1 and is independent of x; $1/x$ is written x^{-1}.

6. Given $x, y \in S$, either $x \geqq y$ or $y \geqq x$.

7. If $x > y$ (i.e. if $x \geqq y$ and $\sim y \geqq x$), then $x + z > y + z$ for any $z \in R$.

8. $x > 0, y > 0 \Rightarrow x \cdot y > 0.$

9. $x \geqq y, y \geqq z \Rightarrow x \geqq z.$

A subset S of R is said to be *bounded above* if there is $s \in R$ such that $x \in S \Rightarrow s \geqslant x$. Similarly, S is *bounded below* if there is $t \in R$ such that $x \in S \Rightarrow x \geqslant t$. S is *bounded* if it is bounded above and below. Also, such an element $s(t)$ is called an *upper* (respectively, *lower*) bound of S. *Infinum* (*g.l.b.*) of S is defined to be the greatest lower bound, whereas the *supremum* (*l.u.b.*) of S is defined to be the least among the upper bounds of S.

The final property:

10. Any non-empty subset S of R which is bounded above (below) has a l.u.b. (resp., g.l.b.).

Although we have been provided with an abstract definition for the set R—also called the *real line*—it may be easy to see that R is made up of N, the set of positive integers, the number 0, the negative integers (see property 4), the rational numbers (see property 5), and the irrational numbers, introduced by property 10. To see the last bit, notice that $S = \{x : x$ is a rational number $x^2 < 2\}$ is a non-empty set bounded above (2 is an upper bound), whence it has a l.u.b.—it is denoted by $\sqrt{2}$, which is irrational.

8.3 Real Linear Algebra

8.3.1 *Preliminaries*

Given the real line R, consider R^n $(n > 1)$. Elements of R^n will be called *n-vectors* as opposed to elements of R, which are *scalars*. An *n*-vector will be written

$$x = (x_1, x_2, \ldots, x_n) \quad \text{or} \quad x = (x_i)$$

where x_i is the *i*th component of x. Using operations on R, we define two operations on R^n:

1 *Sum*: If $x = (x_1, \ldots, x_n)$, $y = (y_1, \ldots, y_n)$, then $(x_1 + y_1, x_2 + y_2, \ldots, x_n + y_n)$ is defined to be $x + y$.
2 *Scalar multiple*: If $x = (x_1, \ldots, x_n)$ and $\alpha \in R$, then the scalar multiple $\alpha x = (\alpha x_1, \ldots, \alpha x_n)$.

Thus, in vector sum, vectors with the same number of components are added component by component; whereas in forming a scalar multiple, each component is multiplied by the given scalar. These operations lead to the formation of new vectors by a process of *linear combination*. Suppose $x^1, x^2, \ldots, x^r$ are vectors in R^n; i.e., $x^j = (\alpha_{1j}, \ldots, \alpha_{nj})$, $j = 1, \ldots, r$. $\alpha_{ij} \in R$. Then, given scalars $\beta_1, \ldots, \beta_r$,

$$\sum_{i=1}^{r} \beta_i x^i$$

is a linear combination of x^i.

We shall use 0 for the scalar zero and the n-vector, all of whose components are zero, and the context should make clear which is being implied. A collection $\{x^1, \ldots, x^r\}$ in R^n is said to be *linearly dependent* if there is a set of scalars $\beta_1, \beta_2, \ldots, \beta_r$, not all zero, such that

$$\sum_{i=1}^{r} \beta_i x^i = 0.$$

If no such β_i exist, then $\{x^i\}$ is said to be *linearly independent*. Define the n-vector $e^i = (0, 0, \ldots, 0, 1, 0, \ldots, 0)$, $i = 1, 2, \ldots, n$; then $e^i \in R^n$ and constitute a linearly independent set.

A subset L of R^n is said to be a *sub-space* if

(a) $x, y \in L \Rightarrow x + y \in L$; and
(b) $x \in L \Rightarrow \alpha x \in L$ for all scalars α.

Given a sub-space L, the maximum number of linearly independent vectors in L is called the *rank* of L. Hence rank $R^n = n$. If rank $L = r$, then any collection of r linearly independent vectors in L is said to be a *basis* for L. Thus $\{e^i, i = 1, 2, \ldots, n\}$ is a basis for R^n. It should also be noted that, if $\{x^i, i = 1, \ldots, r\}$ constitute a basis for L, then any $x \in L$ has a representation

$$x = \sum_{i=1}^{r} \alpha_i x^i \quad \text{for some scalars } \alpha_i, i = 1, 2, \ldots, r.$$

8.3.2   *The Separating Hyperplane Theorem*

Given two n-vectors, $x = (x_i)$, $y = (y_i)$, we define the *inner product* $x \cdot y$ by the scalar

$$\sum_{i=1}^{n} x_i y_i.$$

A rectangular array of numbers $[\alpha_{ij}]$, $i = 1, \ldots, m$; $j = 1, 2, \ldots, n$ is said to be a *matrix* of order $m \times n$ since i, the first index, refers to rows and j, the second, to columns. The ith row $(\alpha_{i1}, \alpha_{i2}, \ldots, \alpha_{in})$ is an n-vector written a_i, whereas the jth column

$$\begin{pmatrix} \alpha_{1j} \\ \alpha_{2j} \\ \vdots \\ \alpha_{mj} \end{pmatrix}$$

is an m-vector written a^j. Thus $a^j \in R^m$, whereas $a_i \in R^n$.

Using the operations defined above, we may define *sum* and *product* of matrices. Consider $A = [\alpha_{ij}]$, $B = [\beta_{ij}]$, two $m \times n$ matrices; then $A + B = [\alpha_{ij} + \beta_{ij}]$, an $m \times n$ matrix. Consider $A = [\alpha_{ij}]$ $m \times r$ and $B = [\beta_{ij}]$ $r \times n$; furthermore, let the ith row of A be a_i and the jth column of B be b^j.

Notice that a_i and $b^j \in R^r$, and consequently the inner product $a_i \cdot b^j$ is defined. Let $c_{ij} = a_i \cdot b^j$; then $C = (c_{ij})$ is defined to be the product $A \cdot B$, an $m \times n$ matrix. Two of the most common forms of matrix products used are

$$x \cdot A$$

and

$$A \cdot y$$

where A is $m \times n$; x is $1 \times m$ (*row-vector*), and y is $n \times 1$ (*column vector*).

Using the rule for matrix product, $x \cdot A$ is $1 \times n$—a row vector; $A \cdot y$ is $m \times 1$—a column vector; and $x \cdot A$ is a linear combination of rows of A whereas $A \cdot y$ is a linear combination of columns of A. (Henceforth we shall write the matrix product $x \cdot A$ and $A \cdot y$ as xA and Ay, respectively.)

Given $A = (\alpha_{ij})$ $m \times n$, it can be shown that the maximum number of linearly independent rows of A is equal to the maximum number of linearly independent columns of A. This common number is called the *rank* of A.

Given a system of equations

$$Ay = b,$$

we may wish to solve for y. Given an arbitrary A and b, equations such as the above may not be solvable. Notice that, in essence, we wish to express column b as a linear combination of columns of A. This is possible if the r linearly independent columns (where $r = \text{rank } A$) generate a sub-space containing b. If b does not belong to this sub-space, we should be able to construct $\bar{x}$ such that $\bar{x}A = 0$ and $\bar{x}b = 1$. Conversely, if no such $\bar{x}$ exists, then $Ay = b$ must have a solution.

A diagram may help to explain why this is so. In Figure 8.1, if A is just a single column, then $Ax = b$ has a solution if and only if b is a scalar multiple of a^1 (the only column). But b lies either on the ray through a^1 or outside it—so only one of the following alternatives must be true: either $Ay = b$ has a solution, or $xA = 0$, $xb = 1$ have a solution. In Figure 8.1, since b is not a scalar multiple of a^1, note that there is z such that $za^1 = 0$ and $zb > 0$. Clearly, $\lambda zb = 1$ for some $\lambda > 0$.

I shall now state a fundamental result in connection with non-negative solutions of equations of the type discussed above, using the following notation for $x \in R^n$:

x is *non-negative*, $x \geqq 0$, if $x = (x_i)$, $x_i \geqq 0$, $i = 1, 2, \ldots, n$;
x is *semi-positive*, $x \geq 0$, if $x \geqq 0$ and $x_i > 0$ for some i;
x is *positive*, $x > 0$, if $x_i > 0$ for all i.

THE SEPARATING HYPERPLANE THEOREM (*SH*): Only one of the following alternatives must hold:

either $Ax = b$ has a solution, $x \geqq 0$;
or $yA \geqq 0$, $yb < 0$ have a solution.

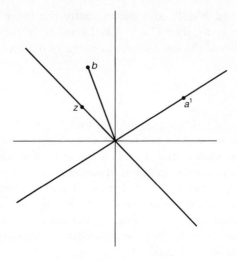

FIG. 8.1

Again, a diagram may be used to explain why such a result may hold. In Figure 8.2, if b lies in the shaded region, then b may be expressed as a non-negative linear combination of a^1 and a^2. If b lies elsewhere, then it should be possible to construct y making an acute angle with a^i and an obtuse angle with b, as shown. Some corollaries of the above follow.

SH1: Only one of the following alternatives must hold:
   either $Ax \leqq b$ has a solution $x \geqq 0$
   or $yA \geqq 0$, $yb < 0$ have a solution $y \geqq 0$.

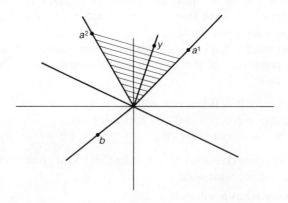

FIG. 8.2

SH1 follows from SH if one notices that

$$Ax \leqq b \quad \text{for } x \geqq 0$$

$$\Leftrightarrow \quad (A, I)\begin{pmatrix} x \\ z \end{pmatrix} = b \text{ for } \begin{pmatrix} x \\ z \end{pmatrix} \geqq 0$$

where

$$I = [e_{ij}], \quad e_{ij} = 0, \qquad i \neq j$$
$$= 1, \qquad \text{otherwise, } i, j = 1, \ldots, m.$$

Let A be $m \times n$; thus (A, I) is $m \times (n + m)$, and

$$\begin{pmatrix} x \\ z \end{pmatrix}$$

is $(n + m) \times 1$—the first n components making up x and the remaining m components making up z.

Next, we have

SH2: Only one of the following must hold:
either $Ax = 0$ for $x \geqslant 0$
or $yA > 0$ has a solution.

Once again, if A is $m \times n$, and $u = (1, 1, 1, \ldots, 1) \in R^n$, then

$$Ax = 0 \text{ for } x \geqslant 0 \Leftrightarrow \begin{pmatrix} A \\ u \end{pmatrix} x = \begin{pmatrix} 0 \\ 1 \end{pmatrix} \text{ for } x \geqslant 0,$$

and once more an application of SH establishes SH2. Finally

SH3: Only one of the following must hold:
either $Ax \leqslant 0$ for $x \geqslant 0$
or $yA > 0$ for $y \geqslant 0$.

This follows from SH1 by using an argument similar to the one employed to illustrate SH2.

8.3.3 *Determinants and Quadratic Forms*

We have seen some properties of solutions to equations involving matrices that need not necessarily be square. We can construct, for each square matrix, a number called the 'determinant' of the matrix by operations which, though tedious, may be familiar. We shall sometimes use properties of determinants, and it may be useful to have them collected at one place. In this section, all matrices are *square*.

Consider a square matrix $A = (a_{ij}) i, j = 1, 2, \ldots, n$; whenever $a_{ij} = 0$, $i \neq j$, $a_{ii} = 1$ for all i, we shall designate the resultant matrix by I. We associate with

A a number d(A), or *determinant* of A, or det A, which satisfies the following properties:

(i) if B is obtained from A by replacing ith row a_i by αa_i, then d(B)=αd(A);
(ii) d(A)=0 whenever two rows of A are identical;
(iii) d(I)=1.

It may be shown that these three properties specify d(A) and that

$$\text{d}(A) = \Sigma \pm a_{1i} a_{2i}, \ldots, a_{ni}$$

where the sum is extended over all permutations of

$$1, 2, \ldots, n,$$

and where for each permutation, say $i_1, i_2, \ldots, i_n$, the term

$$a_{1i}, a_{2i}, \ldots, a_{ni}$$

appears with a plus or minus sign depending on whether the permutation is even or odd, i.e. on whether the number of transpositions (exchanges) necessary to pass from $1, 2, \ldots, n$ to $i_1, i_2, \ldots, i_n$ is even or odd. There may be many sets of transpositions that convert $1, 2, \ldots, n$ to $i_1, i_2, \ldots, i_n$; but, given a particular $i_1, i_2, \ldots, i_n$, the remarkable fact is that the number of transpositions used to pass from $1, 2, \ldots, n$ to $i_1, i_2, \ldots, i_n$ is always even or always odd, no matter which set of transpositions is used. For example, 7, 6, 8, 3, 5, 1, 4, 2 is a given permutation which may be obtained from 1, 2, 3, 4, 5, 6, 7, 8 by the transpositions 1 and 6, 2 and 8, 3 and 4, 4 and 7, 6 and 8, and 7 and 8, i.e. six transpositions. Any other method would also use an even number of transpositions, and hence the given permutation is an even permutation.

One may deduce that

(iv) if B is obtained from A by an interchange of rows, then d(B)= $-$d(A);
(v) if B is obtained from A by changing rows into columns and vice versa, then d(B)=d(A) (such a B is writtten as A^T);
(vi) if the word 'rows' in (i), (ii), and (iv) above is replaced by 'columns', the statements would still hold;
(vii) By virtue of (i), it is expected that

$$\text{d}(A) = a_{i1} A_{i1} + a_{i2} A_{i2} + \ldots + a_{in} A_{in}$$

where A_{ij} are numbers independent of the ith row. A_{ij} are called *co-factors* of the i–jth element and are defined by

$$A_{ij} = (-1)^{i+j} \text{d}(D_{ij})$$

where D_{ij} is the matrix obtained from A by deleting the ith row and the jth column. Sometimes D_{ij} is referred to as a *minor* of A of order $n-1$.

The number d(A) is called the determinant of A. It turns out that d(A)$\neq$0 implies that rank $A = n$, and such matrices are called *non-singular* or *regular*; whereas if $d(A) = 0$, then A is *singular*. For non-singular matrices A, define $B = (b_{ij})$ where

$$b_{ij} = A_{ji}/\det A$$

and A_{ij} is the co-factor of the i–jth element in A. Then we can see that

$$AB = BA = I.$$

Given a system of n equations in n unknowns, $Ax = b$, if $d(A) \neq 0$, then the unique solution is given by *Cramer's Rule*:

$$x = A^{-1}b$$

or

$$x_i = \frac{1}{\det A} \left\{ \sum_{j=1}^{n} A_{ji} b_j \right\}.$$

Given a square matrix A, the *characteristic equation of* A defined by

$$d(A - \lambda I) = 0;$$

it is a polynomial of order n in λ and has n roots, $\lambda_1, \ldots, \lambda_n$. Each such λ_i is called a *characteristic root* of A. If λ is a characteristic root, then $d(A - \lambda I) = 0$, whence rank $(A - \lambda I) < n$ so that there are $\bar{x}$ and $\bar{y} \neq 0$ such that

$$(A - \lambda I)\bar{x} = 0$$

$$\bar{y}(A - \lambda I) = 0.$$

$\bar{x}$ is a *column characteristic vector* and $\bar{y}$ is a *row characteristic vector* corresponding to λ. We shall require some properties of characteristic roots and vectors, when the matrix A has non-negative elements.

A square matrix $A = (a_{ij})$, $i, j = 1, 2, \ldots, n$, is said to be *symmetric* if $a_{ij} = a_{ji}$ for all i, j; for a symmetric matrix A, the expression (where x' is $1 \times n$ and x is $n \times 1$)

$$x'Ax$$

is called a *quadratic form*. The quadratic form is said to be *definite* if $x'Ax$ has the same sign for all $x \neq 0$; thus it is

positive definite if $x'Ax > 0$ for all $x \neq 0$;
negative definite if $x'Ax < 0$ for all $x \neq 0$.

Sometimes we shall use the term *positive (negative) semi-definite* to describe cases where $x'Ax \geqslant 0 (\leqslant 0$, respectively) for all x.

If a quadratic form $x'Ax$ is positive (negative) definite (semi-definite), then A is defined to be positive (negative) definite (semi-definite).

Regarding symmetric matrices, it should be noted that their characteristic roots are real numbers; moreover, for a positive (negative) definite matrix, all its characteristic roots are positive (negative). While a positive definite matrix is non-singular, a semi-definite matrix may be singular. There are some properties of positive and negative matrices that are of some interest. However, before we can state them, we need the following notation. Given

$$A = (a_{ij}),$$

$$D_{1j} = d\begin{pmatrix} a_{11} & \cdots & a_{1j} \\ a_{21} & \cdots & a_{2j} \\ a_{j1} & \cdots & a_{jj} \end{pmatrix}, \quad j = 1, 2, \ldots, n,$$

clearly, $D_{11} = a_{11}$, $D_{12} = a_{11}a_{22} - a_{21}a_{12}$, and so on. Also, let

$$D_{ij}^k = d\begin{pmatrix} a_{ii} & \cdots & a_{ij} \\ a_{ji} & \cdots & a_{jj} \end{pmatrix}, \quad i < j, \quad k = 1, 2, \ldots, n,$$

where k signifies that there are k rows and columns in the matrix on the right-hand side. Then we have the following rules:

A symmetric matrix A is

$$\text{positive definite} \Leftrightarrow D_{1j} > 0 \text{ for all } j;$$

$$\text{negative definite} \Leftrightarrow (-1)^j D_{1j} > 0 \text{ for all } j;$$

$$\text{positive semi-definite} \Leftrightarrow D_{ij}^k \geq 0 \text{ for all } k, i, j, i < j;$$

$$\text{negative semi-definite} \Leftrightarrow (-1)^k D_{ij}^k \geq 0 \text{ for all } k, i, j, i < j.$$

8.3.4 *Dominant Diagonal Matrices and Non-Negative Matrices*

In this section some useful results are presented which follow from SH (Section 8.3.2). First, a square matrix $A = (a_{ij})$, $i, j = 1, 2, \ldots, n$ is said to have a *column-dominant diagonal* (c.d.d) if there are $t_j > 0, j = 1, 2, \ldots, n$, such that

$$t_j |a_{jj}| > \sum_{i \neq j} t_i |a_{ij}|, \quad j = 1, 2, \ldots, n. \tag{8.1}$$

Let $B_A = (b_{ij})$ be defined by

$$b_{ij} = -|a_{ij}|, \quad i \neq j$$
$$= |a_{jj}|, \quad \text{otherwise.}$$

Then

$$A \text{ has a c.d.d. iff } tB_A > 0 \text{ for some } t \geq 0. \tag{8.1a}$$

A is said to have a *row-dominant diagonal* (r.d.d) if and only if A' has a c.d.d., i.e. if there exist $c_j > 0, j = 1, 2, \ldots, n$, such that

$$c_i |a_{ii}| > \sum_{j \neq i} |a_{ij}| c_j, \qquad i = 1, 2, \ldots, n, \tag{8.2}$$

or, alternatively, if

$$B_A c > 0 \text{ for some } c \geqq 0. \tag{8.2a}$$

It may be shown first that

1: A has a c.d.d iff A has a r.d.d.
2: If A has a dominant diagonal (d.d.), then A is non-singular.

Matrices such as B_A will play an important role in our analysis. We shall refer to matrices such as these, i.e. with non-positive off-diagonal entries, by the term *B-matrices*. For a B-matrix, $B = (b_{ij})$, the above considerations imply that B has a d.d. with $b_{ii} > 0$ (positive d.d), if and only if

$$Bt > 0 \quad \text{for} \quad t \geqq 0. \tag{8.3}$$

Moreover for any B-matrix, $B = (b_{ij})$, we have:

3: $Bx = c$ has a unique non-negative solution for any $c \geqq 0$ iff B has a positive d.d.
4: For a B-matrix, $B^{-1} \geqq 0$ iff B has a positive d.d.
5: For a B-matrix, B has a positive d.d. iff

$$\text{d } B_k = \text{d} \begin{pmatrix} b_{11} & \cdots & b_{1k} \\ \vdots & \vdots & \vdots \\ b_{k1} & \cdots & b_{kk} \end{pmatrix} > 0, \qquad k = 1, 2, \ldots, n. \tag{HS}$$

Let $A \geqq 0$ be a square non-negative matrix of order n.

$$F(A) = [\pi : \pi I - A \text{ has a positive d.d.}].$$

For any π, $\pi I - A$ is a B-matrix and hence the above results apply. Moreover, for any $A \geqq 0$, $F(A) \neq \varnothing$, since any π larger than the maximum column sum of A must be an element of $F(A)$. Also,

$$\pi \in F(A) \Rightarrow \pi \geqq 0.$$

Hence

$$\pi_A^* = \inf_{\pi \in F(A)} \pi$$

exists. We shall drop the subscript and write π^* whenever the context makes it clear. First of all, it may be noted that

6: $\pi^* \notin F(A)$, $\pi^* \geqq 0$; $\pi > \pi^* \Rightarrow \pi \in F(A)$.

Thus $F(A) = (\pi^*, +\infty)$. Moreover,

7: π^* is a characteristic root (c.r.) of A; $|\alpha| \leqq \pi^*$ for any other c.r. of A.

8: There is $x^* \geqq 0$ such that $Ax^* = \pi^* x^*$.

9: $(\pi I - A)^{-1} \geqq 0$ iff $\pi > \pi^*$. Further, $L_{ij}(\pi) \geqq 0$ for $\pi \geqq \pi^*$ where $L_{ij}(\pi)$ is the co-factor of the i–jth element in $(\pi I - A)$.

10: If $A \geqq C \geqq 0$, then $\pi^*_A \geqq \pi^*_C \geqq 0$. Moreover, if C is any principal minor of A, then $\pi^*_A \geqq \pi^*_C$.

Collecting the above results, for any non-negative matrix A,

(i) there is $\pi^* \geqq 0$ such that π^* is a c.r. of A, and for any other c.r. α, $|\alpha| \leqq \pi^*$ (see result 7);

(ii) $(\pi I - A)^{-1} \geqq 0$ iff $\pi > \pi^*$ (see result 9);

(iii) there are $x^* \geqq 0$ and $p^* \geqq 0$ such that

$$Ax^* = \pi^* x^*$$

$$p^* A = \pi^* p^* \quad \text{(see result 8 and application to } A')$$

(iv) $Ay \geqq \alpha y$, $y \geqq 0 \Rightarrow \alpha \leqq \pi^*$.

The above set of results is referred to as the *Perron–Frobenius Theorem*.

Some of the above may be strengthened if we impose some additional properties on A. One such property is that A should be *indecomposable*. Let $I = \{1, 2, \ldots, n\}$; if there is a non-empty proper subset J of I (i.e. if $J \neq \varnothing$, and there is $i \in I - J$) such that

$$a_{ij} = 0, \quad i \notin J \quad \text{and} \quad j \in J,$$

then A is said to *decomposable*. If no such set J exists, then A is said to be *indecomposable*.

Under indecomposability of A, one may show that results (i) and (iii) may be strengthened to

(i′) $\pi^* > 0$; π^* is a simple root of the equation

$$d(\pi I - A) = 0;$$

(iii′) there are $x^* > 0$, $p^* > 0$ such that

$$Ax^* = \pi^* x^*$$

$$p^* A = p^* \pi^*$$

and, further,

$$Ax = \pi^* x \Rightarrow x = \alpha x^* \text{ for some scalar } \alpha,$$

$$pA = p\pi^* \Rightarrow p = \theta p^* \text{ for some scalar } \theta.$$

In addition, one may show that, if A is indecomposable, then

(v) $Ax = \pi x$ and $x \geqslant 0 \Rightarrow \pi = \pi^*$;
$pA = \pi p$ and $p \geqslant 0 \Rightarrow \pi = \pi^*$;

(vi) $A \geqslant C \geqslant 0$, $A \neq C \Rightarrow \pi_A^* > \pi_C^*$; and hence, if C is a principal minor of A, $C \neq A$, then $\pi_C^* < \pi_A^*$;

(vii) $(\pi I - A)x \geqslant 0$ for some $x \geqslant 0 \Rightarrow (\pi I - A)^{-1} > 0$.

8.4 Topological Properties of R^n

8.4.1 *Preliminary Concepts*

This section does not contain a comprehensive account of the topology of R^n; however, it does contain the results that we shall require for our analysis. First, recall that R^n is the totality of all n-vectors, called the n-dimensional Euclidean space. The notations $R_+^n = \{x \in R^n : x \geqslant 0\}$ and $R_{++}^n = \{x \in R_+^n : x > 0\}$ will be used often. $x \in R^n$ will be referred to as a point of R^n. We define, for $x \in R^n$,

$$\|x\| = \sqrt{\sum_i x_i^2} : \quad \text{the } \textit{length} \text{ of } x \text{ or } \textit{norm} \text{ of } x.$$

Using this definition, we may define the *distance* between any $x, y \in R^n$ by

$$\delta(x, y) = \sqrt{\left\{ \sum_i (x_i - y_i)^2 \right\}} : \text{ \textit{Euclidean distance}}.$$

The distance function allows us to define a *neighbourhood* $N_\varepsilon(x)$ of x by means of

$$N_\varepsilon(x) = \{ y : \delta(x, y) < \varepsilon \},$$

where $\varepsilon > 0$. Given a set $S \subseteq R^n$, $x \in S$ is said to be an *interior point* of S if, for some $\varepsilon > 0$, there is a neighbourhood $N_\varepsilon(x) \subseteq S$. A subset S, every point of which is an interior point, is defined to be *open*. Given $S \subseteq R^n$, x is said to be a *limit point* of S if *every* neighbourhood $N_\varepsilon(x)$ of x contains a point of S different from x.

A set S is defined to be *closed* if it contains all its limit points. Alternatively, let $\bar{S}$ denote the set of limit points of S; then *closure* of S is defined by $S \cup \bar{S}$; in case $\bar{S} \subseteq S$, $S \cup \bar{S} = S$ and S is closed. Note that S is closed if and only if $R^n - S$ is open. For example, $S = \{1/n; n \text{ is a positive integer}\}$; then $\bar{S} = \{0\}$, $\bar{S} \not\subseteq S$, and S is not closed; but $S = \{y \in R^n; b_i \geqslant y_i \geqslant a_i, i = 1, 2, \ldots, n\}$ is a closed subset. Making the inequalities strict, i.e. $b_i > y_i > a_i$ for all i, would make our set open. In addition, note that any subset S containing finitely many elements is by definition closed; also, if x is a limit point of S, then S must contain infinitely many elements.

Consider any collection of open sets $\{O_\alpha\}$ in R^n; then their union is also open. However, the intersection of only a finite number of open sets is open.

A subset S of R^n is said to be *bounded* if there is some number M such that $x \in S \Rightarrow \|x\| < M$. A fundamental property of bounded non-empty infinite subsets of R^n is contained in the following.

BOLZANO–WEIRSTRASS THEOREM (BW): An infinite bounded non-empty subset S of R^n has a limit point.

To understand the implication of *BW*, consider an infinite subset S, whose members can be written in the form $\{x^1, x^2, \ldots, x^n\}$; i.e., specifying an integer n singles out a specific element of S, and, conversely for any element of S, there is an integer assigned to it. Such a subset is called a *sequence*. $\bar{x}$ is said to be a *limit* of the sequence if, for any $\varepsilon > 0$, there is an integer N such that

$$\delta(x^n, \bar{x}) < \varepsilon \quad \text{for all } n > N.$$

This can be written

$$\lim_{n \to \infty} x^n = \bar{x}.$$

A limit is hence a limit point, and the only limit point for a sequence. BW asserts that, if S is a non-empty bounded subset, then there is $\bar{x} \in R^n$ and a sequence x^n, $x^n \in S$ for all n, such that

$$\lim_{n \to \infty} x^n = \bar{x}.$$

Bounded subsets of R^n which are also closed have certain interesting properties. Let $S \subseteq R^n$; a collection of open sets $\mathcal{O} = \{O_\alpha, O_\alpha \subseteq R^n\}$ constitutes an open covering of S if

$$S \subseteq \bigcup_{O_\alpha \in \mathcal{O}} O_\alpha;$$

if

$$O_1, \ldots, O_N \in \mathcal{O} \quad \text{and} \quad S \subseteq \bigcup_{j=1}^{N} O_j,$$

then $\{O_1, O_2, \ldots, O_N\}$ constitute an open finite sub-covering of S.

A subset S is defined to be *compact* if every open covering of S contains a finite sub-cover.

HEINE BOREL THEOREM (HB): Every closed and bounded subset of R^n is compact.

Compact subsets have, among other properties, the following:

If $\mathcal{S} = \{S_\alpha; S_\alpha \subseteq R^n\}$ is a collection of compact subsets of R^n such that every finite set of members of $\mathscr{S}$ has a non-empty intersection, then

$$\bigcap_{S_\alpha \in \mathscr{S}} S_\alpha \neq \varnothing.$$

8.4.2 Convex Sets and a Separation Theorem

Let $S \subseteq R^n$; then S is convex if

$$x, y \in S \Rightarrow \lambda x + (1 - \lambda)y \in S$$

for all λ, $0 \leqslant \lambda \leqslant 1$. We can now state the following theorem.

SEPARATION THEOREM (ST): Let S and T be two disjoint (i.e. $S \cap T = \varnothing$) non-empty convex sets; then there is $p \neq 0$ and a real number α, such that

$$px \geqslant \alpha \qquad \text{for all } x \in S;$$

$$px \leqslant \alpha \qquad \text{for all } x \in T.$$

(The plane $px = \alpha$ divides R^n into two parts, one of which contains S and the other, T.) This result is a general version of SH mentioned in Section 8.3.2.

Given any set $A \subseteq R^n$, we define con A to be the smallest convex set containing A; con A is the *convex hull* of A. Formally, since R^n is convex, we know that the family $\mathscr{S}_A = \{S \subseteq R^n : A \subseteq S \text{ and } S \text{ is convex}\}$ is non-empty for any A. Also, since the intersection of any collection of convex sets is convex,

$$\text{con } A = \bigcap_{S \in \mathscr{S}_A} S$$

since $S \in \mathscr{S}_A \Rightarrow A \subseteq S$, $A \subseteq \text{con } A$. Note that A compact $\Rightarrow$ con A is compact.

8.5 Functions on R^n: Continuity and Differentiability

A real-valued function $f(\cdot)$ on R^n is a rule that assigns to each $x \in R^n$ a unique real number $\alpha \in R$; this is termed the value of $f(\cdot)$ at x, and we write

$$f(x) = \alpha.$$

Sometimes a function may not be defined for all of R^n but only over $S \subseteq R^n$; the set on which a function is defined is called the *domain* of f. Similarly, it is not necessary that every element of R be taken on as a value; the subset of R from which values are assumed is called the *range* of f. For example,

$$f(x) = \frac{1}{1 + x} x \geqslant 0$$

has as domain the entire non-negative real line, but its range is $[0, 1]$, or $0 < f(x) \leqslant 1$ for all $x \geqslant 0$.

Sometimes the notation $f: R^n \to R$ is also used. Let $x^0 \in R^n$; we shall say that

$$\lim_{x \to x^0} f(x) = A \qquad \text{where } A \in R$$

whenever, for any $\varepsilon > 0$, there is $\eta > 0$ such that

$$|f(x) - A| < \varepsilon \qquad \text{whenever } \delta(x, x^0) < \eta$$

where $|f(x) - A| < \varepsilon$ stands for

$$A - \varepsilon < f(x) < A + \varepsilon$$

and $\delta(\cdot)$ denotes the Euclidean distance introduced earlier.

A real-valued function $f: R^n \to R$ is said to be *continuous* at $x^0 \in R^n$ if

$$\lim_{x \to x^0} f(x) = f(x^0).$$

Otherwise, the function is said to be discontinuous at x^0. Notice that continuity at x^0 entails that

(a) the function must be defined at x^0;

(b) $\lim_{x \to x^0} f(x)$ should be defined;

(c) the two must be equal.

Let S denote the set of points of R^n at which $f(\cdot)$ is continuous. If S is compact, then so is $f(S)$, where $f(S)$ is defined by $f(S) = \{y \in R: \text{there is } x \in S \text{ and } y = f(x)\}$. Given any function $f: R^n \to R$, define $g: f(R^n) \to R^n$ by

$$\text{for } \alpha \in f(R^n), \, g(\alpha) = x \in R^n \text{ such that } f(x) = \alpha.$$

However, in general, $g(\cdot)$ need not be a function; e.g., $y = 4ax^2$ associates with each $x \in R$ a unique y; but, given a y, there are two possible x's: $\frac{1}{2}\sqrt{y/a}$ and $-\frac{1}{2}\sqrt{y/a}$. When g also satisfies the definition of a function, g is defined to be the inverse function of $f(\cdot)$; sometimes $g(\cdot) = f^{-1}(\cdot)$ is also used. The following theorems obtain.

If $f(\cdot)$ is a continuous function defined over a compact set S such that f^{-1} is defined over $f(S) \subseteq R$, then f^{-1} is continuous over $f(S)$.

EXTREMUM THEOREM (ET): moreover, if $f(\cdot)$ is a continuous function on a compact set $S \subseteq R^n$, then $f(x)$ has an absolute maximum and an absolute minimum on S; i.e., there are points $a, b \in S$ such that

$$f(b) \leqslant f(x) \leqslant f(a)$$

for all $x \in S$.

This is a very basic result.

8.5.1 *Differentiability*

We assume that, given a function $f: R \to R$ (i.e., a function of a single variable), readers are familiar with the notion of the derivative of $f(\cdot)$ at $\bar{x}$, denoted by $f'(\bar{x})$. When we consider $f: R^n \to R$, we consider *partial derivatives* of f at $\bar{x} \in R^n$; these are denoted by

$$\frac{\partial f(\bar{x})}{\partial x_j} \quad \text{or} \quad D_j f(\bar{x}), \qquad j = 1, 2, \ldots, n$$

and are defined by

$$D_j f(\bar{x}) = \lim_{x_j \to \bar{x}_j} \frac{f(\bar{x}_1, \ldots, \bar{x}_{j-1}, x_j, \bar{x}_{j+1}, \ldots, \bar{x}_n) - f(\bar{x})}{x_j - \bar{x}_j}$$

whenever the limit exists.

Although, for a function of a single variable, the existence of a derivative at a point implies continuity of the function at that point, the existence of all partial derivatives at a point need not imply continuity of $f(x)$ at that point. It turns out that, for this purpose, the existence of the differential of $f(\cdot)$ at x is sufficient.

Define $\nabla f(\bar{x}) = \{D_1 f(\bar{x}), D_2 f(\bar{x}), \ldots, D_n f(\bar{x})\}$ whenever the partial derivatives exist. Let $df(x; t) = \nabla f(x) \cdot t$ for any $t \in R^n$ ($\cdot$ denotes inner product). Now if $D_j f(x)$ exist for all j and are continuous at x, then, for any $\varepsilon > 0$, there is a neighbourhood $N(x)$ such that

$$|f(y) - f(x) - df(x; y - x)| < \varepsilon \delta(y, x)$$

whenever $y \in N(x)$, $y \neq x$; $df(x; t)$ is then the *differential of* $f(\cdot)$ *at* x and $f(\cdot)$ is said to be *continuously differentiable* at x.

Let $x \neq y$, $x, y \in R^n$; then

$$L(x, y) = \{z : z = \theta x + (1 - \theta)y, 0 < \theta < 1\},$$

is the open line segment (which incidentally, is not an open set if $n > 1$). We then have the following theorem.

MEAN VALUE THEOREM: If $f(\cdot)$ has a differential at each point of an open set $S \subseteq R^n$, and if $x, y \in S$ such that $L(x, y) \subseteq S$, then there is $z \in L(x, y)$ such that

$$f(y) - f(x) = \nabla f(z) \cdot (y - x).$$

Partial derivatives of the second order are defined by

$$D_{ij} f(\bar{x}) = D_j \{D_i f(\bar{x})\}$$

$$= \frac{\partial}{\partial x_j} \left\{ \frac{\partial f(\bar{x})}{\partial x_i} \right\},$$

provided derivatives exist. If, for example, in R^2, $D_1 f$, $D_2 f$, and $D_{21} f$ exist and are continuous, then $D_{21} f = D_{12} f$. Now the matrix $\{D_{ij} f(x)\}$ is denoted $\nabla^2 f(x)$; if continuous second-order partial derivatives of $f(\cdot)$ exist on an open set S then $f(\cdot)$ is *continuously differentiable of the second order* on S. We then have

TAYLOR'S THEOREM:

$$f(y) - f(x) = f(x) \cdot (y - x) + \tfrac{1}{2}(y - x) \cdot \nabla^2 f(z) \cdot (y - x)$$

for some $z \in L(x, y) \subseteq S$.

The Mean Value Theorem and Taylor's Theorem are often used to approximate the value of a function at a point. But some care is necessary to draw correct inferences from such an approximation. For example, suppose x, y satisfy the statement of the Mean Value Theorem for a given function $f(\cdot)$; then

$$f(y) = f(x) + \nabla f(z) \cdot (y - x)$$

where $z \in L(x, y)$.

Consider $w_\theta = \theta y + (1 - \theta) x$, $0 \leqslant \theta \leqslant 1$; then $w_\theta \in L(x, y)$, and for any θ, $0 < \theta < 1$,

$$f(w_\theta) = f(x) + \nabla f(z_\theta) \cdot (w_\theta - x) \qquad \text{for some } z_\theta \in L(x, w_\theta)$$

$$= f(x) + \nabla f(z_\theta) \cdot \theta(y - x).$$

Now for θ small enough, we may use the following approximation:

$$f(w_\theta) \approx f(x) + \theta \cdot \nabla f(x) \cdot (y - x).$$

If we wish to conclude that $f(w_\theta) > f(x)$, then we must have $\nabla f(x) \cdot (y - x) > 0$. If $\nabla f(x) \cdot (y - x) \geqslant 0$, we *cannot* conclude that $f(w_\theta) - f(x) \geqslant 0$.

Finally, suppose that $f_1, f_2, \ldots, f_n$ are each real-valued functions $R^n \to R$; then $f = (f_1, \ldots, f_n)$ is a vector-valued function $R^n \to R^n$. By the *Jacobian* of f at $x \in R^n$, we mean the determinant

$$d\{D_i f_j(\bar{x})\}.$$

It may be shown that the following theorem obtains.

IMPLICIT FUNCTION THEOREM: Let $f = (f_1, \ldots, f_n)$ be a vector-valued function defined on a compact set S in R^{n+k} with values in R^n (i.e., each $f_i : R^{n+k} \to R$); also, suppose that each f_i has continuous partials $D_j f_i$ for all $j = 1, \ldots, n + k$. (This is sometimes expressed by the statement that f is C^1) for all points in S. Let $(\bar{x}, \bar{t}) \in S$, $\bar{x} \in R^n$, $\bar{t} \in R^k$, and let $f(\bar{x}, \bar{t}) = 0$, for which

$$d\{D_j f_i(\bar{x}, \bar{t})\} \neq 0, \qquad j = 1, \ldots, n; \quad i = 1, \ldots, n.$$

Then there is a k-dimensional neighbourhood T of $\bar{t}$ in R^k and a unique vector-valued function g, defined on T, having values in R^n such that

(i) g is C^1 on T;
(ii) $g(\bar{t}) = \bar{x}$;
(iii) $f\{g(t), t\} = 0$ for all $t \in T$.

8.5.2 *Some Special Functions*

In the course of our analysis some special functions appear. First, there are *homogeneous* functions. A function $f: R^n \to R$ is said to be *homogeneous of degree r* if $f(tx) = t^r f(x)$ for any scalar t and for all x.

We shall be concerned with mainly homogeneous-of-degree-0 and homogeneous-of-degree-1 functions. For homogeneous functions, we have the following result:

$$x \cdot \nabla f(x) = r t^{r-1} f(x),$$

obtained by differentiating the earlier defining equation with respect to t. Evaluating at $t = 1$, we have the well-known *Euler's Theorem* for homogeneous functions of degree r,

$$x \cdot \nabla f(x) = r f(x).$$

A function $f: R^n \to R$ is said to be *concave* if, for any $x^1, x^2 \in R^n$,

$$f\{\lambda x^1 + (1 - \lambda)x^2\} \geqslant \lambda f(x^1) + (1 - \lambda)f(x^2) \qquad \text{for any } \lambda, 0 \leqslant \lambda \leqslant 1.$$

$f(\cdot)$ is said to be *convex* if $-f(x)$ is concave. For differentiable concave functions $f(x)$, an immediate consequence is

$$f(x^1) - f(x^2) \leqslant \nabla f(x^2) \cdot (x^1 - x^2);$$

further, if

$$F = \left\{ \frac{\partial^2 f(x)}{\partial x_i \partial x_j} \right\},$$

then F is negative semi-definite. (In fact, a stronger statement is possible; for any concave function $f(\cdot)$, the matrix F exists almost everywhere and is negative semi-definite; i.e., the second-order partial derivatives exist almost everywhere, which means that they may fail to exist only at isolated points.) This result has many interesting applications.

$f(\cdot)$ is defined to be *strictly concave* when

$$f\{\lambda x^1 + (1 - \lambda)x^2\} > f(x^1) + (1 - \lambda)f(x^2) \text{ for any } \lambda, 0 < \lambda < 1 \text{ and } x^1, x^2 \in R^n.$$

Similarly, strict convexity may also be defined.

A somewhat weaker type of concavity is also defined by the following: $f: R^n \to R$ is said to be *quasi-concave* if

$$f(x^1) \geqq f(x^2) \Rightarrow f\{\lambda x^1 + (1 - \lambda)x^2\} \geqq f(x^2) \qquad \text{for any } \lambda, 0 \leqslant \lambda \leqslant 1.$$

An alternative definition of *quasi-concavity* involves the following:

Let $Y(x) = \{y \in R^n : f(y) \geqq f(x)\}$. $f(x)$ is quasi-concave if $Y(x)$ is a convex subset of R^n for all x.

For differentiable quasi-concave functions, it can be shown that

$$f(x) \geqq f(y) \Rightarrow \nabla f(y) \cdot (x - y) \geqq 0.$$

8.5.3 *Correspondences and Fixed-Point Theorems*

Up to this point, we have considered functions $f: R^n \to R^m$; now it may be necessary to consider situations when f is such that the image $f(x)$ consists of a set rather than a point. We shall call such an f to be a *correspondence* from R^n to R^m. Thus, a correspondence reduces to a function when, for every $x, f(x)$ reduces to a single point.

Let S be a subset of R^n and T a subset of R^m; for every $x \in S$, let $f(x) \subseteq T$ so that f is a correspondence from S to T; i.e., $f: S \to T$. Let x^q be a sequence of points in S, y^q a sequence of points in T. Let $x^0 \in S$.

f is *closed* at $x^0 \in S$, if $x^q \to x^0$, $y^q \in f(x^q)$, $y^q \to y^0 \Rightarrow y^0 \in f(x^0)$; in other words, if x^q tends to x^0, and if y^q is a sequence in T such that $y^q \in f(x^q)$ for all q and $y^q \to y^0$, then $y^0 \in f(x^0)$.

f is *lower hemi-continuous* (l.h.c.) at $x^0 \in S$ if $x^q \to x^0$ and $y^0 \in f(x^0) \Rightarrow$ there is a sequence y^q such that $y^q \in f(x^q)$ for all q and $y^q \to y^0$.

f is *upper hemi-continuous* (u.h.c.) at $x^0 \in S$ if, for any open set V of T such that $f(x^0) \subseteq V$, there is an open set U of S such that $x \in U \Rightarrow f(x) \subseteq V$.

f is *compact-valued* at $x^0 \in S$ if $f(x^0)$ is a compact subset of T. When S and T are subsets of R^n, R^m, respectively, if f is compact-valued at x^0, then f is closed at $x^0 \Rightarrow f$ is u.h.c. at x^0. Also, f is *continuous* at x^0 if it is both u.h.c. and l.h.c. at x^0. Notice that, if $f(x)$ is a function, u.h.c. and l.h.c. are each equivalent to continuity: u.h.c. at x^0 rules out the 'collapse' of the correspondence at x^0, whereas l.h.c. at x^0 prevents the 'blowing up' of the correspondence at x^0.

Fixed-point theorems are results concerning the existence of points that are contained in the image of the point under f; i.e., these points are left unaltered. The simplest example is that of a function $f: [0, 1] \to [0, 1]$, where, if the graph of $f(\cdot)$ intersects the 45^0 line for some $x \in [0, 1]$, we have a fixed point. Two fixed-point theorems follow (the first is for functions).

> BROUWER'S FIXED-POINT THEOREM: Let X be a compact convex subset of R^n, and let $f: X \to X$ be a continuous function; then there is $x^* \in X$ such that $f(x^*) = x^*$.

KAKUTANI FIXED-POINT THEOREM: Let $f: X \to 2^X$ (2^X denotes the family of all subsets of X) where X is a convex and compact subset of R^n. If $f(\cdot)$ is closed at every $x \in X$, and, further, if $f(x)$ is a non-empty convex subset of X for every $x \in X$, then there is $x^* \in X$ such that $x^* \in f(x^*)$.

8.6 Problems of Maximization

8.6.1 *Unconstrained Problems*

We shall consider real-valued function $f(\cdot)$ defined on R^n. $\hat{x} \in R^n$ is said to be an *absolute maximum* for f if,

$$\text{for all } x \in R^n, f(x) \leqslant f(\hat{x}). \tag{8.4}$$

Similarly, $\hat{x} \in R^n$ is said to be an *absolute minimum* for f if $\hat{x}$ is an absolute maximum for $-f$.

$\hat{x}$ is said to be a local maximum for f if there exists a neighbourhood $U(\hat{x})$ such that,

$$\text{for all } x \in U(\hat{x}), \quad f(x) \leqslant f(\hat{x}). \tag{8.5}$$

Necessary conditions for a local maximum
  1: If $f(\cdot)$ is twice differentiable, $\hat{x}$ is a local maximum implies that

$$\nabla f(\hat{x}) = 0 \tag{8.6}$$

  and

$$x' \nabla^2 f(\hat{x}) x \leqslant 0 \quad \text{for all } x. \tag{8.7}$$

  2: If $f(\cdot)$ is a concave function of x, (8.6) at $\hat{x} \Rightarrow \hat{x}$ provides an absolute maximum of $f(\cdot)$.
  3: If $\hat{x}$ is such that (8.6) holds, *and*, further, if

$$x' \nabla^2 f(\hat{x}) x < 0 \quad \text{for all } x \neq 0, \tag{8.8}$$

  then $\hat{x}$ constitutes a local maximum for $f(\cdot)$.

So (8.6) and (8.7) are *necessary* for a local maximum; but (8.6) and (8.8) are *sufficient* for a local maximum. Twice differentiable is to be interpreted as continuously differentiable of the second order.

8.6.2 *Constrained Problems*

Let $X \subseteq R^n$ and $f: R^n \to R$. Then $\hat{x} \in X$ is said to be a local *constrained maximum* if there is a neighbourhood $U(\hat{x})$ such that,

$$\text{for all } x \in U(\hat{x}) \cap X, \quad f(x) \leqslant f(\hat{x}). \tag{8.9}$$

$\hat{x}$ is said to be an *absolute constrained maximum* if,

$$\text{for all } x \in X, \qquad f(x) \leqslant f(\hat{x}). \tag{8.10}$$

One may similarly define a *local constrained minimum* and an *absolute constrained minimum*.

The set X is called the *constraint set*. We shall now examine some alternative specifications of X. First, consider

A: $X = \{x \in R^n : g_j(x) = 0 \qquad j = 1, 2, \ldots, m\}$, *where each $g_j(\cdot)$ is a real-valued function on R^n.*

We shall assume that the functions $f(\cdot), g_j(\cdot)$ are differentiable functions with continuous second-order partial derivatives.

4: If X is as in A, $\hat{x}$ is a local maximum of $f(x)$ in X; and if

$$G^0 = \left\{ \frac{\partial g_j(\hat{x})}{\partial x_k} \right\}, \qquad j = 1, 2, \ldots, m, \qquad k = 1, \ldots, n,$$

is of rank m, then there is $\hat{\lambda} \in R^m$ such that

$$\nabla f(\hat{x}) + \sum_{j=1}^{m} \hat{\lambda}_j \nabla g_j(\hat{x}) = 0. \tag{8.11}$$

5: If $(\hat{x}, \hat{\lambda})$ satisfy (8.11) and $\hat{x} \in X$, and if

$$x' \{ \nabla^2 f(\hat{x}) + \Sigma \hat{\lambda}_j \nabla^2 g_j(\hat{x}) \} x < 0 \tag{8.12}$$

for all $x \neq 0$ satisfying $\nabla g_j(\hat{x}) . x = 0, j = 1, 2, \ldots, m$, then $\hat{x}$ is a local maximum for $f(\cdot)$ in X.

A stronger set of sufficient conditions, which, together with (8.11), implies that $\hat{x}$ is an *absolute maximum*, is contained in the next two claims.

6: If, for some $\hat{x} \in X$, there is $\hat{\lambda} \in R^m$ such that $(\hat{x}, \hat{\lambda})$ satisfy (8.11), and if

$$L(x) = f(x) + \Sigma \hat{\lambda}_j g_j(x)$$

is concave in x, then $\hat{x}$ provides an absolute maximum of $f(\cdot)$ in X.

7: If $f(x)$ and $g_j(x)$ are quasi-concave differentiable functions, and if, further, $(\hat{x}, \hat{\lambda})$ satisfy (8.11) with $\hat{x} \in X$ and

$$\nabla f(\hat{x}) \neq 0, \qquad \hat{\lambda} \geqslant 0, \tag{8.13}$$

then $\hat{x}$ provides an absolute maximum of $f(\cdot)$ in X.

Proof: Consider $x \in X$; since $g_j(x) = g_j(\hat{x}) = 0$ for all j, quasi-concavity of $g_j(\cdot) \Rightarrow \nabla g_j(\hat{x}) (x - \hat{x}) \geqslant 0$ for all j. Thus

$$(8.11) \Rightarrow \nabla f(\hat{x})(x - \hat{x}) = -\Sigma \hat{\lambda}_j \nabla g_j(x)(\hat{x} - x) \leqslant 0. \tag{8.14}$$

since $\hat{\lambda}_j \geqslant 0$, and $x \in X$.

Suppose now that there is $\bar{x} \in X$ such that $f(\bar{x}) > f(\hat{x})$; hence quasi-concavity of $f(\cdot)$ implies that

$$\nabla f(\hat{x})(\bar{x} - \hat{x}) \geqslant 0;$$

i.e., together with (8.14),

$$\nabla f(\hat{x})(\bar{x} - \hat{x}) = 0. \tag{8.15}$$

By continuity of $f(\cdot)$ there is a neighbourhood $N_\sigma(\bar{x})$ of $\bar{x}$ such that

$$x \in N_\sigma(\bar{x}) \Rightarrow f(x) > f(\hat{x}).$$

Moreover, $\nabla f(\hat{x}) \neq 0$, which implies that there is $\tilde{x} \in N_\sigma(\bar{x})$ such that

$$\nabla f(\hat{x}) \cdot \tilde{x} < \nabla f(\hat{x})\bar{x} = \nabla f(\hat{x})\hat{x}, \text{ by (8.15)},$$

so that $f(\tilde{x}) \leqslant f(\hat{x})$, by quasi-concavity of $f(\cdot)$: a contradiction to the definition of $N_\sigma(\bar{x})$. Hence no such $\bar{x}$ can exist, and the claim is established. $\square$

An alternative sufficient condition is obtained by replacing quasi-concavity of the functions $g_j(\cdot)$ by the convexity of X.

8: If $f(\cdot)$ is quasi-concave and X is convex, then $(\hat{x}, \hat{\lambda})$ satisfying (8.11) with $\hat{x} \in X$ and $\nabla f(\hat{x}) \neq 0 \Rightarrow \hat{x}$ is an absolute maximum of $f(\cdot)$ in X.

See that

$$x, y \in X \Rightarrow \lambda x + (1 - \lambda)y \in X, \qquad 0 \leqslant \lambda \leqslant 1,$$

or

$$g_j(x) = 0 = g_j(y) \Rightarrow g_j\{y + \lambda(x - y)\} = 0 \qquad \text{for all } \lambda;$$

$$\therefore \nabla g_j(y)(x - y) = 0 \qquad \text{for all } j.$$

This allows us to follow the steps of the proof of claim 7. $\square$

B: $X = \{x \in R^n : g_j(x) \geqslant 0, \ x \geqslant 0, j = 1, 2, \ldots, m\}.$

Consider $\phi(x, \lambda) = f(x) + \Sigma \lambda_j g_j(x)$: the *Lagrangean*. In contrast to our earlier characterization of a local maximum, we first seek an absolute maximum $\hat{x}$ of $f(x)$ in X. Before proceeding with the maximum problem, we consider the *saddle value problem*:
Find (x^*, λ^*) such that

$$\phi(x, \lambda^*) \leqslant \phi(x^*, \lambda^*) \leqslant \phi(x^*, \lambda) \quad \text{for all } x \geqslant 0, \lambda \geqslant 0. \tag{8.16}$$

We shall also maintain the assumption that $f(\cdot)$ and $g_j(\cdot)$ are differentiable functions. It is then easily seen that

9: $(\hat{x}, \hat{\lambda})$ constitute a saddle-point for $\varphi(\cdot) \Rightarrow$
  (i) $\phi_x(\hat{x}, \hat{\lambda}) \leqslant 0, \qquad \hat{x}'\phi_x(\hat{x}, \hat{\lambda}) = 0, \hat{x} \geqslant 0 \tag{8.17}$
  (ii) $\phi_\lambda(\hat{x}, \hat{\lambda}) \geqslant 0, \qquad \hat{\lambda}'\phi_\lambda(\hat{x}, \hat{\lambda}) = 0, \hat{\lambda} \geqslant 0 \tag{8.18}$

These conditions follow from (8.16) and result 1, extended to cover corner solutions. (8.17) and (8.18) constitute the *Kuhn–Tucker conditions*.

10: If $\phi(x, \lambda)$ is concave in x given λ, (8.17) and (8.18) at $(\hat{x}, \hat{\lambda}) \Rightarrow (\hat{x}, \hat{\lambda})$ constitute a saddle-point.

Now we have that, if $(\hat{x}, \hat{\lambda})$ constitutes a saddle-point, then $\hat{x}$ provides an absolute maximum of $f(x)$ in X. Alternatively, by virtue of claim 10, (8.17), (8.18), and concavity of $\phi(x, \lambda)$ in x are sufficient for $\hat{x}$ providing an absolute maximum of $f(\cdot)$ in X.

11: If $(\hat{x}; \hat{\lambda})$ constitutes a saddle-point for $\phi(x, \lambda)$, $\hat{x}$ provides an absolute maximum of $f(x)$ in X if, in addition, $\phi(x, \lambda)$ is differentiable.

By virtue of claim 10, we may restate 11, as follows.

12: (8.17) and (8.18) $\Rightarrow \hat{x}$ is an absolute maximum of $f(x)$ in X provided $\phi(x, \lambda)$ is concave in x for any λ.

In general, of course, if $\hat{x}$ is an absolute maximum of $f(x)$ in X, there may not exist $\hat{\lambda}$ such that $(\hat{x}, \hat{\lambda})$ satisfies the Kuhn–Tucker conditions. But for a certain class of problems, i.e. those where the *constraint qualification conditions* are met, the Kuhn–Tucker conditions are necessary, as well. The constraint qualification conditions are properties required of the function $g_j(\cdot)$. One such condition is as follows.

13: Suppose $f(x)$, $g_j(x)$ are concave functions for $x \geqslant 0$; further, suppose that there is $x^* \geqslant 0$ such that $g_j(x^*) > 0$ for all j (*Slater's condition*). Then $\hat{x}$ is an absolute maximum of $f(\cdot)$ in X if and only if there is $\hat{\lambda} \geqslant 0$ such that $(\hat{x}, \hat{\lambda})$ constitute a saddle-point for $\phi(x, \lambda)$.

14: Suppose $f(x)$ is concave and $g_j(x) = a^j x + b_j$ for all j; then $\hat{x}$ provides an absolute maximum for $f(x)$ in X, which implies that there is $\hat{\lambda} \geqslant 0$ such that $(\hat{x}, \hat{\lambda})$ constitutes a saddle-point for

$$\phi(x, \lambda) = f(x) + \lambda'(Ax + b),$$

where $A = (a^1, \ldots, a^m)$, $b = (b_1, \ldots, b_m)$.

To complete considerations, we consider the results when $f(\cdot)$ and $g_j(\cdot)$ are assumed *quasi-concave* only, rather than concave. For such functions, we have

15: Let $\hat{x}$ be an absolute maximum of $f(x)$ in X; if Slater's condition holds and either $g_j(x)$ is concave or $\nabla g_j(x) \neq 0$ for all $x \in X$, then there exists $\hat{\lambda} \geqslant 0$ such that $(\hat{x}, \hat{\lambda})$ constitute a saddle-point for $\phi(x, \lambda)$.

16: If there exist $(\hat{x}, \hat{\lambda})$ satisfying (8.17) and (8.18), then $\hat{x}$ provides an absolute maximum for $f(x)$ in X provided $\nabla f(\hat{x}) \neq 0$, and Slater's condition holds.

8.6.3 *Duality*

A duality theorem in mathematical programming specifies a relationship between the solutions of two programs. There are three aspects of this relationship:

(a) one problem is a constrained maximization problem (M) and the other a constrained minimization problem (N);
(b) the existence of a solution to either problem implies that the other has a solution and that the extrema are equal;
(c) if the constraints of any one of the problems is inconsistent, whereas the constraint of the other is consistent, then there is a sequence of feasible points of the consistent problem on which its objective function becomes infinitely large in absolute value.

Such a duality theorem is presented in this section.

Let $f(x)$ and $g_j(x)$, $j = 1, 2, \ldots, m$, be differentiable functions defined on R^n; further, let $f(x)$ be concave and let $g_j(x) = a_j \cdot x + b_j$ where $a_j \in R^n$ and $b_j \in R$. Define

$$\phi(x, u) = f(x) + \sum_{j=1}^{m} u_j g_j(x), \quad u \in R^m.$$

Then

$$\phi_x(x, u) = \nabla f(x) + \sum_{j=1}^{m} u_j a_j.$$

Now consider the following pair of problems:

$$\left.\begin{array}{ll} \max & f(x) \\ \text{s.t.} & g_j(x) \geqslant 0, \quad j = 1, \ldots, m \end{array}\right\} \qquad (M)$$

$$\left.\begin{array}{ll} \min & \phi(x, u) \\ \text{s.t.} & \phi_x(x, u) = 0 \\ & u \geqslant 0. \end{array}\right\} \qquad (N)$$

We shall show that (M) and (N) have the dual relationship explained above.

Let

$$X = \{x \in R^n: \quad g_j(x) \geqslant 0, \quad j = 1, \ldots, m\}$$

$$Y = \{(x, u) \in R^n \times R^m: \phi_x(x, u) = 0, u \geqslant 0\};$$

and define

$$v = \sup_{x \in X} f(x) \quad \text{and} \quad V = \inf_{(x, u) \in Y} \phi(x, u).$$

It may be noted that

1 $X \neq \emptyset$ and $Y \neq \emptyset \Rightarrow v \leqslant V;$

2   $X \neq \emptyset$, $Y = \emptyset \Rightarrow$ (M) has no solution;
3   if $Y \neq \emptyset$ and $X = \emptyset$, then (N) has no solution;
4   if x^* solves (M), then there is u^* such that (x^*, u^*) solves (N) and $f(x^*)$
    $= \phi(x^*, u^*)$;
5   if (x^*, u^*) solves (N), and if there is $\theta^* \geqslant 0$ such that

$$\psi(x^*, u^*, \theta) \geqslant \psi(x^*, u^*, \theta^*) \geqslant \psi(x, u, \theta^*)$$

for all $\theta \geqslant 0$, $u \geqslant 0$, and all x, then x^* solves (M) and $f(x^*) = \phi(x^*, u^*)$.
(Here $\psi(x, u, \theta) = -\phi(x, u) + \theta' \cdot \phi_x(x, u)$.)

Claims 1–5 establish our duality theorem. As an immediate special case, let

$$f(x) = c \cdot x \quad \text{where} \quad c \in R^n,$$

and consider the standard linear programming problem

$$\max c \cdot x$$
$$\text{s.t.} \quad a_i \cdot x \leqslant b_i, \quad i = 1, \ldots, m \left.\vphantom{\begin{matrix} a \\ x \end{matrix}}\right\} \quad \text{(M')}$$
$$x_j \geqslant 0, \quad j = 1, 2, \ldots, n.$$

This is a special case of (M), as can be seen by writing

$$\max \quad c \cdot x$$
$$\text{s.t.} \quad b_i - a_i x \geqslant 0, \quad i = 1, \ldots, m$$
$$x_j \geqslant 0, \quad j = 1, \ldots, n.$$

There are $m + n$ constraints, and by virtue of our results, consider

$$\phi(x, u) = cx + \sum_{i=1}^{m} u_i(b_i - a_i x) + \sum_{j=1}^{n} w_j x_j$$

with

$$\phi_x(x, u) = c - \sum_{i=1}^{m} u_i a_i + w$$

where $w = (w_1, \ldots, w_n)$. Now given the nature of (N),

$$\phi_x(x, u) = 0 \Rightarrow \phi(x, u) = \sum_{i=1}^{m} u_i b_i,$$

and so the dual to (M') is

$$\min \quad \sum_{i=1}^{m} u_i b_i$$
$$\text{s.t.} \quad \sum_{i=1}^{m} u_i a_i \geqslant c \left.\vphantom{\begin{matrix} a \\ x \\ y \end{matrix}}\right\} \quad \text{(N')}$$
$$u \geqslant 0.$$

The fact that (M') and (N') are duals of one another, in the sense described earlier, constitutes the *Fundamental Theorem of Linear Programming*.

Additionally, x^* solves (M') if and only if there is u^* solving (N'), and

$$a_i x^* < b_i \qquad \text{for some } i = 1, 2, \ldots, m \Rightarrow u_i^* = 0$$

whereas

$$\sum_{i=1}^{m} u_i^* a_{ij} > c_j \quad \text{for some } j = 1, 2, \ldots, n \Rightarrow x_i^* = 0.$$

These claims follow from results 4 and 5, applied to the special case. Finally, one may note that 5 becomes applicable owing to the nature of the constraints in (N'), so that result 14 of Section 8.6.2 guarantees that, at an optimum, saddle-point conditions must hold.

8.7 Game Theory

8.7.1 *Description and Structure*

Any situation that involves at least two decision-makers whose interests are related and whose decisions together determine the outcome may be thought of as a game. The decision-makers are called *players*; the various actions that each may pursue are called *strategies*; and the outcome for each player is called his *pay-off*.

There are three alternative methods of specifying a game: the *normal form*, the *characteristic function form*, and the *extensive form*. The first involves a specification of the strategies and pay-offs; the second involves a specification of what players and coalitions of players can guarantee to themselves; and the third is a specification of the sequence of players' moves. Here a 'move' may be thought of as the actual action undertaken by the player. The particular specification chosen would depend upon the problem being studied. We shall confine our brief deliberations to the normal form.

Depending on the context, a game may be viewed as being *co-operative* or *non-cooperative*. In the former case, all possible coalitions of players are allowed to form, and a consideration of their joint actions is taken into account, while in the latter case no coalition of two or more players may form. We shall deal with non-cooperative games below, and it is the normal form that is often used to define such games.

To define a game in normal form, we need to specify:

(i) $N = \{1, 2, \ldots, n\}$: the set of players;
(ii) S_i: the set of strategies available to $i \in N$;
(iii) the pay-off function π_i, defined over the set $S = \{S_1 \times S_2 \times \ldots \times S_n\}$ for each $i \in N$;

(iv) additional rules for playing the game; e.g., no coalitions of two or more can form.

Thus, given (iv), the collection $\{N, S_i, \pi_i\}$ defines a game in normal form. The main point about the game is that, for each i, π_i is defined over S, so that the pay-off to i depends upon the strategies chosen by the entire set of players. Given a particular i, it would be convenient to denote by $\bar{s}_i$ the array of strategies $(s_1, \ldots, s_{i-1}, s_{i+1}, \ldots, s_n)$ chosen by players other than i;

$$\bar{s}_i \in \bar{S}_i = \underset{k \neq i}{\times} S_k.$$

A particularly pessimistic player i may proceed as follows. For each $s_i \in S_i$, he considers the worst possible $\bar{s}_i$ for him, i.e. the $\bar{s}_i$ which, if chosen by his rivals, would minimize his pay-off if he has chosen s_i. Let us denote this pay-off by $\pi_i(s_i)$; i.e.,

$$\pi_i(s_i) = \min_{\bar{s}_i \in \bar{S}_i} \pi_i(s_i, \bar{s}_i).$$

Thus, i is assured of at least $\pi_i(s_i)$ if he plays s_i. Now i considers playing or choosing that particular s_i for which $\pi_i(s_i)$ is a maximum; i.e.,

$$\pi_i^* = \max_{s_i \in S_i} \pi_i(s_i) = \max_{s_i \in S_i} \min_{\bar{s}_i \in \bar{S}_i} \pi_i(s_i, \bar{s}_i).$$

If the maximum and minimum considered in the above expressions exist, then player i can assure himself of a pay-off π_i^* by choosing the appropriate strategy s_i^*; such a strategy is called a *minimax strategy*, after the well-known contribution of von Neumann in the context of two-person, zero-sum games. Here $\pi_1(s_1, s_2) = -\pi_2(s_1, s_2)$; and for each i

$$S_i = \left\{ q:(q_1, \ldots, q_{m_i}) \geqslant 0, \sum_{j=1}^{m_i} q_j = 1 \right\}.$$

The interpretation being that each player i has a finite, m_i, number of *pure* strategies $\{v_{ij}, j = 1, \ldots, m_i\}$; a player i can choose a probability distribution over these, and all such probability distributions make up S_i. An element of S_i is called a 'mixed strategy'. In addition, von Neumann assumed that

$$\pi_i(p, q) = \sum_k \sum_j p_k \pi_{ikj} q_j$$

where π_{ikj} is the pay-off to i if player 1 chooses v_{1k} and player 2 chooses v_{2j}, the pure strategies referred to above. In this setup, von Neumann's classic result was

$$\max_{p \in S_1} \min_{q \in S_2} \pi_1(p, q) = \min_{q \in S_2} \max_{p \in S_1} \pi_1(p, q).$$

Returning to our general configuration, where games are not zero-sum, while i can certainly guarantee himself a pay-off π_i^*, he may be able to do better if the corresponding $\bar{s}_i$ is a not particularly reasonable choice by the other players. Thus, we need to look at possible notions of equilibria in such situations.

8.7.2 Equilibrium Concepts

An array $(s_1^*, s_2^*, \ldots, s_n^*) \in S$ constitutes a *Nash (non-cooperative) equilibrium* if, for each i,

$$\pi_i(s^*) = \max_{s_i \in S_i} \pi_i(s_i, \bar{s}_i^*)$$

where

$$\bar{s}_i^* = (s_1^*, \ldots, s_{i-1}^*, s_{i+1}^*, \ldots, s_n^*).$$

Thus, given that others do not change *their* strategies, no player has an incentive to change his own strategy.

If

1   N is finite,
2   S_i is a convex, compact subset of R^{m_i} for each i,
3   $\pi_i \colon S \to R$ is continuous and bounded on S for each i, and
4   $\pi_i(s_i, \bar{s}_i)$ is strictly quasi-concave in s_i for any $\bar{s}_i \in \bar{S}_i$,

then a Nash equilibrium exists.

Sometimes we use the notion of a *strong equilibrium*. An array $s^* = (s_1^*, \ldots, s_n^*) \in S$ is defined to be a strong equilibrium if, for any coalition K of players,

$$\pi_i(s^*) = \max_{s_K \in S^K} \pi_i(s_K, \bar{s}_K^*)$$

for all $i \in K$, where

$$s_K = (s_j \colon j \in K), \quad S^K = \underset{j \in K}{\times} S_j, \text{ and } \bar{s}_K^* = (s_j^* \colon j \notin K).$$

Thus, for any coalition K, if players outside K stick to their strategies, then players in K cannot increase their pay-offs beyond $\pi_i(s^*)$.

Note that a strong equilibrium is a Nash equilibrium; but the converse is not necessarily true.

BIBLIOGRAPHICAL NOTES

The results used here are fairly standard, and there are numerous texts containing proofs of the assertions and claims contained above. A sample of the references is provided, for the sake of completeness.

Sections 8.1, 8.2, 8.4, and 8.5: see Apostol (1957, chs. 1–7).

Sections 8.4.2 and 8.5.3: see Berge (1963).

Sections 8.3.1 and 8.3.2: see Gale (1960, ch. 2).

Section 8.3.3: see Debreu (1952); Takayama (1974).

Section 8.3.4: see Mukherji (1985); Nikaido (1968); McKenzie (1960a).

Section 8.6: see Mangasarian (1969); Arrow *et al.* (1958); Malinvaud (1972).

Section 8.7: see Luce and Raiffa (1957); Friedman (1977); Binmore and Dasgupta (1986, ch. 1).

References

Apostol, T. M. (1957). *Mathematical Analysis*. Addison Wesley, Reading, Mass.

Arrow, K. J. (1950). 'An Extension of the Basic Theorems of Classical Welfare Economics'. In *Proceedings of the Second Berkeley Symposium in Mathematical Statistics and Probability* (ed. J. Neyman), pp. 507–32. University of California Press, Berkeley.

—— (1951). *Social Choice and Individual Values*. John Wiley, New York.

—— (1974). 'General Economic Equilibrium, Purpose, Analytic Techniques, Collective Choice'. *American Economic Review*, 64: 253–73.

—— and Hahn, F. H. (1971). *General Competitive Analysis*. Holden-Day, San Francisco.

——, Hurwicz, L., and Uzawa, H. (eds.) (1958). *Studies in Linear and Non-linear Programming*. Stanford University Press.

—— and Scitovsky, T. (eds.) (1969). *Readings in Welfare Economics*. American Economic Association, Richard Irwin, Homewood, Ill.

Barro, R. J., and Grossman, H. I. (1971). 'A General Disequilibrium Model of Income and Employment'. *American Economic Review*, 61: 82–93.

Bator, F. M. (1957). 'The Simple Analytics of Welfare Maximisation'. *American Economic Review*, 47: 22–59.

Benassy, J. P. (1975). 'Neo-Keynesian Disequilibrium Theory in a Monetary Economy'. *Review of Economic Studies*, 42: 503–23.

—— (1982). *The Economics of Market Disequilibrium*. Academic Press, New York.

Berge, C. (1963). *Topological Spaces*, Macmillan, New York.

Bergson, A. (1938). 'A Reformulation of Certain Aspects of Welfare Economics'. *Quarterly Journal of Economics*, 52: 310–14.

Bhaduri, A. (1983). 'Multimarket Classification of Unemployment: A Sceptical Note'. *Cambridge Journal of Economics*, 7: 235–41.

Binmore, K., and Dasgupta, P. (eds.) (1986). *Economic Organisation as Games*. Basil Blackwell, Oxford.

Chipman, J. S. (1965). 'The Nature and Meaning of Equilibrium in Economic Theory'. In *Functionalism in the Social Sciences: The Strengths and Limits of Functionalism in Anthropology, Economics, Political Science and Sociology, A Symposium* (ed. D. Martindale), pp. 35–64. American Academy of Political Science. Reprinted in *Price Theory* (ed. H. Townsend), pp. 341–71. Penguin, Harmondsworth.

——, Hurwicz, L., Richter, M. K., and Sonnenschein, H. (eds.) (1971). *Preferences Utility and Demand: A Minnesota Symposium*. Harcourt Brace, New York.

Clower, R. W. (1965). 'The Keynesian Counter-revolution: A Theoretical Appraisal'. In *The Theory of Interest Rates* (ed. F. H. Hahn and F. P. R. Brechling), pp. 103–25. Macmillan, London.

Coddington, E. A., and Levinson, N. (1955). *Theory of Ordinary Differential Equations.* McGraw-Hill, New York.

Dasgupta, D. (1974). 'A Note on Johansen's Non-Substitution Theorem and Malinvaud's Decentralization Procedure'. *Journal of Economic Theory,* 9: 340–49.

Dasgupta, P., and Heal, G. (1979). *Economic Theory and Exhaustible Resources.* James Nisbet and Cambridge University Press.

Debreu, G. (1952). 'Definite and Semi-definite Quadratic Forms'. *Econometrica,* 20: 295–300.

—— (1954). 'Valuation Equilibrium and Pareto Optimum'. *Proceedings of the National Academy of Sciences,* 40: 588–92.

—— (1959). *The Theory of Value.* John Wiley, New York.

—— (1982). 'Existence of Competitive Equilibrium'. In *Handbook of Mathematical Economics* (ed. K. J. Arrow and M. D. Intrilligator), Vol. II, pp. 697–744. North Holland, Amsterdam.

—— and Scarf, H. (1963). 'A Limit Theorem on the Core of an Economy'. *International Economic Review,* 4: 235–46.

Diamond, P., and McFadden, D. L. (1974). 'Some Uses of the Expenditure Function in Public Finance'. *Journal of Public Economics,* 3: 3–22.

Dierker, E. (1972). 'Two Remarks on the Number of Equilibria of an Economy'. *Econometrica,* 40: 951–5.

Diewert, W. E. (1982). Duality Approaches to Microeconomic Theory. In *Handbook of Mathematical Economics* (ed. K. J. Arrow and M. D. Intrilligator), Vol. II, pp. 535–600. North Holland, Amsterdam.

Dorfman, R., Samuelson, P. A., and Solow, R. (1958). *Linear Programming and Economic Analysis.* McGraw-Hill, New York.

Dreze, J. H. (1975). 'Existence of an Equilibrium under Price Rigidity and Quantity Rationing'. *International Economic Review,* 16: 301–20.

—— and Muller, H. (1980). 'Optimality Property of Rationing Schemes'. *Journal of Economic Theory,* 23: 131–49.

—— and de la Vallee Poussin, D. (1971). 'A Tatonnement Process for Public Goods'. *Review of Economic Studies,* 38: 133–50.

Feldman, A. M. (1980). *Welfare Economics and Social Choice Theory.* Kluwer Nijhoff Publishing, Boston.

Friedman, J. W. (1977). *Oligopoly and the Theory of Games.* North Holland, Amsterdam.

Gale, David (1960). *The Theory of Linear Economic Models.* McGraw-Hill, New York.

—— (1963). 'A Note on the Global Instability of Competitive Equilibrium'. *Naval Research Logistics Quarterly,* 10: 81–7.

—— (1974). 'Exchange Equilibrium and Coalitions: An Example'. *Journal of Mathematical Economics,* 1: 9–15.

—— and Mas-Colell, A. (1975). 'A Short Proof of the Existence of Equilibrium without Ordered Preferences'. *Journal of Mathematical Economics,* 2: 9–15.

Gale, Douglas (1982). *Money in Equilibrium.* James Nisbet and Cambridge University Press.

—— (1983). *Money in Disequilibrium.* James Nisbet and Cambridge University Press.

Georgescu-Roegen, N. (1951). 'Some Properties of a Generalized Leontief Model'. In

Activity Analysis of Production and Allocation (ed. T. C. Koopmans), pp. 165–76. John Wiley, New York.

Graaff, J. de V. (1967). *Theoretical Welfare Economics* (2nd edn.). Cambridge University Press.

Grandmont, J. M. (1982). 'Temporary Equilibrium Theory'. In *Handbook of Mathematical Economics* (ed. K. J. Arrow and M. D. Intrilligator), Vol. II, pp. 879–922. North Holland, Amsterdam.

—— (1983). *Money and Value.* James Nisbet and Cambridge University Press.

—— and Laroque, G. (1976). 'On Keynesian Temporary Equilibria'. *Review of Economic Studies*, 43: 53–67.

Greenwald, B. C., and Stiglitz, J. E. (1986). 'Externalities in Economies with Imperfect Information and Incomplete Markets'. *Quarterly Journal of Economics*, 100: 229–64.

Guesnerie, R., and Laffont, J. J. (1978). 'Advantageous Reallocation of Initial Endowments'. *Econometrica*, 46: 834–41.

Hahn, F. H. (1962). 'On the Stability of Pure Exchange Equilibrium'. *International Economic Review*, 3: 206–13.

—— (1978). 'On Non-Walrasian Equilibria'. *Review of Economic Studies*, 45: 1–17.

—— (1982). 'Stability'. In *Handbook of Mathematical Economics* (ed. K. J. Arrow and M. D. Intrilligator), Vol. II, pp. 745–94. North Holland, Amsterdam.

—— (1984). *Equilibrium and Macroeconomics.* Basil Blackwell, Oxford.

—— and Negishi, T. (1962). 'A Theorem on Non-Tatonnement Stability'. *Econometrica*, 30: 463–9.

Hart, O. D. (1985). 'Imperfect Competition in General Equilibrium: An Overview of Recent Work'. In *Frontiers of Economics* (ed. K. J. Arrow and S. Honkapohja), pp. 100–77. Basil Blackwell, Oxford.

Heal, G. (1984). 'Planning'. In Handbook of Mathematical Economics (ed. K. J. Arrow and M. D. Intrilligator), Vol. III, pp. 1483–1510. North Holland, Amsterdam.

Henry, C. (1972). 'Differential Equations with Discontinuous Right Hand Side for Planning Procedures'. *Journal of Economic Theory*, 4: 545–51.

Hicks, J. R. (1946). *Value and Capital* (2nd edn). Clarendon Press, Oxford.

Hildenbrand, K., and Hildenbrand, W. (1978). 'On Keynesian Equilibrium with Unemployment and Quantity Rationing'. *Journal of Economic Theory*, 18: 255–77.

Hildenbrand, W., and Kirman, A. P. (1976). *Introduction to Equilibrium Analysis.* North Holland, Amsterdam.

Hirota, M. (1985). 'Global Stability in a Class of Markets with Three Commodities and Three Consumers'. *Journal of Economic Theory*, 36: 186–92.

Hurwicz, L. (1984). 'Incentive Aspects of Decentralization'. In *Handbook of Mathematical Economics* (ed. K. J. Arrow and M. D. Intrilligator), Vol. III, pp. 1441–82. North Holland, Amsterdam.

Iritani, J. (1981). 'On the Uniqueness of General Equilibrium'. *Review of Economic Studies*, 48: 167–71.

Johansen, L. (1972). 'Simple and General Non-substitution Theorems for Input Output Models'. *Journal of Economic Theory*, 5: 383–94.

238 *Walrasian and Non-Walrasian Equilibria*

Jones, R. W. (1961). 'Stability Conditions in International Trade, A General Equilibrium Analysis'. *International Economic Review*, 2: 199–209.

—— (1965a). 'The Structure of Simple Models of General Equilibrium'. *Journal of Political Economy*, 73: 557–72.

—— (1965b). 'Duality in International Trade Theory: A Geometrical Note'. *Canadian Journal of Economics and Political Science*, 28: 390–3.

—— and Kenen, P. B. (eds.) (1985). *Handbook of International Economics*, Vol. I. North Holland, Amsterdam.

Kelley, J. L. (1955). *Topology*. Van Nostrand, New York.

Keynes, J. M. (1936). *The General Theory of Employment, Interest and Money*. Macmillan, London.

Koopmans, T. C. (ed.) (1951). *Activity Analysis of Allocation and Production*. John Wiley, New York.

—— (1957). *Three Essays on the State of Economic Science*. McGraw-Hill, New York.

Laroque, G. (1978). 'On the Dynamics of Disequilibrium: A Simple Remark'. *Review of Economic Studies*, 45, 273–8.

Leontief, W. (1951). *The Structure of the American Economy 1919–1939*. Oxford University Press.

Lindahl, E. (1919). *Die Gerechtigkeit der Besteuerung*. Lund, Sweden.

Luce, R. D., and Raiffa, H. (1957). *Games and Decisions*. John Wiley, New York.

Majumdar, M., and Mitra, T. (1985). 'A Result on the Transfer Problem in International Trade'. *Journal of International Economics*, 19: 161–70.

Malinvaud, E. (1971). 'A Planning Approach to the Public Good Problem'. *Swedish Journal of Economics*, 73: 96–112.

—— (1972). *Lectures in Microeconomic Theory*. North Holland, Amsterdam.

—— (1977). *The Theory of Unemployment Reconsidered*. Basil Blackwell, Oxford.

—— and Younes, Y. (1977). 'Some New Concepts for the Microeconomic Foundations of Macroeconomics'. In *The Microeconomic Foundations of Macroeconomics* (ed. G. Harcourt), pp. 62–95. Macmillan, London.

Mangasarian, O. L. (1969). *Non-Linear Programming*. McGraw-Hill, New York.

McFadden, D. (1968). 'On Hicksian Stability'. In *Value, Capital and Growth* (ed. J. N. Wolfe), Aldine, Chicago.

McKenzie, L. W. (1956). 'Demand Theory without an Utility Index'. *Review of Economic Studies*, 24: 185–9.

—— (1960a). 'Matrices with Dominant Diagonals and Economic Theory'. In *Mathematical Methods in Social Sciences* (ed. K. J. Arrow, S. Karlin, and P. Suppes) pp. 47–62. Stanford University Press.

—— (1960b). 'Stability of Equilibrium and the Value of Positive Excess Demand'. *Econometrica*, 28: 606–17.

—— (1981). 'The Classical Theorem on the Existence of Competitive Equilibrium', *Econometrica*, 49: 819–42.

Mirrlees, J. A. (1986). 'The Theory of Optimal Taxation'. In *Handbook of Mathematical Economics* (ed. K. J. Arrow and M. D. Intrilligator), Vol. III, pp. 1197–1249. North Holland, Amsterdam.

Morishima, M. (1964). *Equilibrium, Stability and Growth*. Oxford University Press.

Mukherji, A. (1972). 'On Complementarity and Stability'. *Journal of Economic Theory*, 4: 442–57.

―― (1973). 'On the Sensitivity of Stability Results to the Choice of the Numeraire'. *Review of Economic Studies*, 40: 427–33.

―― (1974a). 'Stability in an Economy with Production'. In *Trade, Stability Macroeconomics* (ed. G. Horwich and P. A. Samuelson), pp. 243–58. Academic Press, New York.

―― (1974b). 'The Edgeworth Uzawa Barter Stabilizes Prices'. *International Economic Review*, 15: 236–41.

―― (1975). 'On the Hicksian Laws of Comparative Statics and the Correspondence Principle'. *Keio Economic Studies*, 12: 41–50.

―― (1977). 'On the Existence of Choice Functions'. *Econometrica*, 45: 889–94.

―― (1985). 'On Some Implications of the Separating Hyperplane Theorem'. *Keio Economic Studies*, 22: 57–62.

―― and Sanyal, A. (1986). 'Price Flexibility and Unemployment: Microeconomics of Some Old Fashioned Questions'. *Keio Economic Studies*, 23: 19–36.

Nayak, P. R. (1980). 'Efficiency of Non-Walrasian Equilibrium'. *Econometrica*, 48: 127–34.

Negishi, T. (1962). 'Stability of a Competitive Economy'. *Econometrica*, 30: 635–69.

―― (1979). *Microeconomic Foundations of Keynesian Macroeconomics*. North Holland, Amsterdam.

Neuefeind, W. (1980). 'Notes on the Existence of Equilibrium Proofs and the Boundary Behaviour of Supply'. *Econometrica*, 48: 1831–7.

Newman, P. (1965). *The Theory of Exchange*. Prentice-Hall, Englewood Cliffs, NJ.

Nikaido, H. (1968). *Convex Structures and Economic Theory*. Academic Press, New York.

Ohyama, M. (1972). 'On the Stability of General Metzlerian Systems'. *Review of Economic Studies*, 39: 193–204.

Patinkin, D. (1965). *Money, Interest and Prices* (2nd edn.). Harper and Row, New York.

Quirk, J. P. (1974). 'A Class of Generalised Metzlerian Matrices'. In *Trade, Stability and Macroeconomics* (ed. G. Horwich and P. A. Samuelson), pp. 203–20. Academic Press, New York.

―― and Saposnik, R. (1968). *Introduction to General Equilibrium Theory and Welfare Economics*. McGraw-Hill, New York.

Rybczynski, T. (1955). 'Factor Endowments and Relative Commodity Prices'. *Economica* (new series) 22, 336–41.

Samuelson, P. A. (1947). *The Foundations of Economic Analysis*. Harvard University Press, Cambridge, Mass.

―― (1951). Abstract of a Theorem Concerning Substitutability in Open Leontief Models. In *Activity Analysis of Production and Allocation* (ed. T. C. Koopmans). pp. 142–6. John Wiley, New York.

―― (1954). 'The Pure Theory of Public Expenditure'. *Review of Economics and Statistics*, 36: 387–9.

Scarf, H. (1960). 'Some Examples of Global Instability'. *International Economic Review*, 1: 157–72.

―― (1982). 'The Computation of Equilibrium Prices: An Exposition'. In *Handbook of Mathematical Economics* (ed. K. J. Arrow and M. D. Intrilligator), Vol. II, pp. 1007–61. North Holland, Amsterdam.

240 *Walrasian and Non-Walrasian Equilibria*

Sen, A. K. (1970). *Collective Choice and Social Welfare.* Holden-Day, San Francisco.
—— (1984). 'Social Choice Theory'. In *Handbook of Mathematical Economics* (ed. K. J. Arrow and M. D. Intrilligator), Vol. III, pp. 1073–1181. North Holland, Amsterdam.

Shafer, W., and Sonnenschein, H. (1982). 'Market Demand and Excess Demand Functions'. In *Handbook of Mathematical Economics* (ed. K. J. Arrow and M. D. Intrilligator), Vol. II, pp. 670–93. North Holland, Amsterdam.

Shephard, R. W. (1953). *Cost and Production Functions.* Princeton University Press.

Sheshinski, E. (1986). 'Positive Second-Best Theory'. In *Handbook of Mathematical Economics* (ed. K. J. Arrow and M. D. Intrilligator), Vol. III, pp. 1251–80. North Holland, Amsterdam.

Silvestre, J. (1982). 'Fixprice Analysis in Exchange Economies'. *Journal of Economic Theory,* 26: 28–58.

Smale, S. (1976a). 'A Convergent Process of Price Adjustment and Global Newton Methods'. *Journal of Mathematical Economics,* 3: 1–14.
—— (1976b). Exchange Processes with Price Adjustment. *Journal of Mathematical Economics,* 3, 211–26.

Sonnenschein, H. (1971). 'Demand Theory without Transitivity'. In *Preferences, Utility and Demand: A Minnesota Symposium* (ed. J. S. Chipman *et al.*), pp. 215–23. Harcourt Brace, New York.

Stolper, W. F., and Samuelson, P. A. (1941). 'Protection and Real Wages'. *Review of Economic Studies,* 9, 58–73.

Takayama, A. (1974). *Mathematical Economics,* Dryden Press, Hinsdale, Ill.

Uzawa, H. (1962). 'Walras' Existence Theorem and Brouwer's Fixed Point Theorem'. *Economic Studies Quarterly,* 8: 59–62.
—— (1971). Preference and Rational Choice in the Theory of Consumption. In *Preference, Utility and Demand: A Minnesota Symposium* (ed. J. S. Chipman *et al.*), pp. 7–28. Harcourt Brace, New York.

Varian, H. (1975). 'A Third Remark on the Number of Equilibria in an Economy'. *Econometrica,* 43, 985–6.

Walras, L. (1877). *Elements d'economie politique pure.* Corbaz, Lausanne. Translated as *Elements of Pure Economics* by W. Jaffé (1954). George Allen & Unwin, London.

Willig, R. (1976). 'Consumers Surplus without Apology'. *American Economic Review,* 66: 589–97.

Younes, Y. (1975). 'On the Role of Money in the Process of Exchange and the Existence of a non-Walrasian Equilibrium'. *Review of Economic Studies,* 42: 489–501.

Yun, K. K. (1979). 'A Note on Some Perturbation Theorems for Price Dynamics in an Exchange Economy'. *International Economic Review,* 20: 359–65.

Index